920   Donaldson   John Cheever,
a Biography

SEP 1 7 1988

OCT 1 3 1988

NOV 0 2 1988

NOV 2 2 1988

DEC 0 6 1988

JAN 2 4 1989
AUG 1 7 1995

DEMCO

ALSO BY SCOTT DONALDSON

The Suburban Myth
Poet in America: Winfield Townley Scott
By Force of Will: The Life and Art of Ernest Hemingway
American Literature: Nineteenth and Early
    Twentieth Centuries (with Ann Massa)
Fool for Love, F. Scott Fitzgerald

Editor, Jack Kerouac, *On the Road*
Editor, *Critical Essays on F. Scott Fitzgerald's*
    "The Great Gatsby"
Editor, *Conversations with John Cheever*

JOHN CHEEVER

JOHN CHEEVER
A Biography

SCOTT DONALDSON

 RANDOM HOUSE NEW YORK

Grateful acknowledgment is made to Macmillan
Publishing Company for permission to reprint an
excerpt from "Shoetown" from *Collected Poems:
1937–1962* by Winfield Townley Scott. Reprinted with
permission of Macmillan Publishing Company (New
York: Macmillan, 1962).

Library of Congress Cataloging-in-Publication Data
Donaldson, Scott.
John Cheever.
1. Cheever, John—Biography. 2. Authors,
American—20th century—Biography. 1. Title.
PS3505.H6428Z64   1987   813'.52   [B]   86-29682
ISBN 0-394-54921-X

Typography and binding design by J. K. Lambert
Manufactured in the United States of America
98765432
First Edition

This book is for Vivian

FOREWORD

WE'D MADE the date by postcard, but there must
have been some mix-up and when I got off the ferry
to Nantucket with the rest of the day-trippers, John
Cheever was not there to meet me. Having come so
far, I went out to the end of the island and knocked on
the door of his room at the Wauwinet Inn. Cheever
was all graciousness: invited me in, took me downstairs for a drink (his was iced tea), and talked about
himself and his work for three hours as we watched
the sailboats sport in the breeze. Almost immediately—did he aim to shock?—he told me about the
"hundred and fifty affairs" he'd had. Later, as he drove
me back to the ferry, he spoke with feeling of his
recently deceased brother. "Some people have parents
or children," he said. "I had a brother." There seemed
no appropriate response. "For a long time I couldn't
take him," he added, and then, quietly, "I still can't."

It took several years of hard digging and harder
thinking to *begin* to understand what those remarks
signified. All biographers know theirs is an impossible
task, for we really cannot understand one another. As
Mark Twain commented, every person's real life "is
led in his head, and is known to none but himself."
With a writer like Twain or Cheever, the long paper
trail suggests the direction of some of that private
cogitation. Patterns emerge, generalizations develop.
But no one goes inside another's mind. And that first

and only meeting in Wauwinet, with its intermingling of confusion and revelation, disappointment and pleasure, warned me to expect the unexpected from John Cheever.

Eventually, I came to see his complicated and difficult life as a triumph. Hurt in childhood, he grew up a man divided against himself. A battle raged inside him between light and dark, celebration and sorrow, love and hate. The tension drove him close to self-destruction, and sometimes he lashed out at those around him. Yet with his victory over alcoholism, the mature Cheever at last rejected the dark and chose the light. Always a writer's writer, toward the end he started getting the kind of public recognition his work had long deserved. Cheever's 180 stories, spanning from 1930 to 1980, tell us more about people in the American middle class during that half century than any other writer's work has done or can do. Among his novels, *The Wapshot Chronicle* (1957) movingly captures the contrast between the often dispiriting present and the past, not perfect but recollected in tenderness, that we like to think we came from. *Falconer* (1977), situated in a prison, lands us smack in the middle of everything that is wrong with our civilization, yet ends in a celebration of the glory of love. And everything bears the stamp of Cheever's vivid imagination and rhetorical magic. He wrote, John Updike observed, "as with a quill from the wing of an angel."

SCOTT DONALDSON

CONTENTS

JOHN CHEEVER

PREHISTORY

T HE MOST remarkable thing about John
Cheever was his capacity for invention. You
could not be with him for fifteen minutes before he would look across the street or the
restaurant, spy an interesting face, and the story
would begin. William Maxwell, the writer who edited
most of Cheever's stories for *The New Yorker,* once
called him a "story-making machine" in the same
sense that a rosebush is a machine for making roses.
Cheever himself compared his talent to the possession
of a pleasant baritone voice. He could not sing, much.
But oh, could he tell stories.

The gift was there from the beginning and lasted all

his life. At seven, he began to entertain his grammar school class-mates with preposterous tales. At seventy, in the last year he lived, he finished his last book of fiction. "I can tell a story," he observed. "I can do . . . little else."

It was, of course, more than enough. As he learned to shape and hone his talent, he became one of the century's masters of the art of fiction. His yarn spinning also made him an enchanting companion. "The truth was not in him," his friend Arthur Spear said of Cheever, with a reminiscent smile. Spear would not have changed him for the world.

As a practical matter, though, Cheever's capacity for invention—his compulsion to invent—sometimes led to difficulties. The man, like the writer, was afflicted by this touch of genius, and in his private life he could rarely be relied upon for the unadorned truth. This was particularly true regarding his family origins, which he tended to redecorate and improve upon when he could be brought to discuss them at all. For an anecdotal man he was surprisingly reticent about his background. Often it seemed that he was trying to muddy his past. "Something back then" must have been troubling him, friends thought. In a few of his early stories never collected in book form, he addressed the subject openly and frankly. Otherwise, most of his fiction romanticized his roots.

According to family legend, John Cheever was descended from Ezekiel Cheever, the schoolmaster at Boston Latin who was so revered that Cotton Mather preached his funeral sermon and called him Master Socrates. Ezekiel crossed the Atlantic in 1637 (the legend had him aboard the *Arbella* in 1630, along with John Winthrop and the Puritan founders of the Massachusetts Bay Colony). He taught first in New Haven, then at Ipswich and Charlestown before the call to Boston in 1671. A commanding figure, Ezekiel drilled the sons of ministers and magistrates in the Latin grammar he himself composed, maintained strict discipline, and punished any show of pretension. "The Welfare of the Province was much upon his spirit," Samuel Sewall noted when Ezekiel died at ninety-four. "He abominated periwigs."

Ezekiel Cheever was a great man, John Cheever loved that remark about periwigs, and so he claimed him for his ancestor. His father had done the same, supposedly searching through "seven or eight generations" in the genealogical records in Newburyport to trace his origins back to the redoubtable schoolmaster. He had seen the papers himself, John said, but thrown them all away. In fact,

he was not directly descended from Ezekiel. The real founder of
the family in America was Daniel Cheever, who emigrated from
England in 1640. Daniel became prison-keeper in Cambridge, as did
his son Israel, also in the direct line of descent. Daniel was a cousin
of Ezekiel's. Ezekiel was a cousin of John Cheever's great-great-
great-great-great-great-grandfather.

If Cheever knew who his progenitors were, he did not acknowledge it. Once he'd adopted Ezekiel he was loath to let him go, and
developed a genuine pride of family based on him. As novelist
Ralph Ellison observed in this connection, "Some people are your
relatives but others are your ancestors, and you choose the ones you
want to have as ancestors." So, like his father and the fictional
Leander Wapshot, John Cheever declared that there was nothing
in his veins "but the blood of shipmasters and schoolteachers." He
told his children about their ancestor Ezekiel, and often mentioned
him in interviews. He used the name in his fiction in two important
instances. The founder of his Wapshot clan, modeled on Ezekiel
Cheever down to his hatred for wigs, is called Ezekiel. The protagonist of his novel *Falconer* is Ezekiel Farragut. In real life he named
a much-loved black Labrador puppy Ezekiel, or Zeke for short.
When his first grandchild was born, Cheever tried—unsuccessfully—to persuade his son Ben to call the boy Ezekiel.

Cheever came to believe in his relationship to Ezekiel so wholeheartedly that he was disturbed to discover a sour apple in that
branch of the family. Ezekiel Cheever, Jr., a schoolmaster like his
father, testified against the accused witches at the Salem trials of
1692. In *The Crucible*, Arthur Miller's 1953 play about the witch trials,
this Ezekiel Cheever appears as an official of the court that tried and
condemned the witches to death. In due course John Cheever
talked to Miller and was reassured that the playwright had simply
happened upon the name in reading documents of the time and that
his role was not historically accurate. In 1978, however, poet and
professor Lewis Turco showed Cheever the records certifying that
Ezekiel Cheever, Jr., had in fact given testimony against the accused women. Cheever was shocked. "The family has suppressed
this information," he declared, and joked that he might destroy the
incriminating evidence. In effect, he achieved the same result by
choosing to ignore it. Ezekiel Jr.'s failings were not admitted into
the legend.

John Cheever's real ancestry was not without its distinctions.
His progenitor Daniel's grandson William Cheever married Mir-

iam Cleveland, an ancestor of Grover Cleveland. And William's son John—a great-great-great-granduncle of the writer—marched against the British troops from Newburyport on April 19, 1775, the day of the shot heard round the world. As for sea captains among his forefathers, two Cheevers, not direct ancestors, owned ships built in John Currier, Jr.'s Newburyport shipyard in the mid-nineteenth century. In addition, Benjamin Hale Cheever, John's great-grandfather, sailed the seas for the China trade, and became the first actual progenitor recognized by the family. The Cheevers named their first son for him. Blue-and-white Canton china that he brought back from his travels was displayed in their Ossining house, along with a red Chinese fan, framed. Born in Newburyport in 1770, Benjamin Hale Cheever became a successful and respected member of the community. In 1820 he was elected a trustee of the Newburyport Sabbath School and Tract Society; he had earned the title Master by the time of his death two years later.

Benjamin Hale Cheever's youngest child was John Cheever's grandfather Aaron, the first in a series of late-begotten children who stretched four generations over more than two hundred years. Benjamin Hale was born in 1770, Aaron Waters in 1815, Cheever's father, Frederick Lincoln, in 1863, and John William himself in 1912, to die in 1982. Aaron, Frederick, and John were all youngest children. Aaron was forty-eight when he fathered Frederick, Frederick forty-nine when he fathered John.

John's father loved to spin yarns about eccentric members of the family. His uncle Ebenezer, for instance, had been an abolitionist before the Civil War in Newburyport, a copperhead town whose livelihood came from shipping. Depending on the story, Ebenezer was either stoned in the streets for his opinions, or tarred and feathered with William Lloyd Garrison, or both. During the war itself, another story went, he might have made a fortune as a purveyor of hardtack to the Union troops, but lost the contract to a fledgling firm that became the National Biscuit Company. Ebenezer played his flute and didn't mind. His wife, Juliana, who played the pianoforte, occasionally assumed the personality of an Indian squaw. In this incarnation she would "braid feathers into her hair, squat on the floor, light a pipe . . . and receive messages from the dead."

These and other family sagas Frederick Lincoln Cheever gladly told, but he said not one word about his own father, Aaron. Once when John and his father were feeling particularly mellow, having drunk "at least a pint of whiskey" each, he screwed up his courage and asked, "Dad, would you tell me something about your father?" The answer was "No."

Under the circumstances, rumors flourished. It was understood that his grandfather had left his wife, Sarah, and their two children, Hamlet (Aaron admired Shakespeare) and Frederick, to fend for themselves. His grandmother subsequently ran a Boston boarding-house, John suspected, though he wasn't told. He did get the distinct impression between the lines of what went unsaid that his grandfather had been a seafaring man in his youth, that he drank, and that he had committed suicide.

In an early story, "Homage to Shakespeare" (1937), Cheever attempted to summon up his grandfather's ghost. According to the story, he had in effect been undone by Shakespeare. At sixteen he shipped out to Calcutta and took with him the buckram-bound copy of Shakespeare's plays that, along with a tintype of himself looking fiercely angry, were the only mementos to survive when he died. The book was heavily annotated, with sonorous speeches underlined where Lear and Coriolanus and Macbeth "damned men for their treachery" and their lack of faith. Admittedly his grandfather was a failure in the eyes of Newburyport, where he retired to reflect, with the encouragement of the Bard, on his own unappreciated greatness. He considered that he had the spirit of a king, and did not deign to work. With Shakespeare, he took dark views. "Gleaming through the vanity of every incident he read the phallus and the skull." Eventually, nagged by his wife, he took up with the bottle and the local barmaids, and she left him for a better life. At the end, the narrator imagines him—"my grandfather," given no other name—still prideful but now beaten, too drunk to find a woman, bumping into lampposts, locked out of his lodgings, "muttering as he stumbled some line from *Timon of Athens* about how men bolt their doors against the setting sun."

So it may have been, or some of it. The available facts are that Aaron Waters Cheever was born in Newburyport on September 18, 1815, the son of Benjamin Hale and Rebekah Thompson Cheever. At thirty-one, on December 5, 1847, he married Sarah A. Nash in Medford. Both bride and groom then lived in Woburn, and he was employed as a cordwainer—a worker in cordovan leather, a shoe-maker. Later he became a patternmaker, someone who sketches the design of shoes. In time the family lived both in Newburyport and in Lynn, where Aaron probably participated in the great shoemakers' strike that began on Washington's birthday, 1860. Frederick Lincoln Cheever, John's father, was born in Lynn on January 16, 1863. Frederick's only sibling, Hamlet, was almost ten years his senior. Soon after Frederick's birth the Cheevers moved to Boston. Evidently Aaron left his wife and children early in the 1870s. He died in Boston on August 2, 1882. The death certificate lists his final residence as 111 Chambers Street in the old West End, a ragged quarter inhabited largely by Eastern European immigrants. (Chambers Street no longer exists, having given way to urban renewal.) The immediate cause of death was "alcohol & opium—del. [irium] tremens." That too was not something John was told.

Left fatherless, Frederick Cheever grew up poor, but the stories he told did not dwell on his poverty. Instead he talked of sleeping in an attic full of ivory tusks and of riding the first horsecar from Newburyport to Amesbury, a trip he celebrated in the laconic style of his journal.

Sturgeon in river then. About three feet long. All covered with knobs. Leap straight up in air and fall back in water. . . . Hold the reins and see the sturgeon leap. Boyish happiness.

He came to Boston with his parents on the *Harold Currier*, the last sailing vessel to leave the Newburyport yards. It cost the family very little, since the ship was being towed in for outfitting; otherwise, they probably couldn't have afforded the trip.

Frederick went to work in a shoe factory full-time the day after he graduated from the Phillips School with honors. In the evenings, wearing mittens against the cold, he studied *The Magician's Own Handbook*, in order, his son concluded, "to make himself socially desirable." One of the tricks was "How to Cook an Omelet in Your Hat." The secret was to make the omelet in advance, hide it in the top of the hat, then propose to perform one's magic when, say, the gentlemen rejoined the ladies after brandy and cigars. "I can cook an omelet in my hat," one was to say brightly, and when challenged produce four eggs, three of them blown through tiny needle holes, drop the one whole egg on a table as if by accident, then take the three blown eggs and "cook" them over a candle in one's hat, eventually—Alakazam—displaying the precooked omelet for the wonderment of one's companions.

In appearance John Cheever's father "was one of those Massachusetts Yankees who look forever like a boy although toward the

end he looked like a boy who had seen the Gorgon." He spoke in
a North Shore accent and kept his *a*s variable. "The ship had a
mahst made of had wood," he would say. He followed a series of
rituals, convinced like the fictional Leander Wapshot "that the
unobserved ceremoniousness of his life was a gesture or sacrament
toward the excellence and continuousness of things." Every morning "he took a cold bath, howling like a walrus." In the evenings
he invariably wore a white shirt and a dark coat. "His concern for
sartorial preciseness was exhaustive," as his son put it. He went
skating on Christmas Day. He went swimming as many days as he
could; at seventy his false teeth were swept away by the Atlantic.
He fancied himself a seafarer, and handled his catboat—though "it
sailed like real estate," he'd complain—as gracefully as a dancer.
But actually he made his living, and then stopped making his living,
in the same shoe business that had given his own father employment.

Frederick Lincoln Cheever either did or did not own a shoe
factory. In his late years, John Cheever certainly said he had, and
said so with the verisimilitude of the storyteller. As a boy, John
reported, he was permitted once a year to toot the noon whistle at
the factory in Lynn. "Everybody then took their sandwiches out
of their paper bags. And that," he observed, "was my participation
in the shoe industry." Yet city directories in Lynn show no record
of Whitteridge and Cheever or Woodbridge and Cheever, as his
firm was presumably called. Moreover, Frederick Lincoln Cheever
is listed in Quincy city directories as a salesman from 1908 until 1922,
then as a shoe manufacturer for several years thereafter. And the
records of Thayer Academy, attended by both John and his
brother, Fred, during the 1920s, give their father's occupation as
"shoe salesman."

It hardly matters, except that it mattered to John Cheever. As he
grew older, he became insistent on his father's status as factory
owner. But there is no mention of this part of his career in the
apparently accurate story/article "The Autobiography of a Drummer," which appeared in *The New Republic* of October 23, 1935. Its
first-person account traces the roller-coaster career of a "commercial traveler" in the shoe business from 1891 to 1931. The unnamed
salesman (or drummer) of the piece was modeled after his own
father, Cheever acknowledged, and the pattern of success followed
by failure was manifestly that of Frederick Lincoln Cheever's life.
Significantly, in the story the drummer fails through no fault of his

own but because of changing economic conditions. In his glory days on the road—and this brief Cheever story anticipates Miller's *Death of a Salesman*—the drummer succeeded through force of personality and the intimate knowledge of the business he'd acquired by going to work at twelve as office boy in a shoe factory. He "often sold two carloads of shoes over a glass of whiskey." He "had ten suits of clothing and twenty pairs of shoes and two sailboats." He gambled at the track and at the table. For three decades, from 1895 to 1925, he traveled all over the United States, living in hotels and clubs and selling "expensive and beautiful" shoes to individual buyers working "for individual firms." But then the structure of the business began to change. Cheap shoes manufactured in mass quantities replaced well-crafted handmade shoes. Chain stores and stores owned by manufacturers replaced individually owned stores. Only a few independent dealers remained, and they did not buy enough to cover the expenses of selling shoes. By 1925 the drummer's income began to drop; by 1930 he was out of work and as forgotten as "those big yellow houses with cornices and cupolas that they used to build." Shaving in the morning, the salesman considers his life "a total loss." He looks at his defeated face in the mirror, and then, he says in conclusion, "I get sick as if I had eaten something that didn't agree with me and I have to put down the razor and support myself against the wall."

This piece, signed like several other early writings by "Jon" Cheever, may have been shaped in part by the anticapitalist requirements of *The New Republic* in 1935. Politics aside, though, it accurately reflected what happened to Cheever's father. By the mid-1920s his career had gone sour, while earlier there had been high old times on the road. Frederick Lincoln Cheever told stories about those days—about oyster sweepstakes in Chesapeake Bay, storms on Lake Erie, breakfasts in New Orleans, horse races and boxing matches and the night he and two companions drank all the champagne on the Boston–New York train. It was an extravagant life, but he brought back the orders.

Things were going well in 1900 when with thousands of others he shot off Roman candles in Boston Common to welcome the new century and decided, at thirty-seven, to get married. Projecting his own experience backward, John later reckoned that his father, "an intensely sensuous and perhaps lascivious man," must have had affairs with lovers of both sexes during his bachelor years. In fact, his dapper father was regarded as something of a ladies' man, though at least in the beginning he obviously adored the woman he married. This too would change; the marriage deteriorated along with the family fortunes.

A decade younger than her husband, Mary Devereaux Liley Cheever was born in England in 1873 and came to this country as a young girl with her parents, William and Sarah A. D. Liley. A tiny woman scarcely five feet tall, she was a dynamo of energy. John Cheever came to resent her, as many American male writers resent their strong mothers, but it was evidently from her side of the family that he inherited his artistic talent. Grandfather Liley died soon after the voyage across the Atlantic; Grandmother Liley survived to become a favorite figure of his boyhood. The daughter (according to her grandson) of Sir Percy Devereaux, a tradesman knighted by Victoria when he became Lord Mayor of Windsor, Sarah Liley began reading him Dickens in his preschool years; he reciprocated by reading to her after she suffered a stroke. She observed rigorous standards and demanded proper English of John. "Did you have a good time?" she would ask him. "An awful good time," he would answer. And then she would say, "A *very* good time," and he would say, "No, it was really an awful good time." John's father rather liked deflating her cultural pretensions. One afternoon she invited a pianist to tea. "Madame Langlois," Frederick Cheever announced, "is about to tickle the ivories."

Grandmother Liley knew how to let the air out of people too. She especially endeared herself to young John by describing his mother as "a little stupid and foolish." That he always remembered, along with the Dickens. Well educated in England and capable of taking tea in French and hemming a pocket handkerchief, his grandmother nonetheless thought of herself as a free spirit. She read widely in current literature, and was a friend of Margaret Ware Deland, the Boston novelist and short-story writer. One day while walking with the Delands in the slums of Boston, she saw women rapping their rings against the windows. "Why are they doing that?" she asked. "Because they are *whores,*" Mr. Deland explained.

Left virtually destitute by the death of her husband, John's maternal grandmother nonetheless managed to send her daughter Florence to art school. John's aunt Florence, called Percy in the 1968 story he wrote about her, did eventually become a painter, though she was forced to abandon her dream of rivaling "the Masters of the Italian Renaissance" in favor of commercially salable magazine covers. She also smoked cigars (though remaining intensely feminine), and married a philandering doctor whom she continued to love despite his frequent amours. She transferred her artistic hopes to their son, Randall, who had a short career as a concert pianist. After Sunday dinner, Cheever irreverently recalled, Randall "would play two Beethoven sonatas . . . and everyone would sit around and belch."

In a 1968 journal entry about "Percy," Cheever chastises himself for any hint of affectation, any trace of a swagger, in the story. The real reason his Aunt Florence interested him was not that she smoked cigars—it was that art ruled her life as it came to rule his own. One of her last requests was to be taken from her sickbed to see the Sargent watercolors at the Boston Museum one final time.

The artistic inheritance of the Lileys bypassed John's mother, but not the drive and enthusiasm behind it. Both for economic reasons and because it suited her personality, she rejected the Victorian role of passive housewife. Mary Liley Cheever was a woman who did things for others. After high school she attended the school of nursing at Massachusetts General Hospital; she became a head nurse there within a year following her graduation. She and Frederick Cheever must have met and fallen in love sometime during the late 1890s in Boston, where he had for many years been living with and supporting his mother. At the time Mary Liley was thought to be "quite beautiful." In one photograph of her as a young woman that John recalled, she had fair hair, wore a long tennis dress, and carried a racket. "Her features had a pleasant, sensuous thickness." She looked something like John himself at the same age. Another photograph he remembered characterized her better, however. This picture appeared on the cover of a luncheon program, celebrating Founders Day at the Quincy Woman's City Club. She was one of the founders, or as John put it with some hyperbole, "she was founder." In this picture of Mary Liley Cheever, now in her late thirties, the features were finer and the hair darker. These photographs have not survived. John's mother did not like to have her picture taken. She had been able to achieve a look of composure in the Founders Day photo, she explained to her son, only by holding him in her lap. "I was cropped," he added.

That rather bitter remark typified Cheever's feelings about his mother. In his view she was too occupied in raising money for the new parish house, financing the library, installing flower boxes, starting progressive schools, and promoting cultural events to devote much time to him. She "always seemed to be out raising money ... rather than being at home when I needed her." Similarly she invited the downtrodden to take Thanksgiving dinner with the family, but had little time or inclination for mundane domestic tasks. She used to sing a lament about having to wash and iron a shirt, John recalled. Another song was "Hands Off." When as in "Independence Day at St. Botolphs," a draft for the opening of *The Wapshot Chronicle,* Sarah Wapshot (Mary Liley Cheever) came home "from a stirring lecture on hospital conditions," she was in no mood to be embraced. Her husband blew down the back of her neck to no avail. Her "lack of interest in sexuality" sorted badly with his passionate nature. Nor was she demonstrative with her two sons. "There were very seldom warm embraces. Her rules of decorum were rigidly observed."

In such an environment John Cheever grew up, in a series of three houses all located in Quincy, Massachusetts, the South Shore city—suburb to Boston—where his parents moved shortly after the birth of their first son, Frederick Jr., in 1905. As old as Boston itself, Quincy was best known for its most famous citizens. Specifically, Quincy was the home—at least in summer—of the Adams family: the two presidents John and John Quincy, then Charles Francis Adams and Brooks and Henry Adams. The name of a still earlier resident, Thomas Morton of Merry Mount, figures less prominently in histories of the community, for he brought infamy with him.

Morton arrived with Captain Wollaston to establish the original settlement in 1625, and upon Wollaston's departure took over command. He set up an Indian trading post at Merry Mount, or Mount Wollaston (both place-names survive in modern Quincy), and conducted himself so recklessly as to call down the wrath of the other English settlements in the New World. A veritable lord of misrule, Morton got the Indians drunk before striking bargains with them, and then sold them guns. In addition, he and his men disported themselves with the Indian women, "the lasses in beaver coats," around the community Maypole. The combination of "neglected Indian husbands, liquor, and gunpowder" threatened to lead to serious trouble, and eventually Miles Standish was dispatched from Plymouth to arrest Morton in the king's name. Morton was deported to England, but soon returned to resume his former practices. The Massachusetts Bay Colony in the form of Governor Endicott then descended on Merry Mount to cut down the Maypole and ship the still-unchastened Morton back to England again, this time permanently. The rebellion of Thomas Morton, involving strong drink and promiscuity, was directed against the accepted mores of his time. The Adams family objected more discreetly and to political rather than social constraints, but they too rebelled against authority. "Resistance to something," as Henry Adams wrote in his *Education,* "was the law of New England nature," and this was true of John Cheever in the 1920s as it had been for Morton in the 1630s and Adams in the 1850s.

Henry Adams's Quincy represented summertime relief from the rigors of winter in Boston. "Town was constraint, law, unity. Country, only seven miles away, was liberty, diversity, outlawry, the endless delight of mere sense impressions given by nature for nothing, and breathed by boys without knowing it." For Cheever, seventy years later, these dual impulses toward freedom and confinement, license and law, nature and civilization fought their way out on the stony ground of Quincy itself. In its most concrete manifestation, he felt a "critical division" between his outdoor world of play and his mother's indoor world of propriety.

The Quincy of his youth was larger and far more of a self-sufficient city than the rural retreat Henry Adams had enjoyed. It had grown by virtue of its twenty-seven miles of shoreline—young Henry could gaze from the hill near John and Abigail Adams's Old House east across Quincy Bay, north to Boston and beyond—and on the strength of the granite industry. Quincy granite sales flourished from the mid-nineteenth to the early twentieth century. Scotch-Irish, Scandinavian, and Italian immigrants came to quarry and cut the granite. The large Fore River shipyard started operating in 1900, attracting still more laborers and managers. The old summer houses were converted to year-round use, as the railroad made commuting to Boston easy. Not all of the growth pleased longtime residents. More people meant more schools, more police, and higher taxes. The Adams family moved out as the Cheevers moved in.

CHILDHOOD

1912-1926

THE Cheevers lived first in the flat part of Quincy, near the trolley tracks. It was there, in a small house at 43 Elm Avenue, that John William Cheever spent the first seven years of his life. He was born on May 27, 1912, almost seven years after Fred. There were no other children. John's parents had not planned on his birth, as he was often to hear in the years ahead. His mother was thirty-nine, his father forty-nine when he was born.

Looking back on his youth in a 1978 interview, John Cheever said that it could be divided into an extremely sunny childhood and an extremely troubled adolescence. The childhood was probably not as happy as all that, however. His mother kept busy, and was not given to shows of affection. His father was often away from home on sales trips, and when in residence devoted substantially more time to John's older brother, Fred, than to him. Fred was so much older that he and John could hardly have played together. Cheever remembered little of those first years. What he did remember suggests that things were less sunny than he stated publicly.

In his earliest recollections of his mother, she almost always appears as dominating if not tyrannical, cruel if not heartless. Much of the time, she was too busily occupied with charity projects and home-front war work to pay much attention to her younger son. Yet it was she who tore him from the arms of a maid he had grown fond of, as she fired her for petty thieving. And it was she who snatched the broom from him, with the exasperated comment that he "swept like an old woman."

By 1920 the Cheevers had moved up the hill to Wollaston, Quincy's solid Ward 5, the Republican stronghold, the best neighborhood in town. For two years they stayed in a two-family house at 396 Highland Avenue. By 1922, however, they were living in their own eleven-room home a few blocks away, at 123 Winthrop Avenue. The house was Victorian, and so was the heavy, comfortable furniture that Mary Liley Cheever installed. Weekdays John walked to Wollaston Grammar School, near the corner of Highland and Beale Street. On Sundays he attended Episcopal Sunday school. The family fortunes were at their peak. Father went off to work in Boston or Lynn, but rarely took long trips on the road. Mother became a clubwoman, a "Madame President." Gentility reigned.

Wollaston in the early 1920s was "very much turn of the century." Draft horses still clopped through the streets, bringing merchants and their wares. The milkman delivered before 5:00 A.M. You set a large square card in the window for the iceman, turned to indicate how much ice you wanted, twenty-five, fifty, seventy-five, or one hundred pounds. Children tagged along behind the ice wagon to cadge a free sample. Mr. Holman the vegetable man, famous for his high-stepping horse, stopped in at kitchens to sell housewives his products. He might have a special on "native grass" (asparagus) or on oyster shells to be spread on sidewalks. Hawkers toured the streets in open delivery trucks with roll-down side curtains in case it rained. "Strawbeeeries! Strawbe-e-e-ries! Forty cents a box," they hollered, and the box held a quart. Junkmen came by with horse and wagon and a spring-operated hand scale to buy scrap metal and bundles of old newspapers. Kids from down the hill sometimes tossed stones or ripe fruit on the Baileys' tennis court, but there was no serious crime. There were no minorities either, except for Jimmy Tab, who ran the bicycle shop and whose son was the only black child at Wollaston Grammar. Otherwise everyone was white and Christian and well-to-do. If anyone deviated from the norm in some way, it was noticed but discussed, if at all, quietly, quietly.

On the surface John Cheever seemed much like the other children on Wollaston hill. He played kick-the-can, hide-and-go-seek, hoist-the-green-sail, and nine-ten-red-light. He climbed the backyard pear tree he named the Duchess. He lost three teeth riding his brother's bike without permission. He went fishing in the summer and skated in the winter. He swam naked in the woods beyond Furnace Brook Parkway. He loved swimming in the brook, in Black's Creek, and in Quincy Bay off Wollaston Beach. Black's Creek joins the sea at the south end of the beach, and there, his friend Rollin Bailey distinctly remembers hearing, Cheever once threw a ring into the creek and "thus married the creek near where it married the ocean." That was so curious a tale that Bailey stopped telling people about it. They didn't believe it or couldn't imagine such a gesture or didn't know John Cheever anyway.

The theatricality of the gesture fitted Cheever's boyhood personality even as it suggested a lack of emotional bonding within the family. Young Cheever spent much of his time in fantasy worlds. He loved playacting. On one Washington's birthday, he saw to it that all the neighbor youngsters were outfitted in Revolutionary War regalia. As organizer he reserved the role of General Washington for himself. When others took over charge of neighborhood play, he was assigned less glamorous roles. In the Robin Hood band that Rollin Bailey organized, for instance, he was cast as Friar Tuck, and logically so. Like the good friar, he was roly-poly and affable.

When he was still in grade school, Cheever suffered an attack of pulmonary tuberculosis. His mother had the disease herself and may have communicated it to her son. Yet she neglected him in his distress, the boy thought, and he never forgave her. For a time thereafter, he became an indoor child and brought his fantasy world inside with him in the form of puppet shows. At their simplest these were performed in the attic for one or two other children. Sometimes there were more public presentations. The tiny theater with its colorful backdrop was his own creation. "He built his own puppet theater, designed the scenery, and dyed the materials for the costumes," next-door neighbor Helen Howarth remembers. She was enlisted to sew the costumes, advertise the shows, and take in pennies and safety pins. Then John would take over. "He did the talking (in appropriate voices for the characters), manipulating them and narrating the story themes before the acts."

Fiction was his passion and also, he was to maintain, his salvation. "Perhaps the first thing in the world that I can remember," he told an interviewer in 1980, "is being read a story." In those "twilight Athenian years," reading provided the family entertainment. His grandmother read him Dickens, and he was also read *Treasure Island* and *The Call of the Wild* and some of the Tom Swift stories. As soon as he could, he tackled the books on his own. Even before that, though, he had begun to tell stories in school, without puppets or props. "If we did our class work satisfactorily then a period would be set aside during which I would tell a story." Sometimes these were serials. Usually they were "characterized by exaggeration, moving into preposterous falsehoods." When he walked to the front of the class, he often had no clear idea of what the story would be about. He simply started talking, and the story came.

At eleven he decided he wanted to be a writer, and told his parents. That was fine, they said, so long as he didn't expect to win fame or fortune. No, he said, he didn't care about such things. From the first, he found that telling stories had a therapeutic effect as relief from "a volcanic and early adolescence." Yet art was not merely an escape from his troubles, it was also a source of joy and understanding. Both the romantic and the realistic offered epiphanies, though of different nature. He was taken to hear the Boston Symphony Orchestra play Tchaikovsky's Fifth and thought, "That's tremendous—that's the way I feel about life." He was taken to see Ibsen in repertory and became almost sick with excitement at the shock of recognition. His own fiction—sometimes fantastical, sometimes virtually photographic—helped him, as he often said, "to make sense of his life."

The capacity to be moved by art—not entertained or laved by sentiment but genuinely moved—is rare enough, and when aligned with Cheever's still more remarkable ability to invent his own stories, it set him apart from other children. So Robert Daugherty, who was his classmate for the first eight years of school, thought of the public yarn-spinner and puppeteer as an introvert. What he meant, specifically, was that the chubby youth with the engaging manner and the stories in his head was not athletically inclined and rarely participated in such team sports as baseball and football. Baseball, especially, he avoided like a pestilence, and revealed why in "The National Pastime" (1953), another of those uncollected autobiographical stories in which he explored his origins.

The difficulty started with his father. Frederick Lincoln Cheever, who reached fifty before his younger son's first birthday, generally made it clear that he could be expected to do very little for the boy. He had formed a bond with his older son and namesake, Fred—often taking him sailing in Quincy Bay, for example—but John was born too late. One son was enough for his father, and perhaps for his mother as well. "If I hadn't drunk two manhattans one afternoon," she told him, "you never would have been conceived." But it was his father, she also told him, who wanted him aborted and who went so far as to invite the abortionist to dinner. The unwanted-child motif crops up repeatedly in Cheever's fiction. The abortionist appears at the dinner table both in *The Wapshot Chronicle* and in *Falconer*. "Farragut's father, Farragut's own father," the latter novel reflects, "had wanted to have him extinguished as he dwelt in his mother's womb, and how could he live happily with this knowledge . . . ?"

It cannot have been easy, either for Ezekiel Farragut or for his creator. In "The National Pastime" Cheever confronted his feelings about his father openly. Usually the fictional father figure is romanticized in his eccentricity. In this story, though, he is cruelly selfish, too wrapped up in himself to teach his son to play baseball.

"To be an American and unable to play baseball is comparable to being a Polynesian and unable to swim," the story begins in generalization, and then moves rapidly to the unnamed boy and his father, Leander (the story belongs to the Wapshot saga, but was not included in *The Wapshot Chronicle*). According to this story, he was nearly *sixty* when his son was born. Moreover, he has become nearly suicidal about his failure in business. Despite these extenuating circumstances, his thoughtlessness toward the boy is hardly forgivable. At nine the youth decides he will be a professional baseball player, acquires some equipment, and asks his father to play catch with him. At first he refuses, but the boy's mother overhears, and after they quarrel, Leander comes out to the garden and asks the boy to throw the ball to him.

What happened then was ridiculous and ugly. I threw the ball clumsily once or twice and missed the catches he threw to me. Then I turned my head to see something—a boat on the river. He threw the ball, and it got me in the nape of the neck and stretched me out unconscious. . . .

When he comes to, his father is standing over him. "Don't tell your mother about this," he says, and leaves. The boy now has a problem to deal with.

In school one spring day, the gym instructor takes the students outdoors. He is carrying some baseball gear, and as soon as the boy—whose very anonymity suggests his identification with Cheever—sees the bats and balls, "the sweet, salty taste of blood" comes into his mouth, his heart begins to pound, and his legs go weak, and to escape the game he sneaks under the field house. Lying there, he feels "the horror of having expelled myself from the light of a fine day" but also feels the taste of blood "beginning to leave his mouth." The fault, he decides, is his father's, and he decides to ask him again. "The feeling that I could not resume my responsibilities as a baseball player without some help from him was deep, as if parental love and baseball were both national pastimes." Leander once again fails to help his son over this rite of passage. He is asked, to be sure, after he has returned from selling some of his own father's and grandfather's books to help support the family. And had he looked more closely, the narrator acknowledges, he "might have seen a face harried with anxiety and the weakness of old age," but instead he expects his father "to regain his youth and to appear like the paternal images" he's seen on calendars and in magazine advertisements.

"Will you please play catch with me, Poppa?" I asked.
"How can you ask me to play baseball when I will be dead in another month!" he said.

Leander does not die in the following month, nor for years thereafter, and neither does the baseball phobia. The narrator hides inside a shed the next time the class goes out for baseball, neatly buries a ball to avoid a picnic game, and some years later is fired from a teaching position when, forced into playing and having struck the ball, he runs toward third base and knocks down a teammate coming in to score. Yet the story has a happy if improbable ending, when the narrator—now grown with sons of his own—

takes them to Yankee Stadium and makes a one-handed, bare-handed catch of a foul line drive off the bat of Mickey Mantle. The pain is excruciating, but is "followed swiftly by a sense of perfect joy. The old man and the old house seemed at last to fall from the company and the places of my dreams, and I smelled the timothy and the sweet grass again. . . ."

So in fancy Cheever resolved the predicament bequeathed him by an inattentive and unsuccessful father. In actuality, the resolution may never have been achieved. In *The Wapshot Chronicle* he tried to make his peace with his father, but he knew well that he'd touched up the picture to make Leander more sympathetic. Privately he always felt that his father had failed him and resolved to do better with his own two sons. His son Federico recalls his father spending "endless afternoons" with him, "playing catch with half-inflated footballs or chewed-up softballs." It never did much good, Federico added: the practice did not make a ballplayer out of him. But those afternoons on the lawn were important to a father who was nearly forty-five when Federico was born yet was determined to give him the proper athletic instruction.

Aside from his bouts with tuberculosis and the national pastime, Cheever led an active boyhood life. He played with his dog, an Irish terrier that he loved. He went on summer trips to New Hampshire, and then to Cape Cod. He went to Boy Scout camp. He went to school.

His memories of New Hampshire centered on his mother. She took him to the Cutter House in Jaffrey, where one Sunday, after chicken dinner, the hotel went up in flames. Thereafter they stayed at the Monadnock Inn, named for the nearby mountain. All one July they communed with Mount Monadnock, John's mother at a respectful distance, the boy by climbing it day after day. It was there, too, that he learned to ride horseback.

Back in Quincy, Cheever was happiest outdoors. With other boys he snuck into the woods to smoke cigarettes made of cedar bark and toilet paper. One memorable day he went to Paragon Park at Nantasket Beach in Hull, a ten-mile trip from Wollaston, and rode the bumper cars and the whip and saw himself distorted in the hall of mirrors. At twelve he was spirited off to Camp Massasoit, located on three ponds—Gallows, Long, and Little Long—eight miles below Plymouth in heavily wooded territory. There he lived in a tent for a month during the summers of 1924 to 1926, and had a wonderful time. The summer's highlight was the appearance of a Quincy banker named Delcevare King, whose family, then as now, served as benefactors to the Boy Scouts. For the occasion, King took off his three-piece suit and, dressed as an Indian chief, led the campers in Indian songs. Cheever remembered the words all his days, and remembered too the swimming, sailing, canoe trips, and nature hikes, and the joy of friendship.

At camp he solidified his relationship with Faxon Ogden, the closest friend of his youth. The two boys played marbles together and swam together and slept in the same tent and confided in each other. In the fall they went to school together. They were together so much that they even began to look alike, people said.

Cheever's school—his only school, after Wollaston Grammar— was Thayer Academy, in nearby South Braintree. Thayer was named for General Sylvanus Thayer, a superintendent of West Point who left a bequest for the founding of the academy. Coeducational from its beginnings in 1877, Thayer was designed to "offer to youth the opportunity to rise . . . from small beginnings to honorable achievement." John's brother, Fred, graduated from Thayer in the spring of 1924 and went off to Dartmouth that fall. At the same time John himself entered Thayerlands, the new junior school adjacent to the academy.

Thayerlands would not have existed at all without the beneficence of Anna Boynton Thompson, a distant cousin of John's father and another in young Cheever's gallery of impressive and eccentric women. A spinster, Anna Boynton Thompson taught Greek, history, and literature at Thayer for forty-four years, from its opening in 1877 to 1921. She earned her bachelor's and master's degrees from Radcliffe and her doctorate from Tufts while carrying a full teaching load. On her summer travels she dug for ancient artifacts in Egypt and continued her studies at Oxford and in Greece. She brought back a collection of Greek casts and friezes from one such trip, and installed them in the halls of the main building at Thayer. She donated her salary one year to enable trustees of the school to purchase land for playing fields. And she bequeathed her home, at her death in 1922, for use as the new junior school, Thayerlands. It could be said, justly, that she devoted her life to the school.

As John Cheever reconstructed her passing, it became more dramatic. In fiction and in personal reminiscence both, he wrote that Anna Boynton Thompson starved herself to death out of sympathy for the hungry millions in Europe and the Near East following

World War I. She had come to Thanksgiving dinner at the Cheevers' and was repelled by the sight of the turkey and the ham. "How can you do this? How can you have turkey while half the people in the world are starving?" she demanded. Silence descended, the Irish terrier barked, Mrs. Cheever announced that her Thanksgiving had been spoiled, and Mr. Cheever escorted his cousin home, where she stopped eating entirely. The minister was dispatched, and the Cheevers themselves called with chowder and hot bread, but cousin Anna would not be dissuaded. "I cannot live contentedly in a world where there is famine," she declared, and six weeks later died in her cold, classical library in Braintree, Massachusetts. Cheever added a coda to "The Temptations of Emma Boynton," the 1949 version of this story that ran in *The New Yorker:*

... while everything in our power had been done, a member of our family, a member of the middle class, for reasons of conscience that even to my mother, who knew their origins, seemed eccentric and mysterious, had starved to death.

That does sound improbable, and Cheever may well have invented this account of her demise. Anna Boynton Thompson had paid for two Red Cross ambulances in France during World War I, but as Lillian Wentworth of Thayer Academy points out, her giving was both "altruistic and practical." Bequeathing her own home for Thayerlands certainly met that standard. John's parents were among those sponsoring the school. In September 1924 he rode the bus to South Braintree with the other children who made up the first seventh-grade class at Thayerlands.

During his two years at the junior school—now the Thayer Academy Middle School—Cheever demonstrated a talent for writing and playacting, along with a lack of interest in the customary academic pursuits. No transcript of those years survives, but Grace L. Osgood, who taught him history and geography, remembers the "chubby little fellow" as an average student with a flair for storytelling. His spelling, she recalls, was "unusual, to say the least." Miss Osgood instructed him that if he planned to have a career as a writer, he would have to learn to spell. "His reply was that he expected to have a secretary to take care of that problem. I guess he did." (Actually Cheever was by no means the worst speller among major American writers—about on a par with Hemingway, better than Fitzgerald.)

Thayerlands aimed to be a progressive school that encouraged its students' creative instincts. In Miss Osgood's class, the children were challenged to re-create historical scenes from earlier times in their own words. The seventh graders put on a Thanksgiving pageant, Cheever costumed as a Puritan, and a month later presented their version of *A Christmas Carol,* with Cheever decked out in long trousers and swallow-tailed coat to play Fred to friend Fax Ogden's Scrooge. In the spring the whole class saw Marilyn Miller in *Peter Pan.* Mrs. Southworth, wife of the Thayer Academy's headmaster, Stacy Baxter Southworth, brought her radio to the school early in March 1925 so that the children could listen to the inauguration of President Calvin Coolidge. As a Yankee and a Republican, Coolidge was admired. Everyone's parents had voted for him. *The Evergreen,* Thayerlands' semiannual student publication, printed an anecdote about "Johnny"—not Cheever, just any Johnny—bringing home a poor report card.

"Don't you know," his father demanded, "that when Cal Coolidge was your age he stood at the head of his class?"

Johnny thought for a while. "Yes," he agreed, "and when he was your age, he was President of the United States!"

Several of Cheever's poems appeared in the 1924–26 issues of *The Evergreen.* In the eighth grade he was named poetry editor. Two of these poems showed promise.

THE BROOK

Against the cold and the icy snow
Trickles a quiet little stream.
Hid in a nook where the winds won't blow
It goes on and on like a dream,
Arched with birches in Gothic style,
Traced in crystallized rain,
Like a tall and slender window
In Notre Dame on the Seine.

Morning, noon, and night it goes,
Singing its one little song,
Tossing a laugh to the birches
As it cheerily ripples along.
Sometimes it's golden with cowslips,
Sometimes, the deepest of blue.

It stands for the spirit of Thayerlands
So loyal, so brave, and so true.

Even assuming that the school colors were blue and gold, those last
two lines are pedestrian and anticlimactic. But the nice figure of the
icy birches arched over the brook, the rendering of rhymed verse
in coherent sentences, the vivid verbs, above all the sensitivity to
both sound and the natural world—these were remarkable in a
thirteen-year-old.

The other poem, which appeared in the Commencement 1926
issue of *The Evergreen,* implicitly makes the case for Cheever's chosen career. Called "The Stage Ride," it depicts the stagecoach—"a
ribbon of brown in the colors of fall"—making its way to a country
inn where the driver alights and regales the guests with his stories.

He tells them of storms and of wrecks,
Of robbers and holdups and things,
And how a rich old lady
Lost two of her diamond rings.

The driver then jumps to his box,
And the boys look at him with dismay,
The crack of a whip and the blast of a horn,
And the stage goes again on its way.

So Cheever the storyteller left Thayerlands and moved on to
Thayer Academy across the street. Beneath his picture in the commencement issue, his classmates recognized him as "one of our
class poets," ribbed him about his spelling, and concluded that
"John never has a grudge against anyone, and is always a good
sport." *Never* a grudge, *always* a good sport: he must have tried hard
to please. This copy of *The Evergreen* disclosed two other facts about
him. He was author of the winning slogan for Good Posture Week,
"Make it Posture Week, not Weak Posture," but not on the Posture
Honor Roll. He had also written one of the three best short stories
in a school contest, but unlike the other two his was not printed.
Probably he had lost it or thrown it away. The previous year, his
Thanksgiving poem—one of five read at the pageant—also went
unprinted in the magazine with the explanation "Unfortunately,
John Cheever's poem was destroyed." The family custom was to

dispose of all paper as rapidly as possible, and as a boy Cheever had some difficulty of his own keeping track of things. Presumably with irony, the Thayerlands Class Will predicted that he would be "head of the Lost and Found Department of Washington D.C.'s largest department store."

At graduation time, the school issued no diplomas. Instead Cheever received a print of fir trees in the snow with the inscription "John, be true to yourself." He did his best, as the world came crashing down around him.

ADOLESCENCE

1926-1930

THE ties that held John Cheever's universe together began to unravel when his father lost his position in the shoe business in the mid-1920s. What happened to Frederick Lincoln Cheever was not unusual, for the Depression struck New England shoe and leather manufacturing well in advance of the 1929 crash. In "Shoetown," a poem about Haverhill, Winfield Townley Scott recorded the effects of the collapse on his hometown.

> Mr. Forrester shot himself
> at the bank; Benny Goldstein
> Lost his apartment houses; the stores

took back the Armenians'
Rugs and furniture; the Italians moved on with the shops; the
Irish got on relief, and the Yankees voted for Hoover.

But Quincy, unlike Haverhill, was not dependent on the shoe business for its livelihood, and so, though John's father certainly voted
for Hoover, his idleness and want of useful occupation were the
more conspicuous and the more costly in psychological as well as
financial terms.

Frederick Cheever's income had already peaked by 1922, when he
assumed the mortgage on the handsome house at 123 Winthrop. A
few years later, in his early sixties, he found himself unemployable.
He applied for dozens of jobs, but nothing worked out. Perhaps he
aimed too high. He must have felt it was too late to start over. In
frustration he wrote a series of angry letters to the Massachusetts
Registry of Motor Vehicles, the bureaucracy that dealt a final blow
to his pride by reassigning his low-digit license plate to an Italian-
American politician. 3088 was his number, and the state had no
right to take that away too.

In 1923, Mr. Cheever had piled the neighborhood children in his
touring car with the top down and raced a train at the terrific speed
of thirty-five miles per hour. By 1926 those same children saw that
everything had changed, though in accordance with Yankee reticence such matters were not openly talked about. Sixty years later,
the friends of Cheever's youth follow the same standard. "We all
knew about John's father's difficulties but they were not discussed
in front of us," one writes. "Vaguely in our minds we knew that
John's father was not like other dads," another recalls. How was he
different? What were his difficulties? The most perceptive children
noticed that "he always seemed to be sitting down" and that he was
subdued, "like a rubber band" that has lost some of its elasticity.
But the two facts about Frederick Lincoln Cheever that made him
unlike the other fathers, that caused his troubles, that sapped his
vitality, still went largely unarticulated. He was out of work. He
drank.

Liquor was almost always involved in John's memories of his
father, but most of the anecdotes celebrated his drinking rather
than deploring it. His father was debonair, he was hilarious, he had
drunk Robert Ingersoll and James O'Neill under the table at the
old Adams House, and no blame was attached. There was the
time—undoubtedly apocryphal—when he'd finished the sherry in

the parlor and pissed the decanter full to avoid detection. Soon
thereafter the pastor stopped by and Mrs. Cheever served him
moldy pilot crackers and piss. There was the tale—more plausi-
ble—that one drunken Christmas Eve he smoked a cigarette in
church. There was the morning, real enough, when John woke his
father from a sodden sleep; the old man, still comely, was wearing
a necklace of seventeen champagne corks. When awakened, his
father slung the champagne corks across the room. "Will you forgive me?" he asked. John said he did, and would have if he could.

Finally there was the evening, retold in both *Falconer* and "The
Folding Chair Set," when he drove frantically to Nagasakit to
rescue his father from suicide by drowning. Noticing there were
only two plates at dinner, John indiscreetly asked, "Where's Dad?"
At this his mother only sighed and continued serving the red-
flannel hash and poached eggs. When he asked again, she revealed
that there had been a quarrel. His father had drawn up a twenty-
two-item indictment enumerating her failures "as a woman, a wife
and a mother." She'd thrown it in the fire, and the old man, en-
raged, announced that he was going to Nagasakit to drown himself.
Though he had no driver's license, John jumped in the car and
drove to the beach as fast as he could. When he got there, he saw
no sign of his father until—drawn by the music from the amusement park—he finally discovered him riding the roller coaster,
"pretending to drink from an empty bottle and pretending to contemplate suicide at every rise" while a crowd watched in fascination. He then persuaded the attendant to stop the ride, so when his
father got off, he saw his "younger son and killjoy." "Oh, Daddy,"
John said to him in his fictional account of this incident, "you
shouldn't do this to me in my formative years." That remark,
worded humorously to disarm all condemnation, came from the
heart, as did his bland rendering of his mother's callousness. Making it light became Cheever's way of confronting—of evading—his
problems.

The children of Wollaston who did not know what to think of
John's father were unanimous in liking his mother. They thought
Mrs. Cheever charming and pleasant—"a very sweet, wonderful
person—so much a lady." Above all they admired her for her re-
sourcefulness in supporting the family after her husband had lost
his livelihood. Her son John refused to be impressed.

It could not have been easy for Mary Liley Cheever, grown stout
in her fifties, to give up her position as community clubwoman and

make a go of a gift shop downtown, but that is what she did. She first opened the Mary Cheever Gift Shoppe in 1926, and it was this shop, located first at 9 Granite Street and then at 1247 Hancock just north of Quincy Square, that supported the family and paid John's way through school. (Frederick L. Cheever wrote the ninety-dollar check for the semiannual tuition payment to Thayer Academy in the fall of 1926, and Mary L. Cheever paid thereafter.) At the least, it could be said of her that she made the best of a bad situation.

In his writing and conversation, however, John Cheever consistently denigrated his mother's accomplishment. "I suppose that the gift shop was our principal if not our only source of income," he acknowledged, but he did not think much of the place. Mrs. Cheever ran a high-class store, it was true. "You'd go to Woolworth's for souvenirs, but to Mary Cheever's for nice things," Doris Oberg recalls. It was her good fortune, she used to say, to be surrounded by lovely things, but to her son's eyes they were anything but lovely. He spent many an adolescent afternoon amid the clutter and debris in the back of her shop, waiting for his mother to close up. At Christmastime especially, she devoted her energies to the gift shop and not the home. John knew that it had to be that way, and resented it.

Mrs. Cheever's manner as a saleswoman seems to have been unusually aggressive. After greeting customers with a smile, she had a disconcerting way of making up their minds for them about what they should buy. If someone chose a gift that she thought did not match his or her personality, she would do her best to discourage the purchase by suggesting alternatives. Often enough this did not work. She would then sell people what they wanted in the first place, reluctantly, or even with a hint of disapproval.

Still the shop survived, and as time wore on Mrs. Cheever branched out into other ventures. In 1929 she opened a dress shop, the Little Shop Around the Corner, also in downtown Quincy. The shop featured copies of smart French frocks, hats, and costume jewelry. It was launched, according to the *Quincy Patriot-Ledger,* to satisfy the demand of Mary Cheever's patrons for a dress and accessory shop that would reflect the "exclusiveness and beauty . . . already evident in her gift shop." Her entrepreneurial drive also led her to launch two restaurants, one in Jaffrey, New Hampshire, and the other in Hanover, Massachusetts. Both soon went under. Later Mrs. Cheever began a number of cottage industries. She manufactured and tried to merchandise large cloth bags, for instance. When these didn't sell unadorned, she painted roses on them, and that led her into painting roses on other household objects and offering them for sale. There were not many takers, but she kept going. In her old age, she ran a small lampshade shop out of her home.

Whatever the outcome of these endeavors—and to John it seemed as if "the odor of failure" clung to them all—it is clear that Mary Cheever was a woman of tremendous energy who cherished the independence that her gift shop had earned for her, and protected it as need be. Once she drove off an armed robber with a candlestick. Late in life, John Cheever began to understand what that independence must have meant to his mother, but he could not entirely forgive her for it. The very word "antique" would set his teeth on edge. He deeply hated the fact of his mother's gift shop.

For one thing, his mother's highly visible employment as shopkeeper called attention to the family's financial predicament, and hence its difference from others. Though around the country women were beginning to break away from the drudgery of housekeeping and take jobs of their own, it is safe to say that the Cheevers were the only householders in Wollaston and John the only boy at Thayer with an unemployed father and a mother in trade. He felt the social humiliation, patent if unexpressed, and could take no pride in his mother's accomplishment. Worse, he became convinced that her very vitality and strength functioned to demean and unman his father. There was no question as to which parent had the controlling personality.

His mother, John invariably said, was a strong person: dominant, eccentric, opinionated. In middle age she abandoned the Episcopal Church for Christian Science, and suffered her way stoically through any physical ills that befell her. Her weakness was claustrophobia. She could not enjoy a concert or the theater or the movies; the minute the doors closed, she was on the verge of hysteria. Otherwise she was afraid of nothing. As Coverly Wapshot told the psychiatrist in *The Wapshot Chronicle*, where he came from the women were "very powerful. They [were] kind and they [meant] very well, but sometimes they [got] very oppressive. Sometimes you feel as if it wasn't right to be a man."

Cheever regarded his parents' marriage as a struggle for dominance, and his mother as the victor. Caught in the middle, he consistently took his father's part, especially after the loss of his job and his wife's ascendancy as breadwinner robbed him of his power.

"My sympathies all lay with him. And I worried terribly about what would happen to him," John said. His father was a self-made man who suddenly "found himself helpless, unable to support his family." John was afraid he would commit suicide.

In story after story, he reenacted the quarrels that raged between his parents. In "Publick House" (1941), old Mr. Briggs rails at having to wait for his dinner until all the customers in his wife's tearoom/gift shop have been fed. "I'm sick and tired of being pushed around," he says, loud enough for the customers to hear. "You've sold all my things. You've sold my mother's china. You sold the rugs. You sold the portraits. . . . What kind of business is that—selling the past?" In "The Jewels of the Cabots" (1972), a family of three sits down to a Sunday dinner and the son's father starts to carve the roast. As he makes the first cut, his mother sighs so profoundly that it seems her life is in danger. "Will you never learn," she asks, "that lamb must be carved against the grain?" Then the battle ensues. After half a dozen wounding remarks, his father waves the carving knife in the air and shouts, "Will you kindly mind your own business, will you kindly shut up?" She sighs once again, surely "her last breath." But no: to close the argument she gazes at the air above the table and says, "Feel that refreshing breeze." There is no breeze.

Another bitter dinner-table dispute in "The Edge of the World" (1941) sends the teenage son out of the house and on the road. Back home the argument ends when his mother cuts herself, his father binds her wound, and in a paroxysm of passion they make love. But to the boy theirs was a love contaminated by hate, and in his eyes the hate prevailed and made him feel insignificant. "They spend all their lives hating one another," he tells a companion.

"They torture one another. They fight and then she tells me not to feel sorry for him. She tells me that he never wanted to have any children. Then he tells me she never wanted to have any children. Then she tells me that he spent all her money. Then he tells me that she spends all his money. Sometimes I don't think they know who I am; I don't think they know my first name."

They were so wrapped up in hating each other, he thinks, that they had forgotten all about him.

Cheever felt much the same way as the boy in this story. In a journal entry, he writes of coming home from school to find "the furnace dead, some unwashed dishes on the table in the dining room and at the center of the table a pot of tulips that the cold had killed and blackened." Anger had driven his parents out of the house. Their "detestation of one another had blinded them to their commitments to the house and to him. . . ." It was as if he'd been exiled.

Cheever did not run away from home. He found other ways of protesting against lack of love from his parents, against his father's downfall, and against his mother's shopkeeping. Years later he would look back on Quincy occasionally in his journal, a repository for innermost thoughts, or in his fiction. But he went back in person only on visits while his parents were alive, and not at all after they died. It was a painful place for him. He had been unhappy there. His family had been poor there. He did not want to face that time openly, without the scrim of invention.

Besides, his adolescent home was inhabited by the ghost of the father who had never had enough time for him and who in his decline sacrificed his self-respect. "The greatest and most bitter mystery in my life was my father," Cheever wrote in 1977. He was convinced that his father had never loved him, and he revisited the sorrow and the pain of that conviction in almost everything he wrote.

Half a century earlier, in the Massachusetts suburbs south of Boston, the fifteen-year-old knew that his father failed him time and again, but he did not know whose fault it was. His tendency was to assign the blame to economic causes, or to his mother's domineering ways, or to any convenient explanation that would leave his father free of culpability. In the New England society of the day, you didn't tell your father off, and you didn't allow yourself to think he should be told off. In effect, he denied his father's failure and romanticized his shortcomings, repressed his own anger and acted out his own frustrations in the series of disasters that, he said, constituted his own adolescence.

Even in relative poverty, the Cheevers kept up certain appearances. Mrs. Cheever continued to invite to Thanksgiving dinner all of the strays she had been able to collect on "trains and buses and beaches and in the lobby of Symphony Hall during the intermission." When the last guest left, Mr. Cheever would stand by the door and exclaim, "The roar of the lion has ceased! The last loiterer has left the banquet hall!" The ritual was important. Like having a maid who was the daughter of an Adams coachman, it seemed to bespeak the family's secure status in a society of early settlers. As an adolescent, Cheever was keenly sensitive to social slights, both real and imagined. On Thanksgiving morning, he pointed out, he played touch football with the Winslows and Bradfords, who were willing to overlook the fact that his ancestors had not, like theirs, arrived on the *Mayflower*. He claimed that he'd never learned to play tennis, though, because the Baileys, who lived slightly above the Cheevers on Highland and who had a tennis court, never asked him up to play.

His mother did what she could to make sure he was invited wherever he should have been and knew how to act when he got there. There were some advantages to knowing the forks early in life. Even as a kindergartner he had mastered social skills unusual in children of any age. Upon leaving a party one day, Bertha L. Wight recalls, young John was the only child who spoke to the hostess. "Thank you for inviting me," he said. "I enjoyed it very much and I *mean* it!"

As he grew up, he was sent as a matter of course to dancing classes and to the junior and senior assemblies that succeeded them—experiences he memorialized in a 1937 memoir for *The New Yorker* entitled "In the Beginning." The central figure in the memoir is Miss Barlow, a venerable dancing instructor who wore jet-black dresses that hiked up a little in the rear and who spoke as if addressing hundreds. Every Saturday afternoon during his middle school years, John had trouble finding the serge bag that held his patent-leather dancing shoes. He would kneel and pray to God that he'd find the shoes in time to be driven down to the Masonic Temple for the two-o'clock class. There ensued the same drill followed by upper-middle-class youngsters in every American city of the time. The boys gathered in the locker room, the girls in the ladies' room. They then marched upstairs, entered the ballroom in pairs, and bowed to the observing matrons. After an hour of instruction, the children practiced what they had learned by dancing in couples.

When Cheever was fifteen, he graduated to the junior assemblies held at the country club. These "began at eight and ended at eleven, and you could clap as hard as you wanted to but the band wouldn't play any encores." Miss Barlow insisted on at least one cotillion and one elimination dance, the latter usually won by a good-looking boy who danced on the balls of his feet. Next came the senior assemblies, which were formal and lasted from nine to one. By this

time the stock market had crashed, and along with it "most of the
institutions our fathers had lived by." But Miss Barlow did not
change. She still wore the same black dresses and the same ankle-
high beaded shoes; she still carried a corsage in her left hand and
a whistle in her right. She was seventy at least, and had her dignity.
One evening in her last season, she had the ballroom decorated
with balloons. Seeing their opportunity, the teenagers began to
break the balloons with matches and penknives. Miss Barlow
sounded her whistle and commanded their attention with her sarcastic voice. "This is extraordinary," she said. "I can't understand
you young people." Never before, she told them, had her guests
taken so much pleasure in destroying her decorations. "Your
amusement is really a revelation. Next week we'll have rattles.
Alphabetical blocks the week after that."

Cheever himself was the cause of Miss Barlow's final outburst.
He used to dance a lot with a girl named Hope, and one night she
asked the band to play "Diga-Diga-Doo"—so he wrote—and they
"went all over the floor until that shrill whistle blew" and he heard
Miss Barlow's confident and stagy voice address him. "John
Cheever," she said, "your dancing is atrocious." She had seen a
great deal of dancing, but never anything like his. "I am ashamed
of you, John. I am ashamed of you. I'm glad your mother isn't here.
I will give you an illustration of your dancing." The illustration
was not funny at all, and he did his best to dance on the balls of
his feet the rest of the evening.

That night he went home and dreamed that Miss Barlow had
died. A week later he found out that the dream had come true. "Of
course I killed her," he wrote in hyperbole, and he thought about
it sometimes when he was with a girl who danced as if she had been
taught in the assemblies "outside of Buffalo or Baltimore or Boston
or Philadelphia." He thought about the corsage and the whistle,
and the dance music that had been popular, and the smell of the
locker room, "and the black elms and the mansard roofs, and that
whole world that has become . . . fugitive and strange. . . ."

He did not so much want to return to that world as to memorial-
ize it, and to understand his feelings. He did not long for his youth,
ever. And it was not by accident that he had helped to burst the
balloons and had sailed around the dance floor in an exhibition sure
to elicit the dressing-down he got. He could not change his family's
circumstances, nor even talk about them. What he could do was to
act out his frustration, to rebel not against his parents but against

surrogate authority in whatever form it presented itself: the black-
clad figure of his dancing instructor, and still more obviously, the
teachers and administrators of Thayer Academy.

The most dramatic fact about Cheever's prep-school experience
is that he was expelled in the spring of 1930, during the second term
of his junior year. A long history led up to the expulsion, for the
academic promise he had shown at Thayerlands seemed to vanish
in the upper school. Louise Saul, who taught him freshman English, remembers him as a student who was "sloppy" about punctu-
ation and who "didn't take well to discipline." The sloppiness
extended to his appearance as well. He looked so shaggy that at
least once his classmates collected a few pennies and escorted him
to the barbershop.

His grades ranged from mediocre to terrible. In the 1926–27
school year, he got Cs and C-minuses in English and ancient history, but flunked both Latin and Algebra. ("His math was horrendous," classmate Robert Daugherty remembers.) The next year
followed a similar pattern. He earned Cs in English, Latin, and
medieval history, and flunked French and math. During 1928–29,
whether because of family finances or Thayer Academy policies, he
went to Quincy High School, where his grades were 55 in English,
45 in French, 0 in Latin, and 63 in plane geometry, with a D in
physical education. In the fall of 1929, he was back at Thayer as a
"special" student on probation, and at the time of his expulsion he
had a B-plus/C-minus in an English literature course, a C in grammar, and a D in German, and was once again failing French. This
1929–30 course schedule, without any math or science or Latin, was
most unusual and probably designed to give Cheever a chance to
shine.

Grading standards were strict at the time, and it was possible for
a C student at Thayer, like John's brother, Fred, to be admitted to
Dartmouth, but a failing grade was a failing grade, and eventually
the school asked Cheever to leave. He was in his own words "an
intractable student" who did the assigned work when and if it
pleased him. "John was not happy at Thayer nor was Thayer
happy about his lack of achievement or his attitude," teacher Grace
Osgood recalled.

The roster of brilliant people who have failed in school is a long
one—Churchill comes to mind, and F. Scott Fitzgerald—and every
year, hundreds of students are dismissed from American prep
schools. But Cheever was probably the only one to use such a

rejection as a way of launching his career. He sat down and wrote a story about it, applying a thin veneer of fiction to his own experience. Then he sent the story, called "Expelled," to Malcolm Cowley at *The New Republic* and had it accepted for publication.

Surely this was one of the most unusual across-the-transom acceptances in magazine history. A youth in Quincy, Massachusetts, barely eighteen, is kicked out of school and writes a story about it that justifies himself by attacking the dullness and lockstep curriculum of the college preparatory system in general and his own institution in particular. In 999 cases out of a thousand, such a submission would have turned into a political harangue and been rejected without a second glance. But Cheever's tale was different. There was something about it that caught Cowley's attention and held it.

He knew how to start, for one thing: with a promise of revelations to follow and an economy of language and incisive wit reminiscent of the early Hemingway stories Cheever had been reading. "It didn't come all at once," "Expelled" begins. "It took a very long time. . . . The first signs were cordialities on the part of the headmaster. He was never nice to anybody unless he was a football star or hadn't paid his tuition or was going to be expelled."

The eighteen-year-old author also understood that it would be wrong to issue any diatribes. Instead, he drew a series of portraits that illustrate the school's problems far more effectively than he could possibly describe them. A former army colonel comes to make the Memorial Day speech. Usually a politician did the job, and told the boys that theirs was the greatest country in the world, and they should be proud to fight for it. But the colonel has seen his friends die in the Great War and cannot supply the expected sentiments. He describes the terrors of battle, then breaks down and begins to whimper. Everyone is embarrassed. Next Memorial Day, the school will be sure to invite a mayor or governor to speak. The charismatic Laura Driscoll, a history teacher who refuses to acknowledge that history is dead, is dismissed for speaking out in defense of Sacco and Vanzetti. English teacher "Margaret Courtwright was very nice," but she "pulled her pressed hair across her forehead" to hide the fact that she was slightly bald; her interpretation of *Hamlet* "was the one accepted on college-board papers," so that no one had to get a new interpretation.

As for the headmaster himself, his is the inside world of the office, with chairs arranged in a semicircle and "gravy-colored" brocade curtains. When he tells Cheever of his dismissal, the youth gazes longingly out the window. "I was tired of seeing spring with walls and awnings to intercept the sweet sun and the hard fruit. . . . I wanted to feel and taste the air and be among the shadows." The tension is strong between the confinements of school and the freedom of the natural world. The pull of the outdoors, "elegant and savage and fleshly," would stay with Cheever always, and nearly always it would be opposed in his mind to the limitations imposed by ordinary existence, by house and workplace, commitment and duty.

Finally, the writer of "Expelled" knew how to win the sympathy of his audience. It is August now, he writes, and he is At Home as the fall approaches:

Everyone is preparing to go back to school. I have no school to go back to.

I am not sorry. I am not at all glad.

It is strange to be so very young and have no place to report at nine o'clock.

When the story appeared in the October 1, 1930, issue of *The New Republic*, a left-wing periodical rarely consulted by Thayer students, their parents, or the faculty, it outraged the sensitivities of all three groups. Cheever had not been fair to the school, they felt. He had distorted the truth, they insisted: there was no crying colonel, and the history teacher had not been fired for political reasons. He had been cruel to Harriet Gemmel (Margaret Courtwright) and Stacy Baxter Southworth (the headmaster), they maintained. The only good thing was that he had not mentioned Thayer by name. The school's partisans were right to object, perhaps, that Cheever had taken liberties with the truth, and exaggerated the school's stagnation. But it was a story he was writing, after all, and a remarkable one coming from a student who had been expelled in his junior year. Without Stacy Baxter Southworth, Cheever was to say many years later, he might have ended up pumping gas. And "Expelled" might as well have been called "Reminiscences of a Young Sorehead," he also observed. But that was to minimize the accomplishment of the story, an achievement so unusual as to make one wonder whether the failure in the classroom was his alone.

The evidence of "Expelled" and of Cheever's transcripts strongly argues that he was dismissed for poor scholastic performance. As he reconstructed the story in later years, however, the immediate offense became smoking. He was caught with a cigarette ablaze and, he maintained, he wanted to be caught. He did start smoking young. As he wrote in "The Jewels of the Cabots" (1972), a bluestocking came to the school to make a choleric chapel speech against the vice. Could the students imagine Christ on the Cross, lighting a cigarette? Could they picture the Virgin Mary smoking? Didn't they know that a tiny drop of nicotine would kill a full-grown pig? In short, she "made smoking irresistible." Smoke he did, undoubtedly, but there is nothing in the records at Thayer or in the memories of those there at the time to suggest that it had anything to do with his dismissal.

On rare occasions Cheever proposed yet another explanation. According to this version—and it was not unusual for him to supply alternative accounts of events in his own life—he was expelled for homosexuality, or as he once said extravagantly, because he had seduced the son of a faculty member. Probably he meant to shock his audience. But whatever the merits of this interpretation, and again there is no hard testimony in its support, it is significant that Cheever articulated it at all. Smoking was a subject that might be taken lightly. For a man of his generation, homosexuality was not. The issue troubled his last decades.

BROTHER

1930-1934

JOHN CHEEVER grew up at risk. From a father dominated by his wife, he inherited a propensity to strong drink, an extraordinary sense of smell, a talent for yarn spinning, and a nagging fear of failure. His mother, fiercely independent, left him her vast fund of energy and strength of will, along with an acute social sensitivity and a deep resentment of powerful women. Both parents shared in bequeathing their second son the most unfortunate legacy of all: the conviction that he was not loved. As Cheever's wife, Mary, came to believe, "that was the trouble" with her husband. "He never had any love. His parents never paid much attention to him."

In part, this was simply the Yankee way. In the Massachusetts of Cheever's youth a chilly formality reigned. Even within the family, physical contact was taboo. This restraint had its effect on most New England writers. Emily Dickinson's brother bent to kiss his father in his coffin, something he had never dared do while his father was alive. In inland Maine, E. A. Robinson wrote in some exaggeration that "children learn[ed] to walk on frozen toes" and thought passion "a soilure of the wits." No more than fictional cousin Honora in *The Wapshot Chronicle* would John's parents have wanted to be caught in "an open demonstration of affection." When drinking, his father would sometimes fondle his mother and blow down her neck, but these attentions were not encouraged. For the most part his parents did not hug, did not kiss. John was brought up not to touch his face, much less any other part of himself, much less anyone else.

In the case of the Cheevers, the physical reserve mandated by New England mores worked to conceal even as it confirmed the split within the family. At least in public, John adopted a similar conspicuous restraint (and later extended it to his own marriage and family). Understanding the cost of the coolly turned cheek, he turned his own first.

There were times when he would gladly have repudiated his heritage. When Leander Wapshot smokes a cigarette in church, his son Coverly—the character in the Wapshot novels most closely modeled on Cheever himself—wishes he were the child of Mr. Pludzinski. Issuing from a position comfortably inside the dominant culture, the remark bespoke something of the author's sense of alienation. His mother often cautioned him not to forget that he was "a Cheevah," but neither parent had provided him with a clear image of what that was. He had no sure sense of himself, or of his own worth.

The problem of identity was complicated by confusion about sexuality. From the perspective of hindsight—the knowledge that Cheever became vigorously bisexual during the last decades of his life—it seems likely that he must have had both homosexual and heterosexual stirrings in his youth. His journals confess as much, and so did his fatherly advice to his son Federico at thirteen. "You are coming to an age," he told the boy, "when you won't know who you want to go to bed with, but you'll get over it." So it must have been for him, except that he did not entirely get over it.

His parents, who did not much concern themselves with young

John otherwise, were troubled by what they regarded as his tendencies toward homosexuality. In a number of ways, he fit into patterns associated in the public mind with growing up gay. He was the product of an unhappy marriage in which the mother had become the dominant figure. He was short (about five feet five at full growth) and as his boyhood pudginess disappeared rather slight. He was not very well coordinated, and played on no athletic teams, preferring to swim or hike or skate or bike in contact with the natural world. In the only hint of effeminacy about him, he spoke in rather curious mid-Atlantic tones that blended his mother's English with his father's Yankee accent. He was interested in—even passionate about—the arts, as both a participant and a spectator. Dorothy Ela remembers him as a tease who used to pull her curls at Thayerlands, but there seem to have been no memorable girlfriends during his high school years. His closest friend was Fax Ogden; he missed him a good deal when Fax was sent off to Culver Military Academy in Indiana. John's parents thought any such attachment unhealthy. "I did not respond consciously to the anxiety my parents endured over the possibility that I might be a pervert," he wrote in 1968, "but I seem to have responded at some other level. . . . had they been less anxious, less suspicious about my merry games of grabarse I might have had an easier life."

The difficulty was, of course, that he shared his parents' revulsion against homosexuality. He had heard the words of opprobrium even before he knew what they meant. Queen, queer, fag, fairy, pansy—these were the epithets used to describe others, and others at a distance. It was unthinkable that they should apply to oneself. The attitude of Coverly Wapshot, in his comic preemployment interview with the psychologist in *The Wapshot Chronicle*, probably paralleled Cheever's own.

"Well, I guess I know what you mean," Coverly said. "I did plenty of that when I was young but I swore off it a long time ago. . . . There's one in this place where I'm living now. He's always asking me to come in and look at his pictures. I wish he'd leave me alone. You see, sir, if there's one thing in the world that I wouldn't want to be it's a fruit."

He has also had "bad dreams," Coverly admits. "I dream I do it with this woman" who looks like the women on barbershop calendars. "And sometimes," he adds, blushing and hanging his head, "I dream that I do it with men. Once I dreamed I did it with a horse."

In retrospect it is clear that homosexuality formed a central element in Cheever's fiction both before and after the trials of Coverly Wapshot. But often—as in the example above—the topic is treated humorously, as if it were of slight importance. Cheever assumed much the same posture in discussing his own situation. "Well, have you ever had a homosexual experience?" his daughter, Susan, asked him in a 1977 interview, taking over the role of the *Chronicle*'s psychologist. "My answer to that is, well, I have had many, Susie, all tremendously gratifying, and all between the ages of nine and eleven," her father answered. Elsewhere he spoke casually of rolling off "his last naked scoutmaster." Such humorous hyperbole was contrived to shock and amuse, and to forestall inquiry. It also provided the mature Cheever, who like most men of his generation had been raised to despise homosexuals, with a way of confessing his inclinations. As a boy he could say nothing at all.

Though uncertain about his sexuality, he knew very early what he wanted to do with his life. He had made the decision to become a writer at eleven, and it lasted. Books became his consolation, as he began educating himself for his chosen career by reading among authors not taught at Thayer. He found the books downtown at the Thomas Crane Public Library, a handsome Romanesque building designed by Henry Hobson Richardson. There he discovered Joyce, whose explorations of human sexuality had appalled Miss Gemmel. He read Flaubert in translation (or possibly, as he later said, in the original). *Madame Bovary*, whose protagonist seeks to escape from an ordinary marriage in a provincial community, became his favorite book, his "Yale College and his Harvard." He read the Garnett translations of Dostoyevsky and Tolstoy as they came out. He started reading Proust, who both enchanted and shocked him. Through John Donne he fell in love with poetry, and read Yeats and Eliot and the Romantics. He read Hemingway, and appropriated some of the taut sarcasm of his early writing for "Expelled." He had yet a great deal to learn, but had already found out that he would have to teach himself and that his masters would be those who spoke from within the covers of a book.

The other great solace of Cheever's adolescence was provided by his brother, Fred, who came home to Quincy in the spring of 1926 after two years at Dartmouth. (With his father unemployed, Fred's college tuition became a real burden.) The two years apart had changed the relationship between the two brothers. Now the difference in their ages seemed of less consequence. They began going to the beach together, and hiking into the hills for long talks about sex and art and politics. Fred reassured his younger brother that his sexual development was perfectly all right, and encouraged him to venture into Boston for the burlesque shows at the Old Howard. In effect they formed their own bond as their parents' marriage unraveled before their eyes. As the autobiographical story "The Brothers" put it, "in trying to make something of their lives, to bring some peace and order into the household, they became deeply attached to each other."

Fred took a number of jobs to try to shore up the family income. When John reached sixteen and got his driver's license, he went to work also, driving a newspaper truck for the *Quincy News*. He hung around the linotype room until the papers were printed, and then drove to the neighboring villages, tossing out bundles of papers at candy and stationery stores. At World Series time the *News* brought out a second edition with the day's box scores, and John delighted in retracing his route by dark, bringing the news of the day's game to the towns along the shore.

At home, matters were worsening. It seemed to the brothers that their mother was "completely absorbed in despising her husband." As for their father, he began to retreat into fantasy, particularly after the 1929 crash wiped out those few stocks he held as his "anchor to windward." Frederick Lincoln Cheever "lost all of his money and some of his mind" in the crash, John said. At first he protested as his wife stripped the house clean of anything that might possibly be sold at the gift shop. Then he took to pretending that nothing untoward had happened. Their ship would come in again soon, he said, as he smoked his favorite cigars and told stories about the glorious past. At the same time he became apprehensive about burglars. One night he shot at Fred, who was coming home late and had climbed in a window to avoid disturbing the family. Luckily, he missed.

When John was eighteen, and his parents were separated for the time being, he lived with his father in the old house at Hanover, a small town south of Quincy on the South Shore. John did the heavy work around the place, while his father discoursed on the sins of his mother. One day he came upon his father sniffing at a yellow rose. "I can no longer smell a rose," he lamented. For father as for son, the way the world smelled was of great importance. If he couldn't smell a rose, the old man went on, he couldn't smell rain coming and he couldn't smell smoke and the house might burn down and trap him inside. The house went soon enough, but not by fire.

Once John had left Thayer, he and his brother oriented themselves toward the wonders of Boston. There they became the Cheever brothers—Fritz and Joey, Joey and Fritz. Fritz the businessman was beginning to establish himself in advertising. Joey was to be the writer, taking odd jobs on occasion—in the summer of 1930 he worked as a stock clerk in a downtown department store, later he had a job as a reporter and occasional reviewer on a Quincy paper—and otherwise relying on Fritz for support. In appearance and personality they were very different. Fritz was outgoing: he used to greet the city's Irish cops by name. He dressed conservatively, as his job required, but he had a hearty appetite for the pleasures of life and was not at all unintellectual. He and Joey went to a sculpture class at the Museum of Fine Arts together, for example, and Fritz drank and talked comfortably with the writers and artists they met. Joey was, as he said, "some kid in those days," with long hair and a big ring. He was shy in conversation, with a wonderfully engaging humor, "a lovely wry way of taking things." When he laughed, his eyes crinkled up in amusement. He liked to flirt and was getting good at it.

Boston was developing its reputation for censorship at that time. In 1928 the New England Watch and Ward Society succeeded in keeping Eugene O'Neill's *Strange Interlude* off the stage, and the company packed up and moved to Quincy, where the play had a successful run. In 1929 Boston police confiscated copies of *Scribner's* magazine containing the serialized version of Hemingway's *A Farewell to Arms*. Still, the city had its attractions, and the Cheevers went together to the theater and the opera, to cabarets and the Old Howard (where they got acquainted with the stripper Boots Rush). Mostly, though, John's orientation was toward the literary and radical element of the community—toward Boston's Bohemia, such as it was.

Rollin Bailey recalls going into the city with John—this may have been as early as 1928 or 1929—to a party in a second- or third-floor apartment. On hand were a number of "volatile and athletic young men" engaged in "some fencing matches," with "much exuberance and horsing about." There were also a few older women, who struck Bailey as "foreign, perhaps Nordic, Italian, lively, friendly." The atmosphere of the place was "genuine and uninhibited." Bailey, a year younger than John, had never seen anything like these people "who had the temerity to be themselves and to express openly how they felt." Boston's bohemia, and its radical fringe, was not generally impoverished. One teatime on Beacon Street, Cheever recalled, the aristocratic left-wing poet Jack Wheelwright tossed sandwiches into the fire as unsuitable and caused his pretty Irish maid to cry. Wheelwright had been talking about his favorite uncle, Henry Adams, but on the way home Cheever could think of nothing but the smoking sandwiches and the weeping maid.

In such literary and intellectual circles Cheever met and befriended Henry Wadsworth Longfellow Dana and Hazel Hawthorne Werner. Harry Dana, the son of Richard Henry Dana III and Edith Longfellow, was a drama professor closely allied with Communism. He had been dismissed from Columbia's faculty in 1917 for his pacifist sentiments. By the early 1930s, when Cheever came to know him, he was lecturing across the United States for the League Against War and Fascism and paying extended visits to the Soviet Union. When in Cambridge, he lived at Castle Craigie, the historic high Georgian house at 105 Brattle Street where Washington had lived in the eighteenth century and Henry Wadsworth Longfellow in the nineteenth. Dana took an interest in Cheever's career and even subsidized him modestly. According to Cheever, Dana was also interested in his person, and pursued him through the halls of Castle Craigie demanding, "How can you be so cruel?"

Hazel Hawthorne Werner, wife of the M. R. (Morrie) Werner who had been biographer of P. T. Barnum and herself a talented fiction writer, also served as a patron to Cheever. She introduced him around in Boston's literary community and took him to Cape Cod to see Provincetown and its playhouse. It was through the Werners that he met E. E. Cummings for the first time. Some of the political passion of Dana and the Werners (Morrie had written a history of Tammany Hall and was working on a record of revolutionary activity since 1848) apparently rubbed off on Cheever. With brother Fred, he attended meetings of the John Reed Club. And in his second published story, "Fall River" (1931), he attempted a proletarian theme. This story, appearing in the second number of a short-lived journal called *The Left*, sketched the gray outlines of the Massachusetts mill town whose mills had closed. Cheever described the effects of poverty and hunger in Fall River, and warned that the rumblings of the workers sounded "like thunder beneath the hills." Wealthy people in Boston were nervous, but there was not much they could do about it. Cheever's piece conformed to *The Left*'s announced belief in "the disintegration and bankruptcy of the capitalist system." Artistically, though, "Fall River" was a failure, since it consisted almost entirely of descriptive passages, with little plot or characterization to command interest.

Cheever's early literary career moved along slowly. He had started near the top, with "Expelled" in *The New Republic* at eighteen, and it took time to develop his craft and locate his market. Since leaving Thayer, he had been keeping the journal that was to become a lifelong habit. In addition, he was turning out stories, but during his first half-decade as a writer only three were published, and two of those in publications that did not pay. He faced the problem that invariably confronts the young writer: lack of material. He already had a lively awareness, characteristic in his best work, of the way that fantasy impinged on reality, but of the real world itself he had little experience. The literary contacts he made in Boston led to the appearance of "Late Gathering" in a new quarterly called *Pagany* (1931) and "Bock Beer and Bermuda Onions" in the better-known *Hound & Horn* (1932), but both stories drew on Cheever's family situation for the subject matter.

In late 1930 Cheever and his brother spent an evening drinking a bottle of bathtub gin—a spider was embalmed inside—with Richard Johns, the editor of *Pagany*. Soon thereafter Cheever sent Johns the typescript of "Late Gathering," along with a note disparaging its quality. When Johns not only accepted the story but noted it in a list of upcoming items, Cheever wrote to thank him. The letter, typed without the use of capital letters (and hence written after Cheever had met Cummings, almost certainly), also bemoaned the difficulty of getting started as a writer, with little but rejection notices to show for his efforts.

He was not even exactly sure what "Late Gathering" was about, Cheever told Johns, suggesting that he was turning out a good many stories at the time. In fact, the story focuses on a woman named Amy who maintains a summer hotel, probably in New Hampshire, and on two young men named Fred and Richard, not identified as brothers but so close that they spend "whole days in the hills lying on the sharp grass wondering about one another." It is autumn and Amy dreads the loss of paying guests during the winter ahead. Among the guests is a Russian lady who talks about how beautiful the mountains in Switzerland are; she is describing Switzerland on the basis of "milk chocolate advertisements," the narrator decides. This is amusing, but there is not much by way of characterization and no real drama. "Late Gathering" risks making no statement whatever.

"Bock Beer and Bermuda Onions" again takes up the character of Amy, now further depicted as a forty-five-year-old widowed in World War I who lets rooms at her house in the country. As she awaits the coming of spring and the return of tourists, some "Indians" make a bargain to camp in her meadow for five dollars a week. After an attempted rape of one of her guests, the Indians flee and she discovers that they weren't Oklahoma Cherokees at all but a band of Gypsies masquerading as Indians to finagle cash out of the locals. The story is little more than an anecdote, for Amy—based on Cheever's mother—is not well realized and the whole lacks focus.

"Bock Beer" appeared in the same issue with a story by Hazel Hawthorne Werner. Lincoln Kirstein, who was editing *Hound & Horn* in Cambridge, took both young authors to lunch, over which Cheever became argumentative and startled Hazel by contradicting Kirstein on the subject of Henry James. Later he told her he'd been drinking all morning to screw up his courage for the lunch.

Whatever the merits of Cheever's story, its publication in *Hound & Horn* earned him considerable prestige. In its short existence the quarterly attracted submissions from a number of the leading writers of the day. The issue of October–December 1932, for example, printed a long article by M. R. Werner on why collectivist Communism would not work in individualistic America, together with work by T. S. Eliot, Marianne Moore, and E. E. Cummings. Cummings, a Yankee who had moved to New York, provided Cheever with an exalted view of his calling. "A writer is a prince," he said in his "beautiful windupthechimney voice." He also told the young Bay Stater to leave Boston. "Get out of Boston, Joey," Cummings said. "It's a city without springboards for people who can't dive." New York was the place for a writer.

Cheever did not go to New York when Cummings advised him to, probably early in 1931. In refashioning the details of his past, Cheever eventually maintained that he had struck out for New York at eighteen, soon after leaving prep school. He did make one brief trip to New York in 1930, to meet Malcolm Cowley. But he did not actually move there to pursue his career until four years later. He spent the interim period in Massachusetts, living with his parents through 1930 and 1931 and sharing apartments with his brother in Boston from 1932 to 1934.

The relationship between the brothers intensified during their hiking trip to Germany in the summer of 1931. Fritz had landed a new and better job beginning in the fall, and on the strength of that prospect the brothers set off for their abbreviated *Wanderjahr*. Joey was still a teenager, and Fritz a man of the world, who wore a mustache and played bridge for high stakes. The militarism they encountered everywhere in Germany caused a quarrel; it troubled Fred not at all, John a great deal. But such arguments were smoothed over during the summer months of travel together. In looking back on that period late in his life, Cheever sometimes hinted that he and his brother had become lovers, and it may be that this happened during their 1931 trip. He told his agent Candida Donadio, for instance, that he had first been deflowered at nineteen, without indicating whether it was a man or a woman who was involved. She rather thought it was a man. "It's apparent to me now," Cheever said in a 1979 interview, "that [Fred] was instrumental in my growing and so instructive in the nature of love." At the very least his older brother cared for him and nurtured him as his parents had not.

Soon after their return from Europe, the brothers moved into an apartment at 6 Pinckney Street in Boston. Until that time John had been at least nominally in residence at 123 Winthrop Avenue in Quincy, but his parents' quarreling and his own desire for independence drove him to depart. He was also annoyed by his parents' unrealistic expectations for his work. "Have you been writing today?" they would ask. "Isn't that nice?" Then they would tell everyone from the charlady to the president of the women's club that their son John was going to write a book, any minute now.

Mrs. Cheever kept a firm rein on her emotions as her sons left the family home. She even arranged, cheerfully enough, for their furniture to be sent to the apartment in Boston. Yet as they backed down the driveway with the last pile of belongings stowed in the car, the headlights struck her face for a second and both brothers saw her face gleaming with tears. Neither of them said anything about it, to her or to each other.

In mid-1932 their mother faced yet another trauma when the bank moved to foreclose on the Quincy house. In a 1936 story called "In Passing," Cheever vividly depicted the anguish of dispossession.

The woman of the story is distressed when surveyors come to look the place over in advance of foreclosure, and she sends her son outside to order them off the property. For a moment, she breaks down. "I can't stand it any longer," she cries. "It's too much to ask of anyone. This is our house. . . . For thirty years we've been working, saving, trying to find something, anything. And now it's all gone. . . . We haven't a place to rest in, to die in. We may die in a hotel. On the street. . . ." Then she recovers herself and makes her son promise not to say anything to his father about her outburst. As it happened, the loss of the house led also to a temporary separation between Cheever's parents. His mother moved to a small house on Spear Street in Quincy, near the public library; his father went to live with his cousin Mary Thompson on her farm in Assinippi.

In Boston, Fred took up his new job and continued to support his brother's struggle to make a career as a writer. Success did not come easily. In fact, there was a three-year gap between the publication of "Bock Beer" in the spring of 1932 and the appearance of "Brooklyn Rooming House" in the May 25, 1935, issue of *The New Yorker*. It was not that Cheever was not trying. He was sharpening his craft and storing up material, in Boston and out. For example, he and Charles Flato rented Prescott Townsend's studio in Provincetown at off-season rates during the winter of 1932. A victim of polio who was later to achieve a distinguished record in government service and public relations, Flato was also trying to write fiction. Conditions on Cape Cod were less than salutary, however. "It was March," Flato recalled, "on a wharf without heat and the floorboards wide enough to see the water at high tide. We tried to type wearing our overcoats and gloves. . . ." For food they depended on the generosity of their fisherman neighbors, and on the supplies that brother Fred brought down on the weekends.

By the following year, Cheever was more eager than ever to see what he could accomplish with a change of venue. From New York his benefactor Malcolm Cowley encouraged him to seek a residency at Yaddo, the artists' colony in Saratoga Springs, and in the spring of 1933 Cheever wrote colony director Elizabeth Ames. He was still learning his craft, he acknowledged, and his goals were modest enough: if granted a residency, he hoped to produce "a handful of good short stories." Unhappily there was no room at Yaddo that summer. In writing to tell Cowley the news, Cheever again emphasized how little he expected from his immediate ef-

forts. He was glad that Cowley had not seen fit to publish the
stories he'd sent him. He wasn't even sure yet what direction his
writing might take. It could be five years before he turned out
"anything worth publishing."

Meanwhile, Cheever was immersing himself in the cultural life
of Boston and Cambridge, where the presence of T. S. Eliot in the
winter and spring of 1933 had, he said, been "equally sterilizing and
stimulating." Eliot, who had returned to the United States after
seventeen years to deliver the Charles Eliot Norton Lectures, chose
as his topic *The Use of Poetry and the Use of Criticism.* The "shadow
of discipline" that Eliot had cast over criticism was undoubtedly a
good thing, Cheever thought, if only because it should cut down on
the amount of criticism produced. But he was troubled by Eliot's
celebration of impersonality in art. His critical machinery would
break down, he felt, when applied to Hart Crane or Cummings.

The next year Cheever tried for Yaddo again, was admitted, and
began an association that was to last the remainder of his life. The
letter of application, written from the brothers' new apartment at
46 Cedar Lane Way, indicated Cheever's interest in the collapsed
glories of Boston and the surrounding area. He had lived all his life
within view of the city and "nearly every day of the last two years
within" it. In his writing he would try to deal with the way relics
from the past consorted uneasily with modern life in Boston. Nothing Cheever wrote quite fit this prospectus, but almost everything
he wrote is pervaded by a sense of the intermingling of past and
present there articulated. He was finding his way, and Yaddo was
a fine place for that.

Located on several hundred acres between the Saratoga racetrack
and the Northway interstate, the estate that became Yaddo was
donated by Spencer and Katrina Trask. According to legend, a
vision came to Mrs. Trask as she and her husband were walking
around the grounds on a summer afternoon in 1899. As the prose
of Marjorie Peabody Waite described it, she suddenly foresaw the
estate as a place of inspiration for writers and other artists who
were "city-weary, who [were] thirsting for the country and for
beauty, who [were] hemmed in by circumstances and [had] no
opportunity to make for themselves an harmonious environment.
. . . At Yaddo they will find the Sacred Fire, and light their torches
at its flame. Look, Spencer! They are walking in the woods, wandering in the garden, sitting under the pine trees—men and
women—creating, creating, creating!"

Actually a quarter of a century intervened before the creating started. Meanwhile Spencer Trask died in a railroad accident on the last day of 1909, Katrina Trask married George Foster Peabody in 1921 and died the following year, and Peabody fell in love with and adopted the Marjorie Waite whose enthusiastic history of Yaddo is quoted above. Marjorie's sister was Elizabeth Ames, and another legend has it that one day as Peabody was considering who should be chosen to run the colony, a halo of light shone down on Elizabeth's hair. It was a fortunate omen. Mrs. Ames was in charge when Yaddo opened its doors in 1926, and stayed on the job for more than forty years. The estate itself consisted of a fifty-five-room gray stone mansion, "all cupolas and porches and bay windows on the outside, stained glass and oiled floors and marble statuary within," a garage with living quarters, three smaller houses, and several studios. In addition, Yaddo contained four small lakes, a rose garden open to the public, miles of paths through hundreds of acres of woodland, a tennis court, and eventually—at Cheever's insistence—a swimming pool.

Katrina Trask had originally thought of the colonists at Yaddo as houseguests, and Elizabeth Ames, a woman of considerable presence, sought to maintain an air of gentility about the place. The "guests" were expected to dress for dinner, and improprieties of all sorts were discouraged. Cheever, who had youth, good manners, and a winning wit, soon became one of her favorites. For him, Yaddo served as a refuge, almost as a home. He visited there for three full months in 1934, and for at least that long during each of the four years that followed. At Yaddo he met and talked of the profession with other, more established writers. He also learned to demand a regular daily production from himself, in conditions that could hardly have been more ideal.

As at the MacDowell Colony and other artists' havens, the program at Yaddo encouraged results by eliminating outside distractions. Then as now the daily routine consisted of breakfast from eight to nine, followed by seven uninterrupted hours for work. In solitude, each colonist took a box lunch back to his or her room or studio. Visitors were unwelcome from nine to four, and only emergency phone calls were put through. In the evening there was a communal dinner, with no organized social activities thereafter. Some wonderful art emerged from Yaddo under these circumstances. There Cheever produced much of his best fiction. There he formed some of his closest and most important friendships.

James T. Farrell was at Yaddo that first summer of 1934, finishing his *Studs Lonigan* trilogy, and with him his wife, Dorothy, who had somehow managed to escape Elizabeth Ames's usual prohibition against spouses. For a time, in fact, Dorothy functioned as Elizabeth's assistant. A precocious college actress at the University of Chicago, she was seven years her husband's junior and had eloped with him when she was only seventeen. That made her almost exactly Cheever's age, and as the two youngest colonists they became fast friends. In the late-summer afternoons they sometimes went rowing on Saratoga Lake. In the evenings they all traipsed into town to assemble at a wonderful, now-defunct bookstore or at the bar of the New Worden Hotel, also departed. Even in those years Cheever drank a lot. Among the first things Dorothy Farrell noticed about him were the gin bottles stowed outside his door for the maids to dispose of. But he was clearly a worker too, and a charmer, with an engaging effervescence about him. He was short but walked very fast. He did everything fast, as if he were out to enjoy life and glad of companions along the way. For Dorothy Farrell, he was mostly a playmate. For Elizabeth Ames, he was immediately the star boarder.

Cheever was at Yaddo from June 4 through July 28, 1934. When he went back to Boston, he was almost ready to break his bond to Fred. The love he felt for his brother was, as he said a hundred times, "the strongest love" of his life. Boston of the mid-1930s was "so anxious to fortify its own eccentricities" that it rather welcomed the oddly inseparable Cheever brothers. The two even made preliminary plans to buy a small house together at Boxford, whence Fritz would commute to his advertising job at the Pepperell Manufacturing Company while Joey crafted Jamesian novels. But the arrangement began to take on "an ungainly closeness." He and his brother were "morbidly close," John decided, and his own feelings disturbingly "incestuous."

Cheever portrayed this unnatural closeness in "The Brothers," a 1937 story that is patently autobiographical. "That was a true story," Hazel Werner testifies. Kenneth and Tom, the brothers of the title, pay a weekend visit to a farm on the North Shore to see the widowed Amy and her comely daughter Jane. Kenneth and Tom are entirely comfortable with each other. In escaping from their bitterly mismatched parents, the brothers have fallen into a routine that does not admit of quarreling. Jane, who has a yen for Kenneth, goes dancing with the two of them and senses their soli-

darity. "Above everything she felt how accustomed the boys were
to sitting across from each other at table with no one between
them." They have shared so much as to shut out others entirely.
They have even shared girlfriends, in fact. So though she tries
desperately, Jane cannot succeed in wooing Kenneth to herself.

Tom sees Jane's frustration and begins to worry. "He loved his
brother, and this love was the strongest thing in his comprehen-
sion, but it was a love that held no jealousy and no fear and no
increase, and in the beginning it had been as simple as walking into
the sun." Witnessing Kenneth's indifference to Jane, it occurs to
him for the first time "that their devotion to each other might be
stronger than their love of any girl or even than their love of the
world." So he decides to go away, to give up "the little certainty
they had rescued from the wreck of their home. He felt the sharp
thrust of responsibility for them both—they must live and not wear
out their lives like old clothes, in a devotion that would defeat its
own purpose." The following night he takes a bus for New York.
That is exactly what John Cheever did, shortly after returning to
Boston from Yaddo in the late summer of 1934.

"The Brothers" revealed only part of the curious relationship
between Fred and John Cheever, and barely hinted at the animosity beneath the surface. It was a theme he took up repeatedly in his
fiction. "The brothers story I've told fifty times, I guess. Sometimes
I think I am not telling it, but I am." Most of these stories contain
violence. "I strike him in some, I hit him with sticks, rocks; he in
turn also damages me. . . ." Matters were not simple between them,
and at the time of John's departure for New York—despite the
disclaimer in "The Brothers"—they may have been affected by
jealousy.

John saw Iris Gladwin first. Canadian by birth, she had moved
to a Winthrop Avenue house in Quincy as a girl. She was just
John's age, and they surely must have seen each other at Quincy
high school during the 1928–29 year he spent there. Later she attended art classes at the museum with both brothers, as a form of
relaxation from her training as a nurse. Gradually John became
fond of her, and began to take her out. Then Fred took an interest
too, and she chose him. It was the sensible choice. He was a reliable
businessman with a good job, John an insecure artist with no visible means of support. Less than two months after John went to
New York, Fred Cheever married Iris Gladwin.

There was no open rift between the Cheever brothers, however.

To begin with, Fred sent his younger brother a weekly allowance of ten dollars in New York. Once, during his first winter in the city, John awoke to the sound of a snowball plashing against the window of his tiny room, and knew at once that Fred had come to see him. When he went back to Massachusetts, he visited Fred and Iris as a matter of course. Still, he had broken free at last. When he climbed aboard the night bus that rattled down through Worcester and Hartford to the great city on the Hudson, John declared his independence. If he was to be a writer, he would be one in New York, and on his own.

STARTING

1934-1937

I T TOOK courage for John Cheever to leave his
brother behind and strike out at twenty-two, at the
very bottom of the Depression, to gamble on a career as a writer in the metropolis of New York.
Cheever's fictional Coverly Wapshot, a youth brought
up in small-town St. Botolphs, is repeatedly confounded by his first encounter with the city. Coverly
has never seen a high building or a dachshund, a man
wearing suede shoes or a woman blowing her nose on
a piece of Kleenex, a parking meter or a pay telephone.
Unwilling to betray his ignorance by asking directions, Coverly is drawn instinctively to the north, following the crowds from midtown Manhattan through

Central Park to the Upper West Side, past a stickball game in Harlem and finally on the subway farther north still to the outermost reaches of the Bronx. Cheever was not so innocent as that. He had lived in Boston or within eight miles of it all his life. And he had suffered through at least one rite of passage on his 1930 trip to New York soon after *The New Republic* printed "Expelled."

On that occasion the youth went to see Malcolm Cowley, who had accepted the story. Cowley was charmed. "I hadn't ever met before a boy . . . who could speak honestly about himself, and in English," he recalled. "I never afterward met another." He invited Cheever back to a party that he and his first wife, Peggy, were giving. "You must be John Cheever," Peggy said, meeting him at the door. "Everyone else is here." Cheever was offered a choice of two drinks. "One was greenish. The other was brown . . . one was a manhattan and the other Pernod." Eager to appear as sophisticated as possible, he accepted a manhattan. Then he accepted several more. After four or five cocktails, he realized he was going to vomit, but his manners did not entirely desert him. He "rushed to Mrs. Cowley, thanked her for the party, and reached the apartment-house hallway" before throwing up on the wallpaper.

Cowley continued to encourage his career during the next few years. Though he could not accept pieces—part essay, part story—Cheever sent *The New Republic* about the walking trip in Germany and about the deepening malaise among the young, Cowley believed in Cheever's talent. He gave him a novel about prep-school life to review in 1931. He was instrumental in getting him into Yaddo. And in July 1934 when Cheever came to New York alone, Malcolm Cowley was one of the two people he could count on to help him as much as he could.

The other was Hazel Hawthorne Werner, who had moved to New York from Boston with her husband and urged Cheever to follow. The Werners' kindness to him was "exhaustive and indescribable." When he arrived in Greenwich Village, they put him up on the sofa in their fifth-floor apartment on Waverly Place. Cummings stopped by that first night, and so did John Dos Passos. Later Cheever met Sherwood Anderson, Gaston Lachaise, Milton Avery, Walker Evans, James Agee, Edmund Wilson, and others through the Werners. Morrie Werner was also responsible for landing Cheever a part-time job almost immediately.

M-G-M was looking for books that could be turned into successful films, and was hiring writers to read novels and make capsule summaries. Together with James T. Farrell and writer–social critic Paul Goodman, Cheever spent his midsummer days waiting around the M-G-M office for the woman who distributed the books to turn up and hand them out. The going rate was five dollars for a three-to-five-page synopsis, with carbons. That, along with the weekly ten dollars from brother Fred, was the extent of Cheever's income.

Three dollars a week went for rent on his tiny fourth-floor room at 633 Hudson Street in lower Manhattan. The other tenants were mostly unemployed seacooks and longshoremen. Whores used the downstairs toilet. Initially the longshoremen didn't know what to make of Cheever's accent or his gray flannel suit and blue button-down shirts. They encouraged him to take some sort of extension course or an exam for post office work. Paul Goodman, who was "thought to be a genius," misunderstood the situation in a different way. He conceived the idea that because Cheever lived among sailors, he must be homosexual, and made a pass that was gently rebuffed.

The room itself was depressing and the summer heat enervating. In a photograph Walker Evans caught the miserably spare room, illuminated by the afternoon light that seeped around the blind of the single window. Cheever was no sooner settled than he wanted to get out. Within the first week he petitioned Elizabeth Ames for another visit to Yaddo. He was using so much time and energy poring over other people's novels for M-G-M, he said, that it was almost impossible to start one of his own. That was what he planned to do at Yaddo.

Mrs. Ames manufactured an opening at the end of August. Meanwhile Cowley helped him skimp out a precarious existence. Cheever presented himself with a number of other young writers at *The New Republic* offices on Wednesday afternoons. That was the day Cowley handed out books for review and, often, books that were never to be reviewed that the writers could sell. In a small way this helped impoverished young authors keep going. The notorious Joe Gould also came every Wednesday, got a dollar, and left. Bearded and unbathed, his clothes spotted with ketchup, Gould panhandled around Village bars for decades. He was, he said, writing a history of the world. It was never completed.

That summer of 1934, Cheever reviewed Josephine Johnson's *Now in November,* a novel about the Midwestern drought, for *The New Republic.* The author was young, only twenty-four, and Cowley may have thought that Cheever would feel a certain affinity for her work. He did and he didn't. He admired Johnson's "fragile and, in its way, nearly perfect" talent, but chided her for her tranquil tone and her interest in "the little things." The drought was a national disaster. Johnson was "observing the salamanders while the fields [were] burning."

Cowley also sent his young protégé to talk to Harrison Smith, of Cape & Smith, about his prospective novel. Smith had published Cowley's book of poems, *Blue Juniata,* in 1929. Perhaps he could be persuaded to give Cheever an advance. He could not, for a reason that was to have a continuing effect on Cheever's reputation. The short-story writer and the novelist were "two different birds," Smith thought. Cheever refused to be discouraged, and set off for five weeks at Yaddo, determined to bring back a healthy chunk of the novel.

Already the estate in Saratoga was beginning to seem familiar. If the decor did not entirely suit his taste, it was certainly distinctive. Coming down the stairway from his room for breakfast—he occupied many different rooms during his visits to Yaddo— Cheever passed the brass mermaid, the Tiffany window of a woman holding a flower (this was supposed to be Katrina Trask herself), and the cast of Venus he would smack on the backside as he slid down the banister. His room invariably contained some emblem of culture—a charcoal drawing of Dante, perhaps—and was almost always in need of repairs. On one visit, a sign cautioned him to shut the shower door, lest water drip on the piano below. That turned out to be no problem at all, since the shower didn't work. Yaddo was one of a kind, unique, *sui generis.* Room and board were free to those who could not afford to pay. Cheever loved it there and thought it the best place in the world to work.

Despite Yaddo's encouraging ambience, what Cheever wrote during his 1934 visits did not sell. His beginning-of-a-novel failed to attract an advance. Meanwhile, a couple of magazine editors were holding stories. If he could only get one acceptance, he wrote Elizabeth Ames, the other editors might loosen up. In discouragement, he went back to New York to face the hardest winter of his life. "I was cold, I was hungry, I was lonely," he recalled. Though M-G-M gave him an occasional book to write a synopsis of, funds were so short that he subsisted for weeks on stale bread and buttermilk. There were a few houses and apartments he could go to for a meal, but his pride would not let him abuse that privilege.

Cheever had plenty of company in his misery. In the Battery, drifters sat along the docks with their junk bags on mild days, sharing cigarette butts and staring into the water. As it grew colder, they huddled together over small bonfires. Some slept in doorways with newspapers for blankets. As many as twelve hundred a night slept at the Municipal Lodging House, Annex No. 2, in the old ferry shed at the foot of Whitehall Street. Farther uptown in Union Square, poor people ate in cheap restaurants that dispensed plain food for nickels and dimes and quarters, and forgot their troubles in cheap movie theaters that showed double features and gave away dishes during intermission. Cheever himself spent long afternoons in Washington Square, discussing with other hungry men the effects of not having enough to eat. "It was the torpor we objected to," he recalled. Poverty complicated every detail of daily life. Someday when he got some money, his friend Shorty Quirt said, he was going to shave with a new blade and wear clean socks every day.

As Cheever wrote Elizabeth Ames, it had been "a lean strange winter" so far. At least he had two acceptances to report, from *The New Republic* and *Story Magazine*. Both stories drew heavily on his own experience. The documentary-style "Autobiography of a Drummer" read like an apologia for his father's failure. In the much longer and more complex "Of Love: A Testimony," a story about a young woman who unaccountably shuttles back and forth as the lover of two close friends, he tried to work out his feelings about Iris and Fred. At the end he imagines a dim future for the odd man out in the triangle:

Make him employed or unemployed, put him in a strange city without money or on board a train leaving the city.... He is older. His face is lined. His topcoat is shabby. He stands on the platform smoking a cigarette. He has taken the wrong train and there is nobody there to meet him.

In actuality, Cheever was working to construct a happier future for himself than that represented by the bereft odd man out. He had started a novel at Yaddo partly in response to Cowley's suggestion that he try to write a book that would appeal to the younger generation much as F. Scott Fitzgerald's *This Side of Paradise* had fifteen years earlier. But now Cowley had read the completed chapters of this novel, variously titled *Empty Bed Blues* and *Sitting on the*

Whorehouse Steps, and found them disappointing. They read too much like stories, Cowley thought, each chapter reaching a dead end. And they sounded too much like Hemingway—particularly the Hemingway of "Cross Country Snow"—both in style and theme. That was discouraging news, and so was the fact that most of the stories Cheever had written lately were being rejected by the magazines.

On a Friday evening in midwinter, Cowley asked Cheever to come for dinner and a talk about his career. It proved to be one of the most momentous evenings of his life. Cheever obviously needed to make some money from his fiction, both men agreed. His novel-in-progress did not offer much promise along those lines. In addition, the stories Cheever was writing were too long, up to six or seven thousand words. Editors didn't like to buy long stories from unknown writers, Cowley explained. The solution was to write shorter stories.

"It's Friday now," Cowley said. "Why don't you write a story a day for the next four days, none of them longer than a thousand words? Then bring them to me and I'll see whether I can't get you some money for them." It was a labor to daunt any writer, but Cheever agreed at once. On Wednesday afternoon he appeared in Cowley's office with the four stories. *The New Republic* took one of them, an anecdote about a burlesque performer called "The Princess." The other three Cowley sent to Katharine White at *The New Yorker,* and she took two—"Brooklyn Rooming House" and "Buffalo." (The fourth story, "Bayonne," was published in the spring of 1936 in a little magazine.)

So commenced one of the longest and most important publishing connections in American literary history. *The New Yorker,* barely a decade old in 1935, was looking for talented newcomers who could grow along with it and help to build circulation. In Cheever they found what they wanted. He was two days short of his twenty-third birthday when *The New Yorker* first printed a story of his. He was not quite sixty-nine when they printed the last one. Altogether 121 stories by Cheever ran in the magazine, more than by any other author except John O'Hara. In all other periodicals he published only 54 additional stories. William Maxwell, who edited most of his *New Yorker* stories (usually they required very little editing), became one of Cheever's closest friends. Gus Lobrano, who replaced Maxwell for a time, provided conservative counsel and performed the fatherly service of teaching Cheever to fish. Even editor in chief Harold Ross, a gruff man who rarely trafficked with fiction writers, occasionally took Cheever to lunch.

The pieces Cheever wrote for *The New Yorker* in the 1930s bear little relation to the great stories that appeared there in later decades. Long stories like "The Enormous Radio," "Goodbye, My Brother," "The Country Husband," and "The Swimmer" brought whole worlds to life and conveyed a powerful emotional charge. In contrast, most of the early *New Yorker* stories were brief, pessimistic sketches. "Goddammit, Cheever," Ross swore, "why do you write these goddam gloomy stories?" There were reasons enough, and the young writer could hardly change his viewpoint on demand. Looking back on the decade thirty years later, Cheever could only bring the thirties into focus through a filter of grainy darkness. Everything sloped downhill, toward war.

Others more politically committed than he were madly hopeful. Cowley, for instance, has written of the 1930s dream of the golden mountains, of the invigorating sense of living in history with a chance to change it for the better, come the revolution. Cheever witnessed what seemed the last throes of capitalism—no one with eyes could have failed to—but could not summon up the utopian vision of the true believer. His stories of the period tell of poverty and disillusionment, and of his dark belief that neither Communism nor pacifism could rescue mankind from itself.

Time after time the economic crisis forces his characters to compromise their humanity and abandon their hopes. In evocations of the working class thought by latter-day critics to be beyond his ken, Cheever glimpsed the dreary and loveless lives of lunch-cart workers, striptease artists, and sailors down on their luck. More effectively, his tales caught middle-class people trying to maintain their dignity in a time of diminished expectations. An example is "Brooklyn Rooming House," the first of his *New Yorker* stories. The landlady who runs the rooming house has clearly seen better days. It is not even her own house she is in charge of, and since she cannot evict the drunks and hooligans, she pretends that they are gentlemen. In a moving finish, one of her drunken renters collapses on the stairs. At first she purports not to notice. Then she goes to him, bends over, and as the passed-out man lies motionless, politely asks him three times, "Can't you find your key? Can't you find your key? Can't you find your key?" Some of the Cheever family's humiliation speaks in this story, and some of John's own.

With nearly everyone fallen on hard times, it was easy to portray oneself as having once had a genteel background. So in a number of stories, near-indigent characters reminisce about the servants they used to have and the high-stakes bridge games their mothers played in and how those days are gone forever and the best they can hope for is a house in Westchester or Connecticut where they can have a garden and a family and some semblance of a comfortable life, and not many of them are going to reach even that goal.

However unlikely its fulfillment might be, people nonetheless refused to give up their dream—not a dream of the golden mountains where all might thrive but of their private gold mine or at least a place in the country where they might be better off than others. It is this thirst for gain that confounds the Communist Girsdansky in "In Passing" (1936), Cheever's forthright tale of why it won't happen here. With the passion of the committed, Girsdansky "spoke of revolution as if it were something that he would see on the next day, or the next." His great selling point is poverty. "Why should you be poor when you can do away with poverty?" he asks his street-corner audiences. But his voice is dry, he lacks humor and human warmth, and the listeners drift away. Tom, the narrator, is living with European immigrants in Saratoga and working at the five-and-dime. All around him he encounters those who resist Girsdansky's message. The immigrants have come to what they think of as a land of opportunity. The petty gamblers of the town have "nothing in their faces but a love of money, and the incorrigible dream of big money." His younger brother daydreams about travel and making a fortune and lots of women. Even his parents, about to be dispossessed of their home, continue to pursue the ever-receding bonanza. At the end Tom takes the night bus to scratch out a chancy existence in New York City, while Girsdansky continues to preach to the trees and the lampposts.

Communism was not the answer, then, at least not in America. Still, simply surviving in New York remained a trial for Cheever. He might not have made it at all but for the generosity of Yaddo, where he spent most of his time from late 1935 to early 1938. During the long cold winter of '35, he sounded out Elizabeth Ames about the possibility of a summer job running the launch at Triuna, the three-island complex on Lake George owned by the Yaddo foundation. In April he renewed the inquiry. By this time *The New Yorker* had taken the two stories, and he'd acquired as his first agent Maxim Lieber (a man who specialized in representing writers with liberal sympathies). But he needed time to write, he told Ames, and "would be glad to work for the chance." Couldn't a summer job at Yaddo "be fitted in" with writing hours?

This query elicited an unsympathetic reply in which Elizabeth Ames advised Cheever to spend more time at some occupation other than writing. He had to learn to support himself, she said. He should adjust to conditions rather than complaining about them. In some exasperation Cheever wrote back that he had held odd jobs all his life, and had supported himself through the winter doing synopses for M-G-M. But as of May 1935 the supply of jobs had run dry. He had put in applications for everything from busboy to copywriter, with no results.

At this Ames relented. Cheever went to Yaddo for the month of August and Lake George for the month of September. In Saratoga he saw a lot of the racing season, piling up background for future stories. On his way south, Cheever stopped in Boston for two days among the "pale, contrite faces" of the city's lawyers and bankers. With relief he returned to New York, where the problem of gainful occupation was solved, for the time being, by his friend Walker Evans. Evans had been commissioned to photograph an exhibition of American Negro art for the Museum of Modern Art, and he hired Cheever—who had no previous experience—to make prints in a "gruesome hovel" of a studio at 20 Bethune Street. According to the expenses Evans submitted to the Museum of Modern Art, he paid Cheever twenty dollars a week for fourteen and a half weeks during the fall of 1935. Other evidence suggests that the weekly salary was ten dollars and that the job lasted less than three months.

In any event, this was a onetime chore and could not long keep the wolf from the door. Conditions for the free-lance writer could hardly have been worse. By 1935, book royalties had dropped to 50 percent of 1929 rates, and book sales were also cut in half. Magazine advertising linage was dropping steadily; editors were reluctant to build up any backlog, for fear their magazine might go out of business at any moment. The editor of *The Atlantic Monthly* declared in 1934 that he bought only one out of every four hundred manuscripts submitted. Sherwood Anderson, after two decades of professional writing, found himself "always in need of money, always just two steps ahead of the sheriff." For beginning free lances the outlook was still dimmer.

To help brighten this dispiriting picture, the New Deal formed the Federal Writers' Project (FWP) as a branch of the Works Progress Administration (WPA), and appointed Henry Alsberg as national director on July 25, 1935. Exactly two months later, Cheever wrote Alsberg seeking employment. The major undertaking of the FWP was to be the writing, editing, and publishing of guidebooks to each of the forty-eight states and a few of the major cities. He could be of use, Cheever argued, because of the "clarity, ease, and meaning" with which he handled the English language.

He might have been hired at that time—he had not overstated his qualifications, certainly—but ran afoul of a provision of the law requiring that 90 percent of all employees must be on relief at the time they were employed. (Later the figure was lowered to 75 percent.) But he couldn't go on relief, Cheever wrote Cowley late in October, because he didn't have a residence. If Malcolm knew of anything he could do, he'd like to hear about it. Instead it was Yaddo that once more gave him sustenance. He spent the entire winter of 1936 on the grounds, along with Lloyd (Pete) Collins, Collins's dog Oscar, who looked like a dandelion, Leonard Ehrlich, Daniel Fuchs and his wife, Sue—Sue could come, Elizabeth Ames decreed, if she promised not to "disturb the artists"—and of course Elizabeth herself. The group got along famously. Both Fuchses were impressed by Cheever's capacity for friendship. "You felt good when you were with him," Dan said. There was a dignity about him too, and a sense of honor. "He was a man who would have been mortified to hurt or disturb anyone else."

Still, he was restless for success. All four of the men were fiction writers, though only Cheever and Fuchs—author of the Williamsburgh (New York City) novels and later an Oscar-winning screenwriter—were to achieve notable careers. The two of them used to sit in the bar of the New Worden Hotel and talk about the future. "What are you waiting for?" Dan asked Cheever. "For the world and my life to get integrated," he answered. Yaddo housed and fed him, but otherwise he was broke. At *The New Yorker* Maxwell remembers getting a call from Maxim Lieber. "Could he have the check in a hurry?" Lieber wondered. His client was living in straitened circumstances upstate.

Hopefully he started working on his novel again, expanding it to a family saga. It was to be called *The Holly Tree*. For exercise he went skiing on the skis he'd brought with him. He and Fuchs constructed a miniature ski jump in front of the mansion. Cheever sailed over without mishap. Then Dan tried it; first he fell ass over teakettle, next he broke the skis. Cheever made no fuss, but Fuchs, seeing he was distraught, went to town and bought a new pair of skis.

Cheever stayed on at Yaddo well into the spring, earning his way as a kind of all-purpose caretaker. The winter residents departed, to be replaced by Nathan Asch, Eleanor Clark, and Josephine Herbst, all writers and all politically left-wing. Herbst was Stalinist in her orientation and Clark a Trotskyite, but Cheever remained largely untouched by their disputes—"a political innocent," Clark thought. Instead he stuck to the task of writing his book. He finished the novel at his parents' small house in Quincy on May 25. To celebrate he drove to the Cape, where the high waves were crashing. The following week he set out for Triuna to take over the job he'd angled for the previous summer. Simon & Schuster had agreed to give his novel a reading. Waiting for a response at Triuna, he ran the enormous Fay & Bowen motor launch, turned out stories, and generally enjoyed himself.

It was at Triuna in the summer of 1936 that Cheever met Anton (Ref) and Lila Refrigier. Ref, a painter of Russian and French parentage, was teaching stage design at the theater school Yaddo was running to bring in summer revenue. His new bride, Lila, taught costume design. Cheever immediately endeared himself to the Refrigiers by rearranging the sleeping accommodations. Elizabeth Ames had assigned them to a room with two twin beds and had given Cheever quarters with a large double bed all his own. Without authorization he undertook to switch his double bed to their room, a maneuver that, according to Lila, made Elizabeth furious. Lila appreciated that kindness, and liked Joey—as she called him—in other ways as well. He had a "delicious" sense of humor. He was a "very loving man." She could not imagine anyone disliking him. And he took pains with his appearance. He had a pair of gray flannel trousers he wore with an old but well-kept tweed jacket with patches, a button-down shirt with black knit tie, and carefully shined shoes. "He always looked good," she recalls.

Cheever was immediately attracted to Lila, a blond girl with a fetching ponytail. On a trip to Yaddo, they took a walk together around the stables at the racetrack. "The only other woman I've known a horse would whinny at was Dorothy Farrell," he told her. He shared his successes with her, too. When he sold a story to *The Atlantic Monthly,* he smuggled a bottle of warm champagne into Triuna. He and the Refrigiers drank it down in toothbrush mugs to celebrate the sale. "Champagne never tasted better," she remembers. "An extra dollar then meant more than ten thousand dollars later."

At midsummer the theater school collapsed in the wake of a dispute between the faculty and the administration. The students had prepared a play for parents' day, but at the last moment the school's director called it off. When the Refrigiers went to Ames to object, she upheld her director and told them all—students and faculty alike—to go home. As a consequence the Refrigiers left Triuna and rented a house in adjoining Bolton Landing for the rest of the summer. Cheever often came over for dinner, and Lila chided him for staying on. Elizabeth was making a pet of him, she said, treating him like Little Lord Fauntleroy. Why didn't he just leave Yaddo? But jobs were still scarce, and he valued the haven Yaddo provided. In a very real sense the place had come to seem like home to him. He had no permanent residence during those mid-1930s years. There were extended stays at Yaddo. The rest of the time he divided between visiting his parents and brother and sister-in-law on the South Shore and bunking in with friends in New York.

In the city he saw a great deal of Lila Refrigier. Together they explored New York on the cheap while her husband was working on his canvases or on occasional commissions to do nightclub murals. They rode the Staten Island ferryboat for a nickel and rode the Fifth Avenue bus up and down Fifth Avenue from Washington Square to Harlem. They walked up to Central Park to spend hours in the zoo and to go horseback riding. Cheever rode like a jockey, with his stirrups way up. They went to twenty-five-cent movies and to the track at Belmont. Later as he became marginally more prosperous he took her on picnics in his Ford Model A and on visits to see Josie Herbst at her Bucks County house in Erwinna. He also escorted her to cocktail parties at Muriel Rukeyser's and Eleanor Clark's. At Eleanor's, he remembered years later, he was talking with her father when the poet Horace Gregory fell at their feet, drunk. To celebrate sale of one story, he took Lila to Charles's on Sixth Avenue, where they drank half a dozen dry manhattans before dinner and went on to the Brevoort for after-dinner kümmel. He also confided to her his innermost feelings about his family, and particularly about his brother, Fritz, whom he seemed alternately to love and to dislike. In short, they became intimates.

Frances Lindley (Frances Strunsky by birth, and then married to Pete Collins) recalls a poignant conversation with Anton Refrigier about this relationship. He was disturbed because when Cheever telephoned them at their flat in Chelsea—where Zero Mostel "rented" Ref's studio one summer without paying the rent—he did not even speak to Ref but simply asked for Lila. "Frances," Ref said, "I have to ask you something. Is Lila in love with John?" Frances sighed with relief at the way the question was worded. It was a question she could honestly answer "I don't know."

Cheever struck almost everyone who knew him in those years as aggressively heterosexual, very much a woman's man. He was "pretty promiscuous," Frances Lindley reports, but that was hardly unusual in the Greenwich Village of the 1930s. The Village's heyday as a center of political and sexual radicalism had passed, but it was still a place where young artists of both sexes could meet and talk and drink and make love without raising eyebrows. Science also made intercourse less risky. It may be significant that most of the women he knew and was attracted to were married when he met them—this was true of Hazel Hawthorne Werner and Dorothy Farrell and Lila Refrigier and Frances Lindley—and therefore posed no threat to his bachelorhood. Simultaneously he was developing his unusual capacity and need for friendship with women who would cherish and encourage him as his own parents had not. Josie Herbst took on the role of a fond older sister, ever interested in his welfare. Elizabeth Ames became virtually a surrogate mother. On the male side, Cowley acted like a father, advising and advancing the career of a talented son.

Forty years later, Cheever wrote a young gay friend that he and Walker Evans had briefly been lovers when he first came to New York. In a letter he vividly described ejaculating all over Evans's furniture and art works before departing at three in the morning. This account, obviously written to amuse, may contain no truth at all. Frances Lindley, who has read Evans's private papers in her capacity as editor, thinks it highly unlikely. Evans had lovers of both sexes, but nowhere mentions Cheever as among them. Besides, it was clear to her as John's devoted friend at the time that his sexual orientation was toward women.

In particular, Frances liked Johnny (as *she* called him) for his kindness. "There was a kind of sweetness in Johnny that was really very nice," she observed. They had dinner at Malcolm Cowley's soon after Malcolm's mother had died. In bittersweet reminiscence Cowley dug out his childhood silver spoon, and Cheever was im-

mediately tender toward him. On the whole he was less sympathetic to other figures in the literary establishment. He fell asleep
listening to Anderson drone on about himself. Dos Passos he
thought "dull but pleasant." He and Edmund Wilson "detested one
another" on sight. His hero was fellow Yankee Cummings, the tall
patrician poet who bestrode the Village like a Colossus from his
Patchin Place apartment, the lovely Marion Morehouse at his side.
"It was Estlin Cummings who, through at least a similarity in
background, made it clear to me that one could be a writer and also
remain highly intelligent, totally independent, and married to one
of the most beautiful women in the world." That was what he
wanted out of life too.

Cheever hoped that *The Holly Tree* would help him achieve a
measure of that independence. It did not work out that way. In the
fall of 1936 he got word from Simon & Schuster that his book needed
revision. He had submitted a digressive and episodic book with a
shifting point of view; the publishers wanted something much
more conventional. So he headed upstate to Yaddo, aided by a loan
from Cowley, planning to "go over the whole novel again, word for
word." Despite the loan, he had to turn out stories to make ends
meet, and so the novel languished. His financial condition, as of
December 1936, was the worst in two years. At Yaddo, the snow-
drifts were piling up outside and the walls beginning to close in.
He needed to escape, and did.

He spent much of January in Quincy, his longest visit in years.
His father got to reminiscing about the impoverishment of Newburyport after the Civil War. Both parents lamented the more
recent decline of New England. Brother Fred had even written a
book—"not a very good book, but a book"—on the subject, he
reported to Elizabeth Ames. But no one resented the collapse more
than John himself. Even sadness seemed inadequate to deal with
the story, he wrote in a book review for *The New Republic*. "For the
glorious seaboard of the China trade means to most of us now a
four-way turnpike and a few brilliant old women and the main-
stem girls in Portland and empty harbors and fugitive mill towns
and the smell of the tourist camps and a cretin at a gas station." The
glory days might be over, but with his brother he was eager to
declare that the tradition was still vigorous, if temporarily quiescent, that there was more to their native land than crazy old aunts
in the attic.

Cheever next went to New York for a week, where he stayed

with the Werners and saw Dorothy Farrell, now divorced. He'd been away from the city for so long that he felt like a yokel: at the Lafayette he stared at a couple who were drinking champagne and playing backgammon. Either he or Max Lieber must also have had a conference with Simon & Schuster, for the publishers came through with a four-hundred-dollar advance, and by the first of February he was back at Yaddo, revising the novel. He had the time to do the job now, but no matter how he sweated and strained he could not bring it off. His publishers demanded a kind of novel he could not or would not produce. In the end he abandoned *The Holly Tree* entirely, returned to New York, and—according to a latter-day yarn—chucked the only typescript into a trash can. No copy has ever surfaced.

By 1937 the Spanish Civil War was stimulating political passions among his friends in the city. The Refrigiers marched in protest against Franco and collected money for Loyalist Spain. "Come on, join up, Cheever," Ref urged him. He sympathized, yet refused. He did tramp down Fifth Avenue in the May Day parade with Josie Herbst and sixty thousand others, their banners proclaiming Solidarity Forever. And he made plans, at least, to attend the Writers' Congress held in New York later that summer. But he signed no manifestos and joined no political organizations. "John sailed through the thirties without getting allied to any group whatever," Cowley said. His heart was in it, Lila Refrigier observed, but he wouldn't make a commitment. "Security meant an awful lot to him."

Security undoubtedly had something to do with Cheever's reluctance to sign on in the cause. More important still was his persistently gloomy anticipation of the future. For him the good old days had passed and would not return. One day a crowd assembled to gawk at a 1910 Pierce-Arrow in New York. "Don't you dare laugh at this car," the painter Niles Spencer told them. "The world in 1910 was a much better place than you have ever known." Cheever was inclined to agree, and anticipated dark clouds ahead. In "Behold a Cloud in the West," a story that appeared in a collection called *New Letters in America* (1937), edited by Horace Gregory and Eleanor Clark, he depicted the impotence of those who sought peace in our time. An aging pacifist, Dr. Hardwick, goes to a European peace conference full of hope, but he stands no chance against nationalistic rivalries and hatreds. "On the east end of the hall," the AP man covering the conference writes, "stands an old man representing forces that at their best were weak and ephemeral. On the west end of the hall sit younger men representing an armed body of seven million soldiers." The war in Spain was going to spread, and, according to Cheever's fatalistic story, there was nothing to do about it.

Finally, Cheever resisted making a commitment to Communism because he knew that it would militate against his art. He had made the point, in "In Passing," that Communism and the American dream were incompatible. So, he believed, were literature and Communism, or literature and any doctrinaire ideology. Human relations were not so simple as the Party tried to make them seem. The true artist had to write about these and not about abstract relations between classes or societies, about the individual and not about humanity as a whole. *New Masses* singled him out in the thirties, Cheever maintained, as "the last voice of the decadent bourgeoisie." It did not bother him at all. He was "not concerned with social reconstruction." He was concerned "with literature as an intimate and acute means of communication."

MARY

1937-1942

WITH his novel scrapped, Cheever was forced to build his reputation as a writer of stories. *The New Yorker* printed two of his short sketches in 1935, two more in 1936, and one in 1937, but he was not yet wedded to that magazine. During 1937, for instance, he published six very different stories in five different publications: *New Letters in America* (where he shared space with Franz Kafka, W. H. Auden, and Elizabeth Bishop), *The New Republic, The New Yorker, Story,* and *The Yale Review.* The tales ranged from a vignette about an aging stripper trying to keep her job, to a brief, tender story about office girls lonely for love, to the long stories—"The Brothers" and "Homage to Shakespeare"—that looked to Cheever's recent and distant past for their subject matter. By and large, these appearances earned him more prestige than money. Late in 1937 he decided to try a more commercial market with more commercial stories. Drawing on his observations during the races at Belmont and Saratoga, he turned out the first of three racetrack romances for *Collier's*. All are written to a formula: boy meets girl and they fall in love, complications ensue and they part, complications are resolved and they walk off together into the sunset. The first of these stories, "His Young Wife," appeared in the January 1, 1938, *Collier's*. Shortly before publication date, the magazine editors called Cheever at Yaddo, frantic. They had lost his story. Could he send along the carbon? No, he couldn't, having kept no copy of his own. But he rewrote it from memory in a day.

Even with sales to *Collier's*, Cheever's income from stories was hardly enough to support him. In early May 1938, he finally found a fifty-dollar-a-week job with the same Federal Writers' Project that had rejected him two and a half years earlier as insufficiently poor. Nathan Asch, already employed on the project, sang Cheever's merits to FWP director Henry Alsberg, Alsberg hired him, and so he entrained for Washington, D.C., to apply his editorial skills to the mound of material for the American Guide series that was pouring into headquarters from across the United States. Most of the copy that came to Washington had been thrown together by unemployed teachers and librarians and office workers, and it read that way. As a "junior editor," Cheever was set to work rearranging "the sentences written by some incredibly lazy bastards." On the administrative side of the FWP, Alsberg was about as disorganized a director as could be imagined. A genial man with an astute literary mind, he ran a chaotic shop. He did not bother to keep carbons of his own letters. As for correspondence from others, "if he were interested, it went into his desk; if not, into his wastebasket." Moreover, Alsberg changed direction with the wind. What was demanded one month was countermanded the next. Few understood what they were supposed to do, and when, and why.

Neither the work nor Washington itself much appealed to Cheever. The clerks spoke in Southern accents, the streets were full of bureaucrats, everybody dressed alike, almost everybody talked about his civil service rating, the bars were closed on Sundays, and he missed New York.

During his months in Washington, Cheever stayed in Mrs.

Gray's boardinghouse at 2308 Twentieth Street, NW, not far from his office in the WPA building. Asch immediately exposed him to the international social life of the city. At parties he drank with conservatives and radicals, Cubans and Danes. Back at the boardinghouse he took his meals with fellow government employees and one elderly woman who went out of her way to denigrate WPA employees. Cheever pretended to be deaf when she asked him to pass the gravy.

At table he also heard rumors about the mouse in the National Archives and Drew Pearson in other people's beds. Success in Washington, it became clear, depended on connections. The man next door at Mrs. Gray's may or may not have made the chart described in *The Wapshot Chronicle:* a chart that detailed his social progress according to the political prominence of the hosts who had asked him to dinner in Georgetown, or to parties at the Pan-American Union and the embassies. And his landlady may not have been a fallen aristocrat who put on airs and shorted her boarders on butter for the spoon bread, as in a short story he wrote. But it was true that everyone he met "verged on being important or on knowing someone important or on being related to someone important." He could guarantee his future in the government by courting the right girl, the widow of a four-star general told him. "Now [labor leader] John L. Lewis has a daughter," she said. "She's rather stout and she's not awfully pretty but if you rush her, you're made."

Actually the abundance of available girls was one of the things that he liked about the city. He took Anna Keogh out for ice cream sodas on warm summer evenings and, for a time, thought he was in love. Life fell into a regular pattern. On paydays he cashed his check and got his shirts back from the laundry. On weekends he played touch football and volleyball and went to parties with fellow workers at the FWP. When Jerre Mangione and Charles Flato moved into an apartment near the Library of Congress, Cheever bought them a record of Midge Williams singing Langston Hughes's "Love Is Like Whisky, Love Is Like Red, Red Wine" as a housewarming gift. He would never own any possessions that might tie him down, Cheever told Mangione. He wanted security, but he wanted to be free too.

Despite sharing the somewhat compulsive social life of FWP workers, Cheever made no important or lasting relationships among his fellow employees. Instead he relied on Asch and Josie

Herbst for friendship. He spent delightful weekends at Josie's house in Bucks County, drinking mint juleps and watching the brook ripple by. The second of his racetrack stories was about to run in *Collier's*, and he had hopes of selling it to the movies. If he got some money, he'd buy a house near hers in Erwinna, he said. That was his goal: "a house a wife a bottle of whiskey and a chance to work." Work on his own fiction, that is, not repairing the tortured prose of others. The job remained uninspiring at best. There must have been intelligent people around, Cheever later acknowledged, but he didn't see much of them.

One Saturday, fireflies were twinkling as he rode horseback through the Maryland countryside. It was pretty, all right, but the colors could not compare with those of a New England autumn, and he was eager to get back to his "six-by-eight furnished room" in New York. In November he returned to the city, having agreed to stay with the FWP for as long as it took to get the New York City Guide ready for publication.

Unlike most FWP operations, the one in New York was blessed with literary talent. Among those who worked on the New York City Guide, in addition to Cheever, were Vincent McHugh, Richard Wright, Kenneth Patchen, Edward Dahlberg, and Kenneth Fearing. As well as the most talented, New York's was also the most controversial FWP group. The original director, the one-legged poet Orrick Johns, ran afoul of his appetite for liquor and sex. Johns was making his way to his apartment one night for an assignation with an attractive employee, a bottle of brandy under his arm, when the employee's boyfriend knocked him unconscious, poured brandy on his wooden leg, and set it afire. That made the papers, and Johns was fired. Next the writers made news by going on strike in protest against a cutback in employees mandated by Washington. Finally, in the autumn of 1938, the New York unit came under fire from the House Committee on Un-American Activities (or the Dies Committee, as it was known, for Congressman Martin Dies of Texas). The project was "doing more to spread Communist propaganda than the Communist Party itself," the *New York Journal-American* declared. That was an exaggeration. There were Communists in the FWP, but most were liberal Democrats.

Whatever its political coloration, the New York group was lagging behind schedule, and Alsberg was under pressure to prove that his organization could produce the two volumes of the New York City Guide, and soon. He put Joseph Gaer, his troubleshooting executive editor, on the job. Gaer commandeered the services of the project's most capable workers, and with Cheever's help, put both volumes of the guide into production within a few months. Cheever himself, listed as an "Editorial Assistant" in the guide as it appeared in 1939, resigned as of May 25, having spent just over a year in the government's employ.

When Cheever left the Federal Writers' Project, he virtually obliterated it from his mind. His parents in Quincy were undoubtedly ashamed of his having been a WPA employee. The Republican middle class in general regarded the WPA as a make-work outfit that paid slackers to lean on shovels. For them the initials stood for We Poke Along. To have been a WPA employee came to represent, in later years, a confession of personal defeat. For some FWP workers, the memory of their experience became a secret shame. Cheever must have been among these. He rarely drew on the experience for his fiction, though he realized it had possibilities. "The Washington rooming-houses where one lived, the social and athletic life of the project, the diversity of the cast—drunken stringers and first-rate men—the bucking for power, the machinations of the Dies Committee and the sexual and political scandals all make an extremely interesting story but it doesn't seem to be my kind of thing." Only rarely, as time passed, could he be brought even to talk about those days, and then with bitterness. Jim McGraw, who worked with him on the FWP, saw Cheever at the American Academy and Institute of Arts and Letters in 1980, for the first time in forty years.

"Hey, Johnny," McGraw said. "It's a long time since I last saw you on the Writers' Project."

"I don't want to talk about it," Cheever replied.

Liberated from the FWP, Cheever headed north to spend most of the summer at Triuna on Lake George, running the launch and water-skiing behind a neighbor's Gar-Wood motorboat. Eleanor Clark came for a stay, but she was gone by fall, along with all the other tourists. Then Cheever himself packed up, stopping in Saratoga for a visit on his way to New York. The previous year, the *Quincy Patriot-Ledger* had called him a resident of Saratoga. That was not so, but Yaddo and its environs did exert "a terrifying hold" over him. *Lost Horizon* romanticized Shangri-La, but Yaddo had Tibet "licked, hands-down." In the fall of 1939 it seemed a million miles away from the real world, where wounded soldiers were straggling into Paris.

Day by day it became clearer that the United States could not stay out of the war indefinitely. "I feel confident that we are going to be involved . . . and that I will be *killed,* " Walker Evans predicted. With still more intense pessimism, a character in Cheever's "I'm Going to Asia" (1940) anticipates the end of Western civilization. "We're nice people," a young man vehemently tells his mother, "and there isn't going to be any room for nice people any more. It's ended, it's all over." But his mother, who refuses to be troubled, contemplates a trip to Asia. "There isn't any war in Asia, is there? Or is there?"

To a certain extent, the impending conflict may have contributed to Cheever's interest in settling down: people needed a sense of emotional security before going off to war. But he was also reaching an age—he was twenty-seven in the fall of 1939—when it seemed right and proper to be married. Besides, he "didn't want to sleep alone anymore."

As always he had plenty of female friends, and things to do and see. He was passionate about popular music, and took Dorothy Farrell to Nick's on Seventh Avenue for Dixieland and Josie Herbst up to Harlem for jam sessions. He loved the great Benny Goodman band of the late 1930s, particularly the quartet with Teddy Wilson on piano, Lionel Hampton on vibraphone, and Gene Krupa on drums to complement the maestro's clarinet. He rarely had any money, as Frances Lindley recalls, but was "very classy" about it. The two of them spent a wonderful day at the World's Fair in Queens. But he was seeking a more lasting attachment than mere friends could supply. For a while he was interested in Peg Worthington, a beautiful woman a few years older than he. And he courted Dodie Merwin still more seriously. An earthy, good-looking young woman, Dodie was also rather outspoken. She and John had been considering marriage, but one day, driving along the Pulaski Skyway, they had a terrible quarrel, and that ended that. Then he met Mary Winternitz.

Years later, Cheever conjured up a romantic version of this first meeting for his Russian friend Tanya Litvinov. He was sitting in a garden outside a stately home, listening to some marvelous piano music emanating from the conservatory. Then the music stopped, and when the piano player—Mary, of course—came outside he stood there with his arms outstretched, since it was she he had been waiting for all his life. "It was pure Chekhov," he added. It might as well have been. The actual circumstances were that he and Mary

met in a Fifth Avenue office building on a rainy afternoon in
November 1939. He liked to tell that story too:

I met her on a rainy afternoon in an elevator. I'd spent a very pleasant
summer working as a boatman and water skiing, which had just come in.
And I saw a woman in the elevator. And I thought, "that's more or less
what I would like." And then she got off the elevator at the same floor.
. . . And she went up into my literary agent's office. And I asked who she
was. And I was told she was Mary Winternitz. And I asked her for a date.
And presently married her.

Cheever had come to get a check from his agent, Maxim Lieber.
Fresh out of Sarah Lawrence, Mary was working for Lieber temporarily on a nonpaying basis. John, she recalls, was wearing a brown
overcoat too large for him so that it came down over his hands and
made him look smaller and colder and more miserable than he
actually was. He looked like he needed taking care of, and that
appealed to her. She needed someone to take care of her, too.

The girl Cheever saw on the elevator—twenty-one years old, five
foot three, dark-haired with a tendency to freckle, and certainly
pretty—was the daughter of two remarkable people, both of them
doctors. Mary Winternitz's mother, Dr. Helen Watson, was one of
the first women in the country to earn a medical degree. The
Watsons were a prosperous, quirky, and distinguished New England family. Mary's grandmother Watson tacked the legend WORK
IS PLEASURE on the wall of her Cape Cod cabin. Mary's grandfather
Thomas A. Watson was the friend Alexander Graham Bell summoned to his side with the famous telephone message, "Mr. Watson, come here!" At Johns Hopkins, Helen Watson met her future
husband, the brilliant and demanding Milton C. Winternitz, and
gave up her career. Instead she gave birth to five children in rapid
order while Dr. Winternitz made his reputation as professor of
pathology and as dean of the Yale Medical School. In New Haven,
Thornton Wilder's sister Isabel once told Mary, her mother "was
legendary for her beauty and graciousness." But she was also unwell during much of Mary's childhood, and Mary, the fourth of the
five children, thought that her mother favored the others over her.
She knew that her birth had disappointed her father's expectations.
She was the third daughter born; her father had wanted a boy as
a companion for his sole son. This inspired the conception of a fifth
child, who turned out to be the second son he wanted.

Genetics might dare to make Dr. Winternitz wait. Few humans did. He was famous at Yale for his temperamental outbursts against shoddy performance by students and colleagues. In the home as well, Dr. Winternitz was a stern master. Yet he had a capacity to bring out the best in those around him. He was "electric, full of fire," Mary observed. People either loved him or hated him. She loved him very much.

In background, Mary Winternitz was part Jewish and part Salem. At first she didn't know about her father's Jewish heritage. Her parents suppressed this information so well that she was ten before she discovered it. Dr. Winternitz was, according to the pun, ante-Semitic. He was also fiercely intellectual. Mary was born and brought up in a large Italian-villa-style house at 210 Prospect Street, on the fringes of the Yale campus. Down the architecturally eclectic street, under the tall maples, stood the massive buildings where the departments of physics (a castle, with "defenseless battlements") and mathematics ("a lighter Italian fantasy") and zoology ("a hulking cloister") were headquartered. The Winternitz children played happily on the New Haven green a few blocks away, hardly aware that they were absorbing the air of serious academic endeavor. They were, of course, expected to do well in school.

In 1931, Mary's mother died. Within a year her father married Polly Whitney, a socially prominent widow with four children of her own. The ensuing ménage consisted of nine children, a few at college but most at home. Certain tensions naturally arose. "The Whitney children were nice to me and [younger brother] Bill," Mary recalls, "but not to the older children. If you weren't attractive, forget it. They used to say, 'Oh, he's so *attractive,*' but if they didn't say it, you were out." Mary did not get along with her stepmother, whom she regarded as something of a snob. Polly tried to be kind to her, Mary says, "but she was one of those people who couldn't be really nice to somebody she felt was basically inferior." Mary was sent to the International School in Geneva for the last two years of high school, and then spent an additional year in New Haven, remedying a low score on her math college boards. This postgraduate year was made endurable, she says, only by reading the fiction of Henry James.

With relief, Mary enrolled at Sarah Lawrence in the fall. She was an intense and successful student who "wallowed" in social philosophy and literature, especially poetry. The heady experience of college stimulated her political radicalism. During the summer of

1938 she tramped around northern New England for the Emergency Peace Campaign, camping out and making antiwar speeches to churches and civic groups. On the first day of May 1939, she made the short trip into New York from Sarah Lawrence to march in the May Day parade, losing her glasses in the process. That story delighted Polly Winternitz, who liked to regale her friends with the tale of her left-wing stepdaughter who'd lost her glasses in the May Day parade. After graduating the following month, Mary traveled to England and France, where she changed her mind about pacifism. The whole peace movement, she realized, was tied up with religious ideas she didn't share. Moreover, everything she saw in Europe made it clear that the United States couldn't simply sit back and avoid the fight. "You've got to help us," a Frenchman told her on a bus in Paris. "Come over and help us."

Her abandoned pacifism aside, Mary remained strongly liberal in her views when she came to New York in the fall of 1939. At the time, she "thought all people who indulged in commerce were wicked." Still, literary commerce seemed the least wicked, Max Lieber was well known as an agent for left-wing writers, and so it was that she was trying to find gainful employment with him at the time she met John Cheever.

She was living then in a furnished room in an old mansion on East Sixty-seventh Street, where her landlady took to introducing her—rather inaccurately—as "Miss Winternitz of Yale." After it became clear that Lieber was not going to pay her anything, she got a twenty-five-dollar-a-week job working for Thomas H. Uzzell, author of *Narrative Technique* and operator of a small-time version of the Famous Authors School, teaching people to write through the mail. Uzzell was a figurehead, really. His wife critiqued the manuscripts that came in, for a fee. Mary was taken on as secretary and to help Mrs. Uzzell with the critiques. One of her tasks was to type up Uzzell's standard letter to prospective clients who'd sent in a sample of their writing. "Thank you for letting us see your work, which shows real promise," the letter invariably began. "The story line/character development is good but the character development/story line is weak. You would find my book *Narrative Technique* useful. If you are unable to obtain a copy at your bookstore, please let me know and I'll see that one is sent to you." C.O.D.

John and Mary dated only a few times before he drove up to Quincy and Norwell (where Fred and Iris were living) for the

Christmas holidays. Everything conspired to remind him of matrimony. On Christmas Eve he went to a party and saw several of his Thayer classmates "escorting pregnant wives." On Christmas Day itself he and his parents went to Norwell, where Fred's young children "played store, played house, played tea-party" and then proceeded to "destroy the tree ornaments." He returned to New York on December 30 to see his former girl Peg Worthington marry Marshall Best.

In the spring of 1940, Mary was fired when an efficiency expert told Uzzell he didn't need her services. In response her landlady moved her to the back bedroom—once a servant's room—and stopped mentioning her Ivy League connection. John rescued her from the back room and the landlady. He found her a top-floor one-room apartment on West Eleventh Street in Rhinelander Gardens. John himself had a hall bedroom a few steps away. There were two buildings at Rhinelander Gardens, one for famous folk and one for those who were not famous, at least not yet. John and Mary stayed among the less distinguished. Downstairs from them lived the young painter Robert Burns Motherwell, who kept a calling card with his Paris address tacked to his door. "Pretty affected," John and Mary thought. Both were acutely sensitive to the pretentious. And they were very much a couple in love, taking pleasure in the giving and sharing of themselves.

Though the separate bedrooms demonstrated a certain respect for the proprieties, Mary's father and stepmother disapproved of her living arrangements. Polly came down to Eleventh Street and took Mary to lunch. Fixing her womanfully, Polly said serially, "Your sweater's on backwards" and "You're living in sin." "No it isn't," Mary answered serially, "I like it this way," and "No, I'm not." It was none of her stepmother's business anyway, Mary thought. Next the redoubtable Dr. Winternitz came calling and asked John what his intentions were. "Well, I want to marry her, of course," he replied, and that settled matters. Nobody asked Mary if she was sure she was ready for marriage.

There remained the problem of finances. Actually, Mary was in rather better financial condition than John. Her grandmother Watson was supplying an allowance of one hundred and fifty dollars a month. John, meanwhile, was surviving only on checks from the magazines. These became much more frequent soon after he met Mary Winternitz. Partly this was due to his growing reputation among editors, and partly to his increasingly close ties to *The New*

Yorker. But his burst of creative energy was also related, undoubtedly, to his determination to prove to himself—and Mary, and the Winternitzes—that he was ready to support a wife. In 1939, he published only two stories, both in *The New Yorker.* In 1940, he published the amazing total of fifteen stories: eleven in *The New Yorker,* two in *Harper's Bazaar,* one in *Collier's,* and one in *Mademoiselle.*

The climate for fiction was clearly improving, also. Around 1940, Cheever later commented, "there were at least fifteen magazines extremely anxious to find serious fiction—and twenty-five first-rate people were sending stuff to *The New Yorker"*—his friends Bill Maxwell and Dan Fuchs and Eddie Newhouse, for example, and soon thereafter Vladimir Nabokov and Jean Stafford, J. D. Salinger and Irwin Shaw. One of the good things about the magazine was quick publication and quick pay. Cheever could finish a story, put it in the mail on Tuesday, and by the weekend see the story in print on the newsstands, with a check on the way. As Newhouse expressed it, *The New Yorker* was "a lifeboat" for a number of young writers in those days.

The two lovers were separated for most of the summer of 1940. Mary went north to Treetops, the family compound of hillside cottages in the New Hampshire mountains above Newfound Lake. In June, John spent a week at Yaddo. It was "like coming back to a place you've dreamed about," he wrote Mary. In New York, he took up residence for the summer in Muriel Rukeyser's apartment on Bank Street. The accommodations were not all they might have been. He was "holed up" in the bedroom trying to write over the noise of the carpenters working in the living room and the amateur musicians practicing at his doorstep. Bedbugs disturbed his sleep. The summer heat was oppressive.

On the bright side, Cheever had plenty of companionship in the Village. His mother came down from Quincy on a buying trip for her gift shop, and John gave her a short, inexpensive tour of the city. One night he dropped in at a party Pete and Lib Collins were throwing, but left when "Hungarians and abstract painters" began to arrive. Another evening he spent listening to writer-artist Charles Norman discuss the genius of Charles Norman. He went to dinner with Carson McCullers and George Davis, editor of *Harper's Bazaar.* He dined with the Bests, where "a little, drooping, small-voiced man"—William Shawn, *The New Yorker*'s managing editor—played boogie-woogie.

Despite the company, John missed Mary terribly. He stayed in New York for two reasons: to try to write an outline and one long chapter of a novel for Houghton Mifflin, and to look for a job.

The novel was to deal with the people he'd known over the last four years. He set about the outline with high expectations, but these soon came crashing to earth. "The book is a pain in the neck," he announced at midsummer. There wasn't much point in starting on something he wasn't enthusiastic about, he realized, and he didn't really know whether he wanted to write a realistic or a romantic novel. Despite these difficulties, he stuck to the project. A novel might earn some money, after all, and he'd been unable to locate a job.

What he had in mind was an editorial post on *The New Republic*, where Malcolm Cowley could be counted on to serve as his advocate. First a man named Carleton Brown was hired for the job, and then—after Brown became ill and had to resign—"another ghoul" beat him to the magazine offices to take over Brown's job. He realized he ought to have a regular position, since free-lancing wasn't enough to get married on. For the moment, though, free-lancing was his only source of income, and he did it with vigor.

On the first of August, Cheever fled from the heat and the bedbugs of New York. After a night of trying to sleep in the bathtub, he left Bank Street at six in the morning and went north to Quincy. The New England countryside "looked like God's own," compared to the city in summer. He drove his mother down to Cape Cod, where despite the commercialization of the "quaintee countree," the ocean remained beautiful as ever. En route he "tracked down the aromas" of an inn called the Pemaquoddy House and put them into a story called "A Border Incident." He wrote "the Pemaquoddy saga" for *Harper's Bazaar* and a Christmas story for *Mademoiselle*; both magazines paid rather better than *The New Yorker*.

His fame had preceded him to Quincy. A reporter from the *Quincy Patriot-Ledger* came by to write a feature on the local boy. As he was often to do in later years, Cheever spoke only briefly about himself before getting away from the subject. He was an "author of exceptional modesty," the interviewer reported. He really hadn't "written anything worth reading yet," he told her. It took years to get anywhere, he added. You had to keep polishing until you had something. That was what he had been up to—that, and working on a contemporary novel he hoped to finish by the following spring. Actually he was making no progress on the novel at all. By the time he left Quincy he was ready to abandon it in disgust.

Back in New York, Cheever continued cranking out stories. He was scheduled to go to Treetops late in August, and he suggested that perhaps Mary could drive back from New Hampshire with him and they could stop in Saratoga. Clearly, he hoped that she might come to share his fondness for the place. In any case, he felt sure that he and his bride-to-be would have "a wonderful and beautiful life."

At Treetops, Cheever charmed everyone. Polly immediately recognized that he had the right clothes and manners, and adopted him as an amusing drinking and gossiping and backgammon-playing companion. Winternitz, impressed by the stories his future son-in-law was publishing in *The New Yorker*, spirited him off for long talks in the study. They both were surprised, Mary thought, that she had managed to snare so acceptable a catch. John himself responded as to the parents he might have wished for: an accomplished and well-respected father, an engaging and socially prominent mother. The scenery and weather at Treetops were magnificent. Best of all, John was briefly reunited with Mary after long absence. But she stayed in New Hampshire when he left, his car packed with flowers and vegetables from the gardens at Treetops. These were deposited with his mother in Quincy, much to her delight. Then John kept going down the coast to New York, where he wrote Mary that he hardly knew how to thank her parents. He'd had a wonderful time.

Privately he harbored a few reservations about marriage. The problem wasn't with Mary. He talked glowingly of her; in his eyes, she could do no wrong. He worried about himself. He wondered, after observing the country gentleman's life at Treetops, whether he could provide for Mary in the fashion to which she must have become accustomed. He wondered, too, if he would be able to live up to the image of male sovereignty projected by her father. He understood that he was marrying up the social ladder, and so did most of his friends. "When John decided to marry," Lib Collins (the artist Elizabeth Logan) commented, "he picked a nice girl from a respectable upper-middle-class family." It seemed to Lib that by doing so he aimed to work his way back into the social position his own father had drunk and failed him out of.

"A Present for Louisa," his Christmas story for *Mademoiselle*, addresses the issue of whether to get married without a firm financial footing. Roger and Louisa are considering marriage, but he's not making enough money, and though she has a college degree she can't find a job. They ought to hold off, Roger thinks. "Marriage isn't a lark. It's a serious contract between two adults." In the end, though, love has its way and they take the plunge.

By the time John and Mary were married in the spring of 1941, they were in rather better shape than his fictional characters. Through her father's connections, Mary landed a job at G. P. Putnam's Sons. She worked first as a secretary to T. R. (Timmy) Coward, but lacked the requisite typing and shorthand skills and was transferred to editing and proofing manuscripts for the publishing house. (She stayed on the job until shortly before their daughter, Susan, was born in 1943.) John, meanwhile, continued his remarkable outpouring of publishable stories, mostly but not entirely for *The New Yorker.* Never again would he match the creative fecundity of the time of his courtship and early marriage. After the fifteen stories of 1940, there were eleven more in 1941 and ten in 1942.

In the fall of 1940, John and Mary resumed their premarital domesticity in Greenwich Village. They even acquired a cat named Harold, after Harold Ross; the name was changed, after a revelation from the veterinarian, to Harolde or Harriet. John paid a last bachelor pilgrimage to Yaddo in the dead of winter. He was ashamed of himself "for gallivanting off" while Mary worked, he wrote her, but the setting was as stimulating as ever. Sharing his pleasure, among others, were his good drinking companion Flannery Lewis and Katherine Anne Porter. At breakfast he heard Porter put down the overtures of a leering playwright. Porter was wonderful, he decided. A few nights later he and Lewis and Porter went downtown to the bars, where she held forth in self-inflating style on her friendships with the great. Porter wasn't so wonderful, he decided.

He had a far better time the night he went to an amateur talent show with Nathan and Carole Asch. Writing Mary about that, he sang Saratoga's praises. Living was cheap, and there were plenty of civilized people to talk to. Why didn't she come up for the weekend and have a look?

On March 22, 1941, John Cheever and Mary Watson Winternitz were married at the Winternitz home in New Haven. The Reverend Sidney Lovett, chaplain and "Uncle Sid" to decades of Yalies, performed an ecumenical ceremony to suit Cheever's Episcopalianism, Dr. Winternitz's Jewish background, and Mary's lack of religious commitment. It was not a large wedding, or a conventional one. Fred served as his brother's best man. Mary's sister Elizabeth was her only attendant. Serious-minded radical that she was, Mary "didn't believe in white or a veil." She wore a severe gray dress with a corsage at the shoulder. Polly organized "a very nice house wedding" with little sandwiches and champagne. John's parents came down from Quincy. His father seemed a little fuzzy mentally, and Mary's pretty stepsister Louise was deputized to look after him. Everything went smoothly. Afterward John and Mary Cheever returned to Greenwich Village and their new apartment at 19 East Eighth Street.

In reporting on the wedding, the Quincy newspaper was inexact about the educational accomplishments of the Cheevers. "The bride-elect was educated in Switzerland and New York," the story read, while the groom "attended Thayer Academy and studied at Harvard." The effect was to imply that John was Mary's equal in educational background, though she graduated from Sarah Lawrence and there is no record of his having enrolled at Harvard. This imbalance created certain tensions, even during the halcyon days of courtship. One night in the fall of 1940, they had dinner with Helen McMaster, who (along with Horace Gregory) had taught Mary in writing courses at Sarah Lawrence, and with a young male instructor from the college. The two academics took the occasion to attack Cheever's *New Yorker* fiction, particularly a story called "Happy Birthday, Enid" that was based on one of Mary's willful stepsisters. Confrontation was the style at Sarah Lawrence. At college Mary was encouraged to express her opinions even when— especially when—they ran counter to received wisdom. But with John and the other men they saw—almost all of them older than John, who was six years older than she—Mary learned to hold her tongue. When she did speak up, they would say, "Oh, that's just Sarah Lawrence" by way of dismissal. The peculiar timbre of Mary's speaking voice also militated against her being taken seriously. Her voice is high and sweet, rather like that of the pianist-singer Blossom Dearie. And since she sounded like a little girl, people were often deceived into thinking her intellectually immature. Nothing could have been further from the truth.

Once they were married, John was eager to make himself the breadwinner of the family. He had "very old-fashioned ideas" about marriage, Mary said, foremost among them the conviction that the male should earn the money and the female should make the home. The example of his own family undoubtedly solidified this feeling. His father had not succeeded as provider, his mother had gone to work, and to John's mind, this reversal of roles had disastrous consequences. So, although Mary had a job when they first were married, he wanted to establish himself, start a family, and relieve her of the obligation/privilege óf working as soon as possible.

For the most part, he and Mary were very happy together as newlyweds. John possessed then what he always had: the capacity to say the surprising thing. "Most people say what's expected of them, and you can anticipate what's coming," Mary points out. It was not that way with John. The way he talked about things and people was so amusing, and so beautifully said, that it more than made up for their occasional disputes. As Bill Maxwell recalls from visits to their Eighth Street apartment, "in those days John was terribly funny and charming, and certainly not like anyone else."

Social life in the Village involved a great deal of drinking. John drank more than Mary, but she participated too. They drank at the party the Werners gave to welcome Mary to their literary and artistic circle. They drank with artists Niles Spencer and Stuart Davis at the marble tables of the Lafayette, where Spencer, "a darling gentle man," liked to play bagatelle. They drank with Flannery and Claire Lewis, who lived above a nightclub called the Black Cat. Lewis had been banished from Yaddo, the story ran, for drinking too much and urinating into the pool outside the mansion. They drank with Pete and Lib Collins, who were always broke but had a lot of style and didn't mind that the Cheevers were somewhat better off. They drank and ate at the parties Dorothy Dudley used to give on Friday nights. Dorothy, a large hospitable woman with a down-Maine accent and a good job at the Museum of Modern Art, loved to cook. At her invitation the Cheevers and Collinses came over on Thanksgiving eve to stuff the turkey. Lib cut herself slightly on a piece of dry bread, put a small Band-Aid on her finger, and continued stuffing the bird. When the job was done, the bandage had disappeared. All four of them hoped it might turn up in the helping of one particularly stuffy guest the following day, but it never turned up at all. After Thanksgiving dinner Cheever and Edward Lazare, who ran a bookstore nearby, lay down on the floor, themselves stuffed.

Throughout the summer of 1941, the Cheevers spent their weekends looking after Josie Herbst's place at Erwinna in her absence.

Venery Valley, they called it, and some drinking was done there too. John worked around the house himself, and hired a neighbor called Foolish—who showed them his "collection of twisted roots" that resembled lewd animals—to mow the field and weed the garden. Just how much these outings in the country meant to John and Mary is suggested in a midsummer 1941 story called "Run, Sheep, Run." Dave and Ramona, the couple in the story, are flat broke, but Dave steals eight dollars from a Greenwich Village bookstore, enough to pay for a Sunday journey by train and bike to the fresh air of Bucks County. All too soon it is time to go back to the city.

"I wonder where we'll get the money next time," Ramona said when she heard the train whistle.

"Don't you worry, honey," Dave said. "We'll get it."

With the bombing of Pearl Harbor, all merely personal matters faded into insignificance. John and Mary heard the news at Edward and Monie Lazare's on Sunday, December 7. Within a week the country was at war with Japan, Germany, and Italy. "Never before," President Roosevelt declared, "has there been a greater challenge to life, liberty, and civilization." The draft was extended to all men between eighteen and sixty-four. By the first of the new year, both Cowley and Herbst had gone to work in Washington, and Cheever asked them to look for openings there. When nothing developed on that front, he determined to enlist. He and Mary made a final trip to Josie's place on Washington's birthday where as usual they warmed themselves in bed with hot bricks wrapped in newspaper. Someday, he hoped, they might all foregather there again when the papers were carrying no war news at all. For the time being, though, all the news was bad. Bataan fell on April 9. John and Mary spent a long weekend together at Treetops. Corregidor surrendered on May 6. The next day Cheever went off to war.

ARMY

1942-1943

A T THE Fort Dix reception center in New Jersey, Cheever began to undergo the demeaning process of depersonalization immemorially employed by the military to transform civilians into soldiers. Nearly thirty, he was a good deal older than most of the recruits, but the army was no respecter of years. He stripped naked for the medics, was examined twice for gonorrhea, and was given the first of his shots for smallpox, typhoid fever, and tetanus. He had his hair sheared to regulation length, took standardized tests to measure his mechanical aptitude and general IQ, and put on the GI clothing he'd been issued. He saw the obligatory movie on venereal disease and was read the Articles of War, reminding him that the penalty for desertion in time of war was death.

On his third day in the service he got up at 4:30 A.M. for a fifteen-hour day on KP. Afterward, refreshed by a shower and a glass of beer, he felt completely peaceful and more than a little sad.

Within a week after induction, Private Cheever was shipped south on a troop train to an unannounced destination that turned out to be Camp Croft, five miles from Spartanburg, South Carolina. He was assigned to thirteen weeks of infantry basic training. That would be rough, but—he reassured Mary—there would be plenty of stories to write later; he hoped that he could continue to average forty dollars a week on his fiction even in the army. The army experience itself provided fresh material. Eleven of the fourteen stories he published between the middle of 1942 and the end of 1944 were directly based on characters and incidents he encountered in the service. For the moment, though, he was fully occupied with the business of basic training. Don't bother to send magazines, he told his wife. He didn't know when he'd be able to read them.

Neither John nor Mary liked the idea of his serving as a foot soldier on the front lines. During his three months at Camp Croft he explored three different alternatives to that dirty and dangerous job. First, he looked for a post on the camp newspaper, only to find out that there wasn't even a paper. Perhaps he could start one himself, in due time. Second, he hoped for an assignment—once basic training was over—to *Yank,* the service magazine Harold Ross had recommended him to. Third, he applied for Officer Candidate School. None of these alternatives panned out.

The first few rugged weeks of basic training left Cheever exhausted. There were no three-day passes and no furloughs. The recruits worked twelve to fifteen hours a day, six days a week. Only on Sunday was there respite, when the men were allowed to sleep an hour past their usual 5:30 A.M. reveille—"no hour's sleep ever seemed sweeter," Cheever wrote home—and had the rest of the day pretty much to themselves. The other happy moments came at mail call, when Cheever could count on his daily letter from Mary and sporadic correspondence from Pete Collins, Flannery Lewis, Josie Herbst, Morrie Werner, Eddie Newhouse, and Gus Lobrano and Bill Maxwell of *The New Yorker.* His father, now doddering, sent him advice and counsel based on his experience with the Roxbury Horse Guards, "a fraternal organization that rode at the inauguration of the Governor of Massachusetts and spent an annual bivouac in drinking bouts." Look into your boots each morning, father Cheever reminded son, to be sure no one has put an egg in the toe.

Some days of training were worse than others. On the second Tuesday in camp, John's platoon went on a long march with full equipment. Then they practiced running up and down hills. That night, all he wanted to do, after scrawling a note to Mary, was to collapse on his bunk. Bayonet drill was the hardest work of all, and the bayonet field with its dummies the strangest of sights. Both his feet and his eyes were bothering him, he wrote on May 28, the day after his thirtieth birthday. He felt "every day of thirty."

In addition to the physical strain, Cheever like all enlisted men had to get accustomed to the language and behavior of men very unlike himself and to a region of the country—the Deep South of Carson McCullers and Eudora Welty, as he explained it to Mary—he had never before penetrated. The South, he decided, was not for him. Spartanburg struck him as a depressing army-post town. The heat was murderous. On the radio, commercials promised a cure for malarial fever, and the music ranged from popular hymns to country western laments. A decade later, looking at "the delicate but ungenerous and sallow face" of Randall Jarrell on a book jacket, he was reminded of the "cultural bleakness" he found around Camp Croft.

With his fellow trainees—mostly New Yorkers—he got along well, even though their barracks talk relied largely on one all-purpose adjective. "In a fucking line-rifle company," Farragut recalls in *Falconer*, "you get the fucking, malfunctioning M-1's, fucking '03's to simulate fucking carbines, fucking obsolete BAR's and fucking sixty-millimeter mortars where you have to set the fucking sight to bracket the fucking target." His platoon at Camp Croft was mostly made up of men who had pursued a wide variety of occupations in civilian life. There were longshoremen and ex-cons, busboys and bank clerks, and one terribly sad fellow "who had never done anything. Anything at all." As the weeks wore on, Cheever made friends with Charlie Baxter and Joe Burt and Andy Broznell, men with backgrounds more or less like his own who liked, as he did, to take a drink. But without question, the most memorable figure of basic training was the platoon sergeant who drove them hard and who seemed determined to make everyone as miserable as possible.

The name of this "strange and interesting" man was Sergeant

Durham, a seven-year veteran, and accounts of his peculiar behavior soon came to dominate John's letters to Mary. Durham was passionately determined to shape up his platoon. The way he went about this was to abuse his recruits unmercifully. Nothing they did could satisfy him, and their least lapse aroused his violent temper.

"You work with me, I make you a soldier," Sergeant Durham told his men. "You cross me, you sell your soul to the devil." Then he ran them in the hot Carolina sun until they dropped. He gave them close-order drill after lunch and rifle inspection after dinner and confined them to barracks night after night. He even called them out one Sunday night for shoe inspection. None of the other platoons suffered so many indignities, the troops soon found, and they threatened to rebel. Almost everyone hated and feared Durham for his temper and his cruelty and his obsession that nothing in the world mattered except the performance of his platoon. "I'll kill the son of a bitch" was the refrain that ran through the barracks. Cheever was inclined to forgive him, however. Durham didn't have a friend in the world, he realized. The army was his life. And he was making the platoon into the best one in the company.

Midway through basic training—after they ran through clouds of poisonous gases but before they crawled under barbed wire with live ammunition zinging over their heads—Durham went on furlough and the army seemed almost like a vacation. Cheever wrote long letters to Mary. He worked on his stories. He read a newspaper for the first time in weeks. A few days later, after their fifty-dollar-a-month payday, he and Joe Burt and Andy Broznell and Larry Doheny got weekend passes and hired a taxi driver to take them to the cool, light mountain air of Hendersonville, North Carolina, which was something like New Hampshire and nothing at all like Camp Croft.

Inevitably Durham "came back with a bang." He was drinking now, and seemed not quite right in the head. One night just before taps, he rushed out of his room and began to rouse the men who had gone to bed. In his stupor, he thought it was morning. Maybe he was going crazy, he told his platoon the next day.

Near the end of basic, one of the privates beat Durham up, but he returned, stitches and all, in time for one last humiliation of his troops. On their final day the men were in the barracks relaxing when Durham blew his whistle and they raced to the quadrangle to assemble in ranks. "Not good enough," Durham said. "You've got to fall out in fifteen seconds," and he put them through this routine again and again "until their fatigues were black with sweat." Finally it was time for the recruits to leave, Cheever for Camp Gordon, Georgia. Memories of Sergeant Durham traveled with him, and he decided to resurrect him in a story.

"Sergeant Limeburner," which appeared in the March 13, 1943, *New Yorker*, had to clear both official military channels and the magazine's informal judgment on what kind of army story it should run in wartime. In most particulars, Limeburner bears a close resemblance to the actual Durham. He is wantonly cruel and friendless, susceptible to alcohol, and possibly deranged. He calls his men out for shoe inspection. He marches them in the heat until they drop. He tries to get them to fall out of the barracks in fifteen seconds. But the story introduces an intermediate voice of reason, a Corporal Pacelli, who assures the troops that they are lucky to have Limeburner in charge. "You'll appreciate this training when you get into combat," Pacelli says. And in the final scene, Cheever alters the facts to create a measure of sympathy for the sergeant. He has been publicly beaten up, and is led away sobbing, by an officer who will—it is implied—bust him of his rank and relieve him of his job. "The faces watching him walk toward his judgment were the lean, still faces of the soldiers he had destroyed himself to make," the last sentences read. "In the morning there was another sergeant to take his place."

It took the troop train all of Friday, August 14, to make the short trip to Camp Gordon, near Augusta, Georgia. The camp was big and new and looked something like, "of all places, Harvard." On arrival at Gordon the men from Camp Croft were immediately split up. Cheever was assigned to E Company of the 22nd Infantry Regiment, but he expected any day, he wrote Mary, to be reassigned to a job on *Yank*. While waiting for this call that never came, he acclimated himself to the Regular Army. With basic training over, both the work load and the tension were sharply reduced. At first he slept so much he felt "bloated." There was also time to write stories, and he soon located a typewriter to write them on. He finished one such story only two weeks after arriving at Gordon. "It's not Shakespeare," he wrote Mary, "but Lobrano might buy it."

Financially, the Cheevers were neither well off nor impoverished. In addition to his fifty dollars a month, they could count on Mary's salary from her publishing job and occasional checks from the sale of stories. Mary routinely received these from Maxim

Lieber, and John asked her to wire him money—ten dollars at a time—when he was strapped. As a soldier's wife Mary was also entitled to an allotment from the army.

He missed Mary badly. She had come to see him briefly in Greenville, South Carolina, during basic training, but now he was dreaming about Sunday afternoons together in New York, with Mary fixing dinner in her red smock. So he wrote her, signing off with "Love, Love, Love." On the last weekend in August, he wangled a three-day pass and made the trip to New York. It was all that he'd hoped for. The time apart changed nothing, except that it made him love her more.

At Camp Gordon, Cheever discovered that he was no longer regarded as an anonymous trainee, but as a writer whose talents might be put to use. His company commander asked to see a copy of "Family Dinner," his bittersweet story of a failed marriage that had run in *Collier's* in July. He went into Augusta with Nat Greenstein, the company clerk, and heard that a request was in to transfer him to public relations. He was asked to work as the chaplain's assistant, but turned that down. If he didn't get *Yank*, what he wanted was a post in publications, attached to the field. He liked bivouac and night problems and living in tents. Cheever always enjoyed spending as much time as possible in the open air. This was true even in the countryside around his army posts, where poverty and soil erosion scarred the land. "There is not enough topsoil between Augusta, Ga. and Spartanburg, S.C. to fill a bait can," he wrote Cowley, and used the same line to describe Coverly Wapshot's army surroundings in *The Wapshot Chronicle*.

Augusta itself was much more attractive than Spartanburg, and Cheever spent many evenings there. The town had a population of seventy thousand and a pleasant resort hotel, the Bon Air. On Saturday nights, however, downtown Augusta became an "army town" void of civilians, with a fleet of buses on hand to carry the invading troops back to the post at midnight. Hospitable though Augusta was, it was still "embarrassed"—so Cheever put it—"by our numbers." He was also troubled by lingering signs of Jim Crowism, such as relegating Negroes to the back of the bus. He was relieved to hear on September 10 that Herman Talmadge, running on a racist platform, had lost the election for governor of Georgia. Talmadge, he thought, stood for "everything that we are in training to destroy."

Besides going into Augusta and writing stories, Cheever filled some of his leisure time at the fifteen-cent camp movies. *Mrs. Miniver,* the motion picture that earned Greer Garson an Academy Award, was, he thought, "a clever little piece" of effective propaganda, but nothing in the movie communicated the monotony of wartime training camps. Boredom and frustration repeatedly spawned rumors at Camp Gordon, where the 22nd Infantry Regiment was at full strength and, presumably, ready for actual combat. The rumor in the fall of '42 was that they were slated to fight in the North African desert, where German Field Marshal Erwin Rommel had so far outmaneuvered the Allied forces.

In late September and early October, Cheever got a ten-day furlough. Bus, taxi, and two trains took him to New York, where he arrived at nine o'clock Saturday night. A radiant Mary greeted him, there were plenty of good things to eat and drink in the apartment, and for eight days they "did exactly as they pleased."

Midway through this furlough, Random House offered him a contract for a book of stories. Cheever had been working at his craft for more than a decade now, and at last he could be sure of seeing his fiction between hard covers in a book with his name on it. Publisher Bennett Cerf took him to a celebratory lunch at the Plaza, and afterward he floated downtown on the wings of euphoria. Sometime during this eventful furlough, also, the Cheevers' first child was conceived. It had been a magical time. "I don't think I have ever been so happy," he said.

At Camp Gordon a letter from E. E. Cummings awaited him. Inside was an autumn leaf, a five-dollar bill, and a one-line message from the author of *The Enormous Room:* "I too have slept with someone else's boot in the corner of my smile."

Cheever's joyous mood continued in the afterglow of his Random House contract. He told his fellow soldiers he was going "to have a *book* published," but not many were impressed. For most of them, book meant comic book.

Early in November he and Mary managed a rendezvous in Richmond on a three-day pass. By then he had been promoted to private first class and recruited by the personnel office. Personnel work had its good points and its bad. On the bad side, he much preferred going on problems in the field to typing up furloughs. Besides, some of the personnel men seemed to calculate everything with their personal safety uppermost in their minds. On the other hand, office work fell into a regular routine, unlike the uncertainties of the field; you knew where you'd be and what you'd be doing every day.

Despite his developing literary reputation and New England accent, Cheever was regarded at Camp Gordon "as a very regular guy who used to drink at the PX with the rest of the guys." He had a talent, then and always, for getting along with all kinds of people. His admiration went most of all to the rebellious, to those who broke the rules and took their punishment. He stood prison guard one day, and decided that the prisoners in the stockade were "the finest looking men" in the army, with a kind of fire and dash about them. But it was the ordinary enlisted men he came to know best and to write about in his letters to Mary. Included among them were Dashing John Dollard, the five-goal polo player from Albany; Smitty, the long mountaineer with no front teeth; Sam Jaffe who ran the payday poker game; Caleb Muse who hid a stolen chicken in the boiler room during inspection; and a soldier named Centennial Prescott. But there was no one at Camp Gordon, no one at all, remotely like Sergeant Durham. In his now abundant spare time, Cheever was crafting "the Durham saga." He finished it Thanksgiving morning.

During the holiday season, PFC Cheever felt somewhat bereft. On a brisk and wintry Thanksgiving Day the men lined up in front of the mess hall, and the mess sergeant told them not to eat until the corporal said grace. The tables were covered with the same sheets they would sleep on for the next two weeks. The dinner was served by KPs. It was not the way Cheever would have chosen to spend the day. Perhaps they could be together next year, when they could celebrate as a family, he wrote Mary. Their family was very much in prospect. In his letters he commiserated with his wife about her morning sickness, referred to baby "Geoffrey" or "Tootsie," and encouraged her to find a roomier apartment. He was delighted with the idea of being a father.

Christmas dinner was the same as Thanksgiving with the turkey served on bedsheets. Afterward Cheever took a nap and dreamed of the house he and Mary might inhabit after the war, in the country somewhere amid elm trees. There were presents from everyone—Bill Maxwell mailed him a copy of *Pickwick Papers*—but Camp Gordon was a hell of a place to celebrate Christmas. The months of waiting were beginning to take their toll. Every soldier at Gordon was eager to be sent somewhere.

Early in January 1943 it looked as if the 22nd would be shipped overseas soon. The men were inoculated, again. They were ordered to use an APO return address and to make their wills. Guns were packed away in Cosmoline, machinery in crates. Finally everyone had to sign an embarkation form. "That cinched it," the troops thought, but preparations stopped as abruptly as they had started. On January 10 an order came down to resume issuing passes and furloughs.

Sharing such inexplicable experiences served to draw the men closer together. In E Company, someone stole sixty-six dollars from Herman Nelson, a thirty-eight-year-old wheat farmer from North Dakota. Nelson was about to be discharged because of his age, and had been saving the money for his return home. The thief was not discovered, though the company commander restricted the company indefinitely in hopes of smoking him out. Nelson's fellow soldiers, however, took up a collection of twenty-five dollars to help him on his way. In his story based on this incident, Cheever gives the farmer a farewell speech. "I'm going to miss all you fellows," he says. "I don't want to go away only it's yust I'm not so young. Such fine fellows I never met before in all my life. Such fine fellows."

Cheever himself was transferred from personnel to Special Services, as editor of the regimental weekly paper, *The Double Deucer*. On this job he worked with cartoonist Lin Streeter, "a very nice guy" who once had had a studio near their apartment in the Village. He rather enjoyed the work, and thought it might continue for the duration. Meanwhile, he resumed the attempts to get into OCS he had initiated at Camp Croft. He had not been selected earlier because he did not have a college education and because he had scored below 110 on the Army General Classification Test given to all entering recruits. Now, he thought, his book might substitute for the college degree, but he still had to do something about his AGCT score. Mary sent him some manuals on how to improve one's IQ—he was especially weak on math—and he boned up on long division, nights. Then he took the test again "and passed into group two, which is OCS material." He made it only with some assistance from Dave Rothbart, the personnel clerk who administered the test and was "not entirely scrupulous about the timing." Rothbart admired Cheever's writing but did not think of him as officer material. "If you saw him marching in formation, you wouldn't think, 'Now, there's a soldier.' There was something of a dreamlike quality about him, something of the New England country gentleman, even then."

The Way Some People Live, Cheever's collection of stories, was published on March 8, 1943. Complimentary copies went to the author's parents, his brother, his in-laws, Gus Lobrano, Malcolm Cowley, Elizabeth Ames, Eddie Newhouse, Flannery Lewis, and four of his officers at Camp Gordon. On the dust jacket Random House noted the uncanny ability of Harold Ross and *The New Yorker* to find "new writing stars" like Sally Benson, Irwin Shaw, James Thurber, E. B. White, and now "the bright new luminary of the past two seasons," John Cheever. Cheever was in the army, the jacket copy revealed, but upon his return "the publishers expect that he will be a major figure in American post-war literature."

The book contained thirty stories arranged more or less by chronology. The first twenty-four derived from the prewar period; the last six were written after Pearl Harbor. They could also be separated according to length. Twenty-seven ran to fewer than ten book pages. Many of these read like vignettes or anecdotes rather than full-fledged stories, and almost all of them came from the pages of *The New Yorker.* Two of the three much longer stories, "The Brothers" and "Of Love: A Testimony"—both of them singled out for praise by reviewers—were deeply felt semiautobiographical tales populated by characters that the author (and hence the reader) clearly cared about.

In putting the book together, Random House worked from tear sheets Cheever and his agent supplied. At some stage of this process, the stories dealing with politics and with Cheever's family background were culled out, among them such ambitious and interesting efforts as "Homage to Shakespeare," "Autobiography of a Drummer," "In Passing," and "Behold a Cloud in the West." Also scrapped were the purely commercial racetrack stories and the two overly contrived sketches about burlesque performers. The stories actually included in the book repeatedly touch on the reduced circumstances of middle-class people after the Depression. Usually the tone is lightly ironical, the narrative voice keeping its distance. Usually the outlook is dark.

For the first time Cheever read his reviews, and he survived the ordeal in good humor. William DuBois, in the *New York Times Book Review,* chided him for writing about "Tortured Souls" with "epicene detachment and facile despair," a comment Cheever decided to regard as very funny. The two most thoughtful reviews—a rave by Struthers Burt, an attack by Weldon Kees—he did not dismiss so lightly.

Writing in the *Saturday Review,* Burt called *The Way Some People Live* "the best volume of short stories" he had come across in a long time and "Of Love: A Testimony" "one of the best love stories" he had ever read. After the war, he predicted, Cheever would become "one of the most distinguished writers, not only as a short story writer but as a novelist" and perhaps even as a playwright. He had all the requisite qualities: "the sense of drama in ordinary events and people; the underlying and universal importance of the outwardly unimportant; a deep feeling for the perversities and contradictions, the worth and unexpected dignity of life, its ironies, comedies, and tragedies." The only things he had to fear were "hardening" into a style that might "become an affectation, and a deliberate casualness and simplicity that might become the same. Otherwise, the world is his."

What Burt was warning against, though the magazine's name was not mentioned in his review, was the danger of Cheever's fiction conforming too closely to the *New Yorker* pattern. It was this that bothered Kees in his review for *The New Republic.* Read individually in the magazine, the stories "seemed better than they are; read one after another, their nearly identical lengths, similarities of tone and situation, and their somehow remote and unambitious style, produce an effect of sameness and eventually of tedium." All *New Yorker* stories, he maintained, were written in highly professional prose, yet displayed "a patina of triviality" both in style and subject matter. If he was to escape the formula, Cheever should write more stories like the 1934 "Of Love: A Testimony"—stories in which "he has room enough . . . to work for something more than episodic notation and minor perceptive effects."

The review by Kees was important as the first of many broadsides against Cheever as a "*New Yorker* writer" limited in scope by his association with the magazine. Unlike most later accusations, Kees's had some validity. Since that day when Cowley first suggested he write much shorter pieces, Cheever had in fact been constructing sketches designed to suit the magazine's special requirements. He needed to grow in his craft, to combine the skill of rhetoric and construction evidenced in his early *New Yorker* work with the emotionally powerful effects of his longer stories.

No critic could have been harder on this first book of stories than

Cheever himself eventually became. In effect he repudiated the book, turning down offers of translation rights and allowing none of the stories in *The Way Some People Live* to be reprinted in the 1978 Pulitzer Prize–winning *Stories of John Cheever*. Even at the time of publication, he was curiously dispassionate about the book. Cerf had warned him not to expect much by way of sales, and Cerf was right. Random House printed 2,750 copies and sold 1,990 at two dollars apiece. Cheever made only one hundred and forty dollars in royalties beyond his advance of two hundred and fifty. The book's appearance had other benefits, however. Seeing the stories in a book, as he wrote Mary with due modesty, showed him how much he had yet to learn. More immediately, several of the writer/ propagandists at the Signal Corps Photographic Center in Astoria, Long Island, read *The Way Some People Live* and liked it enough to badger Colonel Leonard Spigelgass into getting Cheever transferred to their unit.

UPTOWN

1943-1950

CHEEVER'S transfer to the Signal Corps unit
at Astoria on Long Island could hardly have
been more fortunate. He was already at Fort
Dix with the 22nd Infantry Regiment, expecting shipment to combat duty overseas, when he got
word of his reassignment in the spring of 1943. Later,
his old regiment underwent terrible losses in the battle for Fortress Europe. The men of the 22nd splashed
ashore at Utah Beach on D-Day morning, and within
five weeks suffered 3,439 casualties, or more than the
original strength of the unit at D-Day. Still worse was
to come. In the fall of 1944, the 22nd fought both at
Hürtgenwald, or "the Death Factory" as the men

called it, and in the Battle of the Bulge. (The regimental commander during those battles was Colonel Charles T. [Buck] Lanham.
And attached to the regiment was Lanham's close friend, war correspondent Ernest Hemingway.) By V-E Day the total casualties
mounted to 9,359. About four out of five enlisted men who served
with the 22nd were wounded. Half were killed.

In later years, Cheever provided varying accounts of his army
career. He wanted to stay in the infantry, he told an interviewer.
He spent "four years as an infantry gunner," he said on one occasion, "two years as a mortar gunner," he said on another. Actually
he was in basic training and attached to an infantry company for
about one year only, and a strange year it was. In retrospect
Cheever found it difficult to "connect his life" at Camp Croft and
Camp Gordon with the man he subsequently became. "That person in the army," he said, "that wasn't me." The South, the garrison towns, even Sergeant Durham faded into the mist.

Life at Astoria—as veterans of the Signal Corps Photographic
Center call their post—contrasted sharply with the restrictions and
rigors of Regular Army duty in the South. Cheever was treated like
a professional there, and granted certain privileges accordingly.
Best of all, he could live at home in New York with Mary, now
seven months pregnant, and commute to his work like a civilian.

In preparation for the baby, the Cheevers settled into a small
garden apartment on Twenty-second Street between Eighth and
Ninth avenues in Chelsea. It was not a fashionable neighborhood
in those days. On their first Sunday in residence, an outraged cry
punctured the morning quiet as Mary served breakfast outdoors.
"Dontcha call me a whore," a whore yelled. That night a drunken
woman wearing a feather boa and carrying a fluffy dog under her
arm stopped to pee in the gutter. Cheever was back in New York.

At three in the morning on July 31, Mary gave birth to a healthy
eight-pound baby girl they named Susan Liley Cheever. John was
on hand during delivery, and held Mary in his arms through the
last of a long labor. Both parents were very proud. Mary "liked
being pregnant . . . and now she likes nursing," John wrote Josephine Herbst. "Mother's bird," Mary called the baby, and attached
a rose over her cradle. As for John, the birth made him "absurdly
happy." Having a child, his father used to tell him, was as easy as
"blowing a feather off one's knee." But Cheever felt a kind of
rapture mingled with justification. Susan's arrival, and later that of
her brothers, Ben and Fred, gave him the family he ardently

wanted. The most exciting days of his life, he was often to proclaim, were the days his children were born.

The Signal Corps Photographic Center where the new father went to work occupied the capacious grounds of the studios at Thirty-fifth Avenue and Thirty-fifth Street in Astoria, Queens. Many of the great silent movies of the 1920s had been made there. Quiescent during the Depression, the studio hummed to life as part of the propaganda war that Frank Capra—deputized by President Roosevelt—was leading against the sophisticated techniques of Joseph Goebbels and the Nazis. In charge of operations when Cheever came on board in 1943 was Colonel Manny Cohen, the five-foot-tall former production chief at Paramount Studios. Stanley Kramer was administrative head. Head writer Leonard Spigelgass directed the work of such professionals as Irwin Shaw, William Saroyan, Carl Foreman, Don Ettlinger, Arnand D'Usseau, Jimmy Gow, John D. Weaver, and Ted Mills. Their primary function was to write scripts for the biweekly *Army-Navy Screen Magazine,* a film series "using fact and humor, animation, combat footage and specially photographed features to answer gripes, clear up confusions and misunderstandings, pass on information about new policies or plans," and in general improve morale among the nation's servicemen. The unit also turned out special films on the D-Day landings, the liberation of Paris, and so forth. As a group the filmmakers felt a strong sense of mission as "shock troops in the idea war," along with an uneasy sense that they were really amateurs at the business of propaganda.

The army mustered the best writing talent it could find, but even in this all-star cast Cheever stood out. After reading a dozen or so scripts, Weaver recalled, he realized that Cheever was "by far the best writer of our group." Mills, sitting at the desk opposite, marveled at the way Cheever sweated over selecting the right verb for the ear instead of the eye, and at "the lean purity" of the language he composed for the voices of such favorite narrators as José Ferrer. He was also extremely productive. "One problem immediately arose," Spigelgass recalled. "There wasn't enough work for him. . . . There never was. He was a writing machine."

The filmmakers at Astoria had an important job to do, but they were determined to be as unmilitary about it as possible. The place soon became a battleground between these free-spirited professionals and Regular Army types frantically trying to impose some discipline. The men were damned if they'd show up for muster at

6:00 A.M. or live in the barracks provided. According to legend, Irwin Shaw and Bill Saroyan did turn out, ostentatiously, for one early-morning muster. Saroyan's play *The Time of Your Life* had made a great deal of money, so he hired a Rolls-Royce with a chauffeur uniformed like an admiral in the Venezuelan navy to drive them to Astoria. At 5:58 A.M., the Rolls pulled up next to the parade ground, the garishly uniformed chauffeur opened the doors, and Shaw and Saroyan fell in with the other moviemakers. Roll call was advanced to a more reasonable hour, and even then the writers usually adjourned to Borden's for bagels, cream cheese, and coffee before settling down to work.

Efforts at shaping up the unit were also compromised by Colonel Cohen's diminutive stature. "The mini-colonel," he was called. In the subway kids used to grab his cap and run with it. One yarn has it that a ramrod-straight major general, a West Pointer, marched into Cohen's office and lectured him on the need for order and discipline. "When a superior officer enters the room, the least you can do is stand up," he thundered. "But, General," the mini-colonel responded, "I am standing up." The general left in disarray, defeated.

Though Cheever did have an unsuccessful interview with an OCS selection committee, and still wished he could serve overseas as a correspondent for *Yank*, he was doing about as well as an enlisted man could expect at Astoria, and remained stationed there for more than two years, until his discharge in November 1945. Along the way he made some of the closest friends of his life, including Weaver, Ettlinger, and producer Leonard Field. For the most part they called each other by their last names. Rank counted for almost nothing, except when they wanted it to. Cheever, Ettlinger, and Mills, for example, dubbed themselves the Three Sergeants. Together they threw a wild New Year's Eve party in Greenwich Village, inviting almost everyone they could think of. To their surprise almost everyone showed up, and all the champagne was gone by eleven o'clock. Cheever then discovered a case of club soda, this was dispensed in lieu of the bubbly, and no one was sober enough to notice the difference. At midnight Manny Cohen made a maudlin speech about the Three Sergeants. On the spot the mini-colonel was made an honorary member of their brotherhood.

A fine spirit of comradeship developed among the amateur propagandists of Astoria, only occasionally disturbed by a sense of guilt that they were having too good a time and not getting shot at. On Wednesday morning they settled down at their desks, and as if on cue whipped out their copies of *Variety*. Once a week or so they made a run across the bridge for lunch at Canarie d'Or in Manhattan, ordering two dry martinis and two *pots de crème au chocolat* apiece in advance. Comedian Herbie Baker did a wonderful imitation of the maître d's suspicious French. Cheever himself perfected a takeoff on the standard VD lecture, warning in his own fake French against the dangers of "le bal bleu." This performance he delivered at parties, where he used to be "the brightest person in the room until ten o'clock, when he fell over drunk." Even in a hard-drinking group, there were those who thought he was over-doing it.

The political stance at Astoria tilted sharply to the left. Three of the men Cheever worked with in Building Six attended Communist cell meetings. Anti-Fascism was the watchword, and there was talk of freedom, liberty, and justice—terms that Senator Joseph McCarthy tried to devalue as subversive a decade later. The Three Sergeants, liberal but decidedly not Communist, were invited to parties in Manhattan given by such glamorous show-business figures as Fredric March, Abe Burrows, Paul Draper, and Moss Hart on behalf of the Citizens Committee for the Arts, Sciences, and Professions (CCASP). Certain attempts were made at these gatherings to recruit Party members, Mills reports. An attractive female Communist he met at one such occasion took him to bed, and after use of an "exquisite instrument" spoke of seeing him at the Party meeting the next day. Mills did not go. Cheever, married, was less susceptible to such means of persuasion. Besides, he resented the "assault on the language" he encountered in the speeches of American Communist leader Earl Browder. Communism was not for him, Cheever decided. He was considering going in for "some form of sun worship" instead, he wrote Josie Herbst.

In the fall of 1944 the Cheevers embarked upon an experiment in communal living, bourgeois-style. Together with two other couples they rented a town house at 8 East Ninety-second Street for two hundred dollars a month, unfurnished. At the time it was virtually impossible to locate roomy apartments for growing families—each of the three couples had a child—and the house on Ninety-second Street offered amenities of space and decoration they could not have afforded separately. It had eight flush toilets and five floors. There was a handsomely paneled library and a morning room. The floor of the downstairs hall was made of black and white marble. Each of the couples occupied a bedroom, dressing room, and bath; each of the children had a bedroom and bath. The only telephone was in the Cheevers' upstairs bedroom. Friends were warned to let it ring a long time when they called.

The other renters were John and Peggy McManus and Reuel and Ruth Denney. Film editor McManus worked with Cheever at Astoria, and his wife had known Mary Cheever at Sarah Lawrence. Denney, later to become a distinguished scholar, worked for Time-Life. From the beginning there were tensions among the tenants. The Denneys were serious, intellectual, the McManuses gay, partyloving. The Cheevers more or less held the middle ground, but in time that proved to be untenable territory. In an effort to secure community of purpose, the three couples decided to take turns cooking dinner. This endeavor failed when one of the three young matrons prepared elegant gourmet meals, another heated up Spam, and the third burned her meat loaf. A child spat at a mother, not his own. Another child wrecked the flower garden. One of the women washed her hair in the kitchen sink. A secondhand bed purchased to furnish the place turned out to have bedbugs that traveled. In the spring and summer of 1945, matters grew even worse. "In the house there has been constant disorder, hysteria, and vermin," Mary reported to Josie Herbst in July 1945, along with the joyful news that she had found an apartment of their own at 400 East Fifty-ninth Street.

However unpleasant things may have been at the town house, Cheever knew how to capitalize on the experience. First he regaled his fellow travelers in the car pool to Astoria with the ongoing story of the house on Ninety-second Street. Then he began to work nights transforming what happened into "funny, funny pieces" for *The New Yorker*. He wrote six of these "Town House" stories, all published between April 1945 and May 1946. Negotiations also began for a Broadway play based on the stories, inspiring visions of a financial windfall.

In April 1945, Cheever finally got a taste of overseas service on a research-and-writing trip to Guam and the Philippines. En route he stopped in Chicago to see Dorothy Farrell. They went out to dinner in her new Ford roadster, which ran about half a block and stalled. Cheever got out to push, and gleefully started berating her.

"I come all this way to see you, and you make me push your car," he said. "How much did you pay for it, anyway?"

"I bought it from my dentist," she said. "I paid seventy-five dollars."

"He's some dentist. Are you sure you've still got your teeth?"

Later that night, Cheever's jocular mood gave way to melancholy, and Dorothy did what she could to comfort him. They were the same age, but it was almost as though she were mothering him. On arrival in Los Angeles, he wrote to tell Mary how much he missed her and Susan. "I have never left anyone so reluctantly." To make the time pass he started reading *The Best Known Novels of George Eliot*.

He stayed in Los Angeles for a week, taking shots for bubonic plague and getting an impression of the city. The motion-picture industry affected almost everything. All the women had conspicuous breasts, wore fancy hats and furs, and ate in drugstores, waiting to be discovered. He and Carl Foreman went to the Brown Derby instead. Then he finished *Adam Bede,* started *The Mill on the Floss* ("a dog," he reported), and flew to the Marianas.

When he landed at Guam at dusk, the public-address system was playing a Strauss waltz. At the edge of the jungle one evening, he heard someone playing Chopin. It was the soundtrack from *A Song to Remember,* with Merle Oberon and Cornel Wilde. Troops in the Pacific were obsessed with collecting Japanese souvenirs, he discovered, and built that observation into a story. Having completed *The Mill on the Floss*—he had only *Romola* and *Silas Marner* left—he was off to the Philippines, where daily existence did not much resemble that on Ninety-second Street. One morning a monkey that had set up headquarters in Cheever's tent bit a native who came by selling bananas. The monkey found its way into a story, too. Manila was a casualty of the war; "there was absolutely nothing over waist-high" in the city.

On V-E Day Cheever was in the Marianas again. There was no celebration on Guam. The war in the Pacific was not over. Early in June he was on his way home, and glad of it. "It seems incredible that I'm finally coming back," he wrote Mary. He had been away just over two months.

Late in July the Cheevers abandoned the ménage at Ninety-second Street to move to their freshly painted East Side apartment in the same neighborhood, if not the same rent district, as Sutton Place. "Here we are," Mary wrote Josie Herbst, "living like the wicked rich surrounded by swells and movie magnates and the reproachful stares of doormen and other dignitaries whom we can't afford to tip." Susie occupied "her little suite, and ours as well, with the ease and airs of a well-kept woman," Mary reported. Often her parents took her along with them in the evening. During a party at Irwin and Marian Shaw's, Susie as radiant toddler shared the spotlight with Ingrid Bergman.

In August the atom bomb exploded over Hiroshima and the war was soon over. Mary and Susie were at Treetops on V-J Day, so Cheever celebrated with Don and Katrina Ettlinger. They hired a taxi and shouted from the windows, *"La guerre est finie."* Like most other servicemen, Cheever was eager to return to civilian life as soon as possible. He was discharged at Fort Monmouth, New Jersey, on November 27, 1945, having served in the army for three years, six months, and twenty days. Cheever was disbursed $187.03 in mustering-out pay and went back to New York "with a wonderful sense of liberation."

During the war years Cheever saw more and more of the Winternitzes and less and less of his own family. His relations with his parents were "correct" but "never intimate," as he later said. Rightly or wrongly he believed that they had rejected him. "I think they were terribly disappointed that I survived the war," he told Pete Collins. One of the most touching of his army stories is about a young soldier who returns home to find that his parents have "adopted" a youth stationed nearby in his stead.

Cheever's father, retired for twenty years, mellowed into a sweet patient man who drew pictures of boats for his grandchildren (Fred and Iris's children) on Sundays. To the end he remained very dapper, with beautiful white hair and bushy eyebrows, and smelled fresh and clean, probably of bay rum. Late in 1945 he died at eighty-two, and John went to Norwell for the funeral at Fred's house. His mother told him on the drive over from Quincy that his father had passed away sitting in a wing chair beside a cup of tea. On a table nearby was another cup of tea with two cigarette butts, stained by lipstick, in the saucer. Whoever had been with him that day never came forward, but they concluded that for her it must have been "a terrible afternoon." At the graveside, Mrs. Cheever wanted John to read Prospero's speech from *The Tempest*—it was something, she said, that his father had requested—but he refused. (Prospero's words, "We are such stuff as dreams are made on," were later engraved on his tombstone.) "It was a very long association," Mrs. Cheever remarked at the graveside.

As a civilian, Cheever had more time to watch his daughter grow, along with an exacerbated awareness of the need to support his family through his writing. Nothing was to be wasted. The Cheevers spent the New Year's holiday at Candlewood Lake with the Ettlingers, where a primitive ski lift jerkily conveyed skiers up the hill. John's "vacuum mind" took it all in: in a story of his, a little girl is caught in a similar ski lift. Susie was in fact unscathed, except that back in New York she became convinced that a lion lived in her room ("The lion is busy," she had heard over the telephone). She took the lion on walks in the neighborhood, struggling to keep him on the leash. The creature stayed in the city when the family went up to Treetops for most of the summer.

Life at Treetops conformed to a regular routine. During the summer up to twenty-five people might be on the grounds, living in individual cottages. Dr. and Mrs. Winternitz occupied Stone House, the large central building the doctor had constructed largely with his own hands. "Winter" was very much in charge; some awe was commingled in Cheever's admiration for him. Polly served as hostess and manager, ordering quantities of detergent, mayonnaise, and toilet paper as if for a hotel. Each morning after breakfast everyone went to the vast vegetable gardens and picked corn or squash or raspberries, whatever was in season. The rest of the day was free, except for lunch and the almost obligatory swim in the lake. Cheever soon began to climb the nearby mountains with Bill Winternitz, Mary's younger brother, and with Joe Hotchkiss, who had married her stepsister Janie. The people he met at high altitudes in the Appalachian Mountain Club huts fascinated him, and eventually he converted his hikes into an article for *Holiday* on the New Hampshire mountains.

Often he and Joe hustled home from their climbing to be in time for the grand social hour at Stone House, which commenced precisely at 6:00 P.M. and ended at 7:00 P.M. with the ringing of the dinner bell. Some hard drinking was done during that daily one-hour cocktail party. On Sundays the Treetops schedule changed. For the Sabbath only, drinking was permitted at lunch, and ordinarily there was homemade ice cream with the meal. Once, Hotchkiss recalls, he and Cheever nearly cranked their arms off trying to make the rum ice cream harden. Polly, it turned out, had poured in too much of the principal ingredient.

Cheever was "nearly always friendly" in those days, Hotchkiss observes, except when he caught a whiff of unkindness in someone else's behavior. He felt strongly about good manners and about the

respect for the feelings of others that lay behind them. And "he was
good with so many different sorts of people," too. Polly adored him,
Winter was very proud of him, and for six to eight years after the
war he felt himself more their son than their son-in-law. He also
got along well with the hired help, as did Susie. She sequestered
herself in the back of the house with the Swedish cook and her
children, acquiring their speech patterns in the process. "Ain't the
Winternitzes got a nice summer place?" she asked her father. Meanwhile, he made friends with a doctrinaire Communist from
Czechoslovakia who farmed the land and took care of the buildings
the year round. Cheever helped him plow the fields, and undertook
to be of assistance by ridding the place of the raccoons that were
eating dozens of ears of corn each night.

As they worked together, the hired man tried to indoctrinate
Cheever in the mysteries of his secular dogma. He would not whip
the balky mare which sometimes refused to pull the plow, but he
also declined to give her a name. Naming farm animals, he proclaimed, was "bourgeois sentimentality." One evening he slipped
a newspaper headline under Cheever's door: LUXURY LIVING WEAK-
ENS U.S., it read. Cheever put these incidents into "The Summer
Farmer," a 1948 story that pictures the Communist as unfairly
wronged by a young gentleman farmer. Spreading out imagina-
tively from this experience, he wrote two other stories—"Vega"
and "How Dr. Wareham Kept His Servants"—sympathetic to the
plight of East Europeans who brought almost nothing to this country except their political passion. These were not really political
stories at all, however. The hills of Vermont and New Hampshire
were, he observed, full of old Communists from Latvia and Estonia
and Russia and Poland and Germany—all of them aliens in a
strange land. It was their alienation that commanded his sympathy.

Back in the city, the Cheevers surmounted the minor crisis of
dispatching Susie to nursery school. Each morning they maintained a cheerfully upbeat demeanor before sending her off to the
Walt Whitman School. Each afternoon they grilled her, unsuccessfully, on the activities of the day. Social life had its hazards as well.
They went to a party at the Fields' where John performed an
"atomic waltz" with Betty Fast, wife of writer Howard Fast. He
carried her on his shoulders; she put out her cigarette in his ear;
he dumped her on the floor.

Life was not all fun and games, however. Now that the war was
over, the thirty-four-year-old Cheever was a full-time writer again,

determined to make a living on the strength of his talent. For purposes of discipline, he established a daily routine. Each morning he dressed in his good suit and hat and rode down in the elevator with the other professional men who lived in the building. They got off on the first floor, however, while he continued to the basement. There he settled to work at a makeshift desk in the windowless storage room. He stripped to his shorts, hung up his coat and pants, and hammered away at his typewriter in the two-fingered style he had taught himself. He put the suit back on at lunchtime and at the end of the day for the elevator ride back upstairs.

His major project was a novel, and now he had a contract to spur him on. Hoping to build on their investment in *The Way Some People Live*, Random House gave him $2,400 of a $4,800 advance toward a novel early in 1946. At first Cheever was optimistic about its progress. It's "coming along nicely," he wrote editor Robert Linscott in September 1946; the first draft should be done by November. He did not tell Linscott that from the start he harbored private doubts about the value of his novel-in-progress. He felt real pressure to produce the book. "I'm the only man in the east 50s who hasn't finished his novel," he wrote John Weaver. At the end of 1947, responding to Linscott's request, he produced an outline for the Random House sales force.

The writing itself he was generally pleased with, Cheever observed in his preliminary remarks. He thought of his novel-in-progress as having the polish and charm "of a greeting card with an obscene message." The New England of his youth came flooding back to him in memory, and it was this that gave his novel-to-be its "greeting card" quality. In subject matter, the book returned to the milieu of *The Holly Tree*. The story was about the Field family, who in 1936 lived on a farm on the North River south of Boston after losing their house to foreclosure. The Fields' poverty, though unmentioned, affects everything in their lives. The principal characters are father Aaron, who had once been successful but lost his money; mother Sarah, "a run-of-the-mill New England matriarch" who has given up her beauty without a struggle and dreams of being invited to the White House; and their sons, Eben, "personable and cruel," and Tom, an "outing-club type" who leaves Dartmouth in his sophomore year to go to work in a textile house.

The "parochial charm" of the family conceals an impulse to violence. Thus Cheever intended to contrast sentimental scenes of such pleasant rituals as berry picking with others depicting the "lewdness and cruelty" that was also part of the picture. Aaron steals and sells his wife's jewelry. Eben leaves home. The gulf between Aaron and younger son Tom grows wider when the father attempts to seduce one of the son's girlfriends. Next Aaron tries to kill himself. Finally he leaves the farm to escape an illegitimate daughter, and the book follows Tom, Eben, Sarah, and others as they search for Aaron in Boston, New York, and Washington. There were some "wonderful girls" in this part, Cheever wrote, "and some wonderful ceremonies."

Meanwhile, Sarah Field opens a gift shop to support herself and what's left of the family. Then, "for reasons that involve them all and that should be rooted in the first words of the book," she commits a terrible murder. Now it is wartime. Tom goes off to serve in the Pacific. Sarah escapes prosecution. Aaron returns home and is drowned while swimming off Cohasset in 1944. The book ends with Tom on his way back for the funeral.

This outline of a novel—the Field Version, to give it a name—pointed forward to *The Wapshot Chronicle* and like that book derived much of its physical and emotional authenticity from Cheever's own background. His grandfather Aaron, like Aaron Field, deserted his family. His own parents lost their comfortable home in Quincy to foreclosure. His mother ran a gift shop. Cheever sometimes thought of older brother Fred, who left Dartmouth to work for a textile firm in Boston, as "personable and cruel." Obviously both the Field Version and *The Wapshot Chronicle* are family sagas, with a concentration on the inner dynamics of a family in economic difficulties and a celebration of ceremony reminiscent of the nineteenth-century novel.

Whatever its merits and whatever it promised of work completed—Cheever nowhere mentions how much actual writing he's done—this outline was greeted enthusiastically by Linscott. "That's a wonderful presentation," he wrote Cheever on December 22, 1947. "You have certainly whetted my appetite for the book, and I shan't be happy until I read it." A long unhappy period awaited both Linscott and Cheever, who was forced to announce delay after delay. He thought he had finished the book late in 1948, but his publishers thought not. More work was needed, and Cheever did what he could. The number of good, durable chapters was steadily growing, he reported in January 1950. Writing novels, he pointed out nine months later, was still his "principal aim in life." But progress was fitful at best, for in the short term he had to write stories to support himself and his family and simply couldn't spare the time or energy to complete his novel. It was a frustrating business, and Cheever became increasingly sensitive about Linscott's inquiries.

Most of the new stories dealt with the Upper East Side he was inhabiting. In them he went beyond the spare unemotional prose of his early *New Yorker* work, and beyond "the funny, funny stories" of the "Town House" series. He was developing his capacity to suggest a whole life in miniature, to connote through significant detail the entire biography of his characters. To this bit of naturalistic legerdemain he now applied his gift for fantasy. In "The Enormous Radio" and "Torch Song," both stories published in 1947, he artfully managed to combine the mundane and the mystical. So persuasive is the anthropological voice at the beginning of "The Enormous Radio," with its revelation that Jim and Irene Westcott "went to the theatre an average of 10.3 times a year" and otherwise fit into "that satisfactory average of income, endeavor, and respectability" reported in college alumni bulletins, that it seems almost natural when the narrator reveals that the Westcotts' new radio transmits the unhappy quarrels of other residents in their apartment building. This circumstance, defying electronic explanation, confronts the Westcotts with precisely those things about their marriage that will not be mentioned in college alumni bulletins—and serves to remind us all of our sometime hypocrisy.

"Torch Song" delves still deeper into psychological aberration. Joan Harris, it is suggested, feeds on the decline and death of the several men she loves and cares for in their final months. But again the world she lives in is so convincingly recognizable and concrete that her vampirism becomes just as real as the furnished room "in the badlands west of Central Park" where Jack Lorey awaits her return as "the lewd and searching shape of death." "Torch Song" is also notable for its depiction of a woman who destroys the men in her life. This powerful female character, cruel if not always murderous, was often to reappear in Cheever's fiction.

At the beginning of 1947, Mary Cheever started teaching English at Sarah Lawrence two days a week. She liked the work so much that by summer she was planning to get a master's degree at Columbia. Family matters interfered with this plan. Susie went through the usual childhood diseases. When she had chicken pox, so did her father, and Mary nursed them both. Then it was clear by the fall, when she was to start at Columbia, that she was pregnant again and the master's degree was abandoned. On May 4, 1948, her thirtieth birthday, Mary gave birth to Benjamin Hale Cheever. A "fine looking, dark-eyed lively boy," he was very unlike Susan as a baby. John was delighted with his arrival, and from the beginning Mary felt a powerful bond to her first son.

In the meantime, work had been going forward on a stage adaptation of Cheever's "Town House" stories. By the fall of 1948, the play was finally ready to open on Broadway. Bernie Hart had purchased the rights as early as January 1946 and put Herman Mankiewicz to work on the script. When this effort failed to pan out, Hart sold the rights, and the play that opened on Broadway was written by Gertrude Tonkonogy, staged by George S. Kaufman, and produced by Max Gordon. With such professionals behind the venture, Cheever had hopes that *Town House* would make his fortune.

In Boston, where the play had its out-of-town opening on September 2, the auspices looked good. Cheever went up in advance to generate hometown author publicity. In a long article he wrote for the *Boston Post*, he radiated enthusiasm for the production. Tonkonogy had done an excellent job of playwriting. Mary Wickes brought "a richness far beyond the ordinary pathos of comedy" to her portrayal of the awkward and shy intellectual housewife. June Duprez was "just right" as the beauty, and Hiram Sherman and James Monks materialized onstage exactly as he "realized them in the stories." Max Gordon called it "one of the funniest plays I have ever had the honor to produce." The Boston audience, full of family relations and former cleaning women, seemed to agree. There was optimistic talk about a big Hollywood sale. At this stage, according to Cheever, Kaufman decided to add more jokes, with disastrous results.

Opening night on Broadway was an absolute frost. The Cheevers went with the Ettlingers and Gus Lobrano, and "the play was terrible," Don recalls, "not at all what John had in mind." The set, which "cost as much to build as a twenty-room house with running water," was magnificent. Mary Wickes was excellent. Otherwise the play was a disaster. *Town House* closed on September 30, after twelve performances. Cheever made fifty-four dollars. The producers lost a hundred thousand.

Even this experience was not a dead loss, however. In three separate stories, Cheever drew on his observation of the New York theatrical scene. All three contrast the simple unpretentiousness of

ordinary people—twice playwrights from the country, once a teenager without affection—with the glossy world behind the foot-
lights. One of these, "The Opportunity," sold to *Cosmopolitan* for
$1,750 in July 1949. That was "a good deal more than I've gotten
before," he wrote Edith Haggard of Curtis Brown Associates, the
agents he had just hired to replace Lieber. He was still free-lancing
precariously, without a successful novel or play or movie sale to
bolster the family finances, and he stuck to his daily writing regimen in the basement.

Often he talked with the men who worked in the building—the
super, the doorman, the handyman—as he made his daily way to
his subterranean cubbyhole. Never were these men so unified and
happy as on the day after Harry S. Truman defeated Thomas E.
Dewey in November 1948. Every inch a Democrat, Cheever sat
around in the basement with the building employees, gleefully
exchanging stories about how stricken the Republican apartment
dwellers looked.

President Truman's election did little to halt the advance of the
postwar Red scare. Earlier that year the left-wing *Partisan Review*
began a brouhaha over the award of the Bollingen Prize to the
pro-Fascist Ezra Pound. In the summer the Russians blockaded
Berlin. In August, Whittaker Chambers publicly accused Alger
Hiss of treason. The climate was right for witch-hunts: in February
1949 Robert Lowell accused Yaddo's Elizabeth Ames of harboring
Communists. Ames was "a diseased organ, chronically poisoning
the whole system," he declared, and he went to the Yaddo board
to ask for her dismissal. Lowell, then in one of his manic phases,
persuaded three other colonists to join him in bringing his indictment. Cheever was among those who rallied to her defense.

The trouble began with a news report alleging that Agnes Smedley served as a contact for a Soviet spy ring. Smedley, a social
scientist with a particular interest in the Far East, had in fact lived
at Yaddo for almost fifteen years as the close friend and confidante
of Ames. But Ames had sent her away nearly a year before the story
broke in the *New York Times.* By the time Yaddo's board of trustees
met late in February, the *Times* had withdrawn the accusation
against Smedley. Lowell persisted in demanding Ames's dismissal
anyway. She had consorted with Leonard Ehrlich, a "proletarian
novelist," it was alleged. Suspicious jokes had been made about
"Molotov cocktail parties." Ames's private secretary, for five years
a paid FBI informant, had heard "people talking very brilliantly

red," and reported them. After thirty pages of testimony of this sort, the board decided to postpone a decision until a meeting in New York on Saturday, March 26.

The delay gave Ames's friends and supporters time to mobilize under the leadership of Eleanor Clark. A group of five—Harvey Breit, Cheever, Clark, Alfred Kazin, and Kappo Phelan—composed a letter to former colonists asking them to sign a petition on behalf of the director. They were firm "anti-Stalinists," the petition proclaimed, but were also "outraged" by the "smear-technique" that threatened the welfare of the Yaddo where they all had lived and worked. Seventy-five letters went out on March 21. Five days later, the group had fifty-one signers lined up. With these documents in hand, the five defenders went down to Wall Street on March 26 and saved the day for Ames and Yaddo. Cheever had been sought out as one of the five organizers, Clark recalled, because of his own apolitical stance and because of his deep sense of loyalty to Elizabeth Ames. "He was wonderful in his loyalties," she said.

Back in his tawdry basement workroom, Cheever managed only an occasional swipe at his novel. What he really wanted to write were some long stories in which he could build on the progress he'd made in "The Enormous Radio," "Torch Song," and others. In November 1950 he applied to the Guggenheim Foundation to sustain him while he wrote these stories. He had been trying to support himself writing fiction since he was twenty-one, Cheever pointed out, and it had been a chancy enterprise at best. His connection with *The New Yorker* helped, but still there was a terrible "financial uncertainty." He was confident that he'd grown in his craft over the years. Now, though, he needed a block of time to make a further advance. He proposed to write four or five long stories, using the material that another writer might put into a novel.

In supporting Cheever's candidacy for the grant, Cowley pointed out that his stories were already "much better than they would have to be to be sold to *The New Yorker.*" And he stressed that the thirty-eight-year-old writer was at a turning point in his career. "He can go on to new things or go back; he can't stand still."

SCARBOROUGH

1951-1955

I GOT the horse right here," one of the gamblers in *Guys and Dolls* insisted on the phonograph. There was bean dip and vegetable curry to eat, and whiskey and gin to drink. No one in the spring of 1951 served wine or water. Like most parties at Margot Morrow's, this one was attended by a mélange of the successful and promising, mostly from the theatrical and literary worlds. The party was for the John Cheevers, who were moving to the suburbs the next day. The William Maxwells were there, as were John Becker, Dr. Dana Ashley, the Paul Osborns, perhaps a dozen others, and the hostess, of course—an attractive divorcée who danced and acted and was for the time "more or less camping out" at her house at 4 Riverview Terrace on New York's East Side.

It was a beautiful May evening, and some of the guests spilled out onto the sidewalk, admiring the view of the East River and the Queensboro Bridge. Cheever sat on the outer sill of a first-floor window, with his legs dangling over the areaway, talking to those outdoors. Then, suddenly, he came flying out of the window and narrowly missed being impaled on the spear-sharp iron fence that enclosed the areaway. His injuries were not serious: he suffered only a bruised knee and twisted ankle. But he might have been killed.

As in all cases of defenestration three possibilities obtained. Cheever knew he had not fallen. He also knew he had not jumped, though in a 1960 magazine article he wrote that he had. He had been pushed, though by whom and why were questions he never knew the answers to. As time wore on, he became convinced that whoever had done it wanted him dead. Perhaps, he speculated two decades later when his long and close association with *The New Yorker* and his friend and editor Bill Maxwell was drawing to an end with a series of story rejections, Maxwell himself had pushed him. But like everything in his experience, the incident was subject to alteration for artistic purposes. In his 1976 novel *Falconer,* his protagonist, Ezekiel Farragut, attributes a similar malevolent act to his brother, Eben, the dark brother—a pervasive figure in Cheever's fiction and thoughts—for whose murder he was serving time in prison.

The actual event, according to one eyewitness, was a good deal less sinister. Some liquor had been drunk. Cheever was installed in the window, looking terribly handsome, and more or less on view. Two friends—psychologist Jack Huber and Stewart Wells, a merchandiser from Minneapolis—were chatting nearby with Mary Cheever, when someone remarked in a joking manner of the figure in the window, "What a pose! Why doesn't somebody give him a push?" So Wells did. None of the three of them, from inside, could see the spiked fence below.

The alternative that he had jumped Cheever adopted in an article he wrote for *Esquire* about the family's move from New York City to Westchester. "The farewell parties were numerous and sometimes tearful. The sense was that we were being exiled . . . to a barren and provincial life where we would get fat . . . and spend our evenings glued to the television set. What else can you do in the suburbs? On the night before we left we went to Riverview Terrace for dinner where I jumped, in an exuberance of regret, out of a first-story window."

"Exuberance of regret" captures something of the ambivalent feelings with which the Cheevers packed for the twenty-five-mile trip up the Hudson to Scarborough. For John Cheever, who had lived in New York City for seventeen years, it may have been the most important journey of his life, but he could hardly have known it at the time. What he felt was a kind of pleasant apprehension—in the words of their Hungarian moving man, "Who knows what brings the future?"—mingled with the city dweller's scorn for the presumed conformities and dullnesses of suburban living. After the party that last night at Margot Morrow's, Cheever reported, he took a long walk to make his private farewells. It was his thirty-ninth birthday.

On a sidewalk somewhere in the Eighties I saw a Cuban going through the steps of a rhumba, holding a baby in his arms. A dinner party in the Sixties was breaking up and men and women were standing in a lighted doorway calling good-by and good-night. In the Fifties I saw a scavenger pushing an enormous English perambulator—a carriage for a princess— from ash can to ash can.

A heady, vernal fragrance rose from Central Park.

In the morning he took a shorter walk, encountering the Italian shoeshine man who was convinced that shoe polish made him randy, and the old lady who fed and watered the pigeons year-round and would become jealous if anyone else did. The city and its inhabitants were "raffish and magnificent," he thought. Westchester, surely, would be very different. At noon the moving men came and the Cheevers—John, Mary, Susan, almost eight, and Ben, three—joined the postwar migration that carried nine million Americans to the suburbs between 1947 and 1954.

Most of the nine million consisted of families with young children, attracted to the suburbs where the air and the schools were better and the youngsters would have room to learn and play and grow. It was odd, then—or it would have been odd of anyone less inclined to countenance both sides of a question than John Cheever—that in his only extended piece of writing about New

York City he addressed the issue of raising children in the city and came down, though rather hesitantly, on the side of growing up urban. The New York he enjoyed most was the one his children knew. "They liked the Central Park lion house at four o'clock on February afternoons, the highest point of the Queensboro Bridge [which they could see from the windows of their apartment at 400 East Fifty-ninth Street], and a riverside dock in the East Forties" where he'd once watched two "tarts playing hop-scotch with a hotel room key." Those were Sunday walks, and on weekdays he'd sometimes take the children up the block past the Nedick's stand to the Japanese store, where they could spend their allowance on boxes with vanishing coins, rubber spiders, and water flowers.

In his article "Where New York Children Play," however, Cheever acknowledged that most children beginning life in the city were "usually set out to play in a naked asphalt lot within a steel link fence." Their mothers came along to keep watch from a park bench and—often enough—to reminisce about their own upbringing in the country or theorize about a future exodus to the leafy exurbs. "Pity the poor children," said passersby. Pity the children, said many of the mothers, unwilling to accept for them an "environment of tugboats and gutter bonfires." Pity the children for their lack of space, air, light, and foliage, said psychiatrists, city planners, architects, doctors, and social workers.

But what of the children themselves? "The air was so bad the plane trees that had been put out by the Parks Department had begun to sicken, but the children's cheeks were red, their eyes were bright, their voices sounded as hard and clear as the voices of country kids." As Christmas approached, they sent and received cards reproducing Currier & Ives scenes of snowy sleigh rides. "Over the river and through the woods . . ." City children would not remember such trips to grandmother's, but they would remember

wishing on the evening star as it appeared above Hackensack; they would remember a moth-eaten lion [Susan's] and that, at the instant the lights go on over the Queensboro Bridge, a double track of light appears in the river. They would remember the smell of back yards in April, the day they wrote their initials in fresh concrete or picked up a dollar bill on the escalator in Bloomingdale's, and they would, perhaps, conclude that memory is not a greeting card, that childhood is where you spend it, and that it is time to discard the country Christmas and the buffalo robe and let the city playgrounds into our consciousness as a legitimate place to begin life.

Holiday ran Cheever's article in August 1951. By then the author and his wife had decided to let their children spend their childhood, if not in the country, at least in the near-approximation that Scarborough offered.

Both John and Mary Cheever felt the pull of the countryside. Some of the happiest times in the first ten years of their marriage had been spent during weekend visits to Josephine Herbst's house in Erwinna, and during long summer weeks at Treetops. Sometimes Cheever left Treetops in midsummer, in order to work alone in the city. These trips were rarely successful. On one such visit the air smelled "like a piece of dirty grey felt." On another the inhabitants looked "like the citizens of hell," and he soon fled northward.

However the Cheevers felt about resuming city life, the very fact that they could weekend in Erwinna and that the children could count on summers in the New Hampshire countryside made staying in Manhattan more tolerable. They might have stayed permanently except for the financial and spatial pressures of apartment living. They moved finally because Susie and Ben were crammed into one tiny bedroom in the Fifty-ninth Street apartment and they could not find a larger apartment they could afford.

It seemed to Cheever, in retrospect, that they had been driven out of the city along with most of the rest of the middle class. Their apartment house changed hands and the new owners prepared to turn the building into a cooperative. The Cheevers were given eight months to find another home. Most of the people they knew, he then realized, lived either in elegant River House flats or in tenements downtown where you had to put out pots and pans when it rained. The search for an apartment of intermediate cost and condition did not go well. In March of 1951 he failed to pay the electric bill and the lights were turned off. The children enjoyed their baths by candlelight, but the dark apartment had a somber effect on Cheever. "We simply didn't have the scratch" to stay in New York City, he decided, even after word came through of his Guggenheim grant. A week later, he went out to Westchester "and arranged to rent a little frame house with a sickly shade tree on the lawn."

The description hardly did justice to their new home in Scarborough, for theirs was no ordinary move to the suburbs. To be sure, the house was not large, though the children had their own bedrooms. Only an eight-foot-high brick wall protected it from the traffic roaring down the Albany Post Road (Route 9) a few yards away. Once a truck crashed through the wall but subsided short of the house. Nor was it in especially good shape: the drains often clogged, the heating plant was infirm, and the roof sometimes leaked. But these were minor disadvantages when measured against their new home's setting as one of the outbuildings of Beechwood, the vast Vanderlip estate on the Hudson.

According to E. J. (Jack) Kahn, Jr., the *New Yorker* writer who preceded the Cheevers in the small house, the Vanderlips "practically created Scarborough." In 1906, Frank A. Vanderlip, of the National City Bank in New York, bought Beechwood. Soon thereafter, he bought much of the surrounding territory, including the Sleepy Hollow Country Club. He even owned the red-brick building in the railway station plaza where John Cheever settled in to write. The Scarborough train stop itself, it was rumored, had been arranged to accommodate Mr. Vanderlip. He installed two granite columns from 52 Wall Street, site of the first City Bank office, in front of the great ninety-room mansion and transformed the interior with furniture and decorations imported from Europe. Presidents Woodrow Wilson and Herbert Hoover came for dinner. The Prince of Wales swam in the pool. Isadora Duncan danced alfresco on the great lawn that stretched down toward the Hudson. Ignace Paderewski came to play at the opening of Scarborough School, a private institution established primarily for the education of the Vanderlip children and grandchildren who lived on the estate or nearby. Sheep grazed in a pasture, and a brook wound through woods and fields. There was a rose arbor, an Italian garden, and, immediately adjoining the Cheevers' house (Beechtwig, it was called, or sometimes—by John—Beechnut), a large converted garage used as servants' quarters. Beechtwig itself had been converted from a toolshed.

The Cheevers came to Scarborough largely through the auspices of Jack and Jinny Kahn, who were good friends of Narcissa Vanderlip Street and her husband, Julian. John and Mary had come to dinner parties at Beechtwig when the Kahns were in residence and met some of their circle. When the Kahns decided to move out and build a house at the corner of Holbrook and Scarborough roads, the Cheevers were invited to replace them as renters, and were instantly accepted as part of the community. Though the great days were over, Frank Vanderlip had died, and the paint was peeling in some of the mansion's rooms, Beechwood still represented a world of wealth beyond anything they had ever known. John was the son of a shoe salesman and manufacturer whose business had failed, and of the keeper of a gift shop in Quincy, Massachusetts. Mary's father had been successful, but hers was a small inheritance and it had not yet materialized. They were making do precariously on the money John Cheever earned as a writer. In Scarborough, where the natural and social amenities were freely extended to the family and the rent remained modest, he sometimes detected a whiff of patronage.

Cheever demonstrated a certain wry humor in describing his new circumstances. "In the spring Mary and I are moving into a garage," he wrote Malcolm Cowley. In fact they were not moving into a garage or even a former garage, but Cheever did not let such nicety of detail get in the way of entertaining his correspondents. He was moving, he wrote author John D. Weaver, his close friend from Astoria days, to a refurbished honeymoon cottage (it had in fact served that purpose for Charlotte Vanderlip, another of Frank's daughters) in "a place called Scarborough which is near Ossining where The Big House [Sing Sing] is." The house was located "behind the manorial garages and right beside the manorial garbage pail, but from the front door we have a nice view of the manorial lawns and the manorial swimming pool. The swimming pool is so big that it has a groundswell and makes waves in a northeast wind." The surroundings were magnificent, but—he assured Josie Herbst—"we haven't forgotten our beginnings."

The situation provided obvious opportunities for social comedy, as on one occasion when the Kahns were still in residence and held a dinner party. They then employed two black sisters as cook and nursemaid, and these women luckily made friends with the butler at Beechwood. When the guests were about to foregather, Edith the cook sent out an SOS to the butler in the mansion for additional silver and wineglasses. He obliged, and Narcissa Street sat down to dinner at the Kahns' table a few hours later, looked around, and said, "I recognize some things at this table." Cheever loved that story, and enjoyed playing the role—knowing it was a role—of lord of the manor. When guests came to call, he took them on tours past the pool, the parade of trees, the greenhouse where Virginia (Zinny) Vanderlip Schoales's husband, Dudley, cultivated orchids.

It was not Cheever's estate, he owned not the smallest portion of it, and yet he seemed to appropriate the surroundings even as he deprecated them. The children, confused, sometimes wondered if they were rich or poor.

In Scarborough, they had moved far enough out to be exurbanites and not suburbanites, as A. C. Spectorsky defined the terms in his 1955 book on the subject. They lived in northern Westchester, beyond the Tappan Zee Bridge and the Cross Westchester Expressway, in an area that was typified—Spectorsky wrote—by a rat race of "local politics, PTA activity, and genteel socializing, not all of it entirely voluntary." The style of life supposedly involved a strong measure of conformity, compulsive participation in charitable organizations, devotion to the Republican Party, long daily commutes to the city, and skyrocketing taxes as the new residents demanded better schools and public safety for their growing families.

This picture may have been accurate for most in northern Westchester, but not for the Cheevers. As renters they paid no taxes. As a writer who worked either in a quiet room at home or a short walk away at the station, John Cheever did not commute. He did not, then or ever, belong to a country club. Both he and Mary were Democrats, and felt no pressure to conceal their political preferences. On the other hand, there was plenty of social life, they did rapidly become involved in various community organizations, and much of daily existence revolved around the children, just as the social scientists had predicted.

Susan and Ben had no difficulty in adapting to Scarborough. They found plenty of companions: Susie played with Sarah Schoales, Ben played with Joey Kahn, both played with the children of the Italian-American gardener who lived in the remodeled garage next door. They roamed the grounds and explored ruins along the Hudson. Nine months a year, they walked through fields and woods and across a brook to Scarborough School, where two exceptional elementary school teachers—Miss Daniels and Miss Sheridan—managed to inculcate in their charges a love of reading and an appreciation of the world of nature. That world was spread out around them.

The first fall in Scarborough, less than an hour from Grand Central on the fast train, was glorious. It was "the only autumn" he'd seen in twenty years, Cheever reported; he was also enchanted, characteristically for him, by the smells. But even the

Beechwood estate could not completely satisfy the fondness for the outdoors that John and Mary Cheever shared. In the summers they drove up to Treetops for the mountain air, and increasingly during the 1950s, they contrived a visit to Martha's Vineyard or Nantucket as well. In the summer of 1952 at the Vineyard, Susie and Connie Morrow were both horse-crazy. When they weren't actually learning to ride, they took turns pretending to be horses, whinnying and galloping about.

The following summer, Susie went off to camp for the first time. John and Mary drove up to Camp Kaioria from Treetops to see her. They watched her participate furiously in a series of camp activities on land and water and horseback. When it was time for her parents to leave, Susie let her father know how desperately homesick she was. When they returned a few days later, however, the homesickness was over, and their distraught daughter was all smiles.

If social life for the Cheevers was not so compulsively organized as Susie's at camp, nonetheless there was a lot of it and, associated with it, a lot of drinking. "I cringe to think how much we drank in those days," Jinny Kahn recalls. The Kahns functioned as the hub for a group that included the Cheevers, Burton and Aline Benjamin, Don and Ginger Reiman, Phil and Mimi Boyer, and David and Sally Swope, with half a dozen other couples occasionally included in the gatherings. As a group it was not particularly literary: Cheever and Kahn were the only professional writers, and they wrote very different kinds of things. But on the whole they were clever, talented, and attractive people who lived either in Scarborough, in Briarcliff Manor immediately adjoining, in Ossining, the city that in the complications of New York jurisdictions swallowed up both Scarborough and Briarcliff for some governmental purposes but not for others, or in Croton, the hilly town to the north studded with lakes.

In the suburbs the weekend served as a release for those who were liberated for two days from the rigors of commuting to the city. The drinking started promptly at noon on Saturday, when Phil Boyer (who was to become one of Cheever's closest friends) pulled into the Cheevers' driveway. Mary did not always approve of these visits: whatever had been planned for the family or needed doing, "the gin had to be drunk first." Still, liquor consumption seemed to do no real harm at the time, and often the parties involved a measure of physical activity that helped work off the effects of the alcohol. There were touch football games and softball games and swimming and skating at the Boyers' pond in Croton or the Kahns' in Scarborough. One night the Kahns held a masquerade party on ice with skating waiters and artificial moonlight. In celebration of such gatherings, Cheever inscribed the Kahns' copy of *The Enormous Radio and Other Stories,* the book of stories he published early in 1953:

> Here's to Jack and Ginny Kahn!
> Bless the chairs they sit upon,
> Bless their Edith, bless their sons,
> Bless their talent for Home-runs,
> Bless their tact, their grace, their glories,
> And teach this neighbor to write better stories.

Much of the partying was impromptu, spur-of-the-moment. "You always wanted to be with the group," as Jinny Kahn says. But there were more formal occasions as well. Dances were occasionally held in the Beechwood mansion. Christmastime summoned forth so many cocktail parties and open houses and tea dances that it was hard to get any work done in Westchester. The grandest party of all was the New Year's Eve dance in the old stables the Swopes owned up in Croton. This was always a costume party with a theme, and preparations were extensive. Cheever didn't much like these parties. He could never find a decent costume himself. And once there was a crisis when Mary drove off with Rod Swope. So at least he recollected twenty years later, at a time when he was often jealous of Mary.

Cheever's own behavior during those early years in Scarborough was circumspect enough. He was flirtatious but also gallant. He disapproved of off-color jokes around the women, and was a stickler for proper manners. "He was certainly the most gentlemanly of anyone in our group," Jack Kahn remembers. "He was the sort of person you would sit next to the dreadful aunt or boring sister-in-law at dinner. He might have too much to drink, and he would probably mumble—for he mumbled even when sober—but he would certainly be polite and do his best to please his dinner partner." Usually he succeeded. Cheever was wickedly funny in conversation, with a keen eye and ear for the pretentious. He loved gossip, and in retailing it used his storyteller's knack to improve on the original version. Mumbling aside, it often struck his listeners that he spoke much as he wrote—in beautifully crafted language. Perhaps the most distinctive thing about him was his patrician accent, more pan-Atlantic than Yankee; some assumed that he had acquired the accent as his fortunes improved, but Mary points out that in her forty-three-year experience he always spoke in those rather gargly tones. He dressed well, favoring Brooks Brothers clothes. He had excellent manners and knew all the forks. With his small and wiry frame—he was about five feet five and weighed 140 pounds—he looked rather like Burgess Meredith. All his life he had great charm.

Other talents he lacked, though: vocal talent, for example. Their first Christmas in Scarborough, Mary was asked to sing in a performance of Handel's *Messiah* at the Presbyterian church just across Route 9 from the Cheevers' house. So too were Phil Boyer and the Boyers' daughter Linda. Mimi Boyer and John Cheever were not asked to sing, and on rehearsal evenings they consoled themselves in the Cheevers' living room by giving private concerts on their recorders. John had an alto recorder and Mimi a "very cheap soprano" one. Neither was anything like expert, but gradually they learned the notes and labored through "800 Years of Recorder Music." They also "drank quite a lot of whiskey during those evenings," Mimi recalls. After the *Messiah* had been duly performed, John and Mimi continued their duets, except that now she determined to stop drinking. She doubts that she would have made it through that first dark and difficult month of January 1952 "had it not been for John and his recorder."

Their relative lack of skill was brought home to them when they went to a musical evening for recorder performers in Croton. The other players opened velvet cases and carefully removed their recorders. "What kind of recorder is yours?" someone asked Mimi as she drew it forth from her purse, in two pieces. "It's a six-dollar recorder," she answered. She and John limped along as accurately as they could, often getting left behind. Halfway through the evening, a loud and very sour note silenced the whole group. "Who did *that*?" someone asked. Blushing, John acknowledged the crime. "My name is John Cheever and I did *that*." He and his recorder were quiet for the rest of the session.

His adventures in music were not ended, however, for with Susan he began to take piano lessons from a woman named Levina McClure. One of the first stories he wrote about Westchester, "The Music Teacher," tells of a piano teacher who gives her male pupils

a simple and annoying finger drill whose maddening repetition
brings their wives to loving surrender. In the end the teacher is
found strangled to death. In actuality, Levina was a genteel lady
who served juice and cookies at her annual party for her pupils.
Then they all gathered around the piano and sang the words to old
songs off yellowed sheet music.

The music lessons did not last long. Neither did the civic activities Cheever took part in upon moving to Scarborough. (Mary was
far more energetic in local politics, especially where environmental
issues were concerned.) He was for a while a volunteer fireman
with the Scarborough Fire Company—"a brotherhood of 29 manly,
hard-drinking, courageous fellows." Activities, according to
Cheever's friend Arthur Spear, "included instruction, exercises in
the field, putting out fires and beer at meetings." Like his character
Nailles in *Bullet Park*, Cheever rejoiced in riding the fire truck over
hill and dale, ringing the bell and blowing the siren. But the appeal
wore off when word was circulated that he was a writer and his
fellow firemen elected him secretary of the company. Shortly
thereafter he recruited Jack Kahn to the cause, saw that Kahn was
elected secretary, and retired.

Cheever's more serious plunge into community activity came as
a member of the board of Scarborough School, the progressive private school his children attended along with those of the Schoaleses
and the Kahns and the Reimans and a number of other families
living between Dobbs Ferry and Croton. At one school board meeting, he realized that Scarborough had much the same potential for
social comedy as "the village of Z in the province of X" in a Russian
novel.

Like F. Scott Fitzgerald in this way as in others, John Cheever
was ambivalent about the very rich. Equipped with a strong sense
of social class acquired in his Quincy boyhood, he could easily see
the ridiculousness of social pretension. He was amused, for example, when the Scotswoman who served as Mrs. Vanderlip's secretary and collected the rents and paid the servants dropped her
"very classy social manner" with Angelo the gardener and said
things like "shadup" and "bullshit." But for Mrs. Narcissa Cox
Vanderlip herself, he felt a certain respect and admiration. She had
married into money—the rumor was that she had started as a physical education instructor—but had not taken advantage of this circumstance to pursue indolence. Instead she became a suffragette
who used to go out with her six children in her chauffeur-driven

Pierce-Arrow and say to other women, "Look, I can raise six kids and still stand up for women's rights. Why don't you?" Eleanor Roosevelt, she thought, was an amateur at such causes. "Eleanor never passed the sophomore stage," she said.

Mrs. Vanderlip accepted Cheever as she accepted few others—an acceptance he had also won from such other commanding women as Elizabeth Ames at Yaddo and Mary's stepmother, Polly Whitney Winternitz, at Treetops. When Mrs. Vanderlip died, after sowing discord among her children as to their due inheritance, her daughter Zinny—who was to become Cheever's intimate friend—told him some of her recollections. There was the night, for instance, when the children put a dime-store pearl in a dinner guest's oyster. Mrs. Vanderlip felt sure that the pearl belonged to her—she'd supplied the oysters, after all—and when the guest did not volunteer to give it up, she pointedly snubbed him for the rest of the evening. Those who know Cheever's fiction will recognize that story. In *The Wapshot Chronicle,* Mrs. Vanderlip and her daughter Narcissa appear, transformed by art, as the five-and-ten-cent heiress Justina Wapshot Molesworth Scaddon and her ward, Melissa Scaddon.

Fictional representations were one thing; at one stage the Vanderlip clan feared far worse from their renter. In the summer of 1953 a rumor circulated that Cheever was gathering material for an exposé of the Vanderlips. This led the family to do some checking into his background; when Cheever heard about this detective work, he indignantly demanded an apology. None was forthcoming. The rich felt no obligation to apologize. ("Never complain, never explain," as Henry Ford II put it when discovered in a compromising position.) Eventually Zinny Schoales intervened to calm tempers on both sides, and the crisis passed.

Of all the people he met in Scarborough, Cheever was closest to Zinny. A tall, gawky, deep-voiced woman, Zinny was probably the brightest of the Vanderlip children. After graduating from Barnard, she worked as assistant publisher of the fledgling newspaper *PM* during World War II. She and Ralph Ingersoll laid out the first issue. Marshall Field III poured eight million down the drain trying to keep the paper going, but in the process Zinny learned a great deal. Later she became her father's secretary, and learned still more. She had married—against her parents' wishes—a handsome Cornell football player named Dudley Schoales. He used to delight the Cheever children by vaulting over the living-room sofa without spilling a drop of his drink, a stunt that found its way into "O Youth and Beauty!"—one of the most moving of Cheever's early (1953) stories of suburbia. The Schoaleses lived in the Cow Barn, a house remodeled from an old barn at the southernmost edge of Beechwood. There Cheever came to call most afternoons to sit and look at the Hudson and tell his tales and listen to Zinny's and—not least—to drink, since they both drank too much and enjoyed doing it together. When she died in 1967, Cheever delivered a eulogy at the memorial service. On the day of the funeral, he saw her son Dudley, who had in his distress just broken the key off in the ignition of his VW bus. "It's okay, Dud," Cheever told him. "We all die young."

Cheever's attraction to the world of the rich was accompanied by his realization that he did not belong there. Part of him liked living on the fringes of the great estate (years later, his daughter, Susan, and her husband, Rob Cowley, actually rented the Beechwood mansion, before it was turned into one of Westchester's most expensive condominiums), but another part stood back and smiled at the spectacle of the middle-class writer mingling with the swells. He was within and without, dancing in the ballroom and staring in from the windows like a child.

His attitude toward life in Scarborough, the magnificence of Beechwood aside, was similarly complicated. In the beginning he hardly knew what to make of the climate of equanimity. No one wanted to quarrel, and he missed the city's spirit of contentiousness. At times, he wrote Eleanor Clark, he longed to break free of Westchester. People kept asking him how it felt to put some roots down, and he wasn't at all sure that he wanted to be rooted. Both Herbst and Clark were liberals whose bias would lead them—as Cheever must have sensed—to regard life in the suburbs with a jaundiced eye. Yet among his correspondents it was Malcolm Cowley who most strongly encouraged Cheever to leave Westchester.

In a January 1953 letter, Cheever characterized his fellow suburbanites as aging children, determined to stay youthful in their middle years. How could he possibly write about their trivial lives, he rhetorically asked, when atomic bombs were threatening whole civilizations? There were, he rhetorically answered, "some damned good reasons." But Cowley was not so sure, and throughout 1953 the two debated the issue in correspondence.

Cowley urged Cheever to read David Riesman's *The Lonely Crowd* and to go abroad. Riesman's concept of "other-directedness," he believed, summed up the lack of inner conviction and consequent oversensitivity to what others thought that Cheever was encountering among his immature neighbors. These were the people he was living among and writing about, and it seemed to Cowley—reading between the lines—that Cheever was getting tired of them and needed new subjects for observation. He ought to go abroad for a year and take the kids; it wouldn't cost any more than living in Westchester and would open his eyes. The idea certainly had its appeal, John wrote back, but he wasn't really tired of the suburbs yet and not at all sure of the validity of Riesman's conclusions. He was reluctant to leave until he felt "saturated" in his Westchester surroundings. In response Cowley argued that it would be all right to get saturated "in the life of the ten-thousand-a-year-plus, upper East Side and Westchester, other-directed segment of American society" if John really liked the people. But from the stories, Cowley suspected he didn't like them or at least didn't like the men, though he had a grudging respect for the women who kept their Smith diplomas framed above the kitchen sink.

There were times when Cheever was inclined to agree with his mentor Cowley. During the summer of 1953 Cheever left Treetops to do some work at the Hotel Earle in New York. The weather was unseasonably pleasant, and the city seemed "glorious and healthy." By fall he was writing Cowley about "the relative unimportance of northern Westchester." For the most part the people led insignificant lives, and many of them were not as content as they seemed. When the Scarborough stationmaster, an old man who looked like a turtle, retired, Mrs. Vanderlip had a tea in his honor. "I didn't like it when I first come here," he said. "I said to my wife, 'I can't stand that bunch.' But I stuck it out for forty years so I guess I must have liked it."

Cheever was also troubled by the facade of gentility that concealed a fierce acquisitiveness. This emerged the Day the Banker Stole Browning, the bronze boar from Florence that Josie Herbst had given Ben. Ben had been playing with the banker's son and left the much-prized trinket behind. Mary found it at the banker's house but returned home empty-handed. The boar belonged to him, the banker told her, and had sentimental value besides: it was a gift from his mother.

Then there was the pervasive conformism that led, one day, to Cheever's being arrested for vagrancy as he walked in his working clothes—a rather sloppy outfit of old sport shirt and torn jeans—

down to his office in the station plaza. What was a man doing, in old clothes and on foot, in the middle of the day in this commuting exurb? Had he been more tractable, there would have been no arrest. But Cheever carried no identification with him, and was angry enough at being stopped for no reason that he stonewalled and refused to say who he was and where he lived until he'd actually been taken in and booked.

Such were the dubious joys of suburbia as Cheever sketched them in his correspondence. Yet the actual fact was that except for trips he was not to leave the patch of northern Westchester where he settled—first in Scarborough, then in Ossining—for the rest of his life. A few years later, when he wrote his *Esquire* article about the move from city to suburb, he was committed to the area. "The truth is that I'm crazy about the suburbs and I don't care who knows it. Sometimes my sons and I go fishing for perch in the Hudson, and when the trains for the city come bowling down along the riverbanks I salute the sometimes embarrassed passengers with my beer can, wishing them Godspeed and prosperity in the greatest city in the world, but I see them pass without a trace of longing or envy." In his fiction, as opposed to his letters, he rarely pilloried the neighbors whose self-importance and narrowness of outlook offered so many opportunities for ridicule. It would have been easy to look down on their foolishness, but Cheever—or part of him—could not help identifying with the situation of his characters. He knew better than to set himself above them, for he shared their hopes and dreams and fears even as he saw how silly these sometimes were. That duality of outlook furnished his suburban stories and novels with much of their potency. Life in Westchester opened up a new vein of material. And he realized, as he told Cowley, that the suburbanites he encountered deserved their own chronicler.

CAREER

1951-1955

CHEEVER came up to Scarborough in the spring of 1951 with his career at a stage of financial and critical stasis. He was well known as a writer of beautifully crafted stories: "The Pot of Gold," for instance, won an O. Henry Award for 1951. But in his twenty years as a professional writer he had not yet produced a novel. Still, he was determined to make his living writing fiction. More than that, he felt compelled to provide a comfortable middle-class existence for his wife and children. (Mary's inheritance, in time, was to contribute from eight thousand to ten thousand a year toward the family expenses, but that was not yet available.)

Pursuing his precarious occupation with the example of his own father ever present in his mind, Cheever was often afraid that he might fail as a provider.

In actual fact, he did not fail at all but succeeded at an extremely difficult task. It is rare in the United States for a writer to make a financial success as the author of what the trade calls "literary" books as opposed to more popular and often inferior ones. This is exactly what John Cheever managed to accomplish, but when he first moved to Westchester such a future was by no means assured. Financial emergencies continually loomed on the horizon. *The New Yorker*'s five thousand dollars a year or so hardly sufficed, and the Guggenheim provided only temporary relief.

The fiction writer's way to wealth, Cheever knew, was through the novel. He might get a thousand or even two thousand for a story, but that was the end of it. A novel might possibly bring in fifty thousand and keep selling for years. Besides, a novel could command the kind of serious critical attention rarely granted short stories. Yet he remained for the time being an advocate of the short story as the appropriate medium for the times. The novel, he thought, depended on a stable social ambience, while the short story was determined by moving around from place to place, by "the interrupted event." That was the way he'd lived his life, so far. Stories also possessed a kind of intensity that the novel, in its sustained length, could hardly achieve. As always in his thinking about fiction, he saw the story as fulfilling an important function in life. "It's the appeasement of pain . . . in a stuck ski lift, a sinking boat, a dentist's office, or a doctor's office . . . at the very point of death, one tells oneself a short story—not a novel."

So it was that practically his first literary act on reaching Scarborough was to write Bob Linscott at Random House and propose a collection of fourteen stories, all of them having appeared originally in *The New Yorker*. The editor, still waiting for the novel Random House had signed up in 1946, was disinclined to settle for anything less. "A book of stories—even yours," he explained to Cheever in June 1951, "is a pretty costly venture for a publisher" and was usually undertaken "either to keep an author who is profitable or as a last desperate expedient to get an author who may eventually be profitable." Since Random House had his novel under contract, it would prefer to publish that first and then think about a book of stories.

This discouraging news sent Cheever reluctantly back to work on the Field Version. Over the years he had become increasingly frustrated by his lack of progress on the novel, but now he plugged away once again. Late in 1951 he sent Random House a hundred pages of the book, and anxiously anticipated the reaction. In his imagination he tried out various editorial responses. Parts of it are fine, they might say. Or we lost the manuscript in a whorehouse, as once happened to E. A. Robinson. Or why can't you write something like *From Here to Eternity?*—then a runaway best seller.

What actually happened was less humorous and more devastating. Random House greeted the manuscript with "a limp handshake . . . and an all around air of profound embarrassment." Cheever was terribly discouraged and deeply hurt. The extent of the injury was reflected in the way he eventually transformed the rejection into a more sinister exchange between himself and Linscott. He went to have lunch with Linscott and talk about the book, this story had it. At the end of the meal, the editor finally confessed that he thought the manuscript was without merit. Then he added, "You wouldn't do anything foolish like kill yourself, would you?"

The 1951 rejection did not drive Cheever to suicide, but it certainly set his career timetable back. It would be two years before he could return to yet another version of his family chronicle, and six years before *The Wapshot Chronicle* actually appeared. Meanwhile, he began looking for sources of additional income.

Television was undergoing a period of tremendous growth in the early 1950s, and Cheever was one of those hired to supply the fresh material the new medium required. Midway through 1952, Ezra Stone—forever famous for his role of Henry Aldrich—was developing a series called *Life with Father and Mother,* based on the Clarence Day, Jr., memoir and the Howard Lindsay and Russell Crouse Broadway hit. As producer, Stone wanted to hire writers whose work was not totally rooted in radio or very early television situation comedy. Looking to *The New Yorker* for talent, he went after St. Clair McKelway, Patricia Collinge, and Cheever. McKelway and Collinge turned him down, but Cheever accepted the challenge. Stone teamed him with John Whedon, an experienced radio writer and "a quiet man with a twinkle," like Cheever himself. The two got on well, came up with a couple of premises, got the go-ahead on one of them, and wrote a script. Each was paid about three thousand dollars, Stone recalls.

By November 1952, prospects for *Life with Father and Mother* looked bright. A CBS television release announced that Dennis

King would star in the weekly half-hour dramatic series, scheduled
to begin "shortly after the first of the year," and Martha Scott was
hired to play Mother to King's Father. Difficulties then began to
emerge. According to Cheever's 1982 account, he and Whedon attended an eight-person conference on their script where they "listened to captious observations on the fall of a line, the possibility
of cretinous misunderstanding, and a good deal of personal reminiscence." At the end of an hour the writers quit in disgust, slam-
ming the door as they left. Actually, Stone remembers, the problem
was not with the script: "that was in the bank." Instead the show
foundered because of rather overzealous supervision from Lindsay
and Crouse and, especially, from Clarence Day's widow. In any
event, *Life with Father and Mother* became *Life with Father*, the whole
project was moved from New York to Hollywood, Fletcher Markle
took over for Stone, and different writers were hired. The show,
a mild television success, ran for a couple of years.

Despite the contrary indications of the marketplace, Cheever
eventually located a publisher for the book of stories Random
House had turned down. It took him over a year, and the publisher
turned out to be a firm better known for printing dictionaries than
fiction. In February 1953, Funk & Wagnalls brought out *The Enormous Radio and Other Stories.* Artistically the stories in this volume
represented a giant leap forward over those in *The Way Some People
Live,* but the collection was not a success, either financially or
critically. A few of the reviews were very bad, and in each of them
he was tarred with the *New Yorker* brush. Book reviewers are often
intellectuals, and intellectuals have consistently tended to under-
value writers identified with the magazine. It took Richard Stern
a long time to discover how good Cheever was, he admits, since he
"was locked in the intellectual's perception of *The New Yorker* as the
home of formula fiction." This prejudice was so strong that it kept
Norman Mailer from reading Cheever's stories until after Cheever
died in 1982. When he did, Mailer found "gem after gem" and felt
"a great sense of woe. Why didn't I know that man?"

The bias against *New Yorker* fiction derived from the belief that
it was a fiction of manners, rather too comfortable and confident
in its social and moral assumptions. The stories that appeared
there, according to one observer, "viewed the worst excesses of
modern civilization with distaste and sometimes with alarm, but
never with despair. For, no matter how black the present, how
fraught with peril the future or how quaint the past, the fiction and

poetry of *The New Yorker* walked forward hand in hand with the advertisements . . . toward the vague, but discernible horizon, the glow of which indicated at least the possibility of The Good Life somewhere up there among the Delectable Mountains and just beyond the reach of the clean fingernails of the Ideal Reader." The magazine's fiction seemed, to such jaundiced eyes as these, to be almost exclusively concerned with the activities of a particular stratum of urban society and to present that milieu in a realistic, hard-edged prose that was content to reveal a facet of character and then fade away. The stories were all cut from the same cloth, people complained. "Nothing happened" in *New Yorker* stories, they said.

In rebuttal, William Maxwell argues that there has never been a typical *New Yorker* story or "a *New Yorker* writer." In what sense, he points out, can contributors as different as Vladimir Nabokov, J. D. Salinger, John O'Hara, Irwin Shaw, Edward Newhouse, Mary McCarthy, Jean Stafford, Daniel Fuchs, Cheever, Maxwell himself, and more recently Philip Roth, John Updike, and Donald Barthelme be transmogrified into one stereotypical *New Yorker* writer? Moreover, even if one could outline a conventional realistic *New Yorker* story, it was obvious that Cheever's fiction, with the emphasis on fantasy and myth that grew stronger throughout his career, did not fit that mold. But Cheever *was* quintessentially a *New Yorker* writer in the sense that he was a writer people associated with the magazine.

Discussions of the *New Yorker* connection in reviews of *The Enormous Radio and Other Stories* ranged from the mildly critical to the vituperative. His characters, one reviewer objected, were all "the middle-class, upper middle-brow, white collar people who subscribe to *The New Yorker.*" Arthur Mizener suspected that the stories were written to conform to a preselected moral of the sort *The New Yorker* liked, and damned the results with faint praise. The stories were clever, ingenious, neat, refined, well made, skillfully worked out. He did not like them. William Dubois's daily *New York Times* review cut even sharper. "The melancholy fact remains that a little Cheever goes a long way. Like all special formulas his is most effective when taken in small doses—preferably in single installments with plenty of [cartoonists] Addams and Arno in between." Dubois thought the stories too narrow in social setting, almost all of them concentrated on the upper-middle-class East Side of New York. They were also too narrow in outlook, full of unhappy characters beset by nerves and the need for something "beyond the concrete coffin they inhabit" yet lacking the willpower to escape.

The people were expertly presented, DuBois conceded, a point that James Kelly concentrated on in the Sunday *New York Times Book Review:* "No American writer in business today is more on top of his genre than Mr. Cheever. He can reveal New Yorkers to themselves or explain them, just as persuasively, to the reader in Steubenville, Ohio." Yet the stories, almost all of them written before the move to Westchester, focused on a depressing urban world that sometimes resembled hell. Cheever was chided, in reviews and correspondence, for the pessimism of his outlook. (It did no good, he commented, for self-appointed intellectuals to tell him to "cheerup, cheerup.") Only Morris Freedman, in *Commentary,* detected the light of hope that Cheever had left shining in these stories. "At first reading," Freedman commented, "one comes away with a sense that Cheever's characters are sunk in a mire of unrelieved hopelessness. . . . But the volume as a whole reveals the secret of coping with the eternal imminence of disaster which is living." The secret as always in Cheever's fiction was love, and most often love within the family, as in such stories as "The Pot of Gold," "The Cure," and "Goodbye, My Brother." In "Clancy in the Tower of Babel," Cheever also invested homosexual love with a saving grace.

In effect, Cheever laid ten years of his best work on the line in *The Enormous Radio and Other Stories* and was largely rebuked for the effort. (The reviews in Great Britain, where Victor Gollancz published the book, were much better.) It is tempting in retrospect to deprecate the blindness of most reviewers to a book that contained two of the century's best short stories—"The Enormous Radio" itself and the superb "Goodbye, My Brother"—and half a dozen other very good ones. Similar cases of shortsightedness abound in literary history, as for example Virginia Woolf's disparagement of early Hemingway and Clifton Fadiman's dismissal of early Faulkner. The effect of the reaction was to drive Cheever yet again back to his unwritten novel. The novel form seemed "bankrupt," he wrote Cowley in mid-1953, but it was apparently the only course open to him. Cowley was not so sure. Cheever could write a play, he suggested in reply, or even a nonfiction book. And if he did write a novel, it did not have to be along conventional lines. He could write a longer fiction book that began with one of his family stories like "Goodbye, My Brother" and worked backward until the characters were fully rounded out. Or he could weave several stories together. Apparently encouraged, Cheever began to work—between stories, hesitantly—on his narrative of the Wapshot family.

However discouraged Cheever may have been by the response of publishers and critics to his work, he was sustained by the knowledge that he was growing in his craft. It is arguable that he wrote the best stories of his life during the half-decade after moving to Westchester. Preeminent among these was "Goodbye, My Brother," the first story he wrote after leaving New York City. As he promised the Guggenheims, he used his grant for longer stories, stories in which he would have the time to explore the intricacies of individual personality and family conflicts.

"Goodbye, My Brother" covers enough ground for a novel in brief. It deals with a subject—the dynamics of family life—and takes place in a setting—a summer home on the Atlantic—that Cheever was especially skillful at bringing to life. An almost painterly light falls over Laud's Head, the summer house where the Pommeroy family has assembled for a reunion. Daily life is splendidly evoked: the swimming, the cocktail hour, the backgammon games after dinner. Against this surface a deeper psychological story unfolds. The trouble begins with the much-disliked Lawrence, or Tifty, one of four Pommeroy siblings assembled, midway through life, for the reunion. The depressing Tifty, who seems to have inherited the dark side of the family's Puritan heritage, apparently does his best to ruin everyone else's vacation. He predicts that the house will fall into the sea within five years. He tells the cook she ought to join a union and demand higher wages. He disapproves of his mother's drinking and his sister's promiscuity and his brothers' gambling. Finally his carping becomes so unbearable that the narrator, one of his brothers, strikes him from behind, knocks him down, and bloodies his head. Tifty then leaves, and the story ends as the narrator's wife and sister come out of the ocean "naked and unshy," their uncovered heads "black and gold" in the water.

"Goodbye, My Brother" obviously represents an attempt at exorcising the dark brother. What is less clear is that the brother lies both within and without, just as Cheever had a brother he simultaneously loved and hated and was himself inhabited by both the demon of depression and the angel of joy. The clue is that Tifty does and says very little to deserve the narrator's judgment that he's a "gloomy son of a bitch." Almost all of his "sad frame of mind" is attributed to him by the supposedly cheerful narrator. But it is easy to miss this point, as most readers have done. In first draft,

"Goodbye, My Brother" was not the story of two brothers at all. There was only the narrator; Lawrence did not exist. And even in the final version the narrator supplies most of Lawrence's opinions. In a widely quoted passage at the end of the story the narrator asks, "Oh, what can you do with a man like that? What can you do? How can you dissuade his eye in a crowd from seeking out the cheek with acne, the infirm hand; how can you teach him to respond to the inestimable greatness of the race, the harsh surface beauty of life; how can you put his finger for him on the obdurate truths before which fear and horror are powerless?" These questions are directed not at any second party, but at a portion of himself—and the narrator, almost surely, spoke for the author.

The close and curious relationship between Cheever and his real brother was complicated when, in 1952, Fred and Iris Cheever and their four children moved to Briarcliff Manor, the town adjoining Scarborough, and the brothers became neighbors. As advertising manager of the Pepperell Manufacturing Company, Fred had been working out of New York and weekending at his home in the Boston suburbs for several years. When he decided to move the family to Westchester, it was natural that he should have found a place near that of his younger brother. John was not pleased, however. He and Mary dutifully entertained Fred and Iris, but John did not want them as intimate members of their social circle. The brothers' wives did not get along at all. Besides, by the 1950s Fred had started the descent to the depths of alcoholism John would later undergo. On one occasion, John arranged a mixed-doubles badminton game at a local gym involving Eddie Newhouse, an accomplished club player, and Fred Cheever, who played only a backyard game. Newhouse and his partner won easily, and then Eddie swatted the bird back and forth with Fred. "Quit clowning around," yelled John from the sidelines. "Why don't you two play a set?" But eight or ten people were watching, Newhouse knew he would have trouble losing a point—much less a game—to Fred Cheever, and he would have none of it. John seemed to want his brother badly beaten, Newhouse thought.

The fratricidal impulse inherent in the bloodied head, the slaughter by shuttlecock, and—as imagined—the near-fatal shove out the window crops up repeatedly in Cheever's fiction. Sometimes the dark brother is a real character, given a name, rivalrous over a girl or a piece of furniture. Sometimes he is an alter ego determined to obliterate all that is valuable and worthy in oneself.

In either case the drive to destroy this other is strong, even though it is accompanied almost always by a corresponding compulsion to care for and nurture him. After the narrator in "Goodbye, My Brother" finally lashes out at his brother Tifty, he is beset by contradictory inclinations. He wants to do away with his saturnine brother, but he also wants to play the Samaritan and bind up his wounds—and that is what he does.

Such contradictory impulses warred within John Cheever as well. "Did you ever want to kill Fred?" his daughter asked him in a 1977 interview. "Well," Cheever replied, "once I was planning to take him trout fishing up at Cranberry Lake, which is just miles away from everything in the wilderness, and I realized if I got him up there he would fall overboard, I would beat him with an oar until he stayed. Of course," he added, "I was appalled by this."

The destructive conflict of that impulse was reflected, less violently, in the duality of spirit that pervaded Cheever's suburban stories. Between 1953 and 1957 he produced the eight stories collected in *The Housebreaker of Shady Hill and Other Stories* (1958). All were located in the suburban Westchester he had come to know and to feel ambivalent toward. The stories were not *about* suburbia, Cheever would insist: they were about men and women and children and dogs who happened to live there. Yet often the emphasis falls on the contrast between their disorderly lives and their handsomely burnished surroundings. Suburbia aimed to shut out the ugly, eschew the unseemly, bar the criminal. But in Cheever's stories, Johnny Hake, who is broke, tiptoes across the neighbor's lawn to steal their money; Cash Bentley, who is almost broke, ritually hurdles the furniture when drinking and is shot dead accidentally by his wife; the philandering Blake is followed home on the commuter train by a girl he has seduced and made to grovel in the dirt before her; Will Pym, jealous of his young wife, knocks down Henry Bulstrode on the station platform.

Best of all among these stories is "The Country Husband" (1954). The story, as Vladimir Nabokov pointed out in admiration, "is really a miniature novel beautifully traced, so that the impression of there being a little too many things happening in it is completely redeemed by the satisfying coherence of its thematic underlacings." The thematic ties involve the contrast between the safe and static world Shady Hill meant to achieve and the occasional desperation of its inhabitants. The plane on which Francis Weed returns from Minneapolis crashes. He survives, but can interest no one—

not even his own family—in the details of the crash. At a dinner party that night he recognizes the maid as a Frenchwoman he had seen humiliated—her head shaved and her body stripped—for cohabiting with German officers during World War II. But he does not tell this story, because the atmosphere of Shady Hill made such a memory "impolite": "the people in the Farquarsons' living room seemed united in their tacit claim that there had been no past, no war—that there was no danger or trouble in the world." Weed next falls uncontrollably in love with the baby-sitter, but there is no one to tell about this (except the psychiatrist). In Shady Hill there is no precedent for moral turpitude or even the breath of scandal. "Things seemed arranged with more propriety even than in the Kingdom of Heaven."

Seemingly driven by perversity, Weed insults old Mrs. Wright-son, who as social arbiter of the community can keep his daughter from invitations to the assemblies. In an argument about this he slaps his wife, Julia, in the face. When she prepares to leave him, he comes to his senses, sees the psychiatrist, takes up woodworking to forget his passion for the baby-sitter, and—in the end—is joyfully restored to health and happiness.

He reaches his epiphany amid a jumble of seemingly disparate images of Shady Hill at twilight. Dinner is over and the dishes are in the machine. "The village hangs, morally and economically, from a thread; but it hangs by its thread in the evening light." A neighbor taking piano lessons begins to worry the *Moonlight Sonata*. A housemaid writes a letter to Arthur Godfrey. Francis Weed is building a coffee table in the cellar. Upstairs his son Toby takes off his cowboy outfit, climbs into a space suit, and flies from bed to floor, "landing with a thump that is audible to everyone in the house but himself." Nearby, Mrs. Masterson attempts to send little Gertrude Flannery home, for everyone knows that Gertrude does not go home when she's supposed to. In the Babcocks' hedged-in terrace the naked Mr. Babcock pursues his unclothed wife. Mr. Nixon shouts at the squirrels in his bird-feeding station. A miserable cat wanders through the garden, wearing a doll's dress. The last to appear is Jupiter, the Labrador, in a passage Nabokov cited as among his favorites. Jupiter "prances through the tomato vines, holding in his generous mouth the remains of an evening slipper." Finally the narrator concludes, in a passage Cheever himself liked to recite. "Then it is dark; it is a night where kings in golden suits ride elephants over the mountains."

Kings, elephants, and mountains in Westchester? Not likely, but then all the images Cheever has called up work against the grain of the community. The little girl who doesn't know enough to go home, the dog with the slipper in its mouth, the naked Babcocks as handsome as any nymph and satyr—all defy the conventional patterns of Shady Hill, and Cheever's admiration goes out to them. He wanted very much to become part of a community that would give him and his family a sense of security. But the real moments of joy came during flights of independence, brief journeys of defiance and escape that ended, usually, with a thump.

It followed that Cheever's political indignation could be aroused—as in the case of the vendetta against Elizabeth Ames—by infringements on individual freedom. During the Army-McCarthy hearings in the spring of 1954, he conceived a deep enmity for the junior senator from Wisconsin and his crusade against Communism and/or for personal aggrandizement. He also spoke out on behalf of Josie Herbst, who was temporarily denied a passport because of her political associations. "Nothing that she ever did or said would have led me, or now leads me, to believe that she was a member of the Communist Party," his affidavit declared, and in due course the passport was granted. Meanwhile he wrote Herbst bewailing "the crazy thread of associative guilt" that had been used to tie her down. In Scarborough, he reported, he'd recently run across a native Fascist. This man, a fishing companion, was strongly opposed to a public library in the community. "I want my children to grow up and be healthy and patriotic citizens," he said, "and they don't need books for this."

It would be wrong to suggest that Cheever—whether in 1954 or at any other time of his life—became politically militant. He had liberal opinions and he rose to the defense of his friends, but he did not march or proselytize or talk in public on controversial issues. He did not know enough to do so. What he did know about was writing, and in the fall of 1954 he began a two-year stint as instructor in creative writing at Barnard College, Columbia's sister school. This job, teaching one class a semester, supplemented the family income and gave him an opportunity to articulate his ideas about the craft.

On Monday and Wednesday afternoons, he went down to 117th Street to meet his class of bright young women. According to English department colleague David Robertson, Cheever "donned the mantle of an academic with seemingly eager interest as well as with grace." He felt a certain pride in teaching on the university level, since he himself had not gone to college at all. Cheever learned the departmental ropes and "was entirely congenial" as a colleague, Robertson recalls, though as an instructor teaching only one course it was not incumbent on him to do so. Privately he was appalled by the politics of the English department, in which creative writing courses were regarded as unimportant, if not frivolous.

In the classroom, Cheever was a success. He spoke, after all, as an established writer. And he spoke without prejudice, rarely belittling the work of his students. Most of them thought he was wonderful. "He was a demon for style," remembers Judith Sherwin, who took Cheever's "English 11, 12. Story Writing" course in 1955–56. In workshop sessions, he wowed his students by taking dull sentences and making them shine with a touch of incongruity here, a gorgeous clause there. He also insisted on certain standards. Students should write about what they knew, he declared, and since most of them were young and (they thought) short on experience, they resisted this advice. Sherwin herself—now a writer and professor at the State University of New York in Albany—felt at the time that this stricture limited her too much, but has come to realize how right her instructor was. For by example as well as precept he showed how it could be done—how it was possible to "mythologize the commonplace" available at most any age. He was, Sherwin believed, the first of the magical realists.

Cheever also functioned to dampen his students' enthusiasm for the wild artistic life. Even in those beat-generation days he invariably came to workshops and individual conferences well groomed, and wearing coat and tie. Moreover, he backed up his conventional appearance and style with knowledgeable advice. They did not have to become bohemian to succeed, he told his young women students. Few of them, he suspected, had a real vocation for drinking. And, he cautioned, it did not pay to sleep with editors in hopes of getting stories or novels published. His students listened with respect if not in entire agreement; their teacher was a professional who was publishing one wonderful story after another in *The New Yorker*.

In 1955, however, his artistic progress was slowed by medical difficulties. As the new year arrived, Cheever was in Phelps Memorial Hospital recovering from pneumonia. Aline Benjamin recalls visiting on New Year's Day and finding John at work on the typewriter. "Nobody," he said, "will give me any champagne." Often he made his drinking a subject for humor, as in the letters he wrote to Phil and Mimi Boyer over the signature of Cassie, the family Labrador, which had been bred by the Boyers. (For a time during Susan's youth, the Cheevers did not keep dogs, for they were thought to aggravate her asthma. Later it was decided that she was allergic only to male dogs, and thereafter a succession of handsome, clumsy, and affectionate female Labradors lived with the family.) In her letter, Cassie said that on the trip up to Treetops there had been an argument over where they should stop for lunch, with the old man holding out for a Chinese restaurant where he could get a martini. This was all in good fun, but liquor and sex already posed real problems for Cheever. Two or three times in the early 1950s, he consulted psychiatrist Bernard Glueck, "complaining of difficulty with the handling of alcohol and homosexual concerns."

At Thanksgiving, Cheever spent another holiday in the hospital, this time to have his "hindquarters rebushed." A pleasant side effect of these periods of physical discomfort was that Mary always "took wonderful care" of him during recuperation. And despite his illnesses he found much to be thankful for: the light in the sky, the miracle of human love. Depression had often been his companion, he wrote Eleanor Clark at midsummer from Nantucket. Until recently, he'd been "an odd mixture of man and cockroach." Now the cockroach seemed to have gone. In gratitude he joined All Saints Episcopal Church.

It was during that summer at Nantucket, too, that Harper & Brothers bought up the contract for his novel from Random House. As Cheever romanticized the tale, publisher Simon Michael Bessie sailed into Wauwinet on his yacht, stepped ashore with a flourish, and made the deal on the spot.

As Bessie remembers it, he and Cheever progressed from social acquaintance to an author-publisher relationship in two less dramatic steps. Though they had met previously at various gatherings, it was during a long lunch at Gerald Malsby's house in 1953 that they talked seriously for the first time. The subject was Saul Bellow, a writer Cheever greatly admired. Bellow was the only important American novelist, he maintained, who wrote neither out of sympathy with nor in opposition to the Puritan tradition. Up to that time, Bessie had thought of Cheever as an extremely gifted but perhaps overfacile chronicler of his middle-class world. Their conversation about Bellow struck a deeper, more illuminating note.

Mike asked him to write an essay on the subject for *Harper's* magazine. Cheever did not: literary essays were not his sort of thing.

Still, that luncheon encounter cleared the way for a favorable response a few years later when Cheever wrote Bessie a note that went more or less as follows:

Dear Mike:

These old bones are for sale. I have a contract with Random House for a novel which I may never write but which I will certainly never write for them. The price of these bones is $2400, which is the advance I've taken against this novel.

"Where do I send the $2400?" Bessie replied.

The contract with Harper generously allowed Cheever up to five years to deliver his novel. And Bessie also agreed never, never to ask Cheever how the novel was progressing. He did not have long to wait, for Cheever was sailing along on his third and marvelously successful attempt to convert the saga of a New England family into book-length fiction. He'd given the book a new name: *The Wapshot Chronicle*. The career that looked so dismal in 1951 was shining bright, and there were still sunnier days ahead.

ITALY

1956-1957

To prizes awarded Cheever's short stories presaged the success that lay ahead. In May 1955 "The Five-Forty-Eight" won the Benjamin Franklin Magazine Award for the best short story of 1954. In January 1956 "The Country Husband" won the O. Henry Award for the best story of 1955. Cheever took pleasure in making light of these prizes. He had to go to Washington to accept the Benjamin Franklin one, for which he received a scroll depicting a naked man "scratching on a tablet." Mary Liley Cheever, dying in a two-family house in Quincy, read the story about the Franklin Award in the *Quincy Patriot-Ledger*. "I saw it in the newspaper that you got a prize," she told her son over the telephone. "Oh yes," John said. "I didn't mention it to you because I thought it wouldn't interest you." "Oh, you are so right," she said. "It doesn't interest me at all." Now "*that* was Massachusetts," Cheever liked to say in telling this story.

His mother suffered through the decade after her husband's death with arthritis, a stroke, and a broken leg. None of these ailments received medical attention. Mrs. Cheever preferred the consolations of Christian Science, and even maintained that a reader in the church had prayed over a tumor and arrested it. At the end she was virtually immobile and alone in her duplex, except for the oppressive company of the claw-footed furniture that survived the loss of the house at 123 Winthrop. John saw his mother shortly before she died on Washington's Birthday of 1956. She spoke calmly about her approaching death. "You must not be upset when I die," she told him. "I am quite happy to go. I've done everything I was meant to do and quite a lot that I wasn't meant to do."

Later he was to say that she ordered a case of Scotch and drank it down to ease her passing, but that story probably had its origins in his own troubles with alcohol. At the time of his mother's death in February 1956, he told no such tale. Like her husband before her, she died at eighty-two. Gus Lobrano, who edited Cheever's early stories for *The New Yorker* and taught him how to fish, died later that same week.

Benumbed by the double loss, he set off for Yaddo to recover by working on *The Wapshot Chronicle.* For twenty years, the novel had been building up inside of him. Now it came pouring out. To make it do double duty, he sold sections of it to *The New Yorker.* "I don't like to cut it into small pieces," he commented, but his financial situation left him no choice, and the magazine was accommodating. Four chunks of the novel ran there in advance of publication.

As his novel grew, chapter by wonderful chapter, so did Cheever's reputation. In April he got word of a thousand-dollar award in literature from the National Institute of Arts and Letters. Malcolm Cowley, then president, signed the citation to John Cheever,

who with constantly increasing precision of style, sharpness of eye, and wry sympathy of heart, has commemorated the poetry of that most unpoetical life, the middle class life of the American metropolis and its suburbs.

He knows the comedy and the pathos of his subject and he is a master of his form.

At the party for grantees and new members in May, Cheever enjoyed himself more than he thought he should have, and afterward he delivered a homily to Susan. Honors didn't matter, he told her, work was all that mattered. But it was not easy to get back to work. Soon yet another distinction descended from Saratoga, where he was elected to the board of Yaddo.

Despite these interruptions, by June 21 the novel was done and in the mail. At least it *looked* like a novel, John wrote Eleanor Clark: it cost more postage than a short story. The other piece of good news came from Hollywood, where Dore Schary of M-G-M bought film rights to "The Housebreaker of Shady Hill" for forty thousand dollars. With that money in the bank, the Cheevers made firm plans to go to Italy in the autumn, a trip they had been contemplating for years. In the meantime they spent six weeks at the house of Arthur and Stella Spear in Friendship, Maine. There Cheever anxiously awaited a reaction to his typescript from Harper & Brothers and engaged in that fictionalizing exploration of other people's houses, other people's lives that was, for him, part of the charm of rented summer places.

These places usually summoned up at least the beginning of a story. Summer cottages revealed their past in the books left behind, or the absence of them, and in the paintings or other displays on the wall. At Wauwinet on Nantucket, pencil markings recorded the growth of children who had lived there for the past sixty years, and Cheever could not resist inventing tales about them. At Nantucket's Surfside, in the Yates-Shepard cottage, Cheever conjured up a divorce. She was a watercolorist and he a slim young man from New York. Why did they quarrel? When did he leave?

Perhaps because he knew the Spears too well, Friendship did not arouse such story-making instincts. The place refused to "unfold" for him. A village sixteen miles south of Rockland, the town featured the capricious weather of the Maine coast. Looking out the windows on a foggy day was like "looking at a stone." Yet when the sun shone, it seemed like "the top of the world." She would recognize Friendship from her Maine days with Robert Lowell, he wrote Jean Stafford: "Bostonians . . . sunsets . . . and at dusk the whole point awash in tea." On July 1, the tea gave way to beer during a clambake on an island in the bay. Everyone drank too much waiting for the lobsters and clams to cook. To sober up, Cheever dived into the sea, often.

The Friendship sojourn was over and the Cheevers back in Scarborough before Harper's responded to his manuscript. While he waited, John composed both congratulatory letters ("Dazzling," "Brilliant") and discouraging ones ("Write it off to experience") in his mind. Finally Mike Bessie called, said how much everyone liked the book, and invited Cheever down to lunch at the Vanderbilt Hotel. Still apprehensive, Cheever announced before the meal that he had two things to say. "First, if you don't really like the book I'll be glad to give you back your twenty-four hundred dollars." At this point Bessie interrupted to reassure him. They thought *The Wapshot Chronicle* was wonderful. Fellow editor Evan Thomas thought it the best thing that had happened to Harper's fiction list for years. "We are proud," Mike said, "to have the chance to publish it."

"Well," Cheever said, "the second thing I want to say is that you may think there are too many smells in the book, and I just want you to know I'm not going to take any of them out. I am a very olfactory fellow." Bessie had in fact noticed the preponderance of smells in the novel—they are used, often, to summon up place and period—but under the circumstances said nothing at all about that. Instead he spent most of the lunch telling Cheever how much he admired him for what he'd done, and what a good book he'd written. So little editing was required that Bessie felt he hadn't done his job.

With *The Wapshot Chronicle* in production, the Cheevers began to prepare in earnest for their trip to Italy. They planned to spend a year overseas. The Scarborough house was rented to young novelist Stephen Becker and his family. Eleanor Clark and Robert Penn Warren, already living in Rome, were enlisted to help look for a suitable apartment. John booked passage on the *Conte Biancamano*, leaving October 17 and arriving in Naples on November 1. It was hard to get any work done with the trip in prospect. All his ideas "turned to smoke at the thought of leaving."

Cheever recorded the details of the voyage to Italy in "Atlantic Crossing," the only one of his journals so far published. Keeping a journal was an important part of Cheever's writing regimen. The habit came down to him, he said, from the sea captains and sailors among his ancestors, men who habitually set down the weather and the events of the day. He used his journals not only to report what happened, but also to warm up for his fiction, to report anecdotes, to chastise others, to daydream about men and women he was attracted to or was having affairs with, and to entertain private thoughts.

"Atlantic Crossing" is much less inward-looking than most of Cheever's thirty-plus journals. Instead it reads like an extended diary, invigorated by the author's sensitivity to places and the people who inhabit them. The family went first class, partly because Mary, thirty-eight, was more than three months pregnant. At sea they ran into a week of bad weather. Nearly everyone got sick, including the orchestra and the assistant bartender, but Cheever did not. The ship itself seemed like "a cross between the Fall River Line and the old Ritz." Cheever swam in the ship's pool, walked the promenade deck, took Italian lessons, read to eight-year-old Ben (who had smuggled his white mouse, Barbara Fritchie, on board), and singled out drinking companions. At night there were hat parties and flamenco dancing and horse races. Susie, thirteen, roamed the ship as if it were what she was meant for, dancing with the officers and sipping ginger ale in the lounge with other girls her age. The talk of the ship was the Belgian beauty with the three-octave laugh. Cheever watched in fascination as she charmed every male on board with her nearly infinite variety. "She is coarse, she is witty, she is a countess, she is a little girl selling matches in the snow." He spoke also with the Southern woman in whose voice could be heard, "not unpleasantly, the notes of a hound dog." He observed the scrawny Dartmouth professor and his boyish secretary with the scarf tossed gaily over his shoulder. "Do they? Don't they?" he wondered.

During its second week at sea the *Conte Biancamano* stopped at several ports of call. They raised Portugal on October 24, and spent a day in Lisbon. Then it was Casablanca, where their guide from Cook's seemed dreary and defeated. "Why is it," Cheever wondered, "that with their command of language, their knowledge of history, their love of beauty and their admirable piety" all such guides seemed down at heel? There was trouble in Morocco, and the Arab quarter was closed because of the riots. Arab boys surrounded them as they waited for their bus. "They make the hoods at home seem gentle, for this is not the contest between youth and age exacerbated into brutality; this is the contest between wealth and grueling poverty, between the Protestant and the Moslem religions, this is the borderline of whole principalities of sexuality, morality, and religion. We return to the boat, our cozy home." His sympathy was with the Arabs against the French, who were selling their houses and businesses and pulling out. Next there was Barcelona, where at an amusement park he saw a young man use the tip of a very clean handkerchief to remove a bit of soot from his very pretty girl's eye, and Cannes, cold enough for an overcoat in the early morning, with snow on the mountains already, and then Genoa, Palermo, and Naples, where they caught the train to Rome in the rain and sliced through a mountain to emerge into a sunny day and—his journal concluded—"a landscape so various, so beautiful, and impressed so on my memory by postcards, paintings, and the pictures hanging on the walls of the first classrooms I attended that there is a kind of reunion."

The night they reached Rome, *Playhouse 90* broadcast a television version of "The Country Husband." Cheever was not sorry to miss it. He had read the script and knew that "they had changed everything but the title." Besides, he was trying to get acclimated abroad. For the first ten days the family stayed in a rather elegant *pensione*. Daytimes John and Mary scouted for a convenient and affordable apartment, and in the evenings the American colony in Rome— including the Warrens, Peter and Ebie Blume, and Bill Weaver— invited them around for cocktails. Then there were the splendors of the city itself: the Forum, the Vatican, the piazzas. It all seemed a blur; not since his first days in the army had time seemed so distorted. Yet by November 10, Mary had located schools for the children, and with the help of Eleanor Clark they had found an apartment.

Cheever was about to sign a lease for a flat on the outskirts of Rome when Clark stopped him. He mustn't do that, she advised. The city's bus service was terrible, and if they lived away from the center they would never see anybody. Taking the problem into her own hands, she found the Cheevers an apartment in the Palazzo Doria across the street from Mussolini's former palazzo. It cost rather more than they'd wanted to pay, but the apartment was well located and certainly grand. The Palazzo Doria was said to have a thousand rooms, and the Cheevers paid rent along with a hundred other tenants, including banks, stores, offices, one church, and an Englishwoman who daily emerged from a hole in the wall, buttoned up her Inverness cape, and bicycled away. Their apartment, on the *piano nobile*, was dominated by a huge salon and a huge master bedroom. "It was all built for giants," Cheever decided. There was only one chair in the salon where he could sit and have his feet touch the floor. The room was drafty and magnificent, with a marble floor and a golden ceiling two stories high. It would make a splendid place for signing treaties, he thought, provided that the kings and generals were tall and did not have to go to the bathroom. And it did make a splendid place for entertaining guests—writers, editors, artists—who were visiting or living in Rome. "Well, it looks just like the Library of Congress," Bill Weaver's mother remarked, and it was just about as easy to take care of. For a month the Cheevers were without help, and then the novelist Elizabeth Spencer sent over her maid, Iole Felici, to help out, and it was love at first sight. The next day, Iole called Elizabeth and asked if she could work for the Cheevers and send her sister to the Spencers instead. *"I Cheever hanno bisogno di me,"* she said, and need her they did. Iole, who had a managerial streak, pretty much took over running the establishment in the Palazzo Doria.

The Cheevers' landlady was the Principessa Doria, "an unmarried beauty of about thirty-five" with wens. She was the sole child of a noble father and the Scottish nursemaid he married. The Dorias had been anti-Fascist during World War II. To escape persecution they dyed their hair, stained their skin, and were sheltered by the poor in Trastevere. It was nothing at all like the stories in Scarborough. In due course he would write about it.

Throughout the fall, Italy was full of rumors of yet another war. The Russians had stepped in to put down the uprising in Hungary, and Europeans feared that the conflict would escalate. The papers ran maps showing how the Russians could conquer Western Europe in a month. *"La guerra, la guerra,"* the vendors called as Cheever walked Susie to her bus stop. Still it was difficult, with his Italian, to understand exactly what was going on. A fine linguist, Mary picked up the language rapidly. Meanwhile, John took language lessons at La Società Nazionale Dante Alighieri, but did not progress as fast as he would have liked. Eventually he gained "a fluent but incorrect" command of the language. There were certain wonderfully pithy phrases he loved, like *senz'altro* ("say no more") and *magari* ("I'd like to if I could").

Susie and Ben were also learning Italian, along with other subjects, at their Roman schools. Susie went to Marymount International, a convent school where the nuns gave her four hours of homework a night as she struggled through an awkward age. On

Sundays, father and daughter went to the Episcopal church on the Via Nazionale. Susie was baptized there one chilly afternoon, with the Spencers serving as godparents. Cheever was alternately proud of his daughter and disappointed that she was not measuring up to his idealized picture of her as a long-legged blond goddess, slim and fetching. When he told Jean Douglas, a friend who took a shine to Susie, that his daughter was not everything he had hoped for, Jean threatened never to speak to him again.

Ben happily attended the Overseas School in Rome, and made friends with a Burmese boy named Ronald Ang-dingh. Italy was too much for Barbara Fritchie, however. John was supposed to bury the mouse in the Borghese Gardens, but the ground was too hard. To assuage Ben's sorrow, he was given two more white mice, which smelled bad and used to bite his father on the ankle as he tried to work, behind a screen, in the gigantic salon. Ben's mice were invited to appear at a Christmas party given by a family from Chicago. Most of the women in attendance were American divorcées. When everyone sang Christmas songs at the end of the evening, some of them cried.

Only rarely were the Cheevers truly homesick. When a letter arrived from Zeke, the son of Cassie that now belonged to the Boyers, the children felt a pang but laughed at the contents. Susie enjoyed telling people that the letter was "from our youngest dog." Cassie herself, back in Beechtwig with the Beckers, had a hard winter. She fell through the ice into the frigid Hudson and was about to go down when Steve Becker, crawling flat on the ice, managed to grab her collar and pull her to shore.

In Rome the Cheevers led a busy social life, though Mary sometimes stayed home during difficult periods in her pregnancy. She wisely chose to do so one day when it rained and poured but the Warrens and Blumes and John drove off anyway on a picnic outing to Grosseto. Eleanor brought the hamburger and Ebie her usual emergency supply of chocolate and whiskey. Soon the travelers were marooned by the flooding Arrone River. Haystacks that looked like bloated sheep came floating down the road toward them. They took refuge in a highway supervisor's roadside house. Eleanor marched in and in her impeccable Italian asked, "Can we borrow your fire?" They could, and so the raw meat was cooked, the roadside family contributed bread, Ebie passed chocolate all around, and when the waters receded the travelers resumed their journey.

The American colony in Rome divided neatly into those who were associated with the American Academy and those who were not. Cheever—who had no official connection to the academy—resented the "very chilly" reception he got from director Laurence Roberts. Sometimes, however, he met distinguished visitors to the academy, at least one of whom, Archibald MacLeish, proved to be almost as proper as the academy itself. MacLeish and his wife, Ada, left their room key behind to embark on a late dinner with the Cheevers and Ralph and Fanny Ellison. Afterward John walked them back to their *pensione,* where the concierge could not be aroused. "Well," John said, "it looks as if you'll have to spend the night in the Excelsior or the Hassler." "Oh, no," responded the MacLeishes, then in their sixties and as respectable a couple as the desk clerk at the Excelsior had ever seen. "They won't let us in. We have no luggage." Cheever loved that story, and was smitten in a different way by the Italian novelist Antonio Moravia, a man less concerned with the proprieties. Moravia and his girl took him to a village whose drawing card for tourists was an exhibition of the foreskin of Christ.

Back in the United States, Cheever's reputation was thriving. Early in December, Farrar, Straus & Giroux brought out a book called, simply, *Stories,* and containing the work of four *New Yorker* hands: five stories from Jean Stafford, four from Cheever, three each from Daniel Fuchs and William Maxwell. Originally J. D. Salinger had been contemplated as one of the four; when he backed out, Cheever suggested Maxwell instead. He and Stafford conceived the idea for this curious volume, somewhere between a collection and an anthology, while drinking gin and water at a party. They regretted, Cheever's preface read, that their number was so small, "but the colleagues they admire[d] were asleep or in Rome [Warren] or Mississippi [Eudora Welty] or at some other party."

It was assumed that the stories would somehow complement each other, and so they did, according to Richard Sullivan in the *New York Times Book Review.* Each of the writers was distinct in temperament and style, yet overall the fifteen stories exhibited "a remarkable consistency of craft and general feeling," he wrote. William Peden, in the *Saturday Review,* gave the book an unqualified endorsement. It contained "more intelligence, more entertainment, and more effective writing" than a dozen highly publicized and commercially successful novels. Best of all were Cheever's stories, "The Day the Pig Fell into the Well," "The Country Husband," "The National Pastime," and "The Bus to St. James's." "There is no finer present-day writer of short fiction than John Cheever," Peden asserted.

That view gained gratifying confirmation late in January when a letter arrived from the National Institute of Arts and Letters announcing Cheever's election "as a member in the Department of Literature." Jacques Barzun proposed him for membership, with John Hersey and Robert Penn Warren as seconders. Barzun's citation placed Cheever within "the tradition of the New England Observers." His short stories displayed "the penetration of the microscopic eye, combined with the spare writing of the born dissector." As his daughter, Susan, has reported, he made light of his election in a humorous ditty, "Root tee toot, ahh root tee toot, oh, we're the members of the Institute." But the recognition meant a great deal to him, and almost at once he exercised his prerogative as a member to nominate another, slightly younger writer for election: Saul Bellow. "No one has done so much to display, creatively, the versatility of life and speech in this country," he said of Bellow. Cheever later twice served on the institute's grants committee for literature. He also nominated or seconded for election or proposed for grants or wrote citations for a number of other writers whose work he admired, among them William Maxwell, Norman Mailer, Philip Roth, Edward McSorley, Jean Stafford, Daniel Fuchs, John Hawkes, Vladimir Nabokov, Hortense Calisher, Thomas Pynchon, Richard G. Stern, Frederick Exley, John Updike, Joan Didion, Toni Morrison, Philip Schultz, James McConkey, Tom Wolfe, and Bernard Malamud.

Election to the institute established Cheever among the nation's literary elite, and in making decisions about his career, he began to consider questions of reputation as well as monetary gain. In New York the Book-of-the-Month Club was hesitating about whether to make *The Wapshot Chronicle* a monthly selection. Ralph Thompson at the club called Mike Bessie and said they liked the book but had one request, one passage the club would like removed—Moses's saying to his wife, when she stalls his lovemaking, that "you've talked yourself out of a fuck." When *The New Yorker* ran that section of the novel, Thompson pointed out, the offending phrase had been removed. Bessie relayed the request to Cheever, who objected to the deletion. "It's different with *The New Yorker,*" he pointed out. "They sustained me when I was just starting out." He did not, of course, want to throw away the additional money from the Book-of-the-Month Club, but what Moses said was in character and part of his natural idiom. "Does it really mean the club won't take the book if I won't change it?" he asked Bessie. Mike said he thought they would take it anyway, and that's the way it worked out. The club's members were offered the novel, unexpurgated.

Victor Gollancz, who had published *The Enormous Radio and Other Stories* in Britain, enthusiastically signed up English rights to the *Chronicle* in mid-January. Cheever "writes like an angel and must be a good and beautiful person," he wrote agent Naomi Burton at Curtis Brown, along with his offer of two hundred and fifty pounds. That was fine, but Cheever soon showed he was no longer willing to accept payment for anything less than his best work. In March, *Cosmopolitan* offered *Collier's* five hundred dollars for resale of a story called "The Ways of Love on Shady Lane." (*Collier's* was going out of business.) Was that all right? Edith Haggard at Curtis Brown inquired. It was not, Cheever replied. He'd never liked the story and now they could scrap it once and for all. He also turned down an offer from a German firm that wanted foreign rights to *The Way Some People Live.* In effect, he repudiated that first book of stories as apprentice work. He wouldn't want to see it in German, he wrote his agents.

Medical complications developed as Mary's pregnancy neared term. With about two months to go, Mary's doctor put her on a diet of greens. When Mary complained that she couldn't stand spinach every day, the doctor said, "But I have gout and that is all I eat." *He* was not going to have a baby, Mary pointed out. "It is not my role in life," the doctor replied with dignity.

Late in February it looked as if Il Baby was about to be born, but that was a false alarm. The eight-and-a-half-pound baby boy arrived ten days later, on March 9, at the Ospedale Salvador Mundi on the Janiculum. Mary, who had been reluctant to go to the hospital, was in the delivery room only half an hour. A German nun in a white serge habit brought the news to the expectant father. "*Un maschio,*" she announced. It took four days to provide the baby boy with a name. The parents had decided to call him Frederick after John's father and brother, but they did not reckon with the Italian bureaucracy or the fact that there is no *k* in the Italian alphabet. So he was registered in the books of the Comune di Roma as Federico Cheever. The offices of the Comune were "like Gogol." There wasn't a typewriter or filing cabinet in sight. Instead, a small army of clerks laboriously copied Rome's vital statistics into massive ledgers.

From the beginning, father was smitten with son. Federico was a very good-looking boy, he thought. "I love him as much as I ever loved Susie," he declared. Perhaps because they were both late-begotten sons, John felt especially close to Federico. Always he looked back on the evening he was born with joy and gratitude. He was never cruel to Federico as he sometimes was to the other children, Mary said, and Federico was the only child who dared talk back to him.

Iole was also enchanted with the new Cheever. He looked like Il Duce, she said, *"piccolo piccolo Mussolini,"* or like a prince, *"un principe inglese."* She attached herself to the baby and became fiercely protective of him. It became clear that she would not easily be parted from Federico.

Two weeks after Federico's birth *The Wapshot Chronicle* was published. The dust jacket featured advance encomiums from Jean Stafford, Francis Steegmuller, Robert Penn Warren, Saul Bellow, and Malcolm Cowley. "Wonderful," they called the book, "compelling," "beautifully written," "a continual delight," with Stafford's comment the most laudatory of all. "This gamey, witty, sad and truthful novel is an admirable, a splendid achievement by probably the most original writer in America," she said. A few reviewers were willing to accept the book on these terms, without quibble. As one of them observed, *"The Wapshot Chronicle* must have been fun to write, it is wonderful fun to read." There, stated exactly and simply, is the reason this novel seems as likely as anything Cheever wrote to survive the test of time. It is great fun to read, enlivened throughout by the author's unique "blend of gusto, nostalgia and profoundly innocent ribaldry." In a very real sense, as Joan Didion remarked, *The Wapshot Chronicle* was nothing less than "a celebration of life."

Most reviewers, however, faulted the book on one of three different grounds. First, while acknowledging its comic merits, they were disturbed that it did not seem to have an underlying seriousness of purpose. What was the message, anyway? Second, they criticized the book for what they regarded as its lack of a coherent structure. "One gets the final impression of a series of related 'sketches,' which do not quite achieve either the impact of the short story or the inner growth and development of a novel," Maxwell Geismar wrote in the *New York Times*. Finally, the book was sometimes regarded as sentimental for glorifying a departed past at the expense of the present. Each objection had some justification. Each misunderstood and undervalued Cheever's accomplishment.

As in the earlier Field Version, the plot of *The Wapshot Chronicle* focuses on the father, mother, and two sons in a New England family of four. But there are crucial differences between the novel and what Cheever had sketched out ten years before. Sarah Wapshot, unlike Sarah Field, does not commit a dreadful murder, though she does emasculate her husband, Leander, by turning his beloved boat, the *Topaze*, into New England's Only Floating Gifte Shoppe. Sons Moses and Coverly do not, as in the earlier draft, go off in search of their wandering father, but rather to make their fortunes, get married, and produce heirs. And in the published novel Cheever hit upon two stratagems to flesh out the Field Version. The first was creation of the eccentric and willful Cousin Honora Wapshot, who by controlling the family purse strings directs the behavior of all her male relatives. The second was the device of Leander's journal, a brilliantly laconic document that works to tie past and present together.

"In a drilling autumn rain, in a world of much change, the green at St. Botolphs conveyed an impression of unusual permanence," the first page asserts, but the impression is false, for the town is declining in population and importance. "Why do the young want to go away?" their elders wonder, though the answer could not be clearer. There is nothing for them to do in the "old river town" of St. Botolphs, nothing for them to become. They leave to make their way in the world. Geographically, Cheever liked to point out, St. Botolphs was a composite location made up of bits and pieces of Quincy, Newburyport, Bristol, New Hampshire, and the geography of his imagination. As to the charge of undue nostalgia for a vanished (or even nonexistent) past, he obviously meant to draw a comparison between the time when a boisterous port like St. Botolphs might prosper and the actual present. "The impulse to construct such a village . . . ," he explained, "came to me late one night in a third-string hotel on the Hollywood Strip where the world from my windows seemed so dangerously barbaric and nomadic that the attractions of a provincial and a traditional way of life were irresistible." However, he did not long to return to such a past so much as to seek his identity and establish his values by relationship to it. He understood that every age has its faults, every community its shame: "if we accept the quaintness of St. Botolphs we must also accept the fact that it was a country of spite fences and internecine quarrels. . . ." Yet we all come from somewhere, and ignore our origins only to our detriment. The headlong changes of modern life threatened to rob us of these roots, to make nomads of us all. "The room with the people in it looked enduring and secure," he writes in "The Day the Pig Fell into the Well," "although in the morning they would all be gone." So it was with St. Botolphs, its exhausted fortunes, failing businesses, and latter-day eccentrics.

Cheever attempted to bring a measure of universality to the ongoing conflict of present and past by carefully removing references to historical events and personages from the novel. Leander Wapshot does not mention the Civil War nor describe the prospecting trip to the Yukon his brother, Hamlet, would have taken. Cousin Honora is not permitted to rant against Franklin Delano Roosevelt. As Cheever pointed out, he wished to escape from the "tyranny of modern history." So time in this novel—and in *The Wapshot Scandal* as well—is not linear but cyclical. *The Wapshot Chronicle* ends as it began, with the Fourth of July parade. This has happened before and is happening now and will happen again, and not only in St. Botolphs.

Similarly, the structure of the novel is carefully calculated to suggest a wide sweep of experience. The book was held together largely "by spit and wire," critics claimed, and yet, according to Cheever's own testimony, it was "the most deliberately written book I know." The title provided an obvious clue to what he meant. It is a chronicle rather than a conventional novel. When Moses and Coverly leave home to fall in love and marry and construct their lives elsewhere, Cheever follows first one and then the other as they travel, returning occasionally to recount the continuing misfortunes of their father, Leander, and to print selections from his journal. These threads are not neatly tied together, for contemporary existence does not come in gift-wrapped packages. Moreover, the story is told primarily from the point of view of an omniscient and genially obtrusive narrator who wanders from one character's thoughts to another without apology and in clear violation of the unities laid down by theorists of the form. To convey the complications of a disordered time, Cheever consciously eschewed the order of the well-made novel. Instead he wrote a book that resembled "a twentieth-century version of an eighteenth-century episodic novel." Joan Didion, as perceptive a reader of Cheever's fiction as anyone, summed up the situation this way: *"The Wapshot Chronicle* surprised some, troubled others, seemed not even a novel to those brought up on twentieth-century fiction. What it was not was a sentimental novel; what it was not was a novel of manners. It was a novel more like *Tom Jones* than *Madame Bovary,* more like *Tristram Shandy* than *Pride and Prejudice.* (And more like any one of them than like the novels commonly written by *New Yorker* writers.)"

The dominant theme of *The Wapshot Chronicle,* as of most Cheever fiction, is love: fraternal love, love between the sexes, and above all filial love. The book was intended as "a loving novel about my father," the author frequently said. In fiction, he was trying to fashion a bond that he and his own father had been unable to construct. Hence the most crucial relationship in the novel is that between Leander Wapshot and his second son, Coverly. Leander obviously prefers his manly and handsome older son, Moses. He is annoyed by Coverly's habit of stretching his neck and by his sometimes effeminate ways. But he does perform certain father-and-son rituals that Frederick Lincoln Cheever neglected with his son John. He takes Coverly on a man-to-man fishing trip in the north woods, for example, though the boy characteristically spoils the outing by bringing along his mother's cookbook. For the most part Cheever is careful to make Leander a sympathetic character. He is painted as the victim of his wife, Sarah, and his cousin Honora, who conspire to take his beloved boat, his only means of livelihood, his only reason for existence, away from him. His journal reveals him as a man who has often been wronged but is rarely bitter, as a philosopher convinced that ceremony gives life its flavor and dignity, as someone who wants, in vain, "to be esteemed."

Above all, Leander is a creature of the sea. Like his legendary namesake who perishes while swimming across the Hellespont to his beloved Hero, Leander drowns in the sea. But he leaves behind a last word in the form of "Advice to my Sons," secreted in his own father's copy of Shakespeare. In part the advice is merely practical—"Never put whisky into hot water bottles crossing borders of dry states or countries. Rubber will spoil taste." In this fashion he instructs his sons how to drink and smoke and dress and behave in the great world beyond St. Botolphs: "Never hold cigar at right-angles to fingers. Hayseed. Hold cigar at diagonal." "Bathe in cold water every morning. Painful but exhilarating. Also reduces horniness. Have haircut once a week. Wear dark clothes after 6 P.M." Then in the final words of the novel, Leander's advice rises to a kind of epiphany. "Fear tastes like a rusty knife and do not let her

into your house. Courage tastes of blood. Stand up straight. Admire
the world. Relish the love of a gentle woman. Trust in the Lord."

Leander is an unequal match for the energy and enterprise of his
wife, Sarah, who—like Mary Liley Cheever—had been a leading
benefactor of the town before opening her gift shop. There is no
doubt whose side the novel takes in this battle between husband
and wife. In the opening chapter the narrator makes sport of all of
Sarah Wapshot's good works, in a passage exactly opposite in rhetorical construction to Leander's final message. His advice begins
with the mundane and rises to the magnificent. With Mrs. Wapshot, standing behind the lectern on the Woman's Club float in the
Fourth of July parade, the language runs the other way around. It
is fitting that she should ride through the streets, we are told, for
there was no one in St. Botolphs who

had had more of a hand in its enlightenment. It was she who had organized
a committee to raise money for a new parish house for Christ Church. It
was she who had raised a fund for the granite horse trough at the corner
and who, when the horse trough became obsolete, had had it planted with
geraniums and petunias. The new high school on the hill, the new firehouse, the new traffic lights, the war memorial—yes, yes—even the clean
public toilets in the railroad station by the river were the fruits of Mrs.
Wapshot's genius.

Leander, we are informed, "did not mind missing his wife's appearance in the parade." And her dignity is punctured when someone
sets off a firecracker under the rump of the old mare pulling her
float and the horse bolts.

He could not publish *The Wapshot Chronicle*, Cheever said, until
after his mother's death. "Independence Day at St. Botolph's," a
preliminary version of the opening chapter that he revised after she
died, provides supporting evidence for that remark. This story,
which appeared in the July 3, 1954, *New Yorker* (while Mrs. Cheever
was alive), paints a far less derogatory picture of Sarah Wapshot
than that in the actual novel. Significantly, her husband is here
named Alpheus, a legendary river god of greater potency than the
ill-fated Leander. Alpheus is characterized as a rake who has been
amusing himself with various women of the town as a consequence
of sexual incompatibility within the marriage. He has stolen
Sarah's jewelry and, his tearful wife is convinced, plans to sell it
and run away with Mrs. Wilson. This turns out to be incorrect—

Alpheus has pawned the jewelry for fifty dollars' worth of fire-
works—but nonetheless Sarah Wapshot is immediately presented
as the injured party in the marital relationship.

In the revised opening chapter of the novel, Alpheus becomes
Leander, much less of a rake, much more of a victim. As it happened, one surviving relative took this fiction literally and was
permanently offended. Aunt Annie Armstrong, recognizing herself in Cousin Honora and her sister Mary Liley Cheever in Sarah
Wapshot, never spoke to John Cheever again.

The women of St. Botolphs, Coverly tells a psychiatrist, are very
powerful. But so are the women from other regions—the beautiful
and inconstant Melissa, the lonely and perverse Betsey—that
Moses and Coverly marry. Like their father before them, the Wapshot brothers are dominated by their wives and confounded by
their moods. During one of Betsey's periodic absences, Coverly is
pursued by a fellow worker named Pancras and begins to worry
about his own sexuality. Cheever treats the subject humorously.
"And now," the narrator warns, "we come to the unsavory or
homosexual part of our tale," one that genteel readers may want to
skip. Coverly does not succumb to Pancras, though he is sorely
tempted by the trip to England Pancras arranges for both of them.
"I can't go to England with you," Coverly finally declares. "I have
to go and see my brother." Thus the bond between brothers provides Coverly with an excuse to avoid Pancras's overtures. In addition, a letter from his father advises him not to worry about his
longings. "Cheer up," Leander tells him. "Writer not innocent, and
never claimed to be so. Played the man to many a schoolboy bride.
Woodshed lusts. Rainy Sundays." In maturity, Leander had been
pursued by a persistent homosexual, and calmed his ardor by
dumping the contents of the commode on him. Still, Leander concludes, "Man is not simple. Hobgoblin company of love always
with us. . . . Cheer up my son. You think you have trouble. Crack
your skull before you weep. All in love is not larky and fractious.
Remember."

On this ambivalent note, the topic of homosexuality is dismissed.
As to love between the sexes, the evidence of *The Wapshot Chronicle*—like that of most of Cheever's subsequent fiction—seems to
argue that men and women are fundamentally irreconcilable. The
act of sex itself, though not described ("Why describe, as if you
were changing a tire, the most exalted human experience?"), is
celebrated for its inspirational and restorative powers. Aside from

that, Cheever's men and women rarely get along, usually because his female characters behave in cruel or irrational ways. What Coverly decides he needs is instruction in a school of love. The curriculum would include "classes on the moment of recognition; lectures on the mortal error of confusing worship with tenderness ... symposiums on indiscriminate erotic impulses." Special courses would deal with the matriarchy and the hazards of uxoriousness. There would be scientific lectures on homosexuality. "That hairline where lovers cease to nourish and begin to devour one another; that fine point where tenderness corrodes self-esteem and the spirit seems to flake like rust would be put under a microscope.... There would be graphs on love and graphs on melancholy and the black looks that we are entitled to give the hopelessly libidinous would be measured to a millimeter." It would be a hard school for him, Coverly knows, but he would somehow graduate and henceforth conduct his life with increasing contentment and success. Unhappily, no such school existed.

Things are not what they used to be, Cheever's first novel proposes. Marriages are seldom happy. Clouds often obscure the sun. Yet, as anyone who has read it can testify, *The Wapshot Chronicle* is basically a blue-sky book, full of high spirits, comic passages, and the wonder of creation. Above all it pulses with life. It is as if Cheever distilled in one book the accumulated vitality of two decades. As Stephen Becker puts it, "*The Wapshot Chronicle* is a first novel in the sense that Brahms's First Symphony is a first symphony": wonderfully prepared for. Even those reviewers who found fault thought the novel invigorating. And the jury of peers who awarded it the 1957 National Book Award for fiction agreed. The novel, they concluded, "records with humor, with candor, with complete originality, a variety of emotions and experiences. It conveys human qualities so intensely that they seem to rub off on everything else—furniture, houses, animals, the weather even." William Maxwell, who served on that jury, was particularly delighted with the "gaslight quality" of Leander's journal, and plumped hard for Cheever's book against such fine competitors as Bernard Malamud's *The Assistant* and James Gould Cozzens's *By Love Possessed.* (Malamud won the following year for *The Magic Barrel.*)

With *The Wapshot Chronicle* out to generally good notices and selling well, and with the children's school year drawing to a close, the Cheevers made plans for an Italian summer away from the heat and bustle of Rome. John bought a car, and they spent spring weekends touring the countryside. They were in Venice for the *festa* of San Marco, when the bells rang all day long. They traveled to the medieval hill town of Anticoli, where farmers fished for trout from the bridge. They drove to La Rocca, the ruined fortress at Port'Ercole with a mountain above, and the sea all around. It was, Cheever thought, the most beautiful place he had ever seen, which was just what the Warrens had said. They arranged, through Eleanor Clark, to rent it for the summer.

At Susie's graduation from convent school, the girls wobbled down the aisle in their high heels to the slowest rendition of "Pomp and Circumstance" Cheever had ever heard. For two weeks thereafter, the move to La Rocca was delayed because of rumors of polio in the vicinity. On a scouting trip, Cheever talked to a doctor who said there was no sickness in Port'Ercole. Carrying the good news back to Rome, he stopped at the Alan Mooreheads' house in Albano to meet Bernard Berenson, ninety-three. By July 4 the Cheevers were settled at the fortress, where the sea was purple and the fishermen were golden. John could not seem to write there, but he hadn't been working in Rome either, and at least he continued studying *la bella lingua* with their tiny landlady. Aside from the signorina everyone was beautiful, the views were glorious, and on Saturday nights there was dancing on the beach. The place seemed like paradise, and then there was servant trouble.

By this time the family entourage included two maids, Iole and Vittoria. They did everything except "shave me and lace my shoes," Cheever said. Moreover, they were mortified when he performed any task—taking in the wash from the balcony, for instance—they regarded as beneath his dignity. At such times he presented a *brutta figura*, and they hung their heads for shame. Cheever was willing to get used to this kind of pampering, but unprepared to cope with the battle that was soon joined between Iole and Ernesta, the servant who with her husband, Fosco, took care of La Rocca year-round. Ernesta was in charge of La Rocca, Iole was in charge of the Cheevers, and neither would willingly submit to the domination of the other.

After a month of cordial detestation the feud erupted. Iole emerged as victor, having persuaded the Cheevers that Ernesta was cheating them financially and mistreating the children. Ernesta was serving them food fit for peasants, Iole insisted. Fosco was siphoning gas from the new car and charging admission to show

German tourists around the fortress, she maintained. The final blow came on August 9 when Ben and Susan picked some figs from the tree near the lighthouse. The children were busily filling their Venetian straw hats with the fruit when Ernesta started screaming at them. At this point Iole—who had been minding Federico— began to yell at Ernesta, and the two women shrilled insults at each other until the Cheevers intervened, collected the children, and left the most beautiful place in the world within the hour.

Three weeks later they left Italy as well, sailing from Genoa on the *Constitution*. Mary wanted to remain overseas another year, but John thought such an extended stay might be bad for the children, and so back they came to Scarborough. Iole came with them, and Ben brought back his two mice, Giuseppe and Pepe le Moko.

During their ten-month sojourn in Italy, Cheever wrote very little fiction. It was a strange new land to him, and he was too busy soaking it in to write about it. In the long run, though, his work benefited from the shocks to his senses, and to his Yankee sense of the proprieties, that he encountered there. Eventually he turned this material to account in several short stories and in a substantial section of his second novel. In years to come, also, Cheever returned to Italy a number of times. He came back, he said, because he could speak Italian, because he loved the country and the people and swimming in the Mediterranean, and because he had been very happy there.

In Italy he could restore himself and renew his pleasure in life, yet it was the image of Tasso's oak that came to dominate his vision of Rome. Torquato Tasso, the sixteenth-century epic poet, lived a miserable life. At the height of his powers he was imprisoned in Ferrara for seven years, either because of his unwise love for the noble Leonora d'Este, or because he would not accommodate his poetry to prevailing political and religious beliefs, or because—the official reason—he was certifiably mad. On his release, Tasso roamed from city to city without a resting place. At last he came to Rome, fell fatally ill, and in March 1595 took refuge at the Monastery of Sant' Onofrio on the Janiculum. There he finally achieved peace, and spent his last days in quiet contemplation, sitting in the garden. One of his last acts was to plant an oak tree there, and as a pathetic tribute to the poet, the tree—though struck by lightning and obviously dead—has been preserved through the centuries, held up with steel beams and cables to the highest naked branches. Cheever saw this curious memorial and was fascinated by it. He

watched with enthusiasm as Peter Blume fashioned his painting—
the largest he ever did—of the oak. In New York he came to the
opening where the painting was exhibited, and brought the whole
family along.

For Cheever as for the English romantic poets, the story of Tasso
had a special resonance. Byron visited the poet's cell in Ferrara, and
later wrote his "Legend of Tasso." Shelley also took him for a
subject. To these romantics, Tasso exemplified the hypersensitive
creative artist at odds with society and punished for his differences,
loving hopelessly beyond his station, wandering restlessly without
a home, chained in a lunatic cell. For Cheever, Tasso combined
within himself the homelessness and confinement he dreaded. The
dead oak tree, manacled against the forces of nature in eternal
bondage, stuck in his mind as an emblem of those twin misfortunes.

HOUSE

1957-1961

T he *Wapshot Chronicle* began a period of remarkable productivity. Between 1957 and 1964,
Cheever published five books of fiction: the
two Wapshot novels and three collections of
stories. This accomplishment brought with it both
recognition and responsibility. Cheever was clearly
becoming a figure of importance on the American
literary scene. He was a director of Yaddo, and soon
(1958) was to serve on the committee that decided
which artists to admit. He was a member of the National Institute, and soon (1959–62) was to serve his first
term on the committee that decided which writers
should be admitted to that august body. He was taken

into the Century Club (1958) on the nomination of Cabell Greet, who had been his English department chairman at Barnard. The ceremonial dinner of admission went off smoothly, except when— Cheever reported in jest—he clamped his carnation between his teeth.

A moment of greater glory came on March 11, 1958, when the forty-five-year-old author accepted the National Book Award for fiction for *The Wapshot Chronicle.* In his brief speech, he described the novel as "one of the few forms where we can record man's complexity and the strength and decency of his longings, where we can describe, step by step, minute by minute, our not altogether unpleasant struggle to put ourselves into a viable and devout relationship to our beloved and mistaken world." This, of course, was exactly what the *Chronicle* in its vivid cheerfulness aimed to do. Cheever also spoke that day about the loneliness of his craft, and one of its consequences. "Most businesses and many professions," he said, "thrive on good company but the writer asks people to be quiet, asks to be left alone, asks not to be called to the telephone so that he may spin out an interminable tale that will translate the pain and ecstasy of life into understandable terms; and left alone so much he will be insatiable—and rightly so, I think—in wanting to know what value this tale has to others. Most than most people writers desire the good opinion of strangers." This was in part his way of saying thank you, but that last remark confessed to a hunger that would not easily be appeased. Like Leander Wapshot, like his own father, John Cheever wished to be esteemed.

On a subway platform, immediately after the National Book Award ceremony, Cheever met Bernard Malamud for the first time. Malamud congratulated him on the NBA, Cheever spoke admiringly of *The Assistant,* a contender for the award, and a long though not intimate friendship was begun. A number of radio and television interviews followed, including an appearance on the Dave Garroway morning show with Robert Penn Warren, who had won the National Book Award for poetry. As Cheever recalled the day, both he and Warren were upstaged by another guest on the show, a chimpanzee named Joe who was "much better dressed" than either of the two writers and "much more composed." The Garroway show was televised in a storefront of Radio City, with people outside mugging for the camera and holding up signs. Garroway in his relaxed baritone asked Warren to explain why he sometimes wrote fiction and sometimes poetry. "Ah scratches where Ah itches," Warren replied in his Kentucky twang.

As Cheever's reputation grew, so did the critical and public desire to fix him within the confines of a stereotype. He had for a while been labeled a *New Yorker* writer whose stories dealt with upper-middle-class people on the East Side. With the publication of *The Housebreaker of Shady Hill and Other Stories* in September 1958, he became known, overnight and always, as a chronicler of suburban life. It did not matter that he moved on to write about Italian expatriates and prison inmates—a great many people had pinned their butterfly to the wall and would not let him free. He was John Cheever, who wrote those funny-sad stories about the suburbs for *The New Yorker.*

As a characterization of *Housebreaker,* that was accurate enough. This is the most unified of Cheever's collections, and the unifying factor is the suburban experience of cookouts and commutation, dinner parties and dances at the country club. In large part, critics found this subject matter distasteful. Life in the suburbs was dull and conformist, they had been told by social scientists, and therefore unworthy of serious fiction. What right did Cheever have to make suburbia's inhabitants interesting?

Still more objectionable, to some critical eyes, was Cheever's refusal to judge his characters or condemn their way of life. Occasionally he allowed someone to lash out against suburbia's failings. "God preserve me," Charles Flint reflects, "from women who dress like *toreros* to go to the supermarket, and from cowhide dispatch cases, and from flannels and gabardines. Preserve me from word games and adulterers, from basset hounds and swimming pools and frozen canapés and Bloody Marys and smugness and syringa bushes and P.-T.A. meetings." At this stage the narrator interrupts to assert that "there was absolutely nothing wrong with the suburb from which Charles Flint was fleeing," yet soon backtracks to admit that "if there was anything wrong with Shady Hill, anything you could put your finger on, it was the fact that the village had no public library." In the title story, the housebreaker, Johnny Hake, defends the village he lives in. "Shady Hill is open to criticism by city planners, adventurers and lyric poets, but if you work in the city and have children to raise, I can't think of a better place." Still, Johnny Hake steals from his neighbors to maintain his own home in Shady Hill, and one may legitimately wonder how far he should be trusted as the author's spokesman.

What seems to be true is that Cheever saw both sides of the argument. Shady Hill, he knew, had its pretensions and was not nearly so stable and burnished as its inhabitants would like to think, but it had its advantages too—blue sky and sunshine and swimming pools among them—and he refused to issue any doctrinaire judgments against the people who lived there and were doing their best to develop "an improvised way of life" within commuting distance of New York City. Save for Cash Bentley, who dies in mid-hurdle from his wife's starting pistol, and the exploitive Blake, who is reduced to groveling before the office girl he has taken advantage of, his characters survive their crises of love and money and are not even punished for their sins. Francis Weed takes up woodworking and forgets his passion for the baby-sitter. Refreshed by a rain shower, Johnny Hake gives up burglarizing. Will Pym knocks down a village roué on the station platform and so disposes of his jealousy. Charles Flint forgives his wife, Marcie, her adultery and comes home after all. And in "The Worm in the Apple," a final story Cheever wrote especially for the collection, no one can find anything at all to disturb the Crutchmans' happiness. Everyone in Shady Hill assumes they must have a flaw—sexual recklessness, lack of money, too much drinking, trouble with the children—but in fact no one can find the worm in the apple. The Crutchmans are simply very happy. In this story Cheever thumbed his nose at the prevailing view that existence in the nation's upper-middle-class suburbs must be either dull or miserable. "A toothless Thurber," Irving Howe called him, conniving in "the cowardice of contemporary life."

Once restored to Westchester, Cheever began to write stories about Italy. He published six of these, five in *The New Yorker,* between March 1958 and May 1960. All of them focus on the clash of cultures, on what it is like to inhabit a foreign culture. His expatriated Americans find everything in Italy different. The rain that pounds on the roof in Nantucket falls silently in Rome. The wind does not sound the same, the light in the sky and the smells of the street are strange, and, of course, the food is not at all what one is accustomed to: one of his forlorn expatriates daydreams about a bacon, lettuce, and tomato sandwich. The language difference, most crucial of all, he explored in the best of the Italian stories, "The Bella Lingua."

Wilson Streeter is fiftyish, divorced, and working in Rome for one of those companies that go by an acronym. He enjoys the social life and feels a certain sense of release in Italy, but understands neither the country nor the people. Once he masters the language, he feels sure, he will reach such an understanding. So he sets out to learn Italian despite his rusting middle-aged memory and his lack of talent for languages. Streeter runs through a series of instructors before discovering Kate Dresser, a widowed American whose Italian he can almost always understand. She guides him safely past *Pinocchio* and on to *I Promessi Sposi*. He is making excellent progress, Kate tells him. Then he takes a weekend trip to Anticoli, where he hears a young woman sing rapturously in the garden outside his hotel. It is a beautiful song, and he cannot make out a word of it.

Streeter is also troubled by the casual attitudes toward love and death he encounters. One Sunday afternoon in Rome he walks home alone after his language lesson, and is subjected to a series of shocks. A beautiful young whore speaks to him, but he tells her in broken Italian that he already has a friend. Then he sees a man struck by a car, and the driver runs away while a crowd—not solemn at all but garrulous, excited—gathers around the dying victim. Next, a young man offers a cat a piece of bread with a firecracker concealed inside. When the booby trap explodes, the cat leaps in the air, "its body all twisted," and streaks away while the man and several others who have been watching laugh at his trick. Finally a hearse careens by, driven recklessly by a man who looks like a "drunken horsethief." The hearse rattles and slams over the stones, and behind it the mourner's carriage is empty. "The friends of the dead man had probably been too late or had got the wrong date or had forgotten the whole thing, as was so often the case in Rome." Streeter knew then that "he did not want to die in Rome."

Kate Dresser's fifteen-year-old son, Charlie, has a different problem: he does not want to *live* there, but instead to go back to Iowa where he can stay with his Uncle George in "a nice clean house [with] lots of nice friends and a nice garden and kitchen and stall shower." Nothing, not even a shower bath, will keep her from "wanting to see the world and the different people who live in it," Kate indignantly tells her son. Besides, she knows that in Krasbie, Iowa, people would still call her Roller Coaster for her sharply upturned nose. Nobody in Rome does that. So she lets her son go back to the States while she stays on, giving Italian lessons and thrilling to her occasional contacts with the nobility.

A more remarkable story, technically, is "Clementina," told

from the viewpoint of an Italian *donna di servizio* who goes to work for an American family in Rome and then accompanies them to the United States. For Clementina, it is the American way of life that is foreign to everything she has known. She is enchanted by all the labor-saving devices: the washing machine and the dishwasher and the electric frying pan and the *frigidario* and the deep freeze and the electric eggbeater and the vacuum cleaner and the orange squeezer and the toaster and the TV. Listening to the machines doing all the work makes her feel powerful. She cannot understand, however, why the signora "who in Rome had lived like a princess, seemed in the new world to be a secretary" always talking on the phone and writing letters and raising money for good causes. The religion of the New World also bewilders her—the priest gives her "the tail of the devil for not coming to church every Sunday of her life" and people put up a tree for the *festa* of the *Natale* and they take collection three times every Mass.

The comforts of American life prevail, however, and Clementina decides to marry an old *paisano* named Joe in order to remain in the United States. Her American master tries to stop this marriage, for she does not love Joe and he thinks it is wrong for her to marry without love. Clementina is more practical than that. He talks like a boy with stars in his eyes, she tells the signore. "If people married for love, the world . . . would be a hospital for the mad." So she marries Joe, makes him happy and herself comfortable, and one day when she meets her former signore at the racetrack she finds that he and the signora have divorced. "Looking into his face then, she saw not the end of his marriage, but the end of his happiness. The advantage was hers, for hadn't she explained to him that he was like a boy with stars in his eyes, but some part of his loss seemed to be hers as well." At that moment the Italian maidservant and her American signore share a moment of recognition, linked by their common humanity across the barrier of alien backgrounds.

The actual experience of Iole Felici, the nursemaid-cook who came to the United States with the Cheevers, bore some resemblance to that of Clementina. She left a lover behind in Italy, but he died soon thereafter, and she wanted to stay in this country. One evening at dinner, she spoke of the possibility of marrying Saverio (Sam) Masullo, an old gardener who worked on the Vanderlip estate. If she did marry him, Iole said, she would clean his house and cook but would not make love to him. At this news Cheever became angry. If not love, marriage at least demanded cohabitation, he declared. She would have to sleep with Sam. On that understanding they got married, and despite occasional fights—once Iole persuaded Sam to sign a document promising not to be jealous—they stayed married for the remaining twenty years of Masullo's life. Though she had a house of her own, Iole remained an extraordinarily loyal and vigorous family retainer to the Cheevers. Federico especially was devoted to her, and she to him. He saw so much of her during his first few years that he grew up bilingual, with a preference for Italian. "See the horsie," his father would say. *"Non c'e un* horsie," the two-year-old would correct him. *"C'e un cavallo."*

Shortly after their return from Italy, the Cheevers began to consider different living arrangements themselves. They had been tenants at Beechwood for nearly a decade, and Mary yearned for a house of her own. "I wanted it so badly," she recalled. "I was tired of living in someone else's playpen." Besides, John was sensitive to some people's assumption that he was the pet writer of the rich Vanderlips, who rented him his outbuilding at reduced rates. "He hated that," Mary said, and so did she. On the other hand, as a child of the Depression he could hardly forget the disaster that had befallen his parents in Wollaston. He regarded a mortgage as a pernicious document, and they certainly did not have enough money to purchase a house outright, particularly in upper Westchester. Houses in Saratoga Springs were much cheaper, and periodic visits to Yaddo to attend board meetings and to write revived his love affair with the place. He began to lobby for a move to Saratoga.

It seemed to Cheever that nothing about Yaddo ever changed. Even the flowers in the vase looked as they had when he first came there in 1934. He was treated rather like the lord of the manor. "Only dogs, servants, and children know who the aristocrats are," he joked, and imagined the help saying, "Master John's back, Master John's back." Over the years he developed close relationships with practically everyone who worked there—with Elizabeth Ames herself, who defied nature by continuing to bloom as she grew older; with Pauline (Polly) Hanson, for many years Elizabeth's assistant; with caretaker George Vincent and his wife, Helen; with Minnie Woodward the laundress. It became a ritual for him to invite Minnie for a dinner date at the New Worden Hotel. There she would say strange and wonderful things. "People don't realize how intelligent and loving cows are," she said. "Just look in their eyes." She also told John about the carrot shaped like a man's parts, and that anecdote went into *The Wapshot Chronicle*.

Another *Chronicle* episode led to some embarrassment, first at Beechwood and then at Yaddo. Mrs. Vanderlip, reading about Moses clambering over the roofs of a mansion to make love to Melissa, assumed that Cheever was writing about *her* mansion, and became rather upset with him. At the Yaddo dinner table, Cheever spoke about this, and of how he had insisted to Mrs. Vanderlip, "No, no, that is not your place at all, that's Yaddo," only to realize that Elizabeth Ames was regarding him narrowly. At this point he rapidly reversed himself. It had been Beechwood all along, he assured Elizabeth, and he'd only mentioned Yaddo to quiet Mrs. Vanderlip's suspicions. Elizabeth seemed satisfied, and in any event Cheever was a favorite with her.

When he did go to Yaddo, he usually came back home restored. In the winter of 1959, for instance, he wrote two stories in two weeks, skied every afternoon, and put on ten pounds. There was no place he worked better: he followed a schedule, and there were no interruptions. Invariably he was the first one down for breakfast, which he would eat very quickly with very little talk. Then he went back to his room or studio to write. At one-thirty or two in the afternoon, he emerged and, in most weather, made the six-mile-round-trip walk into Saratoga to buy a bottle. "John goes into town and out to deserve his pint," Elizabeth said, and that was all right with her too. Alternatively, depending on the season, he got his exercise and put "some blue sky" back into his head by skiing or swimming in the afternoon. Then there was conversation at dinner, Ping-Pong afterward, a spell of reading, and early bedtime.

This routine invariably helped him work, but it also separated him from his family. At Yaddo he missed the disturbances of home—a dog in his lap, a baby in his arms—and at Scarborough he missed the fields and the quiet. If they only lived in Saratoga, he came to believe, he could combine the pleasures of home life with the pleasures of writing. So he looked around and found an inexpensive old three-story house on Union Avenue with a porte cochere out front and a carriage house in back where he could work. The whole family drove up one sunny day to see the house, and drove right back to Scarborough. The schools were not good enough for the children, Mary thought. The house was in sad repair. They did not move to Saratoga.

In the summer of 1959, Dr. Winternitz fell desperately ill at

Treetops, and Mary made a number of visits to his bedside during a long siege marked by sudden relapses and temporary recoveries. By this time the relationship between Cheever and his father-in-law had soured. Mary's father, John decided, was a tyrant whose dark spirit compromised their marriage. "I have come to think of Winter as the king of a Hades where M. must spend perhaps half of her time," he confided to his journal. "There is no question that he is a source of darkness in our affairs." At midsummer he escaped the vigil to attend a writers' congress in Germany and revisit Italy. Everything in Europe looked healthy and cheerful. An old lady sold roses in a Frankfurt doorway. Little girls in dirndls gathered mushrooms near Kitzbühel. Alan and Lucy Moorehead put him up in their beautiful house in Asolo, and sent him off to swim in the Adriatic at the Lido. Finally he returned to Rome, this time as a guest at the American Academy, where he had felt himself snubbed two years earlier. On the flight back an engine caught on fire, but nonetheless the trip had been invigorating. Why did he like Italy so much? Mike Bessie asked him. "When I walk down Fifth Avenue," Cheever replied, "I know all the faces. She's Vassar '46, and I know where and how she lives. But in Rome it's not like that at all—the faces are mysterious, and fascinating."

In September, Mary's father died, and with the passing of that dominant male figure John assumed full responsibility for his wife and family. What he and Mary wanted out of life was what most middle-class Americans wanted: a comfortable and fulfilling life for themselves and the best possible opportunities for their children. A house of their own was part of the package, and so were the best schools for Susan and Ben and Fred. In all three cases, this meant expensive boarding schools and private colleges. The advertising man and the investment banker and the network executive managed to provide these advantages, so why shouldn't he? This was not the sort of existence, to be sure, that most American writers were able to or in some cases even wanted to achieve. But Cheever was convinced—and by his example demonstrated the validity of his conviction—that a real writer did not need to be "an outlyer, like a gypsy" (Ernest Hemingway's prescription). "Genius did not need to be rootless, disenfranchised, or alienated," Cheever persuaded young poet Dana Gioia by example. "A writer could have a family, a job, and even live in a suburb." But he could not do these things—at least Cheever could not—without arousing powerful tensions. A conventional life imposed restrictions, and even as he forged his bonds he was driven to loosen or untie them. In addition, he was almost always under severe financial pressure. This strain was directly involved in his looming confrontation with *The New Yorker.*

During most of their first twenty-five years together, Cheever and *The New Yorker* got along extremely well. Usually his stories were accepted, printed, and paid for as fast as could be expected, and three days later he would start getting appreciative and intelligent letters from readers. No magazine had better or more responsive readers, and few could have had better editors.

The redoubtable Harold Ross, for example, read through Cheever's submitted typescripts, littering the margins with his queries and suggestions. Often his queries were maddeningly literal-minded. If a character sat down, he would inquire, "On what?" If a story covered twenty-four hours or longer, he would want to know what had been eaten and whether people had slept. But there were also times when he supplied exactly the right nuance. In "The Enormous Radio," Ross made an amendment that Cheever not only accepted but applauded. A couple discover a good-sized diamond on their bathroom floor after a party. "We'll sell it," the husband says, "we could use a couple of hundred dollars." Ross switched "dollars" to "bucks," an "absolutely perfect" change.

For the most part, Cheever was very lightly edited at *The New Yorker,* since his copy came in clean and spare. William Maxwell, who succeeded Gus Lobrano as fiction editor, recalls discovering that Gus had not made a mark on "Goodbye, My Brother." And Maxwell also remembers the day when he was lying ill with bronchitis and Cheever came by with a story and waited, talking to his wife Emmy, while Bill had the joy of being the first person in the world to read "The Country Husband." In stories like these, ending with a flourish of celebration, Cheever seemed to communicate "a joyful knowledge that no one else ever had," Maxwell thought. For many years their professional connection approached the ideal in editor-author relationships. The men were close friends, and each respected the work of the other. Cheever admired Maxwell's stories, and his novel of adolescence, *The Folded Leaf;* Maxwell counted it a privilege to edit Cheever's fiction.

Two things eventually compromised the relationship. First, when he was strapped for funds, Cheever often felt that the magazine was underpaying him. Second, Maxwell sometimes had to turn down a Cheever story, either because of its subject matter (*The*

New Yorker's taste was genteel, and as time wore on Cheever wrote about everything under the sun), or because of his increasing drift away from realism and toward the fantastic, or—worst of all— because some of the fiction, written under the influence of alcohol, simply did not measure up. It was Maxwell's job to say no, and though for a long time Cheever tried to keep his editor-friend and the rejections separate, in the end he could not.

The problem of finances came up first. *The New Yorker*'s policy has always been to keep a certain number of fact writers on the payroll, but to buy its fiction at space rates from outside contributors. Hence Cheever never had a salary from the magazine. Instead he was paid by the story, with annual bonuses depending on how much he had contributed during the year. There were times, however, when he became convinced that the magazine should support him the same way it supported its fact writers. But *The New Yorker* could not well afford to put all the fiction writers who contributed stories more or less regularly on a living wage, and it could not make an exception of Cheever without making everyone else furious. As it was, Maxwell understood Cheever's very real need for prompt payment and did what he could. Stories were paid for according to their length in print, but Maxwell would ask the accounting department to make an estimate from the manuscript and issue a check for 75 percent of the total, with the rest to follow after the story was set up in galleys. Cheever could also borrow against future work, like other regular contributors of fiction. He was paid an average of more than a thousand dollars for the 121 stories he wrote for the magazine. But these payments, which varied according to length and to a changing scale of rates, hardly sufficed to support Cheever and his family.

The trouble began, Cheever thought, with what he characterized as Harold Ross's feeling that too much money was bad for fiction writers—that if they stopped eating in cafeterias, they might become "prideful, arrogant, and idle." Cheever strongly disagreed, and occasionally the issue flared up. One day in 1959 he marched into *The New Yorker*'s offices on West Forty-third Street and managed to extract a sum of cash from treasurer Hawley Truax. Later that year the Maxwells came to dinner in Scarborough, and left hurriedly in the wake of a quarrel during which Mary declared, with fervor, that the magazine ought to give her husband more money. These disputes encouraged Cheever to explore other markets. In 1959, he published six stories in *The New Yorker* (including a first fragmentary section of *The Wapshot Scandal*) and one in *Esquire*. In 1960, he published two stories in *The New Yorker* and two in *Esquire*, one of them the superlative "Death of Justina." Wherever he published his stories, however, the marketplace reminded him that only novel writing made sound economic sense.

Early in 1960 he applied for his second Guggenheim grant to help finance his second novel. Cheever's letter of application was remarkably brief: seven short sentences, half a page in total. His project was to write a novel, he declared, but he said nothing about what kind of novel. He was relying on the merit of his last two books—*The Wapshot Chronicle* and *The Housebreaker of Shady Hill*—and on the eminence of his sponsors—Robert Penn Warren, John Hersey, Ralph Ellison, and Cowley—to carry the day with the Guggenheims, and so they did.

The novel he settled down to work on was *The Wapshot Scandal*, a dark sequel to the cheerful *Wapshot Chronicle*. As Cheever immersed himself in the book, his sense of the world around him deepened and dimmed. Everywhere he encountered heedless, headlong change—change that in its rapidity and power transmogrified people as they moved from one abode to another, one job to another, one marriage to another, only to gaze emptily at the ruins of what had been their way of life. This constant mutability promised to rob us of our roots, and without these the wind could blow us away. In short, Cheever's cockroach returned, his cafard came back, his depression reassumed control.

In October 1960 he traveled to northern California to participate in an *Esquire*-sponsored symposium titled "Writing in America Today" with Philip Roth and James Baldwin. Each of these writers struck a pessimistic chord during his appearance on a college campus. Roth, speaking at Stanford, described a bizarre Chicago murder trial as an example of the difficulty of "Writing American Fiction" in a society where the awfulness of reality so often outstripped the imagination. Baldwin, at San Francisco State, was incandescent about the fire next time. "To be a Negro in this country," he said, "is to be a fantasy in the mind of the republic . . . and where there is no vision there is no people." Cheever, at Berkeley, deplored the "abrasive and faulty surface" of the nation during the last twenty-five years. "Life in the United States in 1960 is Hell," he said, and the only possible position for a writer was one of negation. "The Death of Justina," which came out the following month in *Esquire*, illustrated what he meant.

The characters in the story come from the Wapshot provenance, but Cheever chose not to subsume "The Death of Justina" in *The Wapshot Scandal*. It stands too well on its own as a devastating satire on contemporary life, and specifically, on the pervasive climate of commercialism. In an opening reflection, the narrator defines art as "the triumph over chaos (no less)" but questions his ability to achieve such a triumph in a world where "even the mountains seem to shift in the space of a night. . . ." Moses—presumably Moses Wapshot, though the last name is not used—is at work writing commercials for Elixircol when he hears of the death of his wife's cousin at their home in suburban Proxmire Manor. His boss insists that Moses finish the commercial before he takes the train home, and in response he submits a horrendous parody of modern advertising copy:

Are you growing old? Are you falling out of love with your image in the looking glass? Does your face in the morning seem rucked and seamed with alcoholic and sexual excesses and does the rest of you appear to be a grayish-pink lump, covered all over with brindle hair? . . . Is your sense of smell fading, is your interest in gardening waning, is your fear of heights increasing, and are your sexual drives as ravening and intense as ever and does your wife look more and more to you like a stranger with sunken cheeks who has wandered into your bedroom by mistake?

If any of these things are true, Moses writes, you need Elixircol, "the true juice of youth" that comes in a small economy size for seventy-five dollars and a giant family size at two hundred and fifty. It's a lot of scratch, but you can always borrow from your neighborhood loan shark or hold up a bank. He sends this copy in to his boss and catches a train to Proxmire Manor, where he finds a village government trying to legislate against death much as Elixircol purports to stave off the process of aging.

Moses and his wife live in Zone B of Proxmire Manor, where her cousin Justina has just passed away, illegally. The laws of the community specify not only that you can't have a funeral home in Zone B (two-acre lots) but also that you can't die there. Dr. Hunter, who gives Moses this information, suggests that he put Justina in his car and drive over to Chestnut Street, where Zone C begins and it is permissible to die. Otherwise, he'll have to get an exception to the zoning laws from the mayor. Moses next goes to see the mayor, who explains how strict zoning laws protect investments in their homes

Washington's Birthday, circa 1922

A diminutive Cheever at right, as George Washington, poses with other Quincy, Massachusetts, youngsters. From left: Gordon Godfrey, Rollin Bailey, Elinor Godfrey, and Dora Cummings as Martha Washington.

Christmas Play, December 1925

In top hat and swallow-tail coat at left, Cheever played Fred to best friend Faxon Ogden's Scrooge (at right) in a Thayerlands school performance of Dickens's *A Christmas Carol*.

Yaddo and Its Colonists, Summer 1934

Here Cheever (seated at right, first row) is pictured during the first
of many visits to Yaddo, the artists' colony in Saratoga Springs. He spent
entire winters and summers there when he was young and broke, and
returned often later in life. Elizabeth Ames (seated in the white dress, first
row) became a kind of surrogate mother to Cheever, and he stood up for
her when she was challenged for her political sentiments. Others in the
photograph: James T. Farrell (over Cheever's left shoulder); his wife,
Dorothy (seated at left, first row); and Muriel Rukeyser (standing at left).

Mary and John Cheever, 1964

Humor helped hold their forty-one-year
marriage together, and so—Cheever used
to maintain—did the accident of nomenclature: Johns and Marys belonged together.

David Gahr

Father, Daughter, Bear

In this fuzzy snapshot from the late 1940s, John Cheever, home from the wars, holds his first child, Susan, while in turn she holds her stuffed panda.

Cheevers and One Other

Looking somewhat out of place in this 1973 photograph is Donald Lang (second from left), a former inmate at Sing Sing who took Cheever's writing class there and later became a close friend. Clockwise from the top are Linda and Ben Cheever, Mary, with grandson Joshua, Federico, Lang, and John Cheever.

Nancy Crampton

Beechtwig
in Scarborough

In the spring of 1951 the
Cheevers moved from New
York City to this converted
toolshed at Beechwood, the
Frank A. Vanderlip estate just
off Westchester's Route 9.
After a decade as renters, they
bought the house below.

The House on Cedar Lane

Despite a reluctance born of his father's failure, Cheever finally took
out a mortgage on this handsome home in Ossining. In time the
house and grounds took possession of him as well. The addition at
right was completed in 1981, shortly before Cheever's death.

Croton Dam in Spring

In every season Cheever enjoyed hiking
to Croton Dam, about a six-mile round trip
from Cedar Lane. But he especially liked
making the journey in the spring, when the
cataract was in full flow.

Cheever at the Station

"Paint me a small railroad station then, ten minutes before dark": so begins Cheever's 1969 novel, *Bullet Park*. Much of his best writing is situated in suburban locales. He was keenly sensitive to the poignant daily drama of departure and return that millions of commuters undergo.

Howells Award, 1965

Ralph Ellison presents Cheever with the William
Dean Howells Award for *The Wapshot Scandal*,
adjudged by the American Academy of Arts and
Letters as the best work of fiction during the
1960–65 period. Ellison praised Cheever's
duality of vision—his capacity to invoke both
laughter and a tragic sense of reality.

Bay State Road, 1974

In the fall of 1974 Cheever began teaching creative
writing at Boston University. Living by himself in this
spare apartment near the campus, he very nearly
drank himself to death. In April 1975 he underwent
treatment for alcoholism, stopped drinking
permanently, and started writing again.

Aunt Josie

Novelist Josephine Herbst, whom Cheever met at Yaddo in the 1930s, more or less adopted him and his family as her own. Some of the Cheevers' happiest moments were spent at her house in Erwinna, Bucks County.

The Good Neighbor

Sara Spencer, the Cheevers' near neighbor on Cedar Lane, thought that John could do no wrong. He swam in her pool, skated on her pond, and confided in her during their Saturday morning ritual of coffee and croissants.

Cheever fell half in love with actress Hope Lange when he first met her in Hollywood in 1964. Years later they became lovers. This snapshot of her was taken about the same time as she took the one of him below.

The Girl of His Dreams

On one of their first dates in New York City, Cheever, in his best suit, decided to don skates and take what looks like a rather uncertain journey around the rink at Rockefeller Center.

Retreat to Whiskey Island

With the St. Lawrence River in the background, Cheever takes the air with Mimi Boyer during a September 1971 visit. Phil and Mimi Boyer were among his closest friends, and he often traveled north to see them. Second dog from the right is the black Labrador Ezekiel (Zeke), son of the Cheevers' Cassie.

Costume Party, Sort Of

Both Cheever—in one of the Russian fur hats he brought back from the Soviet Union in lieu of royalties—and Mary Dirks, in Abominable Snowwoman garb, seem aware that a camera is pointed in their direction.

Backgammon with Arthur Spear

Perhaps Cheever's best friend was Arthur Spear, a down Maine man of taciturn wit who removed to Briarcliff Manor. They fished and swam together, played backgammon for small stakes together, and together formed the Friday club for male conviviality.

Hiking with Roger Willson

Midwesterner Roger Willson became another good friend; for a time his wife, Maureen, taught with Mary Cheever at Briarcliff College. In this November 1975 photo, the two men set out to exercise themselves and half a dozen dogs.

Mentor

Malcolm Cowley published Cheever's first piece of fiction, guided him through his early career, and remained a valued advocate and adviser until the end.

Editor

William Maxwell, a friend since the 1930s, edited many of Cheever's best stories for *The New Yorker.* Though the relationship foundered in later years, each man respected the other as master of his craft.

Comrade

Though they saw each other infrequently and came from different backgrounds, Cheever and Saul Bellow shared a strong bond of fellow feeling. Their friendship seemed to feed on air, Bellow observed.

Colleague

Often thought of in connection with Cheever, the two-decades-younger Updike got to know the older writer during a 1964 trip to Russia. In his memorial tribute, Updike celebrated Cheever's artistic certainty and personal gallantry.

B. A. King

Last Light

Carrying the MacDowell Colony medal he had just been awarded, Cheever in this August 1979 photo makes his way alone across a field.

and is disinclined to grant an exception until Moses threatens to dig a hole in the backyard and shove Justina into it. That night, Moses has a dream in which a crowded supermarket becomes a modern Hell. The shoppers bring their wares to the checkout counters, where brutes push or kick them through the door into the "dark water and . . . terrible noise of moaning and crying" beyond. As he watches in his dream, "thousands and thousands pushed their wagons through the market, made their careful and mysterious choices, and were reviled and taken away."

Once Justina is safely buried, Moses goes back to his office and fashions another mock commercial. "Don't lose your loved ones because of excessive radioactivity. Don't be a wallflower at the dance because of Strontium 90 in your bones. . . . You have been inhaling lethal atomic waste for the last twenty-five years and only Elixircol can save you." His boss is not amused. Rewrite the commercial, he demands, "or you'll be dead." At this command, Moses writes out the Twenty-third Psalm and leaves the office for the last time. In the end, then, he achieves a kind of victory, but at the cost of his job and in a society whose most symbolic gathering place, the supermarket, has been transformed into an updated version of the inferno.

From San Francisco, Cheever went to Hollywood for his first and only screenwriting job. He took the assignment to help finance the house that Mary had at long last found and persuaded him to buy. She had been looking around northern Westchester for three years, but most of the places cost at least fifty thousand dollars, substantially more than they were prepared to pay. Then in September 1960 Mary discovered a beautiful stone-ended house in a valley behind Ossining, with a brook and large trees and a field to scythe, and the search was over. The house with its six acres cost $37,500, and the problem of financing was not easily solved. Cheever was extremely uneasy about going into debt, and when he finally was persuaded to ask the bankers about a mortgage, they ascertained his occupation, considered his prospects, and folded their hands. To warm his reception with the bankers he referred them to *The New Yorker*, where legal counsel Milton Greenstein was anything but supportive. What made a writer think he could afford a house like that? he asked. At this juncture, Dudley and Zinny Schoales came forward to cosign the mortgage, the bankers smiled, and the Cheevers prepared to move the four miles north to their new home on Cedar Lane. First, though, there was a down payment to come up with. Mary contributed some funds from her savings, and the rest came from film producer Jerry Wald.

Two years earlier, in the fall of 1958, John had been prepared to go to Hollywood. The rumor was that David Selznick was going to call him about a screenplay for *Tender Is the Night,* but the phone call never came. In 1960, Jerry Wald did call, or rather Cheever's agent Henry Lewis let Wald know that Cheever was available, and so he was put to work on a screen treatment of D. H. Lawrence's *The Lost Girl.* In Lawrence's novel, a girl from England's industrial midlands meets and falls in love with a penniless young Italian and abandons her provincial roots to marry him and go to live in a bleak mountainous region of Italy. Cheever, with his recent exposure to Italian scenes, was a logical choice to try to transplant the story from the page to the screen. During five weeks in November and December 1960, he produced his treatment. This did not result in a motion picture, but Wald—an extremely energetic producer who often had half a dozen projects going at once—thought enough of Cheever's work to offer him two thousand a week to return. He said no. He had his own writing to do. Hollywood was not his cup of tea.

He was put up during his 1960 stay at the Chateau Marmont on Sunset Boulevard, where the management never let him forget he was living in a suite once occupied by Mitzi Gaynor. (Twenty years later, John Belushi died in a two-hundred-dollar-a-night bungalow at the Chateau Marmont.) He did not lack for company. John and Harriett Weaver lived only a few minutes away, and the three of them had dinner together almost every night, either at the Weavers' or at a nearby Japanese restaurant. At Twentieth Century–Fox he was given a cubicle to write in, and a secretary who spent most of her time taking naps. He was delighted to see that Danny Fuchs, an old friend from the early days at Yaddo, was also on the lot. Over lunch, Fuchs advised him to treat Wald "like a demented child." Ivan Goff and Ben Roberts, colleagues from Astoria, relieved his distress at finding that alcohol was unavailable at the Fox commissary by sharing their emergency rations of gin. At a party at Wald's house, a disembodied voice from beyond the closed front door asked Cheever to state his name, please. He refused, and banged the contraption that issued the request with his shoe. At another party—the highlight of his trip—he met and kissed Peggy Lee, a singer he greatly admired.

Hollywood, he feared, was "a sort of literary graveyard" that

consumed talents like those of Fuchs and Weaver, Al Hayes and
Harry Brown and John Collier. Yet it was homesickness that most
afflicted him there as the Christmas season came on. The smog was
terrible for the Santa Claus parade the day before Thanksgiving.
Santa wore a mink beard, a choir sang "Joy to the World" as the
roses bloomed in a climate—he was told—very like that of Bethle-
hem. A jazz combo played a "knockabout version" of "Good King
Wenceslas." It all seemed wrong somehow. He was glad to get
home in time for a cold Christmas among the fir trees.

In February 1961 the Cheevers moved into the house in Ossining
that was to be his home for the last twenty-one years of his life.
Situated alongside the Hudson, Ossining derived its name from an
Indian word for "stones." The same word was responsible for the
name of the town's most famous structure, Sing Sing prison. The
township, ten square miles in area and thirty miles upriver from
New York City, was decidedly not fashionable: "an unchic address," in the words of *People* magazine, when compared with
upriver estates and affluent bedroom communities to the south.
The Hudson provided the town with its economic rationale, and
during the nineteenth century a downtown community rare in
Westchester sprang up to serve the needs of river commerce. Ossining was also unusual among the county's homogeneous suburbs
because of its wide socioeconomic mix. The town was divided
between the old-line professional white Anglo-Saxon Protestants
who commuted to the city, the blacks who did the heavy work of
the town, and the Italian-Americans who ran the shops and stores
and served as guards at Sing Sing. In her poem "How Much Time
Is a Village?" Mary Cheever traces the breach between the WASP
commuters who live on the river bluffs and the proliferating black
population downtown.

Wonderful vistas opened up from the bluffs: the Palisades far to
the south, the vast span of the Tappan Zee Bridge, the triple-
headed High Tor rising 850 feet above the river to the northwest,
and the rugged Highlands farther north. Except for the Bay of
Naples, Alexis de Tocqueville remarked from the heights at Sing
Sing, "the world has not such scenery." And there were also country roads and hills and trees and lakes and—for Cheever the most
ravishing sight of all—the massive Croton dam and reservoir to
gaze upon. "Nobody knows how beautiful this place is," he said.
His new house shared in the natural beauty, with the Hudson
edging the west and the woods and fields and a brook still closer

at hand. It rather looked, he thought, like Josie Herbst's place at Erwinna.

The Cheevers' house, Afterwhiles, is located near the Cedar Lane exit off Route 9A. Commanding an enclave of other early-American homes, the house itself features a pergola near the brook in front, and a stone terrace to the right. The woods beyond lead toward the river. Originally constructed in 1798, the house was redesigned in 1920 by the architect Eric Gugler. Irregular stones are massed to form the ends, with the rest clapboard. Inside there is no entrance hall, so that you walk into a dining room–living room at the left and a good-sized kitchen to the right. In one corner of the living room a sideboard displays the Canton china brought back by Benjamin Hale Cheever. A Paxton on the wall, depicting a woman on the veranda of a summer place, is on permanent loan from Arthur Spear. There's also a winter scene by Phil Rosenthal and a Seth Thomas clock. On the second floor is the master bedroom, a small bedroom, and a library–living room featuring a lowboy from Newburyport with a handsome tortoiseshell finish to the wood, a painting of John Cheever as a boy of eleven or twelve in an artist's smock, drawn by Aunt Florence Liley, and his grand-mother's Chinese fan, under glass. The third floor contains two more bedrooms and a storage area. As his children moved away, Cheever shifted his workplace from one abandoned bedroom to another. In Ben's room he tacked a print of Thayer Academy to the wall. There is no trophy case attesting to Cheever's various honors and awards. Though the highway traffic roars by a few hundred feet away, the house on Cedar Lane seems more rural than subur-ban, an impression seconded by the active presence of the family's large and frisky retrievers. The place has a sense of rootedness about it.

In the first months, though, Cheever found it difficult to take possession of his new home and to enjoy it. But as he lived there and put his labor and mortgage payments into it, he eventually forged a symbiotic bond with the place that involved a mutual possession. Time and again in the years ahead, Cheever was to comment on the hold the house had over him. He could contem-plate divorce with equanimity, he would say, but—like the protago-nist in "A Vision of the World" (1962)—he could not bring himself to leave the rooms he had painted and the soil he had turned. His chains, made "of turf and house paint," bound him in a confine-ment he both wished for and resented. He was always worried about meeting payments on the house, and paid off the mortgage prematurely, losing some tax deductions in the process. He and the house owned each other.

Saul Bellow was surprised by the regularity of the world that Cheever chose to occupy: the fine house, the well-kept grounds, the family heirlooms. On the surface he led a rigorously conventional life, while Bellow knew—as he came to know Cheever better—that he was drinking and having affairs. It was the old story, he supposed, of trying to escape from restrictions that one carefully crafts for himself.

OSSINING

1961–1963

A N INNOCENT motorist, angling his car
between the stone gateposts of Afterwhiles
to catch a glimpse of the handsome house
below, would be unlikely to think it the
home of a writer. It looks more like the house of an
advertising or PR man (Cheever bought it from an
"exploded" public relations executive) or perhaps a
banker (a banker sold it to the PR man). Writers were
supposed to suffer and create in unheated garrets: how
could anyone suffer and create in such a lovely setting?
The answers were that genius could not be circumscribed geographically, that after all Cheever started
out in a cold-water flat on Hudson Street a quarter of

a century earlier and worked his way up to Cedar Lane, and that there was plenty of misery to go around even in the most comfortable of upper-middle-class environments. Cheever could write there as he could write—had to write—anywhere. Every time he put his foot out the door a story started to unfold in his imagination, and he could not conceive of running out of tales to tell.

Westchester had its quota of prosperous Philistines, but Cheever rarely wrote about them. It would have been too easy to satirize them in print; instead they became the victims of private jokes. There was the stockbroker in plaid trousers who used to tell Cheever how much he envied him, being a writer. If only he could find the time, the broker said with a sigh, he'd be a writer too. And at one party he had the following dialogue with his dinner partner.

"What is it you do, John?" the beautifully gowned woman asked him.

"I'm a writer," he admitted.

"How interesting," she said. "What do you write?"

"Oh, stories, mostly."

"Well," she said, "I'm sorry, but I only read *The New Yorker.*"

Yet there were also a number of gifted and intelligent people around, beginning with his wife, to stimulate his imagination. Ossining was also the home of actors José Ferrer and Howard da Silva, and over the hill from Cheever's was the house where Aaron Copland used to live, now occupied by a charming Italian writer named Antonio Barolini. Barolini had some difficulties with the English language. "I am loving the Beatles," he told Cheever. He had in mind their Croton neighbors George and Helene Biddle. Further confusion developed the day Barolini finished a story called "The Beautiful Hussle," about "the beautiful Hussle River."

The Cheevers kept a busy social calendar. "I wish to Christ I led a more private life," he sometimes said, but on the other hand he loved the parties and the gossip and the laughter, much of it generated by his wit. Most of his friends in Ossining were those he had made during the decade in Scarborough. The Kahns had moved away, but the Benjamins and Swopes and Reimans remained, along with such others as Alwyn and Essie Lee, John and Mary Dirks, Tom and Mimi Glazer, Barrett and Jane Clark, and Roger and Maureen Willson. Cheever felt closest of all, though, to Phil Boyer and Arthur Spear.

A Harvard man with a hearty manner and a love of the outdoors, Phil Boyer was married to the daughter of a Morgan partner and had grown up with the kind of wealth and position Cheever could only dream of. In addition to raising dogs, both Phil and Mimi Boyer were interested in exotic birds. At their home in Croton they kept a toucan in a cage. When the toucan squawked for attention, Phil would take a tennis ball from the basket by his chair and fling it at the cage. In time their interest took a more serious direction. Wherever the Boyers went—to Whiskey Island on the St. Lawrence in the summer, or to Guatemala or Texas or Arizona in the winter—Mimi made paintings and woodblock prints of the birds they saw, and Phil became expert at photographing them. The museum in Clayton, New York, four miles from their island retreat in the St. Lawrence, reserves a room for a joint display of "Boyers' Birds": Mimi's paintings and Phil's photographs. In 1964 Cheever wrote an admiring commentary on Mimi's work for her exhibit in New York City.

The Boyers were very much John's friends. Mary did not share in the friendship. In the summers when she was at Treetops, he often journeyed to Whiskey Island. On a clear day at Whiskey—one of the Thousand Islands—you could see New York on one side and Canada on the other, with steamers, freighters, pleasure boats, excursion launches, and fishermen's skiffs going by. On stormy days you could see nothing at all; a freighter crashed into the rocks during one of Cheever's visits.

Mimi's family—Carters from Virginia—owned both Whiskey and a neighboring island, and John reveled in the patrician surroundings. Sleeping in the big house on Whiskey, he communed at night with the ghosts. These happy spirits crowded the upstairs landing, he told Mimi, and in describing them he brought to life with uncanny accuracy the absent and deceased members of her family. He loved the water, especially when aboard the *Wild Goose*, a boat of almost Edwardian splendor. "I don't think the Kaiser will declare war, do you?" he once asked Mimi from his magisterial position in the stern. Other activities had less appeal. When a baseball game started up on the next-door island, he not only wouldn't play but hiked out of earshot to the very tip of Whiskey. Tennis was just as bad: he hated the sounds of games he couldn't play.

As best he could, Cheever reciprocated the Boyers' hospitality to him. Along with St. Clair McKelway, he sponsored Phil for the Century Club. He read and critiqued Phil's writing, and encouraged their son David to go to his agent with what turned out to be a book of stories, *The Sidelong Glances of a Pigeon Kicker* (1968). He and Mimi made long-range plans to go to college, both for the first time, when they reached seventy.

Arthur Spear, like the Boyers, was unusually attracted to birds. At one time he installed an aviary at his home in Briarcliff Manor. When this became a nuisance, he and John spent a hectic afternoon trying to catch all the birds and transport them to a tropical-bird store in the Bronx. As if forewarned of their relocation, the birds flew all over the house to avoid being caught. The last one they retrieved from under the upstairs radiator. In the early 1960s the Cheevers themselves kept ringneck doves, and some of their off-spring found their way to the Spears' house as well. The most remarkable feature of that home, though, was surely the "cow room": a downstairs sitting room, just off the kitchen, with every inch of wall space occupied by pictures of cows and every orna-ment and knickknack accenting the bovine theme. Spear was like Cheever a Yankee, in his case a down-Maine Yankee, and they wasted so few words in conversation that Arthur's wife, Stella, sometimes thought they must be angry with each other. Cheever would call for a lunch date. "Hello," Arthur answered the phone. "Tomorrow," said Cheever. "Noon," said Arthur. "Sellazzo's," said John, and both hung up. Some of the pithiness of Leander's journal in *The Wapshot Chronicle* derived from the *Journals of Heze-kiah Prince, Jr., 1822–1828,* Arthur's ancestor.

Both Spear and Cheever loved the outdoor life. Together they used to go fishing at Mahopac, stopping on the way at a Greek monastery to buy good black bread and macaroons from the monks. Regularly they made the six-mile-round-trip hike along the aque-duct to the Croton dam, with a pint of liquor in pocket. A first drink was permitted at a cut through the rocks they dubbed the Ambuscade Room, and a second at the dam itself as they contem-plated the falls while imbibing bourbon or Gilbey's gin, otherwise known to them as mother's milk. Cheever dogs usually accom-panied them on the hike. "Now don't go playing with the Croton-ville dogs," John warned them in mock seriousness. "They're not the right sort."

Occasionally Arthur accompanied John on longer trips. In Sep-tember 1963, the two drove up to Saratoga, visited Yaddo, stayed at the Gideon Putnam, and spent a hilarious evening with Frank Sullivan, the town's resident humorist. "Wherever we went," Ar-thur recalled, "John made it amusing." They played backgammon together, for the small stakes both preferred. They commiserated with each other over injuries, illnesses, and deaths. They kept in touch even when apart. Arthur reported from Friendship on the performance of his beans and tomatoes and laying hens; John wrote chattily from each of his increasingly frequent stopping places overseas. In short, they were the closest of friends. Among the affinities that bound them—though theirs was not really a literary friendship—was an interest in the language and in the making of books. Spear was for many years an executive of the World Book Company, a right-hand man to its president William Cross Ferguson. Soon after Harcourt Brace purchased World in the early 1960s, however, he was summarily dismissed. Cheever, feeling deeply for his friend, dramatized his dismissal in a 1964 story called "The Ocean." Brutally fired, the man in the story holds his emotions under control until he can get to the men's room, lock himself in a cubicle, and weep in private.

The Yankee friends made an annual ritual of swimming on Patriot's Day. No private pools were open on April 19, and often the waters of the pond or river were bone-chilling at that date, but in they plunged each year in commemoration of their common heritage and the shot heard round the world. Cheever was not a man to test the temperature with his toes.

He did much of his warm-weather swimming at Sara Spencer's. An attractive divorcée, Sara lived across Cedar Lane in a beautiful hillside house with an artesian-fed pool for swimming and a pond for skating. When she learned that Cheever, whose stories she greatly admired, was to be her neighbor, she sent him a postcard of welcome. He phoned and asked her to cocktails, she had a dinner party for the Cheevers, and soon a close companionship developed. No place was handier for swimming and skating, and no one more warmly disposed toward him than Sara Spencer. In the early years of their relationship, John was often "very urgent" with her sexually, she said, but insisted that theirs was "not a full-scale love affair." There had been an affair early on, John told his son Fred, and then it deepened into something else. With Sara as with Arthur, he practiced a private ritual. At eleven o'clock on Saturday mornings, he would appear at her home with fresh-baked croissants for breakfast and conversation. When he was out of town he sometimes sent a note, as a reminder of their rendezvous, missed. He cared about Sara, and she adored him.

On the surface, Sara Spencer and John Cheever did not seem to have much in common. To begin with, she was Jewish and a few years older than he. In addition, Cheever thought of her as much stronger and more capable than he. She inherited some apartment buildings in New York City, and successfully ran the business from her house in Ossining. She tried to teach John something about finance, but he was an indifferent pupil, affecting to scorn the very subject of money. Sara was also emotionally independent. She had survived a broken marriage and learned to live alone, a condition he could not have tolerated himself.

What she provided for him, most of all, was an entirely sympathetic ear. He told her about his difficulties as they came up, and she gave him her understanding and unqualified support. Whatever the merits of the case, she could be counted on to assure him that he was right. Over time her role became rather like that of a fond mother who will not find fault with her own child. John presented himself to her an unhappy and unfulfilled man, terribly in love with a wife who did not give him the love he deserved. Sara thought him badly treated, and told him so.

New literary friends swam into Cheever's ken during his periodic trips to Yaddo. In the summer of 1963, for example, he met and befriended two young poets, Raphael Rudnik and Natalie Robins. Rudnik was sitting by the Yaddo pool one afternoon, eyes closed against the glare of the sun, when he heard someone reading—as he thought—from a book. It was Cheever, and as he looked up, Raphael saw that he was *talking* in wonderful prose, not reading from a book at all. "I'd better avoid this guy," Rudnik thought. "If he doesn't like my stuff, he could make mincemeat of it." A few nights later, Raphael did a reading at Yaddo. Cheever liked his poetry, and they began to take walks together and—another ritual—to throw a ball around. Raphael had "a great wing," Cheever thought, and he admired him too for his reputation as a horse player who used to sneak into the track next door and return with more cash than he'd started out with. Soon thereafter Raphael started visiting the Cheevers on holidays, particularly Thanksgiving. "It was a celebration to see John," Raphael said. He had a mysterious capacity, he thought, for getting people to produce the best in themselves.

In August 1963 there were very few women at Yaddo, and for the first time in her life Natalie Robins felt really popular. Perhaps she reached out to Cheever then because her own father was dying. Perhaps he sensed in her an unusual talent for friendship with men exclusive of sexual complications. In any event he liked her, she liked him, and almost instantly Natalie became like a member of the family, trekking up to Cedar Lane on holidays along with Raphael and—after her marriage in 1965—along with her husband, Christopher Lehmann-Haupt, book critic for the *New York Times.* At the beginning Natalie felt flattered and awed that an established writer like Cheever should take an interest in her. Later she assumed a stronger position in their friendship, comforting him in his distress.

At home in Ossining, Cheever led an active physical life. He enjoyed hiking and biking, skiing and skating. In his boyhood he learned to skate on the Braintree dam with his parents, and as an adult skating always gave him pleasure. Some winters he skated nearly every day at Sara Spencer's pond, where the golden carp could be seen gliding beneath the surface, or at Max and Marion Ascoli's pond in Croton. He coveted such forms of "rudimentary locomotion" because the ground under his feet gave him a foundation to live and write upon. "The physical world is extremely important to me," he said. "It's the world by which I live."

For the sheer joy of exercise, nothing compared with swimming. Cheever swam in the pools of friends and the pools of acquaintances. He swam in the daytime and he swam at night. He swam at pool parties and at dinner parties. He swam in rivers and lakes and ponds and oceans in the northeastern United States, in Italy, in Eastern Europe, wherever in the world he happened to find himself. As a director of Yaddo he led a persistent campaign to get a pool installed—a campaign that succeeded despite the misgivings of Elizabeth Ames. He wrote his most famous story about swimming: "The Swimmer."

As a landowner he enthusiastically did the outdoor work around his place. He cut wood, both with an ax and a chain saw, and scythed the underbrush in the woods. Yet the ground was never entirely cleared until after his death. It was as if he wanted to keep the job "in a state of process," his son Fred said.

There were always dogs to walk at Cedar Lane. One summer the Cheevers hired a neighborhood youngster to take Cassie for walks, but the Labrador was set in her ways and refused to budge for anyone but John or Mary. Cheever's own mother seemed to survive in Cassie. As she grew older, Cassie used to fix her master with a reproachful stare, and he could hear his mother's voice saying, "John, can't you try to be a little neater?" He himself felt so close to Cassie, and then to Flora MacDonald and to Edgar (female), that he suspected he had been a dog in an earlier life.

Fond as he was of dogs, Cheever could not tolerate cats. In particular he loathed Delmore, a cat presented to the family by Josie Herbst and once the property of Delmore Schwartz's ex-wife, Elizabeth Pollet. Delmore arrived early in 1963 and immediately established his perversity by relieving himself in a box of Kleenex. When he got the cat shit off his face, Cheever drop-kicked him out the kitchen door, and soon the cat began to sulk. After Delmore, Cheever took to declaring that he was "internationally famous for his cruelty to cats." After Delmore, one of his fictional characters puts a kitten in the blender and another—the obese guard Tiny in *Falconer*—massacres dozens of prison cats.

Cheever moved to Ossining with as full a schedule of social, recreational, and domestic activities as the busiest of suburbanites. The difference was that he did not commute to a job in the city but repaired for five or six hours each day to a room not his own where he wrote letters, wrote in his journal, and wrote the fiction that made him famous. Within two months after the move to Cedar Lane, in April 1961, his fourth book of short stories appeared under the title *Some People, Places, and Things That Will Not Appear in My Next Novel.*

Despite including the magnificent "Death of Justina," *Some People* contained fewer excellent stories than any collection since *The Way Some People Live.* Two of the stories—"Brimmer" and "The Golden Age"—are little more than anecdotes constructed to build up to a punch line. A pervasive discontent and disenchantment runs through the book. "What is becoming evident in your work is a sort of apocalyptic poetry," Cowley wrote, "as if you were carrying well observed suburban life into some new dimension where everything is a little cockeyed and on the point of being exploded into a mushroom cloud." David Boroff, in the *New York Times Book Review,* called Cheever "a Gothic writer whose mind is poised at the edge of terror." Frank Warnke in *The New Republic* described his vision as one of nightmare, not of promise.

The final story in the book, "A Miscellany of Characters That Will Not Appear," purports to eliminate a number of subjects that were in fact to recur later in Cheever's career. Cheever announces that he will do away with such golden girls as the one he might have glimpsed—glorious in her shyness and her violet eyes—catching an out-of-bounds kick at the Princeton-Dartmouth rugby game, with all parts for Marlon Brando, with "all scornful descriptions" of ruined American landscapes, with all "explicit descriptions of sexual commerce," with all addicts and lushes, with "those homosexuals who have taken such a dominating position in recent fiction," in short with all topics that suggest a writer has "lost the gift of evoking the perfumes of life: sea water, the smoke of burning hemlock, and the breasts of women." Omitted from this "Miscellany" was one other category described in the *New Yorker* story Cheever published in November 1960: autobiographical characters "under the age of reason" à la J. D. Salinger: "I mean I'm this crazy, shook-up, sexy kid of thirteen with these phony parents, I mean my parents are so phony it makes me puke. . . ."

The thing to do upon publication of one book, Cheever knew, was to put it out of mind and get on with the next. Like a runner, he was much more interested in where he was going than in where he had been. So in the wake of *Some People* he produced some excellent stories and continued work on *The Wapshot Scandal*. Six excerpts from the novel appeared in *The New Yorker* between May 1959 and the book's publication in 1964. That way, readers who counted on seeing Cheever's fiction in the magazine could find it there, even when he was concentrating on a novel.

A rare editorial dispute with *The New Yorker* surfaced in November 1961 in connection with "The Brigadier and the Golf Widow." In this cold-war story, the jingoistic Charlie Pastern gives a key to his elaborate bomb shelter to a neighbor, the plumply seductive Mrs. Flannagan. When Charlie's wife discovers this perfidy, a terrible row occurs. In a final coda the narrator reveals that both the Pasterns' and Flannagans' marriages have collapsed, that Charlie is in jail for grand larceny, and—as a finishing touch—that in the first snow of the winter the now impoverished Mrs. Flannagan comes back to the Pasterns' fine suburban lawn and is standing there, gazing at the bomb shelter in the snow, when the new owner of the house sends out her maid to tell her to go away. Bill Maxwell, who thought this summarizing ending ineffective, had the story set up in galleys without the coda, so that Cheever could see how it read. At this stage Cheever stopped by the office, saw the proofs, concluded incorrectly that the magazine meant to publish the story that way regardless of how he felt, and roared with indignation. Maxwell gave up trying to persuade him, and the coda was restored. The conflict foreshadowed the severing of relations between author and magazine that was to come two years later.

Meanwhile, Cheever was beginning to get his first serious critical attention. Frederick Bracher, a professor at Pomona College in California, published two essays which remain among the best yet written about Cheever's work, in part because they benefited from the correspondence between the two men. In his letters Cheever made it clear that he welcomed and was surprised to receive the attention of an intelligent and reputable critic. Most of the breed, he thought, were guilty of a great deal of trimming and hedging. It was a rare critic who, like Bracher, genuinely concerned himself with the welfare of the literary commonwealth. He liked Bracher's article, "John Cheever and Comedy," so much that it became a kind of family joke. "Daddy's reading Professor Bracher's paper *again*," Susie would say.

Cheever did most of his writing at home during the early 1960s, but he was at Yaddo in September 1962 when word came of Cummings's death. Everyone sat around in the Great Hall after dinner while John and Curt Harnack reminisced about the poet. "I'm not especially pious," Cheever wrote Cummings's widow, Marion, the next day, "but I think he was an angel." As much as anything he admired his fellow New Englander's indisputable style, a style reflected in the manner of his passing. At sixty-seven and despite his arthritis, Cummings was cutting kindling behind his house in New Hampshire. Marion called out to him, "Cummings, isn't it frightfully hot to be chopping wood?" "I'll stop now, dear," he answered, "but first I'm going to sharpen the ax before I put it up." Those were the last words he spoke.

The following year Cheever had his first literary encounter with John O'Hara, another *New Yorker* regular and a writer he was often compared to. The occasion was an *Esquire*-sponsored conference in Princeton, and at a tea party there he met O'Hara, who was wearing yellow plush shoes that seemed to be killing him. "Well," the hostess told O'Hara upon discovering that he was a writer, "you've got the map of Ireland on your face."

Cheever himself was increasingly troubled about his drinking, a vice often associated with the Irish and with writers. In his journals he wrote of excruciating hangovers and dissected his own rationalizations. If he had errands to run the next day, that was a reason to get drunk the night before. If he went to pick up the maid, he could swing by the liquor store for gin. If there were no errands, he struggled to stay at his desk until noon—or at least until eleven—before taking a first drink. To disarm strangers, he took to announcing himself as "a *very* heavy drinker." Whether or not to invite the Cheevers became a real issue among their friends, since his customary good nature sometimes turned to meanspiritedness under the influence of alcohol. The problem was his to deal with every day, for it was up to him to establish his own job discipline. Unlike many modern American writers, most of whom have held regular positions as teachers or journalists, Cheever lacked the benefit of an external schedule to keep him at his desk. He had to make his own appointments and set his own deadlines, and this required tremendous willpower. There were a good many hours in the day, and it was easy to occupy them with drinking, with sex, with anything except work.

His brother, Fred, furnished an example close at hand of the devastation of drink. Liquor was undermining Fred's career and leading to domestic problems, while he steadfastly maintained that it wasn't his fault, that the world was against him.

The Cheever brothers saw much less of each other after Fred moved from Briarcliff Manor to Weston, Connecticut. Yet when it became clear that Fred was in the grip of alcoholism, John felt an obligation to care for him. He and Mary invited Fred down to Thanksgiving. His face swollen with drink, Fred insisted, defiantly, that at least his children loved him. John was immediately angry at the implication—intended or not—that his own children did not love him. But mixed with the anger was a complementary compassion for the brother who was "drinking himself to death in an empty house in Weston." A few months later he woke in the middle of the night, sensed that something was terribly wrong, and drove to Weston, where he found Fred in the throes of acute alcoholism. He rushed him to the hospital at Yale, where Dr. William Winternitz, Mary's younger brother, took charge of the case.

Clouds were hovering over the house on Cedar Lane as well. In the fall of 1962, Mary Cheever took a part-time job teaching English at Briarcliff College nearby. She was hired, Dean Kenneth Shelton assured her, for her own wit and intelligence and integrity, not because she was John Cheever's wife. Though the job paid only a few thousand dollars a year, about enough to cover Iole's occasional domestic services, it gave Mary a sense of herself as a person of value. Teaching "saved my life," she said in retrospect. She was an exceptionally gifted teacher. Raphael Rudnik remembers accompanying her to class one day and being struck at her easy rapport with students who obviously worshiped her. She rapidly earned the

admiration and respect of her colleagues as well: they recognized
in her a professional, and a good one. Invigorated by the college
surroundings, she made new friends, took yoga lessons, and started
to write poetry in earnest.

John viewed his wife's career with scorn and resentment. Sensitive about his lack of education, he thought most academics were
"bitter and ugly" people. At one party, he threw a glass of whiskey
at Mary's department chairman, who was advocating a libertarian-
ism Cheever found odious. He also thought it ridiculous that the
family should in any way be inconvenienced while Mary instructed Briarcliff's Megans and Betsys—most of them, in his opinion, debutantes of limited intellectual capacity—in the mysteries of
freshman composition and creative writing. It was one thing to
teach good students and be properly compensated for it, but why,
he asked her in front of others, why should she waste her time
teaching at an eighth-rate college? "Now, John," she replied, "it's
a fifth-rate college and you know it."

Both of them used humor to smooth over arguments, but tensions were building in the marriage. Perhaps as a consequence of
his drinking, John was troubled with spells of impotence. They
sought counseling for the problem, but nothing seemed to help. In
due course each of them became convinced that the other was not
interested. In a poem, Mary recounted how in a dream people

> young and old can lie naked
> side by side in a single bed
> each one believing he or she alone
> wants to make love.

Both of her parents, according to Susan, sought lovers outside the
home. In any event, John became convinced that Mary was unfaithful to him. "If she does not take a lover," he thought to himself, "she
will be a fool. If she does and I find out, I will wring his neck."

For vicarious amusement, he conjured up dream girls like the
one in his 1961 story "The Chimera." This imaginary creature
(named Olga) appears miraculously to a henpecked husband one
evening after dinner. A waltz begins to play, and there she is,
dark-haired, olive-skinned, just in from California on the train and
sorely in need of his "love, strength, and counsel." Soon Olga
proves unfaithful herself and disappears, but the husband is not
desolated. Since he had invented Olga, what was there to keep him

from inventing others—"dark-eyed blondes, vivacious redheads with marbly skin, melancholy brunettes, dancers, women who sang, lonely housewives?" In another story, "An Educated American Woman" (1963), Cheever took a more direct swipe at his wife's busy calendar. In the story, Jill Chidchester Madison, a graduate of one of the best women's colleges, devotes herself so wholeheartedly to community and educational causes that she neglects her husband and child. In the end, the child falls ill with pneumonia and dies. Mary knew what the story was about. "I did go to one or two meetings of the League of Women Voters," she remarked, "but I do think he should not have killed the little boy."

In the Cheevers' own very literary family, children and adults alike sometimes read aloud after dinner. As a regular weekly ritual, the clan foregathered in the living room at five o'clock on Sunday afternoons to recite poems they had memorized during the previous week. Ben, at seven, was reciting Robert Frost. Despite such pleasant family entertainments, an undercurrent of sarcasm ran beneath the dinner-table conversation. And for a time at least, John was dissatisfied with the progress of his two older children.

Susie, in adolescent rebellion, was unhappy at the Masters School in Dobbs Ferry. Her father used to give her books to read, books not in the regular school curriculum—Stendhal, Flaubert, Dumas, Dickens, Hemingway, Fitzgerald, Bellow's *Augie March*—and then keep her up late at night talking about them. The next day in English class, almost inevitably, she would argue with her English teacher. Occasionally Cheever tried to play the stern disciplinarian. When Susie brought home news that she was on probation, he was upset. When she announced that she didn't care, he was furious. Considering her father's hopes for her as a potential debutante, it did not help that she rarely had dates. When a boy did come to the door, her father welcomed him effusively and told him to keep her out as late as they wanted. She felt as if he were selling off the homely daughter.

In reaction, Susie sought ways to declare her independence. She persuaded her disappointed parents to remove her from the Masters School and send her to the somewhat less social Woodstock Country School in Vermont, where she improved both grades and attitude enough to be admitted to Pembroke. In college she took up the classical guitar and started wearing serapes. Summers she worked as a maid at the inn in Wauwinet, as a clerk at Macy's, and as a teacher of the illiterate poor in Alabama. Charles Shapiro from

Briarcliff College, leader of the group that went to Alabama, remembers Susie as extremely intelligent and biting in her wit.

Like his parents before him, Cheever was sensitive to the least hint of unmanliness in his sons. At Scarborough, Ben had one friend with effeminate manners. "My father hated him," he recalls. "He'd much have preferred my hanging around with the kids who broke into candy machines." In Ossining, John was annoyed by Ben's high early-adolescent voice. "Speak like a man," he used to command him. Once when Ben was sweeping the floor he angrily snatched the broom away. Sweeping was woman's work. Man's work was outdoors, clearing land and splitting wood. At twelve or thirteen, Ben came in from a spell of such yard work at fifty cents an hour and climbed into the detergent bubble bath his mother had run for him. John happened by and saw the boy up to his neck in bubbles. "Who do you think you are?" he roared. "A movie star?" When Ben went off to prep school at Loomis, his father forbade him to take his teddy bear along.

Despite incidents like these, Ben always regarded his father as a good parent. "He could be so loving, so concerned, so solicitous, so entertaining." He used to take Ben fishing, and later the two of them went kayaking on the Croton River. When Ben tackled Dostoyevsky's *The Idiot*, his father began calling him Myshkin, affectionately. And he read Ben all of Joyce's *Dubliners* aloud. Ben recalls especially "The Dead," with the snow, "general all over Ireland," falling lyrically at the end and leaving both father and son limp with tears.

Certain paternal duties proved too much for Cheever, however. One day Ben, fifteen, managed to get his penis stuck in a zipper, and nothing his father could devise would extricate him. Amid general chaos at the house on Cedar Lane, the boy finally freed himself. As the years wore on, the pattern of dependency was reversed, and Ben found he could sometimes be of service to his father, a man brilliant in his art and physically tough, yet barely competent to deal with some of the simplest problems of daily life. On a ski trip with his father and Alwyn Lee, for instance, the teenager showed Cheever how to turn on the tap water in the railway sleeping car. "Isn't it wonderful that I have this son who can figure things out for me?" his father said. He had a way of making people feel needed, and of presenting himself as the one in need. "Don't you wish I was different?" he sometimes asked Ben. "Don't you wish I didn't drink?" Eager to please, Ben invariably

said no, that was all right, whatever his father did was fine with
him.

It was different with Federico, called Picci as a lad and then
simply Fred. Fred was the apple of his father's eye, and he could
say what he pleased. One of his earliest memories is of sitting in
his father's lap at dusk, watching the blackbirds wheel by on their
way to the Hudson to feed on insects. Whenever harm threatened
the boy, John was terrified for him. When the boy came down with
a fever, his father spent the night on the floor of his room. When
Cheever spilled both his son and himself in a bicycle accident in
Nantucket, the damage was minor but both were traumatized. Fred
was well along into adolescence before he learned to ride a bike. As
he grew older, though, Fred asserted himself with his father. In the
corner of the downstairs living room–dining room at Cedar Lane
there is a wooden chair. "That chair was broken twice," Mary said,
"when Fred hit his father in it." It was not that they were enemies,
not that at all. Fred loved his father very much and could hardly
have felt closer to him. But he was frustrated and angered by his
father's refusal to take control of himself. And he was in the house
for the worst of it, after his older siblings were packed off to prep
school and college.

In addition to liquor, Cheever was victimized by phobias. The
worst of these was his fear of bridges, a fear that for many years
kept him from crossing the Tappan Zee Bridge to visit such old
friends as Eddie Newhouse and Don Ettlinger in Rockland
County. In his 1961 "The Angel of the Bridge," this phobia is
associated with a more general condemnation of the ills of modernity: freeways and monotonous housing developments and continuous piped-in music. "It was at the highest point in the arc of a
bridge," the narrator reveals, "that I became aware suddenly of the
depth and bitterness of my feelings about modern life, and the
profoundness of my yearning for a more vivid, simple, and peacea-
ble world." But what could he do? Go back to St. Botolphs, sit
around in a Norfolk jacket, and play cribbage in the firehouse?
Instead he goes on as best he can until one day, on the Tappan Zee,
he picks up a young girl hitchhiker who fetches a small harp from
a waterproof case and sings him across the bridge and into "blue-
sky courage, the high spirits of lustiness, an ecstatic sereneness"
with the folk song "I Gave My Love a Cherry That Had No Stone."

No such miraculous cure rid Cheever of his phobia. In his fiction
he repeatedly attempted to construct bridges between the gro-

tesque real world and the potentially unifying universe of his dreams. In "A Vision of the World" (1962), he explores this obsessive compulsion to forge a link between the two worlds. The troubled protagonist beholds a beautiful woman standing in a field of wheat, wearing the clothes his grandmother might have worn. Like the chimera in the backyard and the folksinger on the bridge, she is an apparition, surely, and yet she seems "more real than the Tamiami Trail four miles to the east, with its Smorgorama and Giganticburger stands." The woman speaks an incomprehensible language, then the rain on the roof wakes the narrator from his dream, and as the healing waters descend he sits up in bed and exclaims to himself, "Valor! Love! Beauty! Virtue! Compassion! Splendor! Kindness! Wisdom! Beauty!" The words take on the colors of the earth, and his hopefulness mounts until the litany, together with the vision, render him "contented and at peace with the night."

Happy endings or not, stories like these confessed to Cheever's deepening dissatisfaction with modern life: its pervasive materialism and weakening ethical standards, its standardized and cheapened mass culture, above all its excessive mobility and rootlessness. No angel appeared to halt his addiction to alcohol, cure his phobias, ameliorate his self-disgust. To some degree, he transferred the self-criticism that cropped up regularly in his journals to a fictional condemnation of contemporary existence in its ugliest manifestations. Throughout 1962 and much of 1963 he was working on *The Wapshot Scandal*, his darkest book and the one in which he most vigorously excoriates the world he inhabits. Writing the novel only intensified his depression. "I can't ever recall having been so discouraged and melancholy," he observed in September 1962, and this "absurd melancholy" persisted up to and beyond publication of the novel in January 1964.

This depression was so powerful as to lead him to the brink of suicide. "After the *Scandal*," as he told Lehmann-Haupt, "I was really in trouble, really suicidal." Despairing, he got up in the night, sat on the edge of the bathtub, and chain-smoked into the early hours. Then in his fitful sleep he dreamed he heard Hemingway saying, "This is the small agony. The great agony comes later." He disposed of all the shotgun shells and tried to sweat out his malaise by scything the woods. Then, still seeking equanimity, he flew off to Rome for two weeks alone. The family, he felt sure, was happy to see him go.

Cheever's lingering despondency was the more ominous in the light of the novel's success. *The Wapshot Scandal*, generally well reviewed, sold over thirty thousand copies in the first two months. Earlier in life, when his cafard (or cockroach) visited him, there was almost always an assignable reason. The dark eminence would surely go away, he thought, if he made some money, if he finished the novel, if he had a house of his own to live in, if he won the award. It was worse when all these things came to pass and the depression hung on, stronger than ever. What did he want? Was there anything that could banish his cafard?

Though *The Wapshot Scandal* is a sequel to *The Wapshot Chronicle* and deals with the same characters, it is in tone a very different book. As George Garrett put it, "the sins of *Chronicle* are original sin. *Scandal* moves inexorably toward the end of the world." The difference is nowhere more striking than in the almost total absence, in the later novel, of those "odors of the world, the flesh and the devil" that proliferated in the earlier one. Love has also disappeared, or almost so, giving way to lust. Melissa Wapshot, obsessively conscious of her mortality, seduces Emile the grocery boy and takes him off to live in carnality and unhappiness in Rome. Moses, devastated, resorts to drink and casual fornication. Dr. Cameron, Coverly's boss at the missile center, contemplates apocalyptic explosions without flinching, but he has treated his own son monstrously and can only feel the chill go off his bones in the arms of his high-priced Italian prostitute. Cousin Honora also finds her way to Italy in an escape from the Internal Revenue Service, to which she has never paid a penny in taxes. She comes home to St. Botolphs to die, however. It is where she belongs, but it is not what it used to be.

Faith is fading even in St. Botolphs. As the *Chronicle* begins and ends on Independence Day, two Christmases in the old town frame the *Scandal*. At the beginning, Mr. Applegate, the rector of Christ Church, receives a delegation of carolers in his home. He has been troubled by religious doubt, but as the carolers sing he "felt his faith renewed, felt that an infinity of unrealized possibilities lay ahead of them, a tremendous richness of peace, a renaissance without brigands, an ecstasy of light and color, a kingdom! Or was this gin?" For Mr. Applegate drinks. In fact, he is quite drunk while delivering the Mass on Christmas Eve to a congregation of four (Coverly included). In a burst of rhetoric he presents much of the novel's message.

"Let us pray for all those killed or cruelly wounded on thruways, express-ways, freeways and turnpikes. Let us pray for all those burned to death in faulty plane-landings, mid-air collisions and mountainside crashes. Let us pray for all those wounded by rotary lawn mowers, chain saws, electric hedge clippers and other power tools. Let us pray for all alcoholics mea-suring out the day that the Lord hath made in ounces, pints and fifths. . . . Let us pray for the lecherous and the impure. . . ."

At this point, the other worshipers leave and Coverly is alone with Mr. Applegate to his amen.

Cheever does not end his novel there, but follows Coverly as he goes back to the Viaduct House to liberate brother Moses from the grip of Dionysus and the arms of the lascivious widow Wilston. The next day, following cousin Honora's old custom, Coverly and Betsey serve Christmas dinner to residents of the Hutchins Insti-tute for the Blind. Once more Leander has the last word, in the form of a scrap of paper found in his wallet after he drowned: "Let us consider that the soul of man is immortal, able to endure every sort of good and every sort of evil." The sentiment is reassuring—it was one Cheever often recited—but it can hardly justify the wider universe of the novel, where evil so consistently predominates over good.

One reviewer of *Scandal* thought the author's epiphanies too fac-ile, another noted inconsistencies in character and tone, and as with *Chronicle* there were reservations about the seemingly haphazard structure. What Cheever was after was a structural pattern that suited his own fragmented times. Linear narrative no longer made sense in a world "distinguished by its curvatures." Conventional narrative was designed "to express a sense of consecutiveness," but he did not regard life that way. So he reached out for something new. *The Wapshot Scandal,* he once said, "was an extraordinarily complex book built around non sequiturs." And in his notes for the novel, "I think of the book as a collection of forlornities. . . . I think of the book as a painting, there is the opening, the overture and then the eye moves from the snow storm to [Coverly's missile base] Talifer. From Talifer to [the suburb where Moses and Melissa live] Proxmire. The Chronicle was all thrust and this is very different. This is your world and I have come to tell you so; I am your prophet." If a prophet, then a Jeremiah with a warning not to be ignored.

In *The Wapshot Scandal* Cheever set out to paint nothing less than a terrifying picture of the times. "I look for a simple world," he commented in his notes,

and I seldom find it. I look for resolute and homely faces, good health and the authority of decision, for wit, vitality and good cheer, but instead I find timidity, the half-formed and sometimes the malformed, suspiciousness, cupidity, and lust. And so I think I see here in these crowds, and in my heart the deep confusions of my nation and my time.

For some time he had integrated dream and reality in his fiction, and now dream turned to nightmare. In his spare time Coverly feeds the poems of Keats into a computer to discover the frequency of word use, and to his amazement (and in defiance of all mathematical logic) the words come out in a comprehensible verse of subterranean darkness:

> Silence blendeth grief's awakened fall
> The golden realms of death take all
> Love's bitterness exceeds its grace
> That bestial scar on the angelic face
> Marks heaven with gall.

"It is as if Marquand had suddenly been crossed with Kafka," a surprised reviewer wrote. The surprise was not really justified, for it was past time for readers to recognize that Cheever's writing constituted "something unique in contemporary fiction," completely outside the *New Yorker* pattern or any other. "The terrible vision you have is of our daily lives in their emotional squalor and incongruity," Cowley wrote him after reading the novel in galleys. "You're getting angrier and angrier."

As the book was coming off the press in December 1963, the simmering antagonism between Cheever and *The New Yorker* came to a boil. The Christmas holidays with their annual financial burden tended to trigger the author's resentment about the prices paid for his fiction. Besides, he felt himself in a strong bargaining position. He'd completed his novel, *Time* was doing a cover story on him, and he had just submitted his magnificent story "The Swimmer" to the magazine. So he went down to New York and asked Maxwell for a raise. Maxwell did not have the power to give him one, and explained that he was already getting the highest fiction rate. A disgruntled Cheever went downstairs to a pay phone and called Candida Donadio, who was not then his agent but was over-joyed to hear from him, and asked if she could do better. A few minutes later Donadio called back. *The Saturday Evening Post,* which had recently lured John O'Hara away on a similar basis, was pre-pared to offer him twenty-four thousand dollars for a first-look contract and four stories a year.

This was about five times what *The New Yorker* was then paying him, so Maxwell and editor William Shawn could hardly match that in their counteroffer. "A key to the men's room and all the bread and cheese I could eat," John Cheever characterized it. He reached an agreement with the magazine, nonetheless. He prom-ised to give *The New Yorker* a first look at his stories in return for his usual rate on acceptance and a tacit understanding that if he wanted to submit any of his fiction elsewhere, the editors would look the other way. On this basis the relationship staggered on, though in the years ahead Cheever was to publish twice as many stories in other magazines, including the *Post, Esquire,* and *Playboy,* as he did in *The New Yorker.* Of his 121 stories in the magazine, 5 appeared in 1964, and only 6 more during the remaining seventeen years of his life.

RUSSIA

1964

1964 was in almost every respect an extremely important year in Cheever's life. He published not one but
two books: *The Wapshot Scandal* in January and *The
Brigadier and the Golf Widow* in October. In March he
appeared on the cover of *Time* magazine, for the first
time emerging as a public figure. The surge of accomplishment carried him on trips to Italy and Hollywood and Russia. In Hollywood he met and fell half
in love with actress Hope Lange. In Russia he got to
know John Updike and conceived an admiration for a
people who—it seemed to him—valued their artists
far more than most Americans.

The *Time* cover story acquainted Cheever with

some of the costs of fame. To begin with, he resisted the idea. "I don't want the story," he said. "We didn't ask," the *Time* people said. Still the project might have foundered except for the involvement of Time-Life editor Alwyn Lee, a gregarious and witty Australian who was one of Cheever's closest friends and drinking companions. Cheever felt he could trust Lee, but he was not prepared for the persistence of the magazine's editors, researchers, and photographers. With characteristic Yankee diffidence, he refused to unburden himself on intimate matters. His technique with interviewers, during those years, was to try to get them drunk, or failing that, to involve them in some form of exercise that made question-asking and note-taking virtually impossible. "Cheever doesn't really like to talk about himself but about other people," *Time* correspondent Andrew Kopkind reported. "When I would say, 'Now we really must talk about you,' he would leap up and say something like 'Let's go tobogganing.'" In fact, Lee and another *Time* staffer did accompany Cheever and his son Ben on a ski trip to Stowe, where they followed him around the trails. Meanwhile, another editor had been at work "asking indecent questions" in Ossining. Altogether it was far from a pleasant experience.

Faced with Cheever's uncommunicativeness, the magazine's reporters widened their contacts with family, friends, neighbors—anyone who could claim acquaintance with the author. They promised to leave his brother, Fred, alone, something Cheever insisted upon, and then broke the promise. Clearly, everyone was fair game. One reporter came to see the Robert Penn Warrens in Connecticut. "I remember that son of a bitch," Warren said. "He was after smut." Another tracked down Fax Ogden in Delaware. "What have you done wrong?" Ogden inquired of Cheever by telephone. "Someone from *Time* magazine is coming to ask questions about you in half an hour."

The legman in Westchester concentrated on Cheever's drinking and sex life. One neighbor was fairly bursting with gossip when —as she thought—this *Time* man finally came to call. She started in immediately with tales of martinis at noon, nude swimming, and other morally reprehensible behavior. When she paused for breath, the man said, "Lady, I'm your Fuller Brush representative." Or so, at least, Cheever claimed in reconstructing the story.

It was not only shyness that made him distrust public recognition. He felt strongly that it was wrong to court publicity, and tried as far as possible to avoid the appearance of calling attention to himself. As Lee noted in the *Time* story, he was "not a writer with a public personality to flourish and exploit, such as Hemingway or Norman Mailer." The story's strongest emphasis fell on Cheever as a kind of latter-day moralist who envisioned the individual "at the center of a system of obligations." Let them neglect these obligations, and his characters might find themselves punished by a black-magical metamorphosis into some creature or object less than human. Cheever would have denied the designation of moralist—he passed judgment on no one, he liked to believe—but certainly his fiction is full of the struggle to build and then obliterate boundaries, and those who try to escape are sometimes consigned to a modern variation of the inferno. The best thing about Lee's story, working with bits and pieces as they trickled in from *Time* staffers, was that it derived from his own intimate acquaintance with John and Mary Cheever. He portrayed them as likable and talented human beings, as complementary yet very different people. "Ovid in Ossining," as the cover story was entitled in an unhappy burst of alliteration, was much better than it might have been.

While the March 17, 1964, *Time* introduced his name and picture to a large audience (the cover portrait showed Cheever at his desk, with the family's pet doves in a cage beyond), the story did him little good with the critics. To the critical establishment, almost all of it liberal, *Time* was associated with upper-middle-class readers and their rather comfortable Republican viewpoints. Appearing on the cover was as likely to harm as to help a literary reputation.

Cheever himself was wary of succumbing to his new celebrity. People kept sending him copies of the cover to sign, and that was flattering, but he knew that *Time* had no power to canonize. In his journals he imagined Susie dressing him down. "Don't think anybody's impressed . . . ," he fancied her saying. "They put all kinds of people on the cover, including broken-down ballplayers and crooks." Soon thereafter two Frenchmen from *Réalités* called for an interview and he consented. "My fatuous vanity," he accused himself, "made their attentions irresistible." Whatever others might think of him, Cheever was rarely free of the harshest criticism from within.

Another avenue to fame opened up early in 1964 when Alan J. Pakula and Robert Mulligan purchased screen rights to the two Wapshot novels for "a moderate amount—about $75,000." The film was never made, though Pakula-Mulligan hired Tad Mosel to com-

bine the two books into one screenplay and did some tentative
casting: Spencer Tracy for Leander, Katharine Hepburn for
Honora, and the then little-known Robert Redford for Moses.
Cheever went to Hollywood to close the deal, and that trip was to
have long-range consequences, for it was there that he met Hope
Lange, then married to Pakula. To get acquainted the Pakulas had
a dinner party for Cheever, and Hope remembers being terribly
nervous, trying to fix dinner and to make sure everything went
smoothly. Cheever arrived rather buttoned up, "with his New
England mumble and suit on." Then she ushered everyone to the
basement recreation room, put *Guys and Dolls* on the record player,
and that did the trick. Cheever sloughed off his carapace of reserve
and they had a wonderful evening.

Among other things he and Hope shared a background in Greenwich Village. She grew up there with her brother and two sisters,
supported by the restaurant—the Minetta Tavern in Washington
Square—run by and named after her mother. "When we'd all been
fed," as Hope puts it, her mother closed the restaurant. The Langes
were a warmly affectionate clan, as free with hugs and kisses as the
Cheevers of Massachusetts were chary of them. John was attracted
by her outgoing nature and found that they could laugh together,
and of course she was very beautiful. He was, in short, smitten. He
was staying at the Beverly Hills Hotel, with Hope's brother David
assigned to drive him around. He got all shined up when he knew
he'd see Hope, David recalls, and started shaving twice a day. "He
was like a kid with an enormous crush." It was as if one of his
dream girls had materialized: married and hence not available, but
certainly interested in him and willing to show it.

David Lange, then in his early twenties and working for Pakula-
Mulligan, saw in Cheever everything he'd ever wanted in a father—a New England Yankee, a writer of consequence, witty and
charming. For his part, Cheever regarded David as a glamorous son
of Hollywood. Half jokingly he proposed to fix him up with Susie,
though he knew the competition was tough: David was dating
Natalie Wood. Cheever was not immune to the appeal of the star
system. On his last night in California, David was driving him
around Beverly Hills, pointing out the homes of famous actors.
When he indicated Glenn Ford's house, Cheever immediately said,
"Let's go see him. I've got to have something to tell the kids." It was
already midnight, but David called Ford up and they went over for
a visit that turned out to be pretty dull, since both actor and author

were basically shy people. The next day, on the way to the airport, Cheever stopped by the Pakulas' to say goodbye to Hope. Honk honk went the auto-horn doorbell, but Hope was out. So he said goodbye to Gus the dog and flew home to Westchester.

There his unshakable cafard awaited him. In May he went into New York City to have lunch with an old school friend. Life had not gone well with the friend; he was dissatisfied with his children and unsuccessful in his work. "The only jobs I could get," he said, "are traveling jobs. A day in Topeka, a day in Chicago, a day in San Francisco, and Johnny, I'm too old to spend the rest of my life in hotel rooms." When they parted, Cheever spent the rest of the day with "the lovely wife of a jealous friend." This should have brightened his spirits, but it did not. Instead he castigated himself for taking so much pleasure in being loved. Wasn't that really a form of self-love?

He and Mary were planning a trip to Italy in June, but not even that prospect pleased. "You don't want to go to Italy with me," she said, and he admitted it was true. She seemed unfriendly much of the time, he thought. But one magical night when a thunderstorm struck and all the lights went out, he and Mary dined by candlelight, and made love on the lawn afterward, and for the moment all the darkness left his heart and mind. Eventually they traveled together to Italy, along with Alwyn and Essie Lee, and visited Alan and Lucy Moorehead at Port'Ercole. Despite the good company and the beautiful countryside, Cheever felt "homesick and uneasy" overseas. He was glad to come home again.

On July 18 *The New Yorker* printed "The Swimmer," a story they'd been holding for midsummer publication. Almost immediately Frank Perry was on the telephone proposing a film version. Cheever had met Perry during the recent trip to Hollywood and tried to interest him in a film about the lives of expatriates in Rome. Sitting poolside at the Beverly Hills Hotel, he sketched out scenes for the movie lifted from his stories. Perry was at least mildly interested in the idea—later he bought screen rights to "Clementina"—but he was bowled over by "The Swimmer." He and his wife, Eleanor, the team that made the prize-winning *David and Lisa*, secured an option and started work on an adaptation right away.

The Perrys were invited to lunch at Ossining to seal the bargain, and Frank Perry remembers being struck by two things about Cheever. The first was his drinking. Then a serious drinker himself, Perry recognized a pattern of behavior in his host that he associated with dependence on liquor. The second was his extraordinary vulnerability. Cheever seemed to him underprotected, almost naked, lacking in insulation.

More than anything else he wrote, "The Swimmer" is pervaded by this sense of vulnerability. Neddy Merrill, the protagonist of the tale, has lost everything: his job, his wife and four beautiful daughters, his friends, his youth. It is drink that has led to his ruin, and he emerges on the page directly out of Cheever's own self-disgust. Even his fondness for swimming parallels that of his creator, as he sets out one hung-over Sunday to negotiate the eight miles between the Westerhazys' pool and his own home in Bullet Park by way of a series of swimming pools, "a quasi-subterranean stream" meandering across the county that he calls the Lucinda River, after his wife. At first Cheever only hints at Teddy's plight. "He might have been compared to a summer's day, particularly the last hours of one, and while he lacked a tennis racket or a sail bag the impression was definitely one of youth, sport, and clement weather." But as he traverses the watery stretches of the fifteen pools ahead and consumes half a dozen drinks, it becomes increasingly clear that things have gone wrong. He has a terrible time crossing Route 424, barefoot among the "beer cans, rags, and blowout patches." He grows cold and weak as day lengthens into twilight, and the pool owners grow increasingly less glad to see him. His former mistress, Shirley Adams, lets him know she is not alone and refuses him a drink. Then it is night, and the stars above are those of Andromeda, Cepheus, and Cassiopeia. "What had become of the constellations of midsummer?" he wonders, and begins to cry.

At the last two pools, he resorts to a hobbled sidestroke and hangs on to the side of the pool for support. He has swum the county, but is stupefied with exhaustion. He arrives at his own house to find it dark, with a rain gutter hanging down over the front door like an umbrella. Since the house is locked, he "shouted, pounded on the door, tried to force it with his shoulder, and then, looking in at the windows, saw that the place was empty." So "The Swimmer" ends. It is a powerful story, and a moving one. Cheever read it in public more than anything else in his fiction. And it ranks, with "The Enormous Radio," as one of his two most anthologized and analyzed stories.

In talking about "The Swimmer," Cheever invariably stressed how difficult it was to write. He completed most of his stories in about three days, he said, but spent two months on "The Swimmer." "There were 150 pages of notes for 15 pages of story." Originally he had in mind a simple story about Narcissus. But it seemed absurd to limit the tale to a tight mythological plot. So he let Neddy Merrill free and "he swam in an immense number of pools—thirty of them!" Then he started to narrow it down "and something began happening. It was growing cold and quiet. It was turning into winter. Involuntarily. It was a terrible experience, writing that story." He was proud of having written it, but it left him—"not only I the narrator, but I John Cheever"—feeling dark and cold himself. It was the last story he wrote for a long time.

"The Swimmer" has received as much critical attention as anything Cheever wrote, and deservedly so, since it is beautifully crafted and carries a powerful emotional charge. Usually he made fun of such critical commentary. The story had one Marxist interpretation and two Freudian ones, he asserted, all three of them nonsensical. The Marxist version: "See, in Capitalist America everybody has a swimming pool, and what are they? Unhappy." Freudian Number One: the Narcissus myth, wherein Neddy courts his own image and finds death. Freudian Number Two: "the water is quite naturally mother," and Neddy's quest is for a return to the womb.

In addition to "The Swimmer" and the title story, *The Brigadier and the Golf Widow* contained the two best Italian stories, as well as "The Angel of the Bridge" with its indictment of the ills of modernity, "The Ocean" with its attack on inhumane business standards, and a number of stories—"The Music Teacher" and "An Educated American Woman" among them—in which the battle between the sexes is bitterly joined. Despite the upbeat ending of "A Vision of the World," with its litany of heartening abstractions, the collection as a whole struck a note of melancholy. There were comic passages, as Orville Prescott pointed out in his *New York Times* review, but dismay was "omnipresent." Prescott admired the subtlety of Cheever's craft in depicting suburban discontents. Others who wrote of similar characters and similar settings did so "in cruder terms, in terms of satirical exaggeration or of sociological documentation." Cheever's fiction was not like that at all. Instead he "smiles, sighs and suggests a whole way of life (a hollow and uneasy one) with a few delicate touches. Why, he seems to ask, are well-educated, prosperous people living in the midst of comforts undreamed of even by their own parents so often lost and adrift?"

Cheever was in Russia when *The Brigadier* came out—he had

been in Italy when both *Wapshot* books were published—and Russia was a revelation. He made the trip as part of an exchange program worked out by the State Department with the Soviet Writers Union. William H. Luers, then a political officer in the American embassy in Moscow, helped negotiate the exchanges that brought Edward Albee and John Steinbeck to visit Russia in 1963, and Cheever and John Updike in 1964. Cheever, traveling alone, came first, and Updike followed later, with their visits overlapping for ten days or so.

When he got off the plane in Moscow, Cheever heard what appeared to be a chant of "cheep, cheep, cheep" from the crowd. It was a delegation of Russian writers, led by Vassily Aksyonov, calling out "Cheever, Cheever" in welcome. He was delighted, and responded warmly to his Russian colleagues. Aksyonov was impressed by his vitality and his wonderful sense of humor. "He spoke to us as colleagues," Aksyonov said. "He could identify with the problems—not the political problems, but the artistic problems—of young writers starting out."

Without question it was Tanya Litvinov who became Cheever's closest friend in Russia. The daughter of the diplomat Maxim Litvinov and the English writer Ivy Litvinov, Tanya had recently finished translating most of the stories in *The Enormous Radio and Other Stories* for a Russian edition of Cheever's work and was, naturally, eager to meet the author. He was assigned like all eminent visitors to an official "minder," Giorgio Breitburd, but soon managed to slip away from Giorgio and his tight schedule to spend more time with Tanya. They first met at a luncheon gathering of *Inostzannaya Literatura* ("Foreign Literature") magazine, which had published a couple of his stories in translation. "Hidden behind a bowl of fruit the dreadful symmetry of which no one cared to disturb," she remembers, the two of them carried on a sotto voce conversation while from the head of the table reverberated the "official boom-booming" about Soviet-American Relations, Culture, Common Aims, Literature in Its Humanitarian Aspect, and so forth. The head of the magazine, droning on about the deficiencies of abstract art, was speaking with indignation of a capitalist in the West who collected pictures made by driving a car over a canvas when Cheever "perked up and asked for the capitalist's address. Nobody seemed to mind."

The next day he and Tanya had lunch at the Hotel Ukraine, where Cheever was staying. It was a high-rise building, sprawling and ornamental, whose lobby smelled like a barnyard. He called it Mother, or Mama Ookraenya, because he could spy the building from afar and "run under its apron when feeling lost or forlorn." They discussed some of the difficulties of translation. Tanya wanted to know if the man in "Torch Song" escaped the ghoulish girl, but Cheever would not say. "He left it beautifully ambiguous," Tanya realized, while "translation pants for certainties." About more concrete matters he was more helpful. He sketched what an American mailbox looks like, for example, and a taxi meter.

Tanya also went along on Cheever's trip to Kornei Chukovsky's dacha in Peredelkino. Chukovsky (1882–1969), who had "discovered" Cheever and suggested that Tanya do some translations of his stories, was "the grand old man of letters" in Russia. He and Cheever hit it off immediately. Chukovsky said the American reminded him of H. G. Wells in the twenties and brought out a pen-and-ink drawing of Wells to prove it. There was a glow about the room only partly attributable to vodka. "We have no old men in America," Cheever told her as they left. That night, Cheever was supposed to go to the Bolshoi, but he and Tanya stole off and walked and talked for hours. At the zoo she showed him where the iron railings had been widened by children squeezing themselves in for free. Cheever would have tried it himself if she hadn't discouraged the idea. They talked politics too, for Cheever had come to Khrushchev's Moscow and one week later left Brezhnev's. The rapid change in power bewildered him, and in her relief at a bloodless change of government Litvinov prophesied hopefully that this was the way it would be in the future: "*they* will be at each other's throats every four or five years, leaving *us* out of it." That seemed rather a waste of effort, Cheever thought. Eventually she took him home to her flat to meet her husband, two of her daughters, and her dachshund. They shared some tomatoes and a piece of boiled meat.

When the Updikes arrived, Cheever spent much of his time with them. In fact, the two writers came to know each other well only during their ten days together on Soviet soil. To a literary public that sometimes assumes a close tie between them in age, background, style, and subject matter, it is worth noting that Cheever was almost precisely twenty years Updike's senior, that he came from Massachusetts and Updike from Pennsylvania, and that in their fiction Cheever's Shady Hill and Bullet Park resemble Tarbox of Updike's *Couples* only slightly and Brewer of the Rabbit novels not at all, and that no careful reader examining a page of their fiction would be likely to confuse a passage of Cheever's with one of Updike's, excellent as they both are in their different ways.

Because of the age difference and his admiration for Updike, Cheever was able to recognize and reward the younger man's work. He recommended that the prolific and talented Updike be admitted to the National Institute of Arts and Letters. As a 1963 National Book Award judge, he pushed hard and successfully for Updike's *The Centaur*. At the NBA ceremony in the spring of 1964, the Updikes and Cheever—Johns and Marys both—began to get acquainted. The two writers got along well, and so did their wives. Mary Updike looked on Mary Cheever as something of a model of how to cope with marriage to a writing husband. In July, however, Cheever was annoyed when *The New Yorker* printed Updike's story "The Morning" on pages 24 to 26, in advance of "The Swimmer" on pages 28 to 34—even though, as he must have known, the magazine normally ran shorter stories ahead of longer ones.

During their time in Russia, Updike was unaware of any competitive overtones. *The Centaur,* like Cheever's book of stories, had recently been translated into Russian, so that both writers were well known to their hosts and both had brought along a good many copies of their books to distribute as gifts. To the extent that any rivalry surfaced between them, it involved a humorous competition to unload as many of these autographed copies as possible. In almost every respect, both John and Mary Updike were charmed by Cheever. His brisk humor "lit up the potentially gloomy Soviet surroundings" and made October in Moscow "as gay as an April in Paris," Updike said. He communicated a kind of restless energy throughout, pacing crowded rooms and suddenly departing for long walks that struck the Updikes as brave if not foolhardy. In Leningrad, the three of them were left mercifully unattended for a morning, and then—Mary Updike recalls—"we behaved like children let out of school, comparing notes, griping about the system, talking to the bug, gossiping, feeling homesick and missing our children." When they said goodbye to Cheever, the Updikes felt bereft.

Both Updike and Cheever were effective cultural ambassadors, Luers felt, and Cheever the more so because he carried "very little ideological baggage." Lacking these impediments, Cheever was captivated by the Russian people. From Moscow his itinerary took him around the country. Everywhere he saw families on weekend

outings, collecting ferns and flowers. Poets unselfconsciously recited their work, singers sang when asked. He shared with the
Russians he met "a taste for hard liquor, enthusiasm, and demon-
strativeness."

The most demonstrative of all was the flamboyant Yevgeny Yevtushenko. Like a dynamo, the poet enraptured adoring audiences
who came to what were tamely advertised as poetry readings but
actually combined—in Mary Updike's phrase—"the more moving
elements of theater, opera, concert, and church." A matinee idol to
these crowds, Yevtushenko was rarely offstage at any time. He
carried himself like the commanding figure he was. In a Communist society, he was treated like nobility. He and Cheever, very
different in his "muttery Waspish manner," were nonetheless
taken with each other. "I think that John was amused by the bucca-
neer in Yevtushenko," John Updike speculates, "and Zhenya (as we
called him) was engaged by the debonair raffish side of John" (or
Chon, as Zhenya called him). With his quick ear, Cheever soon
developed an imitation of Yevtushenko based on his theatricality
and his ego that could "crack crystal at a distance of twenty feet."
Yevtushenko asked him how many letters he got from readers.
"Maybe ten a week, twelve a week, something like that," Cheever
said. "I get two thousand a day," Yevtushenko said. Still, Cheever
felt a genuine affection for the poet that was not always shared by
his fellow writers in Russia. "Yevtushenko is nothing but a flirt,"
they told Cheever, "in your case, a very successful flirt."

The two most vivid memories Cheever brought back from Russia
were of his final afternoon in Moscow and of his visit to Tolstoy's
home. Yevtushenko took Cheever to a tenement on the outskirts of
Moscow where a young artist and his family lived. The artist
showed Cheever a dozen "brilliant, progressive, and heretical"
paintings. As they left, Yevtushenko exclaimed, "So! He cannot
show his paintings. He cannot sell his paintings. My present to you
is the invincibility of his paintings." Rightly or wrongly, Cheever
came to think that the very restrictiveness of Soviet life was necessary to the Russian people and that only under such oppressive
conditions could they and their art thrive. According to this theory,
which owed something to his own experience, Russians were
happy only when confined and suppressed. Give them freedom and
they would be miserable.

Cheever's most unforgettable moment in Russia came at the end
of a pilgrimage to Yasnaya Polyana, Tolstoy's country estate. The

day did not begin auspiciously. It was a long dreary trip, he had a hangover, and at the estate Russian peasants were picnicking on the great man's grave. Yet when he was ushered into Tolstoy's study, Cheever felt the hair rise on the back of his neck in mystical communion. He fell asleep on the long drive back to Moscow, and awoke just at dusk—his head in the lap of his long-haired female interpreter. Looking out the windows streaked with rain, he could see the streetlights of the city winking on. It seemed the most romantic thing that had ever happened to him, and not because of sexual excitement. If anything, the tableau was that of a little boy, asleep on the backseat, sheltered against the weather by his mother as they drove home at last light.

INWARD

1965-1967

THE trip to Russia was the first of three Cheever made to that country, and he was to travel to Romania and Bulgaria also during the years ahead. Meanwhile the occasional trips to Italy continued, interspersed with journeys to the Caribbean, to Ireland, to Spain, to Egypt, to the Far East. Within the United States as well, he began to travel widely in response to the demands of his developing reputation. During 1965, for instance, he went to Washington twice and to Chicago twice. Simultaneously with this wayfaring and allied with it, he was waging an inner battle to understand and come to terms with himself. In his journal and in his fiction, he repeatedly directed his attention inward. And during the second half-decade of the 1960s, he twice consulted psychiatrists at considerable length about his problems: his compulsive drinking, his persistent phobias, his deteriorating marriage, his confused sexuality.

On the return trip from Russia, Cheever made a brief stop in Berlin for the State Department and there met Paul Moor, an American writer and critic. Moor, an admirer of Cheever's work, phoned him at the Hilton and volunteered to show him around during his stay. They saw a good deal of each other during the next few days, enough at least so that it became clear that Moor lived alone with a French bulldog and had no lady friends. On Cheever's last night in Berlin, he invited Moor up to his room at the Hilton for a nightcap, where he said, unexpectedly, "I've had some very pleasant homosexual experiences." Later Moor came to think that with this remark Cheever was signaling him to take the initiative, but at the time it did not occur to him. John had talked glowingly about Hope Lange throughout the visit, and that placed him, Moor thought, firmly on the heterosexual side of the fence. This must have been what Cheever wanted Moor to think, and what he wanted to think himself as he sat in the departure lounge in Amsterdam. He heard "a thrilling sound"—the sound of high heels on stone. And when he wrote Moor from Ossining, early in February, he told of ice skating and drinking the day before and of the subsequent morning-after blues that would not subside until he imagined "a picturesque cottage" and a beautiful young woman who lived there with him.

From Cedar Lane, Cheever launched into long-range correspondence with his new Russian friends. As a way of introducing them to American life, he sent Tanya Litvinov and Kornei Chukovsky copies of *The New Yorker*. It took Kornei a while to get used to the advertisements in this capitalist magazine. After that he enjoyed "looking at all the girls I'll never kiss, the cars I'll never drive, the sweaters I'll never wear, the shoes which will never pinch my toes, the places I'll never visit and the cemetery in which I'll never lie." Tanya passed her *New Yorker* on to her mother, Ivy, who in due course submitted to the magazine—and had accepted for publication—several stories and sketches of her own.

The regularity with which Cheever received mail from the USSR depended upon the state of relations between the two countries. Never was this more noticeable than at Christmastime. When

U.S.-Russian relations brightened, dozens of cards arrived in Ossining. When they darkened, there were no cards at all. Understandably, Cheever worried that his letters to Russia might cause trouble for those he was writing to. He knew, too, that the U.S. State Department was not entirely pleased with his affection for Russia, its writers, and its people, but he did not suspect what proved to be the truth: that the CIA occasionally intercepted letters he posted to the Soviet Union.

Nor did he have reason for such suspicions, since he was publicly recognized in Washington as one of the nation's leading writers. Late in February he was invited to read to "the literati, cognoscenti and intelligentsia" of Washington under the sponsorship of the Library of Congress. James Dickey, poetry consultant to the library, arranged the program, in which Cheever shared the platform with novelist Reynolds Price. Dickey thought Cheever "very well mannered and gentlemanly," and not at all the sort of person you could get close to on short acquaintance. "You could feel some suppression in him," Dickey thought, "some kind of withdrawn and secretive thing." From Washington, Cheever went to read at Pembroke, where he performed without incident and thus quieted the fears of his daughter, Susan, an undergraduate there, that he might drink too much and disgrace himself.

Next stop was Chicago, where he spent a week working with novelist Richard Stern's creative-writing students and giving a public reading at the University of Chicago. Cheever was "excellent," Stern recalls, and extraordinarily generous into the bargain. Mary came along on this trip, and one evening the Cheevers took the Sterns to the Pump Room for dinner, thereby spending much of what John had earned for his week at the university. From the first, Stern detected the tension between John and Mary. A feeling of unhappiness radiated from Cheever, while his wife countered him with power and sharpness. "I felt defensive for him," Stern remembers. He was also struck by the way Cheever's reticent demeanor contrasted with the openness of his talk. This was especially true of his accent, shoved up into his nose and the upper part of the throat, making a unique patrician sound that clashed with the frankness and sharpness of what was said. Stern thought him a curious mixture of external dignity and internal emotional chaos. With Cheever, he said, "you had that sense that you were living in a duplex." As always when in Chicago, during this trip Cheever saw Saul Bellow, another writer who—like Stern—respected his work and felt keenly aware of his vulnerability.

Mary preceded her husband in returning to Ossining. Riding the train alone back to New York, the assertive Cheever took over. He had been taught as a youth that it was perfectly proper to talk to strangers on trains or planes, and so, as the *Twentieth Century Limited* sped toward New York, he struck up an acquaintance with "a fork-lift manufacturer" and two housewives from Evanston. As Sherry Farquharson—one of the Evanston women—recalls, a rather dapper older man approached their table and asked, politely, "May I join you?" He looked faintly familiar, and then she realized she'd seen his picture in *Time*. So join them he did for cocktails and dinner, followed by lethal Rusty Nails in the club car as the night receded behind them on the silver rails. The next day, she walked along the ramp at Grand Central with the worst hangover of her life.

Shortly thereafter, son Ben, seventeen, produced his own woman-on-the-train incident on his way home from prep school at Loomis. Instructed like his father before him to engage traveling companions in conversation, he began to talk to a woman—a divorcée, as it turned out, in her early thirties. She was friendly, and seemed interested in what he had to say. With no thought of sex in his mind at all, he invited her to come home with him for dinner and to spend the night. He promised to show her around Ossining the following day. John and Mary, meeting the train, were horrified that their son had picked up or been picked up by an older woman. Inclined to believe the worst, they were too well mannered to say anything overtly, though at dinner, Ben noticed, his ordinarily charming father was anything but charming to his new lady friend. And the next morning, when Ben awoke to drive her around town, he found that he was too late. His father had gotten up early and put her on the train himself. The incident, dressed out in full comic regalia, found its way into *Bullet Park*, his novel of 1969.

Cheever had begun work on *Bullet Park* soon after publication of *The Wapshot Scandal*. Stories came to him less easily than in the past, and he devoted much of his time to this novel-in-progress. So he must have been singularly encouraged when he was awarded the American Academy of Arts and Letters' William Dean Howells Medal for *The Wapshot Scandal*. The Howells Medal, awarded for the best work of fiction during a five-year period, had previously been won by Willa Cather, William Faulkner, Eudora Welty, and James Gould Cozzens, among others. Cheever's *Scandal* emerged as the winner in close competition with Katherine Anne Porter's *Ship of Fools* and Saul Bellow's *Herzog*. In reaction, Cheever wrote Bill Maxwell that he thought the award somehow unsuitable. It seemed foolish to try to segregate American fiction into five-year periods. And accepting any honor ran against the grain of the New England reticence he'd grown up with.

But of course he was more pleased than he would admit and happily accepted the award in the ceremony on May 19. In his presentation speech, Ralph Ellison stressed Cheever's duality of vision. Ours has been called a comic age, Ellison observed, for in comedy we recognize our common humanity, and surely "it is easier to protect ourselves from despair with laughter, desperate though it might be, than to surrender to the chaos that we've made of our promise." Cheever's achievement, he went on, was to "have made us aware not only of what our laughter is about, but of that tragic sense of reality, that graciousness before life's complexity which is its antidote."

In accepting, Cheever was characteristically laconic and straight-forward. When the novel was finally completed, he began, his first instinct was to commit suicide. Next he thought of destroying the manuscript, but how then, Mary had asked him, could she explain to the children what he had been doing for the previous four years? "Thus," he concluded, "my concern for appearances accounted for the publication of the novel; my concern for disappearances ac-counted for much of the book itself, and that these disparate mat-ters should have brought me here this afternoon gives me the pleasure most novelists take in drawing together unrelated experi-ence." He took the honor bestowed on him "most seriously," he said, and was "deeply grateful." Then he took his solid-gold medal, "as big as a saucer," and sat down.

In June, Cheever paid his second visit of the year to Washington, this time to attend a White House dinner in the company of John Glenn, Stan Musial, and such other writers as Updike, O'Hara, and Marianne Moore. The guests were served cocktails but only "bug juice" with the dinner. Back in Ossining there were no such restric-tions on alcoholic consumption. One night Cheever got drunk and, while biting into a piece of cold meat, apparently swallowed a dental bridge. For a time, he feared that the contraption might nibble away at him internally, but no complications ensued. He must have passed the bridge, hooks and all.

In September he wrote "The Geometry of Love," his first story in over a year, and sent it to *The New Yorker.* In the story an unhappy husband attempts to counteract the tyrannies of his wife by reducing them to understandable geometrical theorems. The experiment seems to be succeeding, but then he is taken sick. His wife comes to see him, tells him how well he looks, remarks that she wishes *she* "could get into bed for a week or two and be waited on," and goes from the hospital to a restaurant and a movie. It is the cleaning woman who tells her, when she gets home, that her husband has passed away. On the literal level, "The Geometry of Love" does not present a convincing picture of reality. The basic idea—that Euclidean geometry can ameliorate a bad marriage—is preposterous, and whether intentionally or not, the episodes are strung together with a conspicuous lack of coherence. On a Saturday visit to Cedar Lane, Bill Maxwell suggested, gently, that the story had failed. The trouble, he thought, was liquor. The stories were still beautifully written, but they had no point, or so Maxwell felt.

Cheever's fiction was still marketable elsewhere, however. On Monday *The Saturday Evening Post* "took exactly ten minutes" to buy "The Geometry of Love," and paid three thousand dollars. Cheever recounted this anecdote in several letters, with the strong suggestion that the *Post* purchase invalidated Maxwell's judgment. But he did not easily forget the incident, and wondered in his journals if Maxwell might not be right after all.

He ended 1965, however, in a burst of brilliance at the Modern Language Association meeting in Chicago, the annual gathering of university teachers of language and literature. For the occasion the American Studies Association sponsored a program on the relationship of the writer and his culture and produced three novelists to discuss this topic. The three were Norman Mailer, Ralph Ellison, and John Cheever. Mailer was very much in the news through his antiwar pronouncements (we should turn LBJ's picture upside down, he declared at Berkeley) and through the well-publicized domestic battle in which he had stabbed his wife with a knife. In *An American Dream,* his novel that had been serialized in *Esquire,* he seemed to argue that violence was a valid form of experience and an appropriate way of responding, personally and politically, to a corrupt world. "In those days," as Mailer said in 1985, "I took

myself very seriously, and was indeed embattled with the establishment." So he was cast as the star, and Cheever and Ellison as
supporting players for the thousand professors who jammed into
the Red Lacquer Room of the Palmer House to See Live Writers
Perform.

In advance, Cheever regarded the event as a one-on-one confrontation. He joked about going five three-minute rounds with Mailer.
"I'll be wearing white trunks" for the bout, he said. As it happened,
he spoke first, and instead of addressing the topic directly he presented "The Parable of the Diligent Novelist." For him almost
anything could set a story in motion, even a request from a scholarly organization to discuss the relationship between the American
writer and his culture. So it was a story he machine-gunned to the
professoriate in his nervous, elegant, witty, dazzling style, a story
designed to parody Mailer's most recent novel.

The novelist in Cheever's tale, like Stephen Rojack of *An American Dream,* goes through life seeking sensation far and wide. He
goes to a seminary, for example. Then he quits and holes up in a
slum. He rapes and knifes and buggers. He becomes a cop assigned
to Central Park's nether world of criminality and sexual perversion. He takes up international spying and in that role meets his
death when struck down by a taxicab in Krakow. The point of the
parable, clearly, was that the novelist's death/bankruptcy/failure
resulted from his "wretched excess" in chasing after every conceiv-
able experience, legal or illegal. Even writers needed to learn the
value of moderation. Cheever told the story so cleverly and so
engagingly—and it was such a relief, in a convention devoted to
close examination of literary minutiae, to actually hear a story
told—that he left his audience "ablaze with pleasure." The academics loved it, though not many realized that he was satirizing Mailer,
giving him a "friendly kick in the ass," as program organizer Robert F. Lucid put it.

Mailer understood well enough, was mightily annoyed, and generated some "fierce eye contact" as Cheever returned from the
rostrum. When it was his turn to speak, he gripped the microphone
like a bulldog and read a corrosive, dramatic, hit-and-run essay
titled "The Dynamic in American Letters," describing the division
of our literature into two rivers, one of manners, one of the voice
of the people, and both running dry. Mailer like Cheever brought
down the house. Immediately afterward there was more eye contact in which Mailer detected in Cheever an unspoken acknowledg-

ment that he, Cheever, had underestimated his opponent. (Ellison, speaking as usual without notes, was outshone by the two of them, at least on this occasion.) Later Mailer led his fellow writers, along with Lucid, to the Playboy Club, and there the animosity between Cheever and Mailer dissipated with the drinks and their mutual interest in the *Playboy* phenomenon. The novelists did better with the professors than with the Playgirls, who wandered in, sized them up, decided there wasn't a movie producer in the bunch, and wandered out again.

What most struck Cheever was the regularity that *Playboy* owner Hugh Hefner imposed on himself, his club, and his employees. Rigorous rules obtained. Bunnies were not to date customers. The bunny who served him was saving up to cure her father of Parkinson's disease. Every day of the week, there was a set menu. "If this is Tuesday, it must be pot roast." Hefner circumscribed his own existence, too, never going out, always wearing pajamas, living in a kind of aphrodisiacal paradise that was also a sort of prison. The whole pattern mirrored Cheever's concern for order in lives that might otherwise go off the rails.

When Mailer, Robert Lowell, and other writers made their 1966 march on Washington, Cheever stayed in Ossining. He was opposed to the Vietnam War, but not at all sure what to do to end it. If he went to Washington, he speculated, he would probably suffer an attack of agoraphobia and/or acquire a hangover. Besides, he doubted whether demonstrating would serve any useful purpose other than "making a physical declaration of where one stands." Actually he came to know the idealism of the 1960s best through his children. A few years later, Ben was to suffer the consequences of just such a public display against the war as his father declined to make. Meanwhile, both Ben and Susan worked for social justice. Susie, now out of college and—during the regular school year— teaching at a prep school in Colorado, spent the summers of 1965 and 1966 as a volunteer instructor in Mississippi. Ben, deep-voiced and handsome in late adolescence, did social work in the black slums of Ossining and settled on liberal Antioch as his college. His children's determination to serve minority causes had its origins, Cheever liked to think, in their family history. After all, hadn't his great-uncle Ebenezer espoused unpopular abolitionist sentiments and been dragged through the streets of Newburyport?

On the social level as in politics, Cheever was not a joiner. He and Mary never belonged to a country club. On the other hand, he was a charter member of an exceedingly informal organization called the Friday Club. The club was simply a vehicle that enabled certain noncommuting males in the area to get together on Fridays for drinks and lunch and conversation. There were no dues, no rules, and to begin with only three members, but Cheever gave them all titles. Arthur Spear, retired but full of energy, was the Founder. Folksinger and songwriter Tom Glazer was the Treasurer, since he could figure out the tab with some accuracy. Cheever himself was the Membership. Around noon on Fridays the three of them would foregather at one of their homes for canapés and cocktails. (Mary, who regarded the club as yet another excuse for her husband's drinking, was less hospitable than the other wives.) Then they went to one local restaurant or another for lunch. The early favorite was a place run by an ambitious Italian and advertised as the Oldest Seafood House in Croton. (Friday Clubbers kept putting a hyphen between Oldest and Seafood.) An irreverent waitress named Pam fit well into the humor of the group. How was the sole? she'd be asked. "I wouldn't advise it today, dearie," she'd answer. She was designated the Ladies Auxillary. For additional humor the club expanded to take in Alwyn Lee, a wonderful raconteur, and he became the Entertainment. Usually the men did not get home until midafternoon, and sometimes, well fortified with liquor, sallied forth on a hike through the woods and hills behind Cheever's house.

From these modest beginnings the Friday Club grew to as many as a dozen members, including among others writer Bill Rickenbacker, sculptor John Dirks (the son of the man who drew the Katzenjammer Kids, Dirks was to replace Lee, after his death, as the Entertainment), foundation executive Roger Willson, and actor Barrett Clark. Cheever's letter asking Clark to join them on Fridays captured some of the flavor of the club. The organization was "about as exclusive as a telephone booth," Cheever acknowledged, but perhaps Clark would join them for Friday lunch anyway, sometimes.

In the summer of 1966 the Perrys were filming their version of "The Swimmer." It was a difficult film to sell, Frank Perry recalls; his wife Eleanor Perry's script circulated for a year before Sam Spiegel at Columbia Pictures decided to buy in, with Cheever getting sixty thousand dollars for film rights. It was also a difficult film to make, since the story resisted the literal lens of the camera. If he were to do it again, Perry said, he would try to make the movie more suggestive of the undercurrents of myth in the story. Burt Lancaster was signed to play the lead role of Neddy Merrill, and initially both Perry and Cheever thought him somewhat miscast, since he lacked the requisite New England background and idiom. In one scene, for example, Lancaster insisted on reading a line, written "I'm going to send you both a check," as "I'm going to send the both of you a check."

The movie was shot in Westport, Connecticut, where the pools were handsomer and less disturbed by highway noise than those around Ossining. Cheever came to the set only rarely. He was impressed during these visits by the way Lancaster managed to seem successively "lewd, tearful, crucified, boyish and infirm." One day the Perrys arranged for Cheever himself to make a cameo appearance in the film. The scene was a pool party, where he shook hands with Lancaster and bussed actress Janet Landgard. It was not Landgard but another actress, the intelligent and sexy Diana Muldaur, whom Cheever developed a crush on. Muldaur was wearing close-fitting "pool pajamas" during the party scene. "Either they've lowered her neckline since yesterday," a production assistant observed appreciatively, "or they've raised her bust."

At Yaddo in the fall of 1966, Cheever had a brief affair with the composer Ned Rorem. They had first met in 1962, also at Yaddo, when Rorem was hobbled by a broken ankle and Cheever was friendly and solicitous about his injury. During the four-year interim, Rorem had published *Paris Diary* with its explicit revelations about his sex life, and Cheever surely knew about the book. He came up to Rorem's room about nine o'clock one night, rather drunk, and made his overtures. At first the composer was reluctant. He was not particularly attracted physically, but Cheever almost broke his heart, he was so wistful. "I simply have to," he said, and when it was over he was "sentimental about it, like a high school boy," Rorem recalled. During their three-day affair, they made love under the Ping-Pong table, in the woods, in the car. Cheever was extremely ambivalent about revealing their liaison. Once as they drove off together, Hortense Calisher saw them leave. "Never mind, I want everyone to know," Cheever said, and then in the next breath, "but oh my God, what will they think of me?"

The unsatisfactory state of Cheever's marriage continued to trouble him. He saw himself in the role of lover and Mary as the beloved. Often he felt "proud of her beauty, her wit, her intelligence, her originality." Yet at times he thought she seemed to despise him, to treat him as cruelly as the wife in "The Geometry of Love." In seeking to know why, he resisted clinical explanations based on Mary's unhappy childhood. Similarly, he repudiated her belief that he had been crippled by his mother. And, he reasoned, even if an unhappy marriage was "a full time occupation," this did not mean that efforts to shore it up were necessarily hopeless.

Liquor gave him at least as much trouble as his marriage. In the summer of 1965, his doctor—Dr. Ray Mutter—put him on tranquilizers as a substitute for alcohol. But the pills left him feeling as "stagnant as the water under an old millwheel" and he soon reverted to bourbon. He saw himself as engaged in a continuous and unavoidable struggle with drink. "I still fight the booze," he wrote Stern, "but the score seems tied." The battle commenced each morning, when the first or second thing he wanted was a drink. He went to his desk, determined to avoid drinking until noon, but it was not easy to stick to that resolve, with the bottles in the pantry calling out to him. Often he moved the noon deadline up an hour or half hour, and once the drinking was begun, it did not end until bedtime. In correspondence and in journals he chided himself for "the bitter and absolutely perfect circle of drunkenness and remorse" he had fallen into. But such self-criticism did not indicate any real desire to change his ways. On the contrary, it was as if the process of shaming himself gave him leave to continue his dependence on drink. And he was also prone to rationalizations, among them the notion that liquor liberated his imagination and so was necessary to his work.

He was hooked, he knew it, yet he did not want to confront his addiction directly. When he was bothered by a sore foot, he was reluctant to consult Dr. Mutter, for fear that he would diagnose some ailment that could only be treated by abstaining from alcohol. When at Mary's urging he did go to a psychiatrist during the summer of 1966, he insisted—"Unicorn in the Garden" fashion— the problem was hers and not his and that if she would act differently, the marriage would be fine and his phobias and depressions and drunken episodes would simply evaporate.

Dr. David C. Hays, who saw Cheever between early July and mid-September, was inclined to disagree. Cheever made it clear at the start that he opposed the idea of treatment and had consented only to please Mary. It cut against his Yankee grain to dig deep and then declare aloud what one found. Besides, he reasoned, how could anyone who had not read his work possibly know much about him? As a partial remedy he brought Hays an autographed copy of *The Wapshot Chronicle*. In their sessions he alternated between trying to appear as earnest as possible and trying to entertain the doctor. Hays was surprised at how quickly he went to the basics. If he wanted dreams, Cheever gave him dreams, including a highly erotic one in which he seduced the boyfriend of an old girlfriend. If he wanted family life, Cheever gave him the power struggle between his parents, with his mother, "the predatory sex," as the winner, and he gave him too the unnaturally close intimacy he felt for his brother. If he wanted bedroom adventures, Cheever gave him a number of affairs and the report that at home he'd "been allowed to have an orgasm." Usually, he said, Mary ignored him, and he complained when she went off to Treetops. In case Hays might fancy schizophrenia, Cheever spoke of the two John Cheevers, the pretended and the authentic one.

Dr. Hays was both dazzled and dismayed by his patient's performance. Admiring Cheever's wit, he wondered what it was designed to conceal. What lay immediately below the surface was scorn. In a letter to Mary at Treetops, John satirically described his most recent visit to the psychiatrist. Hays beamed down upon him, he wrote, like a dentist with a drill. To brighten the atmosphere, he "regaled" the psychiatrist "with idle and meaningless accounts" of his past. Obviously Cheever was not ready to undergo a thorough psychoanalysis. Besides, Mary thought, he "was too smart for psychiatrists. He had so much quicker a mind, and was verbally so much more sophisticated than they were. He'd talk them up a tree."

Cheever's resistance grew stronger as Hays made it clear he thought John ought to work toward "a characterological change." He refused to attend group sessions. He turned up fifteen minutes late for his own appointments. Finally, on September 15, he announced, "I don't like to talk about any of these things," and that was that. Over such a limited period of time, Dr. Hays could hardly arrive at any definitive understanding of his patient, but he did form a strong impression of what kind of man he was. He felt an excessive dependence on Mary, Hays thought, and the multiple affairs, real and imagined, with women and men alike, were undertaken as a way of reacting against that dependence. He wanted badly to be taken care of and nurtured, and was inclined to transfer his resentment against a neglectful mother to his wife, while attributing to other women who paid attention to him—Sara Spen-

cer, for instance—the qualities of the good mother. His marriage
stood little chance of success, Hays told him, unless he was prepared to change. He wanted to change, Cheever replied, to be more
compassionate and understanding and a better father to his sons.
But most of all, he said, turning the tables once again, "I want a
wife." Wasn't he the injured party?

The one person Cheever was eager to talk about in his meetings
with Dr. Hays was his brother, Fred—the older brother who had
once played "mother, father, brother, and friend" to him and who
had recently gone to pieces in front of him: the only Cheever in
worse shape than he himself. After these psychiatric sessions,
Cheever usually went home and talked things over with Susan.
Hays thought it unusual that he should go to his daughter rather
than to his wife with such confidences.

For years John had been simultaneously encouraging and discouraging Susan's romances. Once when she was invited to a house
party in Bucks County, he told her not to go unless she planned to
sleep with the man who asked her. Otherwise, her date would feel
humiliated, he warned. Yet when she brought beaus to the house,
he objected to any displays of affection. By late 1966 all such ambivalence about Susie's boyfriends faded away when she gave up her
teaching job at Colorado Rocky Mountain School and came to New
York to move in with Rob Cowley. Cowley, divorced and the father
of two young girls, was the only son of Malcolm and Muriel Cowley. He and Susie planned to marry in the spring.

Young Cowley grew up worshiping John Cheever, who used to
visit Sherman, Connecticut, once a year or so to see his parents and
such other friends as Peter and Ebie Blume and Matthew and
Hannah Josephson. A lot of literary folk passed through Sherman,
but Cheever was "something special," Rob thought. When Rob was
a teenager, he sat around the dinner table marveling at this engagingly funny man who spoke as well as he wrote, with wonderful
limpidity and without any "ers" or "ums" or unintended repeti-
tions. He liked Mary Cheever too, whose brilliant humor issued
incongruously from her high little-girl voice. Some of his initial
attraction to Susie, he thinks, stemmed from his admiration for her
parents.

When Rob and Susie decided to marry, Cheever found it hard to
visualize his daughter amid "organ music, white lace, flowers,
cakes, and wine." He also wondered whether he should caution her
against getting married. But whatever the trials of his own mar-

riage, he concluded, it would be "obscene" of him to warn Susie "not to marry, not to love."

On May 6 the wedding took place at St. Mark's in the Bowery church in the East Village. A beautifully catered reception followed in the churchyard, with a massive tent erected for the occasion and green felt carpet spread over the graves of the departed. It was a rainy, windy day, and passing derelicts stared through the isinglass peepholes at the festivities within. Inside there was some tension between the two principal families. As Malcolm Cowley recalled, "the Cheever connection drank their champagne on one side of the tent, while the smaller Cowley contingent sat grouped on the other." The Cowleys thought the wedding too expensive and ostentatious, while the Cheevers were determined to give their daughter the best sendoff they could afford. As it happened, Rob and Susie were then able to begin their married life in extraordinarily elegant surroundings, as tenants at the mansion at Beechwood. With the estate tied up in the courts after the death of Mrs. Vanderlip, the place stood idle, and Zinny Schoales installed the young Cowleys as house sitters. Cheever, visiting for dinner at Beechwood Hall, thought that Rob and Susie should work up from a ranch house to a mansion instead of vice versa. When the newlyweds visited Cedar Lane, Rob was taken aback by the competitive atmosphere around their dinner table. Sarcasms flew, and no one was spared. "In that Bear Pit you had to perform," he decided. "Dullness was not tolerated."

In July 1967, Cheever went to Italy to interview Sophia Loren for *The Saturday Evening Post*. Mary and Fred went along, and the itinerary included Sperlonga and Rome as well as Loren's Naples. Sperlonga he liked. Father and son walked along the beach mornings, and watched the daily soccer game in the evening. In Rome he met an American businessman at a United States Information Agency party. The businessman had come to Rome to open an American-style supermarket. "Mr. Shivers," he told Cheever, "Rome needs Minimax and Minimax needs Rome. I'm going to build a supermarket in Rome that will put the Pantheon to shame."

The *Post* paid him "a shirtfull" for the interview with Loren. The actress herself was "what used to be known as an eyeful," with an amazing front and gleaming legs. In Naples as in Rome, he wrote in his article, there were people on their way to one-room basement flats that smelled of drains and cheese rinds who still carried themselves with style and grace. Loren had that quality, and yet there was no trace of artifice about her. She wore "no perfume, no makeup," her dress was simple, and she seemed "sincere, magnanimous, lucky, intelligent and serene." The interview over, she walked him to the door as the bells of Naples rang noon. Before leaving he asked if he might kiss her. "Of course," she said, and so he did. In his notes he reduced the meeting to three words: "See Loren. Pow."

At Yaddo and Saratoga he saw other, more mortal women. Aileen Ward, biographer of Keats and one of the nations's leading literary scholars, met him there during a brief visit, and they forged an instant friendship. Dining together at a restaurant near the racetrack, they rapidly established the feeling that they understood each other. Cheever spoke of his background, seeming somewhat defensive about his lack of education. Yet his manner was so conspicuously that of the upper-middle-class WASP that Ward assumed he was the product of the best prep schools, if not of the best colleges. There was affection between them but no intimacy. He made no overture toward sex, yet she was installed among his gallery of dream girls. "I would suspect," she said, "that really close emotional relationships with women were not easy for him."

In the fall of 1967, Cheever spoke at Skidmore College in Saratoga Springs as the guest of college president Joseph Palamountain and his wife, Anne. Formerly an *haute couture* buyer, Anne Palamountain took her duties as a college president's wife seriously. (She was one of the first wives to be paid a salary for this work.) She was especially concerned that distinguished visitors to the campus be treated right, and so she arranged a dinner party for Cheever, put him up for the night, and generally made him feel welcome. He responded with gratitude and two dozen roses, and a close companionship began. Thereafter the author and the president's wife foregathered regularly when Cheever came to town for meetings at Yaddo. They met for brunch at the elegant Gideon Putnam Hotel or for Big Macs at McDonald's, for cross-country skiing in the afternoon and long confidential talks. "Every woman," as she said, "needs a man other than her husband she can confide in," and Cheever fulfilled that purpose for her. In talking of his own problems, though, he kept it light and amusing. She never was inclined to feel sorry for him. "He carried off his troubles so well, with a kind of detachment about himself."

Within Yaddo itself, the reigning monarch was experiencing difficulties of her own. In her late eighties, Elizabeth Ames was

almost blind, quite forgetful, and often cranky. When the Palamountains called, soon after their arrival in Saratoga in 1965, to ask
if they might visit Yaddo, Ames slammed down the phone on them.
So during Cheever's visit he snuck them into the mansion by the
back door (he knew where the key was hidden), and the three of
them spoke in whispers as they tiptoed around Yaddo's dark halls.
The spirit of Elizabeth Ames seemed to pervade the place, though
she was asleep in Pine Garde cottage a football field away. They
encountered instead Philip Roth, as he came spooking downstairs
to see who was there. As that episode suggests, Ames was threatening to become rather a tyrant at Yaddo, and of course she had
always played favorites. "If she was fond of you," longtime cook
Nellie Shannon remarked, "she'd do anything for you. If she
wasn't, forget it." But to many Yaddo colonists—and to such board
members as Cheever and Cowley—she represented everything that
was valuable about Yaddo. In a sense, she was Yaddo, and they
were reluctant to make her step down until the rigors of old age
made it impossible to act otherwise. Finally it had to be done. After
an extensive search, Curtis Harnack was named to replace her as
director. Cheever was chosen to write a tribute to her accomplishment.

Elizabeth has seen all kinds—lushes down on their luck, men and women
at the top of their powers, nervous breakdowns, thieves, geniuses, cranky
noblemen, and poets who ate their peas off a knife. She has remained
imperturbable, humorous and fair. This is much more than the conscien-
tious stewardship of a will, much more than a friendly feeling for the arts.
This is a life and a triumph.

Cheever's own capacity to derive humor from adversity was
illustrated in late 1967 when he suffered a long episode of prostatitis.
In a letter to Dr. Mutter, he explained that his prostate acted up
in response to erotic stimuli. That whole part of him, he confesses,
"was apt to be foolish."
   At Thanksgiving the family followed a regular ritual. First John
and Fred lined the sloping lawn with tennis-court tapes, and then
the crowd—as many as two dozen—arrived for the touch football
game. Cheever himself was not much of a player. Next there were
drinks for all and then the turkey that Mary had prepared and John
carved, after reciting a grace he constructed out of the Cranmer
Bible and Jowett's Plato.

The Cranmer is loud, resonant and liturgical and cuts into the small talk and the noise of silver. "Almighty God, maker of all things, judge of all men!" Then comes the Plato, even louder. "Let us consider that the soul of man is immortal, able to endure every sort of good and every sort of evil. Thus may we live happily with one another and with God."

The close is incantatory, close to plainsong. "By Whom and with Whom in the Unity of the Holy Ghost all honor and glory be to Thee oh Father Almighty, world without end. Amen."

After dinner everyone took a walk, and after dark they played charades. The pattern was important to Cheever. Like Leander Wapshot, he intended that "the unobserved ceremoniousness of his life" should be "a gesture or sacrament toward the excellence and continuousness of things."

And yet, he sometimes broke the bounds. One holiday dinner he and Natalie Robins slipped away from the dinner table to go shopping at Barker's, the discount store in the Arcadian shopping center nearby. Cheever loved shopping there: the shoddy merchandise, the piped-in variation on "In a Little Spanish Town," the assistant manager "with ash-blonde hair, a grey lace dress and . . . a strong, unfresh smell like old candy" who counted on her fingers. Natalie, who had no hobbies other than shopping for bargains, was delighted to go along. She went off to look for junk clothes, socks, and shoes, while he visited hardware and chatted with Richard Van Tassel, the manager of the store. Both found a small treasure to purchase, and they drove back to Cedar Lane, where everyone was still at table.

In December 1967, Ben was arrested in Cincinnati. Together with a group of other college students, he had blockaded an induction center as a protest against the Vietnam War. All were thrown in the workhouse for disturbing the peace, with bail set at nine hundred dollars. Cheever wired the money as soon as he got word, but meanwhile Ben spent two nights in jail. When he came home for Christmas, he looked at his father "a little distantly" and told him, "You know, you don't know anything until you've been roughed up by the Man!" It was an experience Cheever was willing to forgo, but otherwise he was entirely supportive of his son, who was eventually tried and got off with a suspended sentence and a $150 fine. A few years later, Cheever was invited to appear in Cincinnati. "I won't make a speech there," he declared. "I won't make a *potholder* in the city that arrested my son." Early in April, he and Mary and Susie participated in an interracial march to mourn the death of Martin Luther King: whites and blacks elbow to elbow, united—however fleetingly—in the common bond of sorrow.

DOUBLING

1967-1969

JOHN CHEEVER embodied the paradox of the bourgeois artist. Most of the time he pursued a respectable suburban existence as a family man, but he sometimes played the drunken rakehell and sexual adventurer. Most of his friends in Ossining saw only the Cheever who lived a conventional life. The bohemian exploits generally occurred on the road. This two-sided pattern of behavior was accompanied by a division within his spirit between the celebratory and the deprecatory. Darkness and light competed for preeminence in a continual chiaroscuro. Hypersensitive to beauty and ugliness alike, he "adored everything and deplored everything."

He was, he liked to point out, a Gemini. The legend of Castor and Pollux, those mythical twins in the sky, holds that they alternated between different realms. Castor occupied Olympus one day while Pollux remained in Hades, and on the next day they changed places. A similar duality obtained in Cheever's personality and in his writing. In *Bullet Park,* the novel he was working on until midsummer 1968, he gave Tony Nailles the same birthday as his own, May 27. Tony's high school French teacher tells him he is a Gemini, and adds with seeming casualness, "Gemini determines many of your characteristics and one might say your fate. . . ." This does not mean that Cheever believed in astrology: he did not. It does suggest an awareness of the deep division within himself that is patent in almost everything he wrote.

"I want an environment, a house, dogs, children and love," he observes in one introspective passage. Yet in another he accuses himself of having constructed a museum of a home, where the exhibits depicted only a drab and confining life. "The fully disciplined man," he wrote a young admirer, "is a stick of wood." He was damned if he would be a stick of wood.

Cheever began his extended affair with Hope Lange in the late 1960s. Of necessity they saw each other infrequently. She lived in Los Angeles most of the year, and was often busy in films or plays or starring in the television series *The Ghost and Mrs. Muir* (1968–70) and *The New Dick Van Dyke Show* (1971–74). From the beginning Cheever was proud of the affair, for wasn't Hope one of the most beautiful women in the world? Chatting with Jinny Kahn at Susie's wedding, he confidentially let her know about it. The Friday Club members heard about Hope regularly, sometimes in wildly exaggerated form. Alan Pakula, Hope's husband, was after him with a pistol, Cheever said. Hope had to hide him in the closet once when Frank Sinatra came to call, he maintained. These tales, Hope confirms, were outright inventions.

Cheever began to invoke Hope's name in a mantra that enabled him to get out of bed in the morning during spells of depression. "I'm loved and wanted and there's something to get out of bed for," he assured himself. "Hope is beautiful and she loves me and she's coming to see me." In his imagination he fancied that they lived together happily in a house by the sea. At times he fantasized about leaving home and family for her.

They saw each other, almost always, for liquid lunches at La Côte Basque or Maxwell's Plum or a French bistro. Sometimes, but by no means always, they made love afterward. Either way they had wonderful fun together, Hope remembers. Like a teenager on a first date, he took her skating at Rockefeller Center. She encouraged his sense of the ridiculous, and was happy when she could make him laugh. "When he threw back his head and really laughed," she said, "I knew I was giving him something."

She loved the way he spoke, too, though sometimes when he mumbled she used to think she was partially deaf. And she liked the way he was supportive of her and totally unjudgmental. There was never any jealousy about the men she was seeing. "Whatever I wanted to do was okay," she said. Theirs was not a "great physical love affair," however. She was not strongly attracted to him physically, and rather surprised by how highly sexed he was. There was never enough lovemaking for him; he always wanted more. He was, she thought, "the horniest man" she'd ever known, and at times adolescent in his demands. Once, early in their afair, John wanted to make love and she did not. Quite drunk, he completely lost his sense of dignity and lay down on the floor in the hallway outside her hotel room.

No matter how insistent he was, they were both very much aware that he was married. During their afternoons together, it was important for him to leave at four o'clock to catch the four-twenty train. "I certainly loved John, and would do anything for him," she said, but she realized that he "had to be a hellion to live with": home a lot, sometimes drunk, terribly moody. She'd known enough writers to understand how difficult they could be. She and Mary met perhaps three times, first when she and Alan Pakula went up to Ossining for lunch, later when Cheever read at the YM-YWHA in New York in 1977, and again at a screening of *The Shady Hill Kidnapping* in 1981, and she could sympathize with the wife's role in those awkward meetings. Certainly she was not out to steal Mary's husband. Though she loved seeing John, she was not prepared to make a full emotional commitment to him. What would happen if she let herself become emotionally dependent on him? She was the one who was single (after 1971), and he'd still be catching the four-twenty to Ossining.

Hope appeared often in the journals he maintained after the fashion of his grandfather and father. As he grew older, he came to depend on his journals "to preserve the keenness of small daily sensations." They also served as his confessional. As Richard Stern suggests, writing in his journal was "a consolation, a secret repair shop, a magic ring to rub out his enemies and doubts." If he could write it down, it lost its sting.

So down it went, even to the extent of self-loathing. When he said that he loved his son's track shoes—so he challenged himself— wasn't he really an emotional impostor? Weren't his dream girls a manifestation of "the barrenness of self-love"? And how could he justify the lack of discipline he brought to his work and the cruelties he visited on his family? When Mary—a superlative cook— fixed a roast for dinner, he carved as usual and served her with the choice piece of meat. "I don't want it," she said, but he insisted that she take it. This pattern was a common one at the dinner table, as he constantly reserved the smallest or least attractive cut of meat for himself. Eeyore, Susan used to call him. He knew what he was doing, and in his journals excoriated himself for doing it. These minuscule sacrifices represented an attempt to salve his conscience for larger betrayals. It was as if he were saying, "See how good I am to you, in this trivial way."

Astringent as he could be with himself, Cheever sometimes allowed self-pity to intrude into his journals. Early in 1968, he went through a period of considerable discomfort with his teeth. Some had to be extracted. The remainder were capped. "I don't care about my beauty," he said, "but my dentist does." The dentist was in New York, and one day he stopped in to see Frances Lindley at Harper & Row before an appointment. They had a drink at "21," and then he asked her to come along while he had a tooth pulled. Fully cognizant that she was playing a maternal role, she went along, sat with him on the dentist's couch for a while afterward, put him in a cab, and left. Soon thereafter he awoke in pain in the middle of the night. Worse than the toothache was his despairing feeling that the doors of his own house were being shut against him. On another trip to New York, he went to the public baths after lunch and encountered a male whore. "How did you ever get into this fix?" he wondered. And why couldn't men have ideal friendships without any taint of perversion? Meanwhile his addiction to alcohol grew worse. This became poignantly clear when his brother, Fred—well dressed, alert, and cold sober at sixty-two— came to visit on the eve of his departure for Europe. The brothers talked late into the night, Fred sticking to ginger ale while John downed a bottle of bourbon. Which brother was in trouble now?

In the summer of 1968, Cheever took a vacation in Ireland with Mary and son Fred. He was ready for a holiday, having finished *Bullet Park* after a long siege and completed a number of literary obligations as well. As chairman of the grants committee of the National Institute, he recommended an award for Dick Stern and wrote "a beautiful sentence or two" by way of citation. As an NBA judge he was a strong supporter of William Styron's *The Confessions of Nat Turner*, a book he thought "astonishing" from a man in whose work he found "no bluff at all." He was also lobbying with the institute and the foundations on behalf of Fred Exley, whose poignant *A Fan's Notes* came out in mid-1968.

Happy developments were in prospect for his own work, too, as Cheever left for Ireland. At the Ford Foundation's invitation he applied for a grant to write a play. From Stockholm came a letter from the Nobel Prize people addressed—he said—to "Sir John Cheese, Offining" and revealing the news—he said—that they "wanted to take a look at me and see if I can walk backwards." And in the Emerald Isle he waited anxiously for a cable from the Book-of-the-Month Club about *Bullet Park*.

In Ireland the mountains were blue and green, and there was wonderful swimming and fishing. The place struck him as "haunted," in the best sense. Armed with the Shell guide and a letter from old Ireland hand Bill Maxwell, the Cheevers went to Kenmare, County Kerry, where Michael J. O'Connor, a fine figure of a man of seventy who owned a fishing boat called the *Sea-Elf*, took them fishing for mackerel in the estuary and talked a fine "crack" about his World War II experiences with the Eighth Army in North Africa. They then went to Inishmore and stayed in a farmhouse with such primitive amenities that John and Fred had "to face the wall when Mary pumped ship." Less politely, a horse gazed in at one window, a cow at another.

On the return flight, Cheever stuffed some smoked salmon in the pocket of his sport coat, a subterfuge that led to a terrible midnight scene in customs at Boston's Logan Airport. And for days afterward, he felt violently disoriented, much more so than after trips to Italy. But he loved the Irish people and the Irish gift for language. He and Mary told John and Mary Dirks, then considering a trip to Ireland, that they really had to go and visit Kenmare and look up the brilliant blue-eyed garrulous Michael J. O'Connor and take their tea at Mrs. Hussey's in Sneem.

Though the Ford Foundation and the Nobel Prize Committee

and the Book-of-the-Month Club had no good news to report, his
agent Candida Donadio had already improved his financial position. She negotiated a new and lucrative contract with Knopf beginning with *Bullet Park,* and so ended eleven years, two novels,
and three books of stories with Harper & Row. Cheever felt defensive about a decision so obviously based on financial grounds. It did
not suit his image of himself as an author who was "not a money
player" like, say, his friend Irwin Shaw. As best he could, he made
light of it. So he wrote Frances Lindley that he was changing not
just publishers but everything—his lawyer, doctor, dentist, and
liquor dealer. And to editor Robert Gottlieb at Knopf he made a
mock apology for fussing about money. He hated to admit it, he
explained, but he was subject to dreams of envy about such best-
selling colleagues as Updike and Roth.

At the same time, he could be like a little boy in the presence of
large sums of money. He brought a hefty check from Knopf along
to dinner with Connie Bessie one night, and afterward they decided to see if the St. Regis (where they'd dined) would cash the
check. When the staff said they wouldn't—or rather couldn't—he
was delighted. He was also extraordinarily generous when flush.
"When John felt rich," Mary said, "he'd go out and buy color
television sets or Volkswagens. Three Volkswagens." He did in
fact buy Rob and Susie a Mustang, and with the advance from
Knopf in the bank, he took the entire family to Curaçao for ten days
over the New Year's holiday of 1968–69. Ben had to be persuaded
to come along. At twenty-one, he disapproved of people who were
tan in January. The following summer, there was a still more
expensive family trip to Majorca, Madrid, and Rome, "all first
class." His income for 1969 came to more than sixty-three thousand
dollars, and he spent a large fraction of it on those vacations. When
he had money he spent it. When funds ran low he was reluctant
to part with a dime.

No novel of Cheever's more vividly illustrates his duality of
vision than *Bullet Park.* As critic Samuel Coale has noted, a "distinctly Manichean conflict" runs through his fiction. As with a
reflex light his writing evokes opposites, flashing back and forth
between the polarities of "flesh and spirit, dark and light, the terres-
trial and the weightless, land and sea." He is at once the lyric
transcendentalist and the bitter Calvinist. As John Updike expressed it, Cheever "thought fast, saw everything in bright true
colors, and was the arena of a constant tussle between the bubbling

joie de vivre of the healthy sensitive man and the deep melancholy peculiar to American Protestant males." And John Gardner, writing of *Bullet Park* in particular, observed that the author "sees the world in its totality—not only the fashionable existential darkness but the light older than consciousness, which gives nothingness definition."

The opening paragraph of the novel at once establishes the poignant tone of the book, fluctuating between celebration and mourning. It begins as a kind of urban pastoral that quickly descends to the sorrowful.

Paint me a small railroad station then, ten minutes before dark. Beyond the platform are the waters of the Wekonsett River, reflecting a somber afterglow. The architecture of the station . . . resembles a pergola, cottage or summer house although this is a climate of harsh winters. The lamps along the platform burn with a nearly palpable plaintiveness.

Though we travel mostly by plane, the narrator goes on, the spirit of the country is reflected in our railroads.

You wake in a pullman bedroom at three A.M. in a city the name of which you do not know and may never discover. A man stands on a platform with a child in his arms. They are waving goodbye to some traveller, but what is the child doing up so late and why is the man crying?

The suggestions are somber, yet this is a novel that will end with the almost miraculous rescue of one of the principal characters from a madman bent on murder.

In its barest outline, *Bullet Park* tells the story of three characters: Eliot Nailles, Paul Hammer, and Nailles's son, Tony. In the first half of the novel, Tony succumbs to a deep sadness and is unable to rouse himself from bed. Neither conventional medicine nor quack doctors can cure his malaise. Finally he is restored to health by the Swami Rutuola, "a spiritual cheerleader" who reinvigorates him by persuading him to repeat cheers of place—"I am in a house by the sea"—and love and hope cheers—"Love, Love, Love . . . ," "Hope, Hope, Hope. . . ." In the second half of the book Tony faces another danger in the person of Hammer, who has been sent by his psychotic mother to commit a ritual murder that will arouse the modern world from a torpor induced by drugs and commercialism and rootlessness. At first Hammer plans to kill Nailles, who helps to peddle a mouthwash called Spang. Then he switches to Tony as his victim. In the end, aided by a message from the Swami, Nailles saves his son from Hammer's attempt to immolate him in the chancel of Christ's Church and so "awaken the world."

Casting this improbable plot into viable fictional form was not easy. Cheever began with the legend of William Tell in mind. He wanted to tell an uncomplicated story of a man's love for his son, but it threatened to turn into an indictment of contemporary existence. In their restless rootlessness, his characters die in rapid transit. One woman has to get stoned before venturing onto the New Jersey Turnpike, where she perishes. A commuter, standing innocently on the station platform, is sucked under the New York–Chicago express as it comes helling through; one highly polished loafer is all that remains to signify his passing. And the action takes place in a suburb, Bullet Park, that is a slightly darker version of Proxmire Manor, which was a slightly darker version of Shady Hill.

In his extensive notes for *Bullet Park*, Cheever revealed his distress about the lack of sensual imagery in the book. "Where are the smells, the lights, the noise, the music?" he asked. More intentionally, he omitted the coarser language of sexual intercourse, leaving it to others to write "about cocks and cunts and arseholes." But he could not ignore obscene behavior and casual lust, which are as pervasive in *Bullet Park* as in *The Wapshot Scandal*. Eliot Nailles's wife, Nellie, goes to an off-Broadway show one afternoon, where a man appears naked onstage and unselfconsciously scratches himself. On the way home, she witnesses an episode of love play between two homosexuals, and arrives back in Bullet Park shaken.

The major technical problems Cheever faced in writing *Bullet Park* involved point of view, the novel's ending, and the relationship between Hammer and Nailles. In effect, there are three narrative voices in the book. First of all, there is the basic storyteller, who reports the action reliably and straightforwardly. Second, there is the flat, matter-of-fact, and ultimately sinister sound of Hammer's autobiographical journal: "a quiet stovelid on terror and rage," John Gardner called it. Finally, there is an occasional comment from a narrator who stands above the action, rather like an anthropologist reporting (and sometimes making judgments) on the mores and customs of this late-twentieth-century civilization. At first Cheever planned to develop this third narrator more overtly. He would read about the murder attempt in the newspaper, and go on to interview Nailles and pore over Hammer's papers. This device was abandoned, however. In the novel as it stands the observations of this narrator are made without apology or any explanation of who and where they come from.

Ending the book proved difficult. From notes and editorial correspondence, it is possible to reconstruct four different approaches to a satisfactory finish. At first, Cheever speculated, *Bullet Park* might close with a man on a train, thinking about all the houses he had lived in. Next he proposed that the novel end with Nailles, tranquilized, floating down the tracks into Grand Central like Zeus upon a cloud and beaming "a vast and slightly absentminded smile at poverty, sickness, wealth, the beauty of strange women, the rain and the snow." (This passage eventually appeared midway through the published novel.) Then he added one sentence as a finale: "Everything was as wonderful as it had been."

This conclusion struck Bob Gottlieb at Knopf as rather too abrupt. He did not want to presume as an "Editor," he wrote Cheever, but felt the novel needed "a little more breathing space at the end." Candida Donadio agreed, and Cheever offered three variations on the last paragraph. Instead of "Everything was as wonderful as it had been," he suggested, the book could finish with a liturgical flair, by multiplying the "wonderfuls" and adding "world without end" or "forever and ever."

Still later he composed the final ending to *Bullet Park:*

Tony went back to school on Monday and Nailles—drugged—went off to work and everything was as wonderful, wonderful, wonderful, wonderful as it had been.

That Nailles still needs his daily drugging to ride the train to work undermines the celebratory note, the fourth "wonderful" counteracts the triadic resonance of the original three, and the religious references to "world without end" and "forever and ever" have been stripped away. As a consequence, the novel ends in an ambiguity that invites contradictory interpretations. Did Cheever intend these lines to be taken as "an affirmation out of ashes" or as bitter irony? In his *Time* cover story of 1964, he insisted that he wanted his fiction "to bring glad tidings to someone." Yet he could not bring himself, at the finish of *Bullet Park*, to declare those tidings unambiguously. He was torn, as his novel was divided, between the contrary instincts to praise the wonder of the natural creation and to deplore the chaos that humankind has wreaked upon it.

The world of *Bullet Park* is spiritually arid. Though Nailles goes to his knees once a week in gratitude for "the thighs of Nellie and his love for his son," most religious observances have become a sham and their rituals debased. Attending church with Nailles is the recent convert Mrs. Trencham, who practices "competitive churchmanship." She utters her amens well in advance of the rest of the congregation, surpasses everyone in the grace of her genu-flections and the perfection of her credo and confession, and when challenged throws in "a few signs of the cross as a proof of the superiority of her devotions." The diocesan bishop recommends that churchgoers turn on their windshield wipers to signify their belief in the life to come. Blessed by an evangelist in London, Hammer feels "completely cleansed and forgiven" and ready for whatever purpose life may hold for him, including symbolic mur-der. When Hammer arrives in Bullet Park, the mercenary Father Ransome sizes him up as "good for at least five hundred a year."

Cheever doubted the validity of his own faith at this time. He hadn't taken communion for a long time, but now he did. Death was on his mind. Basically, his was a religion of nature. He took a lyrical delight in the natural creation, and invested his favored characters with a similar sensitivity. "Give me back the moun-tains," Tony says as depression overtakes him. His father, also keenly attuned to nature, loves to see the leaves blowing through the headlights. "I mean they're just dead leaves, no good for any-thing, but I love to see them blowing through the light." When Nailles comes home one night, the rain lets up and he can distin-guish the different sounds that the wind makes as it fills up different trees: "maple, birch, tulip and oak." What good is this knowledge? he thinks, and with Cheever answers the question: "Someone has to observe the world." In this process of observation, natural ob-jects become holier than relics, manifesting the sacred. Which came first, *Bullet Park* asks, "Jesus the carpenter or the smell of new wood?" As Dana Gioia expressed it, Cheever "was less a Christian than a Deist, but one who felt most comfortable worshipping with familiar liturgy in a traditional church." In his own Episcopal churchgoing, he went to the short early-morning Mass and avoided the sermon. The world outdoors awaited him.

The trickiest puzzle Cheever had to solve in writing *Bullet Park* was that of the relationship between Hammer and Nailles. It was one thing to see them as symbiotic, bound together by "the mysterious power of nomenclature." It was another to make that bond convincing and credible. In undertaking that task, he used his brother, Fred, and "the division in my own spirit," yet for a long time he had trouble seeing the men whole.

On the surface, they are very different men indeed. Nailles is an ordinary man with no superior qualities, not heroic or brilliant yet capable of love and blessed with the capacity to admire the creation. Content with his lot, he naively tries to live in a state of prelapsarian innocence and to protect his family from all harm. He wishes his love were "like some limitless discharge of a clear, amber fluid that would surround them, cover them, preserve them and leave them insulated but visible like the contents of an aspic." But he cannot so shield them. Pain and suffering penetrate the cocoon.

If Nailles would be the rational preserver of family and community, Hammer represents the obsessed and deranged destroyer. A bastard with a madwoman for a mother, he is a wanderer, forever in quest of a house with a yellow room that will somehow, he hopes, relieve him of the cafard that travels with him. His wife, Marietta, is a harridan who abuses and emasculates him. Hate rules his existence as love dominates that of Nailles. In his notes, Cheever also sketched out their sexual distinctions. Nailles takes a healthy pleasure in lovemaking. Hammer, on the other hand, repeatedly insists on his masculinity, yet the word "impotence" can make him flinch.

Despite these distinctions, Hammer and Nailles share certain crucial similarities. Hammer's persistent depression, for instance, is paralleled by Nailles's sudden phobia about trains and by Tony's irrational sadness. Far more striking is their joint propensity to violence. On four different occasions, Nailles contemplates murdering someone. Once the intended victim is his beloved son, Tony, the boy Hammer chooses as his victim. Another time Nailles is visited by murderous feelings toward Hammer when he suggests that Nailles shoot his old hunting dog. The implication in the novel is that the impulse toward murder shelters deep in the recesses of ordinary people. "Have you ever committed a murder?" the generalizing narrator asks the readers of *Bullet Park*. "Have you ever known the homicide's sublime feeling of rightness?"

Whether Cheever fashioned his characters that way or not—and he insisted that he did not—Hammer and Nailles emerge as two sides of the same person, as fragments of a single divided psyche. Furthermore, both of these figures, and Tony Nailles as well, represent facets of the author's own personality. He shared a cafard with Hammer, along with a sense that he was mistreated by his wife and an embarrassing habit of falling "suddenly in love with men, women, children, and dogs." He shared with Nailles a devotion to home and family, regular churchgoing, a fondness for working with the chain saw, and the train phobia. Like Tony, he was beset by a lassitude born of depression. "I would like to stay in bed for two weeks," he confided. So he resorted to incantations much like the Swami's "cheers of place" to rouse himself from bed.

In the winter of 1969, while the book was in press, Cheever broke his leg skiing. He was showing off for a pretty woman, he admitted, and ended up in the emergency room. The leg was still in a cast on the eve of publication, when he entertained interviewer Leslie Aldridge from *New York* magazine in the St. Regis Hotel room Knopf was paying for. He ordered up a bottle of gin and another of Scotch, and drank half the bottle of gin while plying Aldridge with the Scotch. He talked engagingly if not entirely reliably about his working routine, his wife and family, his personal finances, even his compulsions. "I chain smoke, I chain drink. I chain everything else. . . . I love to drink. I'm hooked on it. I drink a lot but I don't drink heavily when I've got to work the next day."

That was a stretcher, and so was his drastic assertion about reviews: "I do read reviews of my books but they don't affect me." In his journal, too, he reassured himself that he had done the best he could and hence should not be bothered by criticism. Nonetheless, he was devastated by Benjamin DeMott's review that ran on the front page of the *New York Times Book Review* for Sunday, April 27.

DeMott's review rehearsed the usual objections to Cheever's long fiction. Structurally the book was "broken-backed, parts tacked together as the Hammer-Nailles ploy of nomenclature suggests." Stylistically it read like a short story, which could get by with setting down what happened, and not like a novel, which demanded explanations. Moreover, DeMott thought that *Bullet Park* had replaced the pure energy of the Wapshot books with "a sluggishness, a heaviness, a crude useless film slicking bright wings." The tone throughout was antagonistic. With its "grand gatherum of late 20th-century American weirdos," DeMott conceded, *Bullet Park* might provide "a necessary fix" to the legion of Cheever addicts, since he was "a topline fictional entertainer." Otherwise the novel's discontinuity, its non sequiturs, its "sad, licked lyricism" were disappointing.

In the same issue with this review, the *Times* ran an interview of Cheever by Lehmann-Haupt, and two days later in the daily *Times* John Leonard wrote a favorable review of the novel, but DeMott's front-page Sunday assault had its effect. Sales amounted to thirty-three thousand copies only, and did not earn back the advance.

Unlike DeMott's, most reviews of *Bullet Park* were respectful, though somewhat mystified. Cheever seemed "carried away by the flood tide of his imagination," Anatole Broyard observed. The novel was full of brilliant digressions and incidental felicities, but what was it that the author set out to say? The problem lay in the presumption that a novel, unlike a poem, must not only *be* but also *mean*. Latter-day enthusiasts, determined to rescue Cheever's novel from critical limbo, have struggled to impose a pattern of order on it. It is a religious novel, one argues. The themes of "chance" and "evil" knit it together, another maintains. But the book will not yield to tidy explications. As Stephen C. Moore has divined, *"Bullet Park* is not about a 'mystery,' it is a mystery. . . ." If there are answers to the questions, solutions to the problems, ways out of the quandaries therein depicted, Cheever and his narrators are not at all sure what they are. The book ends in ambiguity, on purpose.

In a very real sense, *Bullet Park* confesses Cheever's own uncertainties and discontinuities. He invests a troubled part of himself in each of the three principal characters, and the criticisms of contemporary culture embedded in the novel may be regarded as projections of his private malaise. As with *The Wapshot Scandal*, Cheever felt almost suicidal when he finished *Bullet Park*. He would never be able to write in that vein again, he knew, and he was rawly sensitive to any implied disapproval of the book. Philip Roth wrote to congratulate him, singling out parts of the novel he liked. "I'm glad you liked those pages," Cheever replied. "I liked all the pages of your book [*Portnoy's Complaint*]." So he did, and regaled his guests one evening with a reading from Portnoy's outrageous adventures. Mary Cheever was wearing a beautiful yellow dress that night, Steve Becker recalls. She looked like a jonquil, her husband told her, and made him feel like a honeybee.

Such glimpses of sunshine were rare. By May his leg had healed, but he still felt crippled by a "massive melancholy." The struggle with drinking also continued. "A day for me; a day for the hootch." The incantations that worked for Tony were not working for him.

I am no longer sitting under an apple tree in clean chinos reading. I am sitting naked in the yellow chair in the dining room. In my hand there is a large crystal glass filled to the brim with honey-colored whiskey. . . . I am sitting naked in a yellow chair drinking whiskey and smoking six or seven cigarettes.

He needed help, and no Swami Rutuola was at hand. *Bullet Park* depicts a series of incompetent and venal psychiatrists—the worst of them circles his patient's chair like a dentist and sells real estate on the side—yet it was a psychiatrist that Cheever consulted in the valley of his depression.

Cheever saw Dr. J. William Silverberg eleven times between May and November 1969. For the most part the treatment stayed on a superficial level. Cheever wanted it that way. He chatted with Silverberg as if they were at a cocktail party, withholding himself behind a facade of charm. And as the psychiatrist acknowledges, he may have been a little awed by this remarkable patient, this man of genius in trouble.

At their first meeting the problem seemed to be alcoholism. Cheever had been drinking before he arrived. He spoke of his phobias, and how he needed a drink to cross a bridge. Susan had told him six months ago that he was drinking too much, he said. At the second session, however, depression seemed to be the most serious problem. His current spell of depression had begun about eight months earlier, he said, or about at the time he put the final touches on *Bullet Park*, but he had been depressed on and off for years. There was also a hint of an identity problem related to the characters in his fiction. "I've begun to feel they're walking into my life instead of my walking into theirs." He discussed his homosexual concerns, too. His relationship with his brother had been "psychologically incestuous," he said. He felt a need "to prove his sexual prowess over and over." He loved the feeling of discharge: of semen, urine, feces, sweat. He outlined the story of his parents: his father's losing his money, his mother and the gift shop, her "dominant, eccentric, opinionated" nature. He gave Silverberg an inscribed copy of *The Wapshot Chronicle*. "A loving novel about my father," he called it, but it contained feelings of hostility toward him as well, Silverberg concluded after reading it.

At subsequent meetings the subject of homosexuality cropped up repeatedly. Walking down Fifth Avenue, he wasn't sure whether he wanted to look at men's or women's behinds, Cheever said. He confessed to a homosexual encounter the previous December in Ossining. He talked at length about Hope Lange as well, making claims about their sex life that Silverberg interpreted as a defense against homosexual desires. Throughout, Cheever kept trying to put the doctor-patient association on a more personal basis. He even proposed that the Silverbergs come to dinner. As with Dr. Hays, he set out to entertain his psychiatrist. He was all charm, entirely ingratiating, and less than forthcoming. He liked to talk about himself if he'd had a drink or two, Silverberg thought, but not necessarily to reveal himself. Given Librium during one session, he would discuss nothing except the party he and Mary had given for 150 people in honor of Rob and Susie. Cheever drank too much on that occasion, and Iole kept summoning Mary to help. "Signora, you must come. Mr. Cheever no good."

Drink, depression, and bad temper also led to unpleasant relations between Cheever and his son Ben, who was about to be married. John spent much of his time with Fred, a boy who in preadolescence resembled his father at the same age—considerably overweight, not especially athletic, and extremely bright. Cheever was "a very good father," Fred thought at twelve, "but he lives in a world of his own." Fifteen years later, as a law student at UCLA, Fred elaborated on the point. As a writer his father "made his own world in relative isolation from most of his kind. . . . No one, absolutely no one, shared his life with him."

That was not quite what Silverberg concluded. His patient, he thought, was basically a childlike man, enclosed within himself and unable to give freely to others. In his egocentrism, love of self and hatred of self were inextricably intertwined. Cheever thought terrible things about himself, and accused himself at length, but did little to modify his behavior. The psychiatrist came to think of him as "this genius character who bedeviled everyone around him."

Cheever resisted treatment with Dr. Silverberg as he had with Dr. Hays. "I have a wonderful time," he told the Dirkses. "I've never told him the truth once." Some years later, he was interviewed for *Westchester* magazine by a woman who asked why he so disparaged psychiatrists in his fiction. In replying, he ventured the opinion that astrology was probably more therapeutic than psychiatry. Only then did he discover that the interviewer was Dr. Silverberg's wife.

BOTTOMING

1969-1973

THE world turned dark for Cheever as he approached his sixties. The light in the sky did not cheer, the rain did not heal. His depressions and phobias grew worse. His marriage turned bitter. He could write little or nothing. There were times when he considered suicide.

Liquor lay near the heart of these problems. The etiology of alcoholism is a subject of dispute, but recent research suggests what was manifestly the case for John Cheever: that drink was more the cause of his malaise than its consequence. One night's alcoholic euphoria led to the next morning's despair, in an intensifying cycle of repetition. Ever greater quantities were required to purchase the daily oblivion. Rob Cowley, stopping over to play backgammon with his father-in-law, joined his host in a full glass of whiskey, with no water and a few ice cubes—and then joined him in another. When Rob got home, he fell downstairs and passed out. His two young daughters thought it was wonderful. "Look," they said, "Daddy's playing a game." But he played the game only rarely. Cheever played it every day, and through habituation could consume large amounts without showing the effects. When he and John Dirks took the same train into New York for David Boyer's twenty-first-birthday bachelor party, Cheever insisted that they stop at the Century Club for two large goblet martinis. After those and subsequent drinks at the party, Dirks was unable to get through dinner and give the customary toast. Cheever performed as expected. Yet he went beyond even his own extensive capacities at times. He showed up at the wedding of Leonard Field's daughter mumbling and incoherent. On his own, around the house, he regularly drank so much that his speech was often slurred. At his worst, he succumbed to incontinence. When the Cheevers invited guests to their house, say, for Sunday lunch, Mary served only a glass of sherry or two.

By the spring of 1971, he was troubled enough by the way drinking affected his writing to consult his old adviser Malcolm Cowley about it. He wasn't getting much work done, he reported. His "seizures of temporary insanity"—three-day bursts that drove him to the typewriter to produce stories—were occurring much less frequently than in the past. The trouble, he thought, was twofold. He drank too much and he'd written too much. In reply, Cowley assured him that slowing down was to be expected as part of aging. "You can't write twenty stories a year any longer, but patience takes the place of that early jism—you can write four or five and they can be damned good ones." But Cheever was not writing four or five stories a year, or close to it. He published one story in 1970, none in 1971, two in 1972, one in 1973. Nor was he working on a novel. *Bullet Park* signaled the end of "a method, a cadence and a perspective," and he had not yet found the new voice and the new subject matter he was seeking.

As for alcohol, Cowley recommended that Cheever follow his own regimen of "one big slug of bourbon" at sundown each day. He also observed, sensibly, that "nobody in God's world" was going to help him or beseech him to stop drinking. "It's completely up to you—and isn't that a relief? A focusing of responsibility?"

Two months later, the Cheevers attended a dinner party at the
Cowleys' in Sherman, Connecticut. On the way home John was
arrested for driving while intoxicated in Somers, New York. According to Mary, John was a good driver even when mildly drunk,
and never had a serious accident. On this occasion, he was stopped
late at night for driving suspiciously slowly and irregularly on
Route 100. He smelled to heaven of liquor, but argued indignantly
with the state police. "Put me in jail," he demanded. "If it's a crime
to drive carefully, put me in jail." That was not what they had in
mind. He was fined seventy-five dollars and his license was suspended for sixty days. Later that summer, still without a license,
Cheever rode down from Yaddo with Curtis Harnack and Hortense Calisher. During the trip he produced a flask, took a healthy
swig, and to Calisher's surprise made no offer to pass it around.
This seemed so unlike Cheever, with his keen sense of ceremony
and doing the right thing, that it occurred to her for the first time
that he must be under the mastery of alcohol.

At parties generally—"I love parties," Cheever said in his 1969
New York interview—he was almost always gay, with a lively sense
of the absurd and a vibrant receptivity to humor. John Hersey, who
saw him both drunk and sober, thought him much the same either
way: a man of "remarkable speed and sunny disposition who was
enjoying himself almost beyond belief." He seemed so much the
soul of gaiety that Hersey found it hard to imagine the pain he must
have been going through. Shirley Hazzard, who with her husband,
Francis Steegmuller, saw the Cheevers at the Warrens' annual
Christmas party and a few times at dinner parties, thought his
persistent jollity a defense against despondency. Moments of authentic contact dissolved in a flow of jocularity that Hazzard saw
as Cheever's repudiation of any close approach to his private—and,
by then, clearly suffering—self. "We always had pleasant exchanges—about writing, about books, about life, and about Italy,"
she recalls, "but even these became repetitious, as if the same anecdotes represented a safe haven and any fresh considerations would
be disruptive."

Cheever was in fact actively contemplating suicide. "I felt my life
and career were over," he said later. "I wanted to end it." Liquor
served him toward that end. In the summer of 1972, when Mary
Cheever was in New Hampshire at Treetops and John Dirks vaca-
tioning in Maine, Cheever used to stop by Mary Dirks's house at
cocktail hour. He refused, he told her, "to be the lonely man eating

in a Chinese restaurant." Besides, Mary Dirks gave him an intelligent, attractive audience and plenty to drink. One evening on the
terrace, Cheever drunkenly fell and gashed his head on a metal
table. Mary picked him up, took him inside, and fed him a spaghetti
dinner that sobered him up. Often he felt bereft. Once, after Friday
Club, he took Tom Glazer back to the house and solemnly introduced him—they had met before, often—to Mary. "I'd like you to
meet my very great and good friend, Tom Glazer," he said in
sarcastic overelaboration. And then, sotto voce, "I have no friends."

Sometimes it seemed to him that he had no marriage, either. It
might be, he proposed in his journals, that he drank as a substitute
for the love he felt deprived of. "I am not allowed a kiss; I am barely
granted good morning." He and Mary rarely got through dinner
without a fight. If the dinner table was a "shark tank," wasn't he
the dolphin and Mary the shark? Or was it true—as Dr. Silverberg
had intimated—that he was incapable of love or could only love
himself? "Scotch for breakfast and I do not like these mornings."

In the winter of 1969–70, Mary went to St. Croix with Sandra
Hochman, a young poet and novelist who lived nearby. Hochman
was a friend of both Cheevers—he contributed one of his rare
jacket blurbs for her 1971 novel, *Walking Papers*—but he was upset
about the vacation that she and Mary took together. Mary looked
on it as an opportunity to escape a tense atmosphere and the slush
of Ossining. "How wonderful to get away from edgy people," she
said on her return.

According to Susan Cheever, her mother had affairs as well as
her father. Considering their apparent incompatibility, that hardly
seems surprising, though Mary Cheever steadfastly denies it. Whatever the truth of the matter, her husband was convinced that she
had been unfaithful to him. During the 1970 Christmas vacation
from Briarcliff, Mary spent the day in New York buying presents
for the whole family. When she got back to Cedar Lane, John—who
had been drinking with Zinny Schoales—accused her of meeting
a lover in the city. She wouldn't have had time, she said, laughing.
She'd been too busy shopping. "I couldn't find your diaphragm,"
he said. "You don't know where to look," she responded. His suspicions were not allayed.

Though Mary Cheever was a success in the classroom at Briarcliff, she was let go along with Mary Dirks (who taught drama) at
the end of the 1970–71 school year. According to Charles Shapiro,
who resigned in protest when the two Marys were fired, the deci-

sion was made on political grounds. Along with Maureen Willson, with whom she shared an office at Briarcliff, Mary Cheever vigorously if unsuccessfully supported for tenure the only really productive scholar on the English department staff. He was denied tenure largely for his liberal views, including his stand on the raging issue of the day: should Briarcliff switch from a single-sex female college to coeducation? The administration and senior staff opposed the change, and those who lobbied for it—including both Marys, Shapiro, and the untenured professor—were regarded as troublemakers.

On a hot mid-May morning when the wisteria was ahum with bees, Mary attended her last graduation at Briarcliff College. But teaching was in her blood, and she went on to teach composition and literature at Staten Island Community College and then at Rockland Country Day School, and—regularly since 1971—to lead a creative writing class in the adult education program of the Briarcliff Manor public schools. The desire to help others, she says of her teaching, may reflect a lack of self-confidence. "When you're working on someone else's problems, after all, you're not working on your own." Actually, though, she was writing her own poetry in earnest by the time she left Briarcliff. She sent her poems for appraisal both to Malcolm Cowley and to Bernard Malamud. Malamud especially fulfilled her need for a mentor, a rabbi, a particular friend in a bad time.

For the most part, the Cheevers respected each other's literary judgment. He frequently read a story or part of a novel to her (and other members of the family) and trusted her response, even when it was unfavorable. Mary didn't especially like his work, he commented in a 1969 interview, but he didn't want an admirer for a wife, he wanted "a critical intelligence, another person," and Mary provided that. As to her poetry, she learned that her husband, who did not pretend to any expertise, nonetheless had "great critical instincts, and could tell quicker than anyone else what was good or bad" about her poems. And she admired his writing more than she was always willing to show. Her husband was "constitutionally unable to write a mediocre line," she thought, but it was not something she told him. He thought her rivalrous and resentful of his success, literary merit aside.

Cheever consoled himself with sex, both real and imagined, as well as with liquor. He seduced one of Mary Dirks's Briarcliff drama students, "an enchanting kid and very experienced." He saw

Hope Lange whenever he could, and when he couldn't he day-
dreamed about her, about Aileen Ward, and about a new enthusiasm, Shana Alexander. Shana met the Cheevers through Zinny
Schoales. In her teens she had been a copygirl and a reporter on
PM, when Zinny was running the financial side, and they had
become friends. In 1970, when she was editing *McCall's*, Alexander
rented a house near Sleepy Hollow Country Club for weekend
rendezvous with her lover H.A.L. (Harry) Craig, an Irish poet and
screenwriter. Both of them liked to drink, and Cheever naturally
gravitated toward them. People who drink need other people to
drink with.

Besides, he was very taken with her, and flirted with her "more
or less outrageously," though her liaison with Craig could not have
been more obvious. Shana liked Cheever a lot, all the same. He was
cute and he knew it, and that was attractive. He was funny, and
that made for wonderful company. He struck her as a small man
with no hangups about his size, "a little nut-brown guy with twinkling eyes who was sparkling all the time." He promised to write
her "A Pure and Beautiful Story" for *McCall's*, and she asked him
down to the Hamptons to discuss it (the story was never written).
"I thought he was marvelous," she said, but there was no physical
relationship between them. "Those are not the sorts of things one
forgets," she pointed out.

She was in any case admitted to his gallery of dream girls.
Cheever often said that he "adored" women, meaning women who
were good to look at. He would never have anything to do with a
woman who was not beautiful, he said. And he liked women of a
certain type, Candida Donadio observed: slim, elegant, nicely featured, blondish, not tall, women with quiet voices. Moreover, he
was strongly attracted to women who were not only beautiful but
accomplished. One writer at Yaddo he found singularly homely.
"And her career has been a disaster, too," he said of her, as if to
prove a point. The women he admired combined good looks and
a successful, often publicly noteworthy, career. This was the basic
pattern with Hope Lange, Aileen Ward, Shana Alexander, Anne
Palamountain, Sara Spencer, and Sophia Loren, and—later—with
painter Susan Crile and Lauren Bacall. Each of them in her own
way outperformed his mother, who had become a career woman
perforce. In his imagination—and sometimes in his conversation—
they became his lovers. And he imagined, too, that they might give
him a mother's nurturing love. In a dream, for example, he envi-

sioned himself ill, in Rome, with Aileen Ward nursing him back to health.

At times, half in fantasy, he conjured up a divorce from Mary and a subsequent dream-girl marriage. In 1971, he called daughter Susan one night and told her he was planning to marry "the most beautiful woman in the world," Hope Lange, but nothing came of it. He spoke openly of Hope as his mistress in social gatherings, even when Mary was present and within earshot. She seemed not to care. One day when he went into New York to see Hope, he returned home for dinner to announce that he loved two women. That was all right with her, Mary said. She was never possessive or jealous about him. If she could help it, she did not intend to let herself be hurt.

As the marriage ties weakened, Cheever formed an ever closer bond with his younger son. In the fall of 1970, Susie and Rob stayed briefly at Cedar Lane upon their return from fifteen months in Spain and England, but soon they moved to a rented house in Armonk, and she began her writing career as a reporter on the *Tarrytown Daily News*. Ben, though living nearby, was virtually separated from his family for the nine years following his marriage in 1969. His wife, Linda, thought he had been given short shrift by his father: when Ben did come by the house, often it was to ask for money. Fred was the only child at home. He and his father spent a lot of time together.

Their relationship was a curious one. John depended on his shy and pudgy son at least as much as Fred did on him. He was as generous with his time as any father could be. They tossed balls back and forth. They sat together and watched television. Once a week in the good weather, they walked the six-mile round trip to the Croton dam accompanied by Hoover, the imaginary dog the boy invented when Maisie went to live with Rob and Susie. On Sundays they occasionally cooked dinner, fashioning Beef Wellington out of a recipe in the *New York Times Magazine* or a ham soufflé according to the instructions in the Waring blender book. They swam at Sara Spencer's pool and went skating on her pond. They did almost everything together.

In time, Fred assumed the function of protecting his father against his baser instincts. When they went swimming, the fourteen-year-old cautioned his father not to swim naked: people might come along. When he came home from Hackley and a losing soccer

game, tired and upset, and his father was drunk and nasty, Fred
yelled at him over the dinner table and struck him in his chair
afterward. The physical threats all went one way, for John was in
terrible shape from alcohol and Fred was much the largest of the
Cheevers. Later, when Suntory sent Cheever a case of their whiskey, Fred poured most of it down the drain. The boy proved his
usefulness time and again as parent to his own father.

Though Cheever had very different relations with each of his
children, it is noteworthy—as Fred points out—that they all stand
up for him. "He always cared enormously, even in the worst times
with Ben." Moreover, he "valued family life more than anyone I've
ever known," Fred observes. Only in domesticity could he feel a
kind of redemption, a sense of his own goodness. Otherwise, as in
his journals, he excoriated himself. In this connection, Fred cites
a story about the philosopher Alfred North Whitehead. Univer-
sally regarded as a brilliant and wonderful man, Whitehead was
talking to himself on a walk across campus when a student came
up behind him and overheard what he was saying. The great man
was cursing himself.

Fred traveled with his parents wherever they went during those
years. In the summer of 1970, for instance, John took him and Mary
along on his trip to South Korea as a delegate to the Thirty-seventh
International PEN Congress. Updike was also a delegate to this
meeting. The American delegation was seated next to the South
Vietnamese. At one session, Updike recalls, Cheever turned to him
and said, "with mixed alarm and delight, that the Vietnamese next
to him was quite crazy." For the most part the trip was a success.
Each delegate was welcomed with silks and flowers and a three-
volume edition of the speeches of General Park, the South Korean
president.

At a geisha house Cheever was "washed, examined, kissed, and
fed by hand." At the National Theater, dancing girls performed for
the visiting dignitaries, and Updike's noticing—upon close observation—that their knees were wrinkled inspired an exchange of
doggerel with Mary Cheever.

Mary addressed Updike as an "eagley American" who

> clasps the legs with languid hands
> of dancing girls in Orient lands.
> Ringed with the stars and stripes he stands.

The wrinkled knees beneath him crawl.
He squirms, he writhes, he climbs the wall
and on his dimpled plumpside falls.

Updike responded amiably:

I hope that I may never seize
Another pair of wrinkled knees,
But if I do, I hope that they
Are somewhere east of Oakland Bay.

The Cheevers stopped again in Japan on the trip home, ignoring the attractions of Expo to look at shrines and cedar forests and waterfalls. The three of them came home refreshed by their travels. The following year, John took Fred along on his second journey to Russia.

The Soviet Writers Union invited Cheever to represent his country at the Dostoyevsky jubilee in the fall of 1971. He and Fred arrived at Moscow in a blizzard. Asked if there was anything he'd like, Cheever said, "I'd really like a swim." His Russian hosts huddled, and then dispatched him to Tbilisi instead of Riga, the headquarters for the Dostoyevsky observances. It was warm in Tbilisi, the leaves just beginning to fall, and father and son swam in the rivers of southwestern Georgia while speeches and concerts in honor of the Russian writer "raged in snowbound Riga." At Homeric banquets the Cheevers were provided with vast quantities of wine and vodka, multiple toasts were offered, and it was considered impolite not to participate. "Heavy drinking was virtually a social obligation in that society," Fred recalls. The boy, only fourteen, had more than enough to drink himself, and contracted a bad case of indigestion. During a half-hour interview show on Georgian television, he discovered—five minutes into the show—that an attack of diarrhea was imminent. He sweated out the half hour, literally, and then, desperate for relief, was led to a floor drain that manifestly would not serve his emergency.

As in 1964, Cheever was impressed by the Russians' hospitality, their fondness for ceremony, and their respect for the art of writing. At the home of the poet laureate of Georgia, the master of the house opened a bottle of wine before dinner and his wife took the bottle and sprinkled a bit of wine on the linen tablecloth as she moved around the beautifully appointed table. Her guests were not to feel embarrassed, she explained, should they spill some wine. From Georgia they flew back to the snow and cold of Moscow and Leningrad for the rest of their two-week stay. Cheever collected six thousand rubles in royalties there, and even after buying nine fur hats and five strings of amber, he had sixteen hundred rubles left. He could not take the money out of the country, and so when it was time to return, he offered to give it to Tanya Litvinov. She couldn't accept it herself, she said, but would take it to help publish samizdats, underground books and pamphlets. At this stage Cheever withdrew the offer.

As he later explained his actions, he feared that if he gave Tanya money for samizdats she might "end up on a Siberian manure pile." In addition, it seemed to him, perhaps naively, that Russia was a country where writers were valued for their work, political considerations aside. He worried that the success of *Bullet Park* in that country was due to its implicit criticism of the contemporary American scene. "If you think that's what the book is about, we've both failed," he told his Russian colleagues. That was not it at all, they assured him. They liked the book because of its evocation of the natural world, the way he described autumn leaves blowing in automobile headlights.

Undoubtedly, too, he was flattered by the attention paid him in Russia, the sense that he was more honored elsewhere than at home or in the United States generally. In Moscow, for example, he was taken to the Kremlin to meet Nikolai V. Podgorny, the president of the Supreme Soviet. (Podgorny kept a shoeshine machine in his office.) At the same time he well understood the repressive side of the government that honored him. In Leningrad he was less reckless on walks than he had been seven years earlier. He was probably a little afraid that the Soviets might kidnap him (and his son), and so "always said very nice things" about Russia, Fred thought.

In October, Cheever went to Chicago on his own, lured by the munificence of *Playboy* to its International Writers' Convocation. Sean O'Faolain, Alberto Moravia, and V. S. Pritchett attended from overseas, along with American columnists, political commentators, sportswriters, and at least one poet—James Dickey. The convocation, held at the Playboy Towers hotel, was "lavish, decorous, and a success." The assembled writers feasted on caviar and rack of lamb, and drank all they wanted in the Writers' Lounge, kept open until 4:00 A.M. each night. There were, however, no bunnies on display, since editorial director A. C. Spectorsky wanted to keep the meeting serious. Futurist Arthur C. Clarke, addressing the group, envisioned a society in which no one would go to the office. "The slogan will be, 'Don't commute, communicate.' " Cheever nodded vigorously in agreement and sailed a paper airplane across the table.

He stole away from such heady thoughts long enough to have lunch with Dick Stern at the Pump Room, where they called Hope Lange from their table. (She wasn't home.) And he visited a steam room with Saul Bellow, where—he maintained—Bellow inspected Cheever's parts while he studiously avoided gazing at Bellow's. The rest of Bellow looked more Olympian, he admitted, but he suspected Saul "was trying." Both enjoyed the steam bath visit. As Bellow observed, "writers don't get a chance to talk with each other naked very often."

Also in the summer of 1971, Cheever began teaching a class in creative writing at the Ossining Correctional Facility, a.k.a. Sing Sing. To begin with he had no idea of gathering material for a novel. He decided to teach at Sing Sing, he said, because someone at a party had said there were two thousand prisoners and only six teachers. Besides, "it was closer than Princeton." On his first day, Cheever was bused inside the prison walls, escorted by guards through the key room and past five clanging gates, unlocked and locked behind them, to a classroom with a yellowed American flag where twenty inmates awaited him. Two of them showed talent, and one of the two, Donald Lang, vividly recalls that first day.

To begin with, Lang was pretty antagonistic. "Who in hell is John Cheever?" he wondered. When Cheever showed up, Lang was disappointed in the way he looked and annoyed by the way he talked. Writers were supposed to look like Hemingway, or at least act like him. Yet here was this little guy with what sounded like a phony accent. "One expects," Cheever intoned New Englandly, and Lang thought to himself, "One *what?*" Was this guy showing off? And why in hell was he coming to Sing Sing now after twenty years in the community? Was this some kind of fashionable thing to do?

Almost immediately, however, Cheever earned the inmates' respect by showing up for class after the riots at Attica, another New York state prison thirty miles east of Buffalo. On September 9, about half of the twenty-two hundred prisoners at Attica revolted, seizing forty guards and others as hostages and taking control of four out of five cellblocks. Four days later, after some highly publicized negotiations with radical figures like Bobby Seale and William Kunstler serving as go-betweens, Governor Nelson Rockefeller ordered the state troopers to attack. Behind a blanket of tear gas, they laid down a fusillade of rifle and shotgun fire. Thirty inmates were killed, and two hundred injured. Nine of the hostages were also gunned down. Word of the riots at Attica circulated on the Sing Sing grapevine, and things were very tense there. The prison population of Sing Sing was then about 65 percent black, and there was a sense—Lang said—that if the blacks found a leader, they'd riot. The place was a powder keg about to go off, and the authorities imposed extremely tight security. Yet Cheever came in to teach right after Attica, and Lang "had to admire" him for that.

"I wonder where a little shit like you gets the balls to come in here," he said.

"I don't think anyone will hurt me, Lang," Cheever answered.

As time went on, Lang and Cheever discovered that they had a lot to teach each other, and not only about writing. Lang had spent seventeen of his thirty-one years behind bars, and knew very little about how to act on the outside. But he could, and did, tell Cheever what it was like on the inside. As a visitor to the prison, Cheever was never in a cellblock or the mess hall or the shops. To learn more about Sing Sing, he sat Don down and had him go over the daily routine and tell him stories about the brutality of the place. There was a goon squad to deal with troublemakers, for example. They'd isolate the offender in a cell, and let four or five other guys in to "put a beating" on him. "Dead," the certificate would read, "by natural causes."

Lang told him too about the sadistic "asshole" guard named Tiny and the stray cats that hung around the mess hall, about the homosexuality and the fights. Cheever stored the anecdotes away, later to emerge in *Falconer,* his 1977 novel set in a prison very like Sing Sing.

Lang and Cheever became close friends after Lang's release from Sing Sing in December 1971. When Lang got out, Cheever and William Campbell were there to drive him to the halfway house in Poughkeepsie. Two weeks later he was back in Ossining, working for Gray Smith's Street Theater and installed as a boarder in the home of John and Mary Dirks. "This little *pale* black Irish type showed up" on her doorstep, Mary remembers, and stayed for almost a year. Lang would look no one in the eye and had no concept of social obligation, yet there was a natural sweetness in him, he was handy around the house, and he was obviously intelligent. He took the Dirkses to see *The French Connection,* elaborating on the fine points of that world of cops and robbers, drugs and pimps. They gave him for the first time a patterned and comfortable life—he had never seen a fire in a fireplace before—and tried to show him how people who built fires in fireplaces talked and acted and used their knives and forks. At one cocktail party, Lang remembers, he and Cheever were "doing some bullshit" when someone walked up and asked, with real wonderment, "Where did you two meet, anyway?" "Oh," Cheever answered, enjoying it, "in Sing Sing."

Cheever took a protective attitude toward Lang, most of the time. When Lang got drunk and knocked out all his teeth falling down a flight of concrete steps, Cheever helped him pay for the dentures. When a car dealer sold Lang a lemon, Cheever went down to the dealer and bitched. When Lang got mixed up in a barroom brawl, Cheever bailed him out of jail. "I would like," he told Lang afterward, "not to do this again."

Cheever made him feel he might do something with his life, Lang said. He encouraged his writing, and recommended his satirical "The Pit-Wig Papers" to Candida Donadio. With the Street Theater Lang demonstrated his talents at carpentry and electricity. He also handled the logistics for a touring company of *Ceremonies in Dark Old Men* that performed—among other places—within the walls of Sing Sing. Then he struck out on his own doing odd jobs for contractors and working occasionally for Cheever and Art Spear. One spring day, he cut Fred Cheever's hair, using some barbering skills he'd picked up in prison. One summer, Fred worked happily with Lang and his crew of (mostly) ex-cons.

Above all it was Cheever's willingness to accept Lang, despite his criminal record, that solidified their relationship. As a mentor he had mixed results. He could not cure Lang of his habit of showing up without calling first. "You can't do that," he'd say. "You're interrupting my work." "What work?" Lang would ask. "I don't see no hammer, no paintbrush." And he could not persuade Lang to embark on a reading program he'd devised. The best teaching method, Cheever found, was that of example. He took Lang to a restaurant in Croton for soft-shelled crabs; after he ate the whole thing himself, Lang reluctantly did the same. "He taught me a lot by association," Lang says. "He didn't tell me, but showed me."

They both enjoyed the outdoor life—hiking through the woods, swimming, ice skating. They made a six-pool journey one day, à la "The Swimmer." Though Lang was, in Cheever's phrase, "a comely man," he was not welcomed at every pool. Iole had her reservations about him, too. She was fixing lunch when Lang was working around the house, and asked Mary Cheever, in Italian, if she was supposed to feed *il ladro* too. Lang had picked up enough street Italian to know that *il ladro* meant thief. Occasionally Cheever took Lang into New York City for dinner, where such questions were not asked. Candida Donadio went out with them one night, where it seemed clear to her that Cheever was smitten by Lang.

Whenever they'd meet, he gave Lang a hug. "It took time to get used to that," Don remembers, but he took it as an indication of Cheever's need for physical affection. He seemed to be terribly lonely. "Do you have any buddies?" Lang asked him. "Arthur Spear's a buddy of mine," Cheever replied. "You mean, you two old guys are *buddies*?" Lang asked incredulously. Cheever didn't seem to have any "tight friends," Lang thought. "I don't know who would be a tight friend except for me."

Once Lang really got to know Cheever, there didn't seem to be any facade to him at all. Lang refused to be impressed by anything he said or did, and with him Cheever shucked off the restraints of suburban middle-class mores. If he wanted to dive into a pond, he did. If he wanted to drink at the Orchid Lounge, a black bar in downtown Ossining, he did that too, matching Lang's beers with martinis and talking away the afternoon. There was a real sympathy between them. "We didn't have to say anything," Lang recalls. "He'd just read it if I was up or down." Cheever felt an affinity for the ex-convict, as for all those who dared to subvert the expectations of organized society. In any dispute between the cons and the guards at Sing Sing, he was all for the cons.

Over a period of time, his weekly visits to Sing Sing became burdensome. In the summer of 1972, when the Boyers moved away from Westchester, they donated some of their books to the prison library, including a set of the Harvard Classics. Cheever delivered the boxes, and had to wait in the hot room for what seemed an eternity while the guards inspected each book, page by page, for possible subversive material. They found two old Christmas cards. In the hot weather the prison seemed "cruel and dangerous." During the 1972–73 year he acquired a couple of new students with talent, but their stories were depressingly similar. More and more he was troubled by "the blasphemy of men building, stone by stone, hells for other men." Going to Sing Sing was like "participating in an obscenity." He stuck it out, though, until the spring of 1973.

With so little fiction issuing from his typewriter, the free-spending side of Cheever gave way to the parsimonious one. When Susie and Ben came to him for loans, they were turned down. In the spring of 1972, he was ready to resign from the Century Club as a luxury he could ill afford. His depression extended beyond the realm of finances. It was as if he were ready to drop out entirely. At a Yaddo board meeting he spoke of his own career as finished. It was time, he said, for younger people to take over.

Privately, he rather resented the competition, particularly from the school of fabulists—John Hawkes, John Barth, Donald Barthelme, William Gass, Robert Coover, Thomas Pynchon—whose reputations were flourishing in academic circles. Barthelme was "taking his space" in *The New Yorker,* he feared. It was unfair to Barthelme as a young writer, he told Morris Lurie, to praise him so highly when he had so far written so little. As for Barth, he used to tell the story of a literary dinner where he, Barth, and Jean Stafford were all in attendance. Stafford drew him aside and remarked, "John, your reputation in American literature is very shaky. God knows what will happen to it, but if you put a knife in Barth's back, you will be immortal."

Television offered yet another threat to his occupation. "Television debases literature," he said in a May 1972 talk at son Fred's Hackley School. TV shows demanded little or nothing of their viewers: they were designed to be forgotten the next morning, if not sooner. "I'd hate to write a book and think I was competing for the attention of a man who was reading and watching football at the same time." Literature was one of the glories of mankind, but this new medium put it in peril and so threatened his whole reason for existence. Only occasionally was he reassured, as by a review of Updike's that made him feel writing fiction was more important than "ironing shirts in a Chinese laundry."

Fred Exley, teaching at the Iowa Writers' Workshop, inveigled Cheever into coming to Iowa City for a reading in the fall of 1972.

Cheever arrived well in advance of the scheduled reading, and for three days he and Exley drank and talked together. John spoke bitterly of the state of his marriage, coughed his way through his reading of "The Death of Justina," and wowed Exley's writing class with some improbable anecdotes. He was more or less enchanted by the twenty-year-old coed Exley had fallen in love with. He was impressed by the interest in writers and writing around the university. People kept greeting Exley on the street in hopes, as he explained, of getting introduced to Cheever. Jack Leggett, director of the writing program, had a dinner for Cheever and proposed that he might want to spend a semester teaching there. Leggett hardly expected an affirmative answer, but he got one. Cheever signed on for the fall 1973 semester. His writing was not going well in Ossining. He hoped that a change of rivers—from the Hudson to the Iowa—would help. In addition, Fred was leaving for boarding school at Andover in September, and it had been Fred's presence at home, more than anything else, that kept his parents from separating during the early 1970s.

In her poem "Gorgon," Mary Cheever in effect declared her independence while summoning up the very powerful, at least slightly malevolent woman whose image, she believed, was pervasive in her husband's thoughts as in his fiction. He identified this woman (probably derived from his mother) with Mary herself, and nothing she could do would displace the image.

> I have sometimes complained, husband,
> that as you feinted, shadowboxed and blindly
> jived to that misty monolithic woman in your mind
> I have been battered, drowned under your blows.
>
> Not knives, not brassknuckles, not poison or needles,
> no weapons, no holds between you two
> were foul or out of bounds.
>
> Now suddenly in the dawnlight
> lying across our bed while you fuss
> and nicker at my breast
> I can feel myself growing.
> I have become immense.
> The shadows curve black from my body,

which is glowing moonwhite.
I am beautiful. God, how beautiful!

Dear, if you should decide to take
the gold rings out of my ears,
you will need a ladder.
I would help you if I could,
but my arms have turned to stone.

Cheever was outraged by the poem, but had it practically by heart.

If Mary was growing stronger, her husband manifestly was not. His heartbeat was wildly irregular, and he was often short of breath. Dr. Mutter put him on Xylocaine to numb the abnormal heart rhythm and on Seconal to sleep, but the symptoms worsened. In May 1973, Cheever collapsed and was taken to Phelps Memorial Hospital in nearby Tarrytown. A heart attack struck him down, Cheever always said, but that was not entirely accurate. He was afflicted by dilated cardiomyopathy, a disease (according to Dr. Robert A. Johnson, who treated Cheever in Boston during the spring of 1975) that is sometimes caused by alcoholism and is often fatal. In cardiomyopathy the left ventricle stops ejecting blood, the heart dilates under the consequent pressure, and the lungs fill with fluid. What hospitalized Cheever, technically, was not a heart attack—EKGs showed no evidence of such an attack—but a pulmonary edema brought on by drink.

In the hospital, deprived of liquor, he began to hallucinate. For three days—Saturday, Sunday, and Monday—he was convinced that he was being held in a Russian prison camp, and tried frantically to get free. He detached the oxygen tubes and ripped out his IV. Family and friends took turns at bedside, holding him down. When he was alone, nurses strapped him to the bed and straitjacketed him. In the delirium of alcoholic withdrawal, he refused to acknowledge reason. Susan brought him a copy of a favorable review of *The World of Apples*, his collection of stories that had just been published, but Cheever thought it was a confession for him to sign and flung it on the floor. Finally, though, he was ready to be persuaded that he was in a Westchester County hospital and not a Soviet prison camp, especially after Fred produced a sign printed in English. "Oxygen—No Smoking" it read.

In a letter to Gottlieb, he made light of his illness, as a consequence of which "wealthy and beautiful divorcées" brought him gifts. Still, the experience obviously scared him. Both Dr. Mutter and Dr. Frank Jewett, a psychiatrist, assured him that if he started to drink again, he would kill himself. In consultation with Jewett, he compared the euphoria of alcohol to that of writing something you really like. He resisted the implications of the observation: that if he wasn't writing anything he much liked, he might turn to alcohol as a substitute. He soon abandoned therapy with Jewett, and refused to join Alcoholics Anonymous. But he was frightened enough to quit drinking, temporarily. He felt delivered from the grave. If it was possible to start a new life at sixty-one, that's what he intended to do. "Alcohol seems no problem," he cheerfully announced early in June. Two months later he admitted to taking three drinks a day.

On May 16, as Cheever lay bound to his bed fancying himself in a Soviet prison camp, five men in New York nominated him for elevation from the National Institute to the American Academy of Arts and Letters. Or, rather, they renominated him, since his name was first proposed in 1971 by Robert Penn Warren, Malcolm Cowley, Peter Blume, John Hersey, and Mark Van Doren. The sponsors were the same two years later, except that Van Doren was replaced by Glenway Wescott. "In a series of stories unsurpassed in his generation and in his excellent novels," Warren wrote in the nominating petition, "John Cheever has reported faithfully a segment of modern America and at the same time has created a world that embodies his personal vision." Not until November did Cheever get word that he had been elected.

Critics as well as his artistic peers were well disposed toward Cheever's work in the spring of 1973. They gave *The World of Apples* a strongly favorable reception, though it is arguable that few of the stories in the book measure up to Cheever's best. Several of them begin or end brilliantly. In each there are passages of limpid iridescence that only Cheever could have written. Yet only rarely do these stories achieve the emotional power of "The Enormous Radio" or "Goodbye, My Brother" or "The Country Husband" or "The Swimmer." The most moving piece in the collection is the shortest, one in a series of vignettes printed as "Three Stories." On a transatlantic plane trip from New York to Rome, a well-intentioned man in the aisle seat tries to conduct a civil conversation with the woman in the window seat, but she rudely repudiates all his overtures. Then the plane lands, and why is the man helping collect her bags and why does he join her in the cab? "Is he the undiscouragable masher that she dreaded? No, no. He is her husband, she is his wife, the mother of his children, and a woman he has worshipped passionately for nearly thirty years." That was a cry from the heart.

Aside from "Percy" and "The Jewels of the Cabots," both of which draw on his Yankee heritage, most of the stories are concerned either with loveless marriages or with sex. His characters are bombarded by exhibitions of pornography and scatology. The world has become so overtly dirty-minded, one story suggests, that pure literature has gone underground and can only be found on lavatory walls. Yet in "Artemis, the Honest Well-Digger" Cheever depicts a man whose innocence protects him from the venality and venery around him. And in the title story, the aging poet Asa Bascomb finally purges his mind of obscene thoughts. In the act of exorcism, he strips naked and stands under the torrent of a waterfall, bellowing with joy, just as his father had done many years before.

In these stories as in much of Cheever's fiction, water has miraculous restorative powers. Two women emerge naked from the sea at the end of "Goodbye, My Brother," and bring back the joy that the despised brother, Lawrence, apparently sought to dissipate. It is the rain on his head, and the smell of it flying up to his nose, that cures Johnny Hake of his Shady Hill housebreaking. The narrator in "A Vision of the World," awakened by the rain, sits up in bed and exclaims to himself, "Valor! Love! . . . Wisdom! Beauty!" Reciting the words and listening to the sound of the rain make him "contented and at peace with the night." Nailles saves his son, Tony, from immolation in the midst of a rainstorm. Artemis the good "loved the healing sound of rain—the sound of all running water—brooks, gutters, spouts, falls, and taps." Stepping out of the waterfall, Asa Bascomb seems at last to be himself. "In the morning he began a long poem on the inalienable dignity of light and air that, while it would not get him the Nobel Prize, would grace the last months of his life." Water and light, light and water—only these kept "the world from flying to pieces."

IOWA-BOSTON-SMITHERS

1973-1975

WITH Fred packed off to Andover, Ben more or less estranged, Susie and Rob's marriage breaking up, and his relationship with Mary worsening, Cheever returned to Iowa City in the fall of 1973 to teach for a semester at the university's famous writers' workshop. The Iowa sky was bluer and clearer than in the East, and the twilights longer. Front porches ran the width of the houses, declaring themselves to passersby. The Iowa River, a ten-minute swim across at its widest, wound through the campus and the town. The cornfields began at the outskirts, but corn—Cheever soon learned—did not presage "vulgarity and provincialism." Students who walked barefoot in the warm fall weather were carrying Wittgenstein and Descartes, *Double-Entry Bookkeeping* and *Basic Italian*. His aspiring writers were extraordinarily talented, his teaching colleagues accomplished professionals. He was in another country, and loved it nearly as much as the long-term settlers. "Don't tell anyone," they warned him. "They'll only spoil it." "Iowa City—Gateway to Nebraska," they called it, in hopes that visitors would keep going to Omaha.

The worm in this Midwestern apple was his small and sparsely furnished room in Iowa House. A four-story red-brick building run by the university, Iowa House resembled nothing so much as a large motel, with a cafeteria downstairs and ice and Coke machines on every floor. The rooms featured motel-standard blue carpeting, green bedspreads, and beige walls. Cheever's had two single beds and a dresser, bolted to which was a nineteen-inch black-and-white television set. It was not much of a home away from home, but the window offered a redeeming view of the serpentine river, the bridge across it, and the people who jogged or strolled along its banks in the morning and evening.

At first Cheever seemed uneasy in his new surroundings. Fellow instructor John Irving, not yet famous for *The World According to Garp*, asked him over on the day of his arrival, and Cheever seemed proper, polite, and unhappy. He wore a navy-blue suit, with the pin of the National Institute on his lapel. Ron Hansen, novelist-to-be but then a student and teaching fellow in the workshop, asked him what the pin represented, and Cheever explained about the National Institute and the American Academy "as if he were prepared to be patient about anything now that he'd accepted a visiting professorship." Yet it was not really necessary, in Iowa, for Cheever to declare who he was. Students and faculty alike eagerly awaited his arrival. The local newspaper ran a feature about him. The president of the university asked him to dinner. He was also invited elsewhere, often. Iowa was proud to have him around, and eager to show him a good time. He was soon caught up in a variety of things to do and people to do them with. He went to jazz concerts and a bluegrass festival. He went to boat races and rugby games and the Big Ten football games on Saturday. He began to get acquainted with some of those curious folk who foregather in university towns—the odd ducks among the professoriate and student body, the graduates who decide, having nothing better to do, to hang around and pursue eccentric lives.

Cheever's closest friendships in Iowa, naturally enough, were made through the writers' workshop. He and John Irving used to watch *Monday Night Football* together while eating homemade pasta. Cheever told Irving, as he told almost everyone, that his marriage was on the rocks, that he suspected his wife of adultery, and that he felt terribly lonely. Irving was touched by his vulnerability, and pleased that such a wonderful writer was willing to treat him as an equal. The bond between them was solidified by the visit to campus of J. P. Donleavy. Both Irving and Cheever admired Donleavy's *The Ginger Man,* but Donleavy himself was something else. Irving picked up the Donleavys at the airport and drove them around, whereupon they began to act like "unhappy royalty in a hick town." Was this Kansas? they wanted to know. Donleavy let it be known that he read the work of no one living, and that he thought writing workshops a great waste of time. Introduced to Cheever, he acted as if he weren't even there. When Cheever tried to engage him in conversation—"and Cheever," Irving pointed out, "was as gifted in conversation as any man I ever met"—Donleavy remained coldly discourteous.

Finally Cheever had had enough. "Do you know, Mr. Donleavy," he said, "that no *major* writer of fiction was ever a shit to another writer of fiction, except Hemingway—and he was crazy?" He and Irving decided not to attend Donleavy's reading, instead retiring to a bar to debate whether the visitor was "a *minor* writer, a shit, crazy—or all three."

Raymond Carver, also teaching in the fiction program at the workshop and living in Iowa House, was gratified to have Cheever for a colleague. "He was a *writer,* not a beginner like myself," Carver remembers, and he had never heard anyone so eloquent and witty in his use of the spoken language. Still, it was liquor that tied them together. Both were serious drinkers at the time, serious enough so that they almost never took the covers off their own typewriters. Twice a week Carver drove them to the liquor store to stock up. Once they made a date to meet in the lobby of Iowa House shortly before the liquor store opened at ten o'clock. Cheever was pacing up and down the lobby when Carver arrived, on time. The clerk was just opening the door when they got to the store, but Cheever clambered out of the car before it was properly parked and was standing at the checkout counter with his half-gallon of Scotch by the time Carver got inside.

"Oh, yes," Mary said of her husband's Midwestern sojourn,

"John went out to Iowa to drink." Liberated from the usual domestic restraints, he was soon drinking as much as he had before the May 1973 collapse, and investigating the sexual revolution. As Allan Gurganus recalls, Cheever "essentially came on to almost every student he found at all attractive," of either sex. This was done with great charm and without dodging, liquor smoothing the way for whatever did or did not happen. At the first private conference with his writing students, Cheever offered them a water glass full of straight Scotch. Gurganus drank his down, dutifully, and reeled out into the early-afternoon sun.

Cheever had two classes at Iowa, one a fiction-writing seminar and the other a literature course built around novels he'd read and liked. The competition for places in both courses was fierce. In the fiction-writing course, especially, Cheever confronted the very best second-year graduate students. Three members of that workshop— Gurganus, Hansen, and T. Coraghessan (Tom) Boyle—went on to become novelists, and all of them knew their way around writing seminars better than their instructor. That class, Hansen reports, had the sharpest competitive edge of any he ever attended. "And yet Cheever managed to make it generally civil through the simple exercise of good manners, propriety, and decorum." Manifestly he did not like arguments. And when he liked a story, he could ill abide unwarranted criticism of it. Tom Boyle, for example, vividly recalls Cheever coming to the defense of a story of his called "Drowning."

In private conferences, Cheever had an uncanny sense for what did or did not work, but was not always able to indicate why. He was very good at fixing sentences and at suggesting character through description and detail. Perhaps a boy "could lick a finger to comb his eyebrows," he suggested to Gurganus, and it could turn out that his parents hated that gesture. Or perhaps an aging man, instead of simply getting fat and bald, might wonder why his knees had begun to feel "squashy."

Meeting his first class at Iowa, Cheever was terribly nervous, and the more nervous he got the more gargly his talk became. He asked the students about their favorite authors. A few mentioned Vonnegut and Barth, which were not the answers he was looking for. Others said Proust and Balzac, and that was more like it. Then he launched his students on a regimen that some of them—already in the process of writing novels—thought unnecessarily fundamental. He asked them, first of all, to keep a journal for at least a week, recording their experiences, feelings, dreams, orgasms, and even such quotidian details as the clothes they wore and the food and drink they consumed. Second, he required them to write a story in which seven people or landscapes that superficially have nothing to do with one another are somehow profoundly allied. Third, and this was his favorite assignment, he told them to write a love letter from inside a burning building. This exercise "never fails," he maintained. In Gurganus's case it led to a piece that went right into the *Atlantic Monthly*. He had but one standard for grading the results: "Is it interesting or is it dull?"

Cheever found teaching at Iowa a tremendously invigorating experience. His students were "brilliant and diverse" and eager to learn. Above all he wanted them to take notice, to be alive to the world around them and the people in it. John Gerber, then chairman of the Iowa English department, persuaded Cheever to speak about writing to a Unitarian group one evening. Afterward someone asked, "What do you look for when you see people? Take John Gerber, for example. What do you see when you look at him?" "No," Cheever replied, "I won't take John Gerber but I'll take you. I notice for one thing that you have a fine and full voice, and I assume that you like to use it . . ." and so on. (In fact, the questioner was a wonderful singer.) Gerber thought Cheever unusual among writing instructors for the interest he took in his students. He didn't just meet his classes and disappear. Some of his students became his intimate friends.

A first-year graduate student from the University of Maine, Lucy Miner, talked her way into Cheever's literature class and soon became his more or less constant companion. The class met at 11:00 A.M., and she came by Iowa House in advance to pick him up and walk to the English and Philosophy Building together. Usually he had begun drinking by that time. In the evenings they frequently went to dinner together, often for a quiet hamburger at the Mill. When someone called to ask him out to dinner, he would say, "I'd love to, but I'm dining with Miss Miner tonight," and both of them would be invited. Eventually people learned to call her and ask if *they* were busy. At parties, she played a proprietary role by getting him home before extreme drunkenness set in. They would settle on a time to leave the Leggetts, say, and when the hour arrived, she would signal him and hustle him away.

Her relationship with Cheever gave her a certain standing among the workshop students. Many assumed they were lovers, and Cheever encouraged the assumption in his conversation and correspondence. According to Lucy Miner, it was not that way at all. At the time he was an alcoholic in very poor health, hardly a robust sixty-three-year-old: their relationship remained platonic, whatever others might have thought. She did, however, learn a great deal from him about writing—and they had wonderful times together as well. In the supermarket, for example, they used to enact a family quarrel for the entertainment of other shoppers. "Listen," he'd yell at her, slapping the back of one hand against the palm of the other to punctuate his tirade. "I've told you (slap) a hundred times (slap) that you're spending too much money. The mink coat (slap) was all right, but the Maserati is going too far. You've got (slap) to think of the children." It is clear that he and Lucy Miner were the closest of friends during his four months in Iowa, and that they later maintained their friendship through the mails. She has letters from Cheever and photographs he sent her— even his Playboy gold card. He had a duplicate set of keys to her car in his desk drawer on the day he died.

While he and Lucy Miner were keeping company in Iowa City, the wife he loved was back in Ossining. When Mary came for a visit, he organized a reception for her at Iowa House, complete with a carved swan on ice. Susan Boyd, wife of the university president, was surprised by the amount of work Cheever put into the reception. "He really wanted it to be something she'd like," she recalls. Moreover, his friendship with Sarah Irwin, a student in his writing seminar, was based largely on what he characterized as his role of loser in love. Mary was the beloved and he the lover, he told Irwin, and since she felt herself in a similar position, they commiserated with each other over a good many drinks of Scotch. Cheever told her, for instance, that he felt powerless to convey the depth of his love to Mary. (Drinking and infidelity sent a contradictory message.) But he and Irwin enjoyed happy hours together too, most notably during Saturday-afternoon football games at Kinnick Stadium. They walked to the game, the impeccably dressed Cheever carrying a lap robe over one arm and a flask under the other. There they emptied the flask and ate hot dogs and peanuts while watching the Hawkeyes lose time and again. Cheever delighted in the pageantry, and especially in a marching bagpipe band that played at halftime one day and followed them across the bridge after the game, playing all the while. In looking back on their friendship, Irwin is convinced that even at his most melancholy Cheever was always a great lover of life, always anticipating a tiny ray of light on the horizon.

Among the professoriate, Cheever's closest friend was the beautiful Indian critic and scholar Gayatry Spivak. Then in her early thirties, Spivak was going through a divorce; she and Cheever got to know each other when they were paired at dinner parties. As a committed intellectual her approach to literature could hardly have been more different from his. She was lecturing on poetry at the time, and was fascinated by the critical insights of European structuralists and deconstructionists. "Why does no one say Coleridge was a critic who could write poems?" she would challenge him. "Why is it always the writer first, and then the critic?" But the world of contemporary criticism, with its post-Marxist overtones, was one he cordially scorned. Spivak was herself stridently Marxist at the time. "Dear girl," he told her, "that's the one note of vulgarity in you." From him as from no one else, she suffered that "dear girl." Ordinarily she talked back to him, and he spoke openly to her of the most intimate subjects. In early-morning telephone calls, he discussed his writing, his fear of death, his sexual successes and failures. "Well, Gayatry, I couldn't get it up," he confessed one morning. "That's all right," she reassured him, "it happens to the best of us." At Walt's Bar they danced together—"badly, both of us"—and he provided her with an explicit and detailed description of his sexual relations with the black attendant at the garage next door.

It was his student Allan Gurganus and not the black garageman that Cheever most coveted, however. Gurganus rejected his overtures. He was worried about the complications of the dual teacher-lover role. And besides, it was clear that Cheever felt "confused and conflicted" about his own sexual orientation. Theirs remained a platonic relationship, and one that lasted. They took long walks together, often to the park to see the bison tethered in a pen: the West's last stand in Iowa City. Or they strolled on the paths along the river. On one outing, they stopped to watch a sandlot football game at a junior high school. An extra football was lying about, and they passed it around for twenty minutes or so, like father and son. Cheever mentioned that afternoon repeatedly in his letters to Gurganus. It was important to him. It made him happy. Their worst time came the night of the masquerade party for gays at the Unitarian church. Gurganus wore a German sailor's hat and navy uniform, and was dancing with a costumed partner when he looked outside and saw Cheever at the window, gazing in like Peter Quint, a rapt and censorious look on his face. Gurganus was furious, and Cheever was disgusted. Whatever he may have told Spivak or Irwin ("Fellatio," he said to her rather ambiguously, "is the nicest thing one human being can do for another"), he was a long way from declaring himself publicly as homosexual, or even bisexual. The overtly gay world repelled him.

Considering his compulsive drinking, Cheever remained surprisingly healthy during most of his semester in Iowa. There was acute bursitis in his shoulder in September, but thereafter no trouble until late in the fall when he underwent what he called "a mild heart attack or stroke." The symptoms were the same as in May, a wildly irregular heartbeat and terrible shortness of breath. He was walking across campus on a mild day when the tangible world seemed to float away. He sank to the grass, unable to cry out, certain that he was dying. He could dimly make out young men and women walking by, and it occurred to him that this vision of youth was the last thing that he would see and that there was a certain appropriateness about that, since it was partly the promise of contact with youth that had brought him to Iowa. Then the spell passed. He made his way back to Iowa House and, a few weeks later, to Ossining.

On December 7, official announcement was made of Cheever's election to the American Academy as the fifth occupant of Chair 17. (The previous occupants, he found, were John Singer Sargent, John Russell Pope, Sinclair Lewis, and Pearl S. Buck.) That was the only cheerful news. Back on Cedar Lane, he was visited by tremendous loneliness. This was not associated with longing for any person or persons, he thought. He simply stood alone, and painfully so. Yet he was writing "love letters to customers of very different flavors" in Iowa. In February he wangled a trip back to Iowa City to write a piece about the town and university for Caskie Stinnett, editor of *Travel & Leisure*. He wanted to be there for Lucy Miner's birthday, he wrote Stinnett (in fact her birthday does not fall in February), and tried to explain how he felt about "flying halfway across the country to see a young girl one-third my age."

Early in 1974 he agreed to accept a professorship at Boston University in the fall. It seemed time to leave home. At Andover, Fred had been transformed from a shy, overweight youngster into a friendly, handsome youth. Susie and Rob were moving toward

divorce. His own marriage, he thought, was virtually ended. Mary
was busy teaching at her progressive country day school in Nyack.
He planned to move to Boston taking "not a shell, not a stone"—
only three suits, half a dozen button-down shirts, and two pairs of
loafers.

Cheever's luck with *The New Yorker* had not been running well.
The magazine had turned down both "Artemis, the Honest Well-
Digger" and "The Jewels of the Cabots," and in the two years since
he'd had little or nothing to submit. So it gave him some pleasure
to introduce Maxwell to the work of Allan Gurganus. Early in
March *The New Yorker* accepted Gurganus's story "Minor Hero-
ism." Cheever called Gurganus in Iowa City with the news that he
was about to be published in *The New Yorker* and become "the most
famous graduate student in the midwest." He was fortunate to have
an editor like Bill Maxwell, Cheever added. Whatever their differences, he thought Maxwell was "the best editor on the scene."

As for his own writing, he had already begun the prison novel
that eventually became *Falconer,* but was making very little progress. Many days he could not stay away from drinking until noon,
or until eleven, or even until breakfast. Mary did her best to hold
down the supply of liquor around the house, but John found ways
of circumventing her attempts. As a fascinated nation watched the
Nixon administration self-destruct in the wake of the Watergate
revelations, Cheever's family and friends witnessed his private
disintegration. On Easter morning he stopped by the Dirkses'.
Company was coming, he said, and the liquor cabinet was empty.
He was unshaven and stinking of booze, but the Dirkses took him
at his word and gave him a bottle of bourbon. Cheever was taking
a slug as he drove away. Soon thereafter Mary Cheever called them.
"How could you do this?" she asked, and for Mary Dirks that was
the last straw. A few days later, she confronted Cheever. "Do you
realize what a mess you are? You look like a Bowery bum. You
don't care about yourself. All your friends are convinced you're
destroying yourself." He listened, and wanted to know if it was
really true that his friends felt that way. "Yes, they do," she said
emphatically.

His body, long toughened by outdoor work and play, began to
turn fragile. Early in April he took a walk, stumbled barefoot, and
fractured his left second toe. Another day that spring, Aline Benjamin happened upon Cheever at the Books 'n Things store in the

Arcadian Shopping Center. He looked awful: seedy, hair un-
combed, full of self-abnegation. He came over, put his head on her
shoulder, and said—nothing at all.

Dennis Coates came to see him often during the spring and
summer of 1974. A Regular Army officer, Coates was teaching at
West Point while finishing his doctoral dissertation on Cheever's
novels for Duke University. Cheever opened himself up in conversation with the young officer, discussing the most intimate family
matters. "I've never gone on so," he wrote the West Pointer, half
in apology. Coates kept telling Cheever that he felt unloved: that
was his problem. "Nonsense," Cheever replied, "just think of all
those who love me: the children, the dogs, even Mary." That might
be true, Coates agreed, but "you don't *feel* loved. You need a great
deal of love and affection, and it isn't there in your life. Isn't that
true?" In response, Cheever launched into a long story of his affair
with Hope Lange. He did not understand himself at all, Coates
concluded.

One memorable afternoon Cheever read him a story, "The
Leaves, the Lion-Fish, and the Bear," that he had just completed.
Coates listened happily as they sat at the dining-room table and his
favorite author read a new story to him. "The Leaves" consists of
a series of episodes arranged as variations on a theme. The most
arresting episode depicts a manly homosexual encounter. "Larry
Estabrook," it begins, "had read about homosexuality in the newspaper and understood that it was confined to biological degenerates
and men in prison." Nonetheless he picks up a hitchhiker on a trip
to Colorado, they are that night marooned by a snowstorm, and in
their motel room they drink whiskey and make love. In the morning, "Estabrook knew he had done that which by his lights he
should not have done but he felt no remorse at all—he felt instead
a kind of joy. . . ." Nor does the encounter affect his own marriage
adversely. "When he returned home at the end of the week, his wife
looked as lovely as ever—lovelier—and lovely were the landscapes
he beheld." Here, for the first time in his fiction, Cheever overtly
suggested that homosexual love might well occur within the context of a normal marriage, and with healthy consequences.

As he read the story, Cheever put his hand over that of Coates.
Then he took him for a walk into the hills behind his house. Atop
a hill overlooking the Hudson, it was very cold. "Hold me,"
Cheever said. That was all right with Coates—he had bundled

together for warmth during Ranger training—until Cheever started to move against him and tried to kiss him. "I'm sorry, John," he said, "but I don't go that way." Cheever was not immediately put off. "I'm no hard-core homosexual," he said. "I don't even know what they do. All I know is it opens up a wonderful world of love." But Coates could not be persuaded, and as they walked back to the house, he began to think about homosexual strains in Cheever's fiction. "It's been in your work all along, hasn't it?" he asked. "Of course it has," Cheever acknowledged. "It's always been there, for all the world to see."

On a bright summer evening, on the sun porch of Burnham and Sue Carter's home in Briarcliff, Mary Cheever, standing up very straight, announced that she and John were planning to divorce. There had been talk of divorce before, and most of the guests at the party had heard it, but this time it seemed more serious. Their marriage was on the brink of coming apart. Cheever's life staggered out of control under the influence of alcohol.

Gayatry Spivak came for a dinner party at Cedar Lane and stayed overnight. In the morning, Cheever poured himself a tumblerful of whiskey for breakfast. "Is this a person who cares about the excellence of the writer?" she demanded. "Now hush up," he told her, gently. "You're in my house now." To change the subject he started talking about the house and its late-eighteenth-century origins. When Richard Adams, British author of the popular *Watership Down*, came to the United States, he expressed a desire to meet Cheever. A dinner party was arranged, but Cheever passed out during the cocktail hour. He arrived late and very drunk for Christopher Lehmann-Haupt's fortieth-birthday party. As a present he brought along a bush for planting, then lost his balance and dropped the bush out of its pot.

During a trip to Provincetown, he reached an emotional nadir. Molly Cook, Mary Oliver, and Roger Skillings, all yeoman workers for the Provincetown Fine Arts Work Center, invited Cheever to do a reading as a benefit for the center. Cook and Skillings picked him up in Ossining for the drive to the Cape. Arthur Spear came along "to save Cheever's life"—that is, to try to hold his drinking down. En route, Cheever pulled steadily on his flask and complained bitterly that his work had been neglected, that *The New Yorker* had mistreated him, that other writers were overrated. Despite this spate of ill feeling and competitive bile, it was clear to everyone that Cheever was not so meanspirited as he seemed. The grievances were part of his cry for help, a cry that grew more distinct once they'd arrived in Provincetown.

The reading itself was successful enough. Though Cheever had so much to drink beforehand that he barely recognized his old friend Hazel Hawthorne, he went up on the platform and read beautifully. After that, it was all downhill. Cheever stayed in Provincetown for several days after Spear left, and continued to reach out for nurturing and comfort. He treated Cook "like his mother or something," crying on her shoulder, wailing that he hadn't any friends, seeking reassurance. At a dinner party Cook and Oliver gave, he persistently showed his affection for Skillings. In front of everyone, he attempted to hold his hand and then pursued him around the house. This seemed amusing at first, but became embarrassing as Cheever did not stop and Skillings did not know what to do. Cheever desperately needed taking care of, Cook decided. One bad day, he told her he'd "lost everything" and sounded suicidal. She called Skillings, who found Cheever on Bradford Street, walking head down, alone and unhappy.

In Ossining, Fred continued to serve as "his father's guardian." He did not hesitate to be stern and got better results than anyone else. In August, Mary went to Treetops, and in her absence Cheever planned to bring Lucy Miner to stay at Cedar Lane. That prompted a vehement father-son dispute. "You can't do it," Fred objected. "This is our house. Anything else is all right, but you can't bring her here." In the end, and despite Cheever's insistent invitations, Lucy Miner chose not to come to Ossining.

In mid-August—shortly before John was due to go to Boston to teach—Fred took the most drastic step of all. "I'll leave home," he threatened his father, "unless you go to the hospital to dry out." Iole assured Cheever that Fred meant it, and on August 20 he was admitted to Phelps to withdraw from liquor. At discharge he was put on ten milligrams of Valium every four hours and a high-protein diet to keep him from drinking. This regimen did not last long.

Once Cheever moved to Boston, there was no one to prevent him from abusing himself in any way he wished. But he did not go there solely to escape his bonds. He went for the money, too. His income, like that of most writers, fluctuated widely from year to year. In 1973, when *The World of Apples* came out, the family's combined income (Mary usually contributed about ten thousand dollars annually) came to more than fifty-five thousand dollars. The next year, it was down to twenty-four thousand, less than half of the sixty thousand a year Cheever thought necessary to keep up house and family and send Fred to school. Cutting back, he resigned from the Century Club. And in negotiating with George Starbuck, director of Boston University's writing program, he drove a hard bargain.

Actually, Cheever asked for two things that the university rarely provided. First of all, he insisted that B.U. provide him with an apartment. After some difficulty one was located at 71 Bay State Road, only a few blocks from the campus. Three full flights up, the apartment was nicely furnished if rather stuffy. The urban neighborhood was far from the paradise that Iowa had been. A line of brick bow-fronts faced him across the street. Break-ins were reported several times a week. Lacking green fields, students sailed their Frisbees at traffic intersections. For exercise Cheever walked the six-mile round trip to the Ritz Bar downtown: past Kenmore Square where the wind howled around the corners of the embalming school, along Commonwealth Avenue with its statues of William Lloyd Garrison and George Washington, Leif Ericson and the President of the Argentine.

The other thing that Cheever asked for—or hinted at, rather broadly—was female companionship. At Iowa, he intimated to Starbuck, he had been "provided" with a graduate student who slept with him. Since that seemed to be the style these days, couldn't B.U. do the same? There was a twinkle in his voice as he made the point, but Starbuck felt sure he was serious about it and might have tried to make such an arrangement if there had been an obvious candidate in evidence. What he did not realize, at first, was Cheever's need for companionship of all kinds. Other visiting writers—John Barth and Arturo Vivante among them—had sought protection against too much collegial socializing. So Starbuck was surprised when Cheever remarked, in November, that he'd hoped to be introduced around.

Within the English department, he felt a certain affinity for poet Anne Sexton ("I'm not the living Sylvia Plath," she used to insist), who stocked her handbag with airline liquor samples for department meetings, and for writer John Malcolm Brinnin ("I knew Cheever intimately but not well," Brinnin cryptically observes), but no one became his close companion or drinking buddy. Beginning what he regarded as a new life, Cheever was avid for human intercourse, but the phone didn't ring. Inexplicably, he'd had the number unlisted.

Starbuck also realized too late how much Cheever craved public recognition. If he had it to do over again, Starbuck observed, he would arrange for Cheever to be honored by the Boston Public Library, make some outreach to the mayor, involve the Athenaeum. As did Willy Loman, Cheever needed attention paid, the more so since he was losing confidence in his abilities. He was working on a novel, he told an interviewer in October. The book would be his tenth and probably his last. Ten made a nice round number, and he would rather stop than publish drivel the way some older writers did. The trouble was, there was no second career for worn-out writers. "Unlike baseball players, they can't sell insurance. Unlike prostitutes, they can't be hostesses."

His writing students in Boston, with a few exceptions, were not as talented as those at Iowa. Besides, there were far too many of them. Cheever was assigned two writing classes, one for graduate students and one for undergraduates: forty students in all. At first, he wrote Coates, his classes were "wonderfully responsive and contentious" and sometimes ran over three hours in length. By mid-October, that initial enthusiasm had dissipated. It was then that James Valhouli came to Boston to see him.

Valhouli, like Coates, did his doctoral dissertation on Cheever's work (Wisconsin, 1973), and during the 1974–75 academic year he was on leave from Bradford College in nearby Haverhill, Massachusetts. He planned to spend the time observing and taperecording Cheever's classes at Boston University, and then to write an article on the author as teacher. On Valhouli's first visit, however, Cheever had difficulty negotiating the walk to class after two hours of drinking Scotch. Inside, he was "visibly uncomfortable" facing grad students who knew very well he was drinking. Valhouli went to class with Cheever twice more, and then abandoned his project. It was too painful.

Valhouli continued to drive down to Boston periodically to see Cheever, however. He saw his role as that of a friend helping another man survive. He tried to cheer him up when Cheever spoke of his "crazy impulse" to throw himself in front of a car or described the dream he had of pallbearers carrying a coffin, with himself inside. He tried to get him to eat, for otherwise he was liable to drink indefinitely. He tried to get him to bed at a reasonable hour. Most of all, Valhouli provided Cheever with company,

since he was "desperately lonely" and badly in need of companionship. By midwinter, Valhouli decided he couldn't keep up the
relationship. It became clear that when he spent an afternoon and
evening with Cheever, he couldn't get back to Bradford without
risking an automobile accident.

Cheever also turned to Laurens Schwartz, the ablest of his writ-
ing students, for care and comradeship. Now a lawyer and author
in New York City, Schwartz had been a student of Robert Penn
Warren's at Yale and eagerly looked forward to working with
Cheever. On September 25, after one of the first class meetings,
Schwartz accompanied Cheever to a bar in a nearby hotel.
Cheever's routine was already known there. The bartender—a
middle-aged blonde in a short skirt—brought him a double vodka
on the rocks as soon as he sat down and kept his cigarettes lit.
Terribly depressed, Cheever began to sob. He was separated from
his wife, he said, and couldn't function on his own. He had been
living on oranges and hamburgers for seventeen days. He had no
clean clothes. His apartment was dirty. On most weekends Mary
came up from Ossining to take care of him, tidy up the apartment,
and stock the refrigerator. She did not regard the marriage as
finished, but rather in a state of disrepair owing to her husband's
alcoholism. Except for her ministrations, he seemed unable or unwilling to care for himself. Schwartz was enlisted to help out: to
fix instant coffee, walk him to class, tell him to go to the doctor.

It was clear that Cheever needed medical assistance. He drank
and smoked steadily throughout his waking hours. His hands shook
so violently it sometimes took him a dozen matches to light a
cigarette. In his stupor he occasionally faded off into another world
for a few moments. Once Schwartz removed a burning cigarette
from his lap. It was very much like taking care of a child, and
yet—as with his son Fred—Cheever thought of himself as father,
not son. He often spoke about procreation. "I want seventy-two
million children," he said, and talented young men like Schwartz
qualified as protégé-offspring. One night Cheever sat down at his
typewriter and started revising a story of Schwartz's. "I'm going
to get it published for you," he announced, and he might have been
able to do so. Even when drunk, he could produce "paragraphs of
pure Cheever," if not entire stories. But Schwartz wanted to be his
own kind of writer. He ripped the paper out of the typewriter.

Early in October, Anne Sexton committed suicide. Though she
and Cheever had not been close friends, her death deepened his

depression. He threatened to resign, then thought better of it and stayed on through the worst days of his life.

On a few occasions Cheever saw John Updike, then living a mile away in Boston and separated from *his* wife Mary. "I tried to entertain him," Updike recalls, "but he was hard to entertain." They drove up to Andover to visit Cheever's son Fred and Updike's son David. They went to see a Garbo film at the Museum of Fine Arts, but it was sold out and instead they dined at Café Budapest, a place Cheever seemed enchanted by. They went, in Boston idiom, "to Symphony." When Updike came to pick him up, Cheever opened the door naked, and for a second Updike was terrified that the door would close and lock behind him. Cheever needed help getting into his clothes, and lasted at Symphony only until intermission. "He was jumpy and needless to say foggy," Updike remembers. Yet even at his foggiest, "a flash of wit and perception would remind you that it was John Cheever in there."

Through the mails he issued calls for help. "I lost my vicuna coat in a bar," Gurganus remembered him writing. "Three people had to bring me home." "Death is—like drink—sometimes an irresistible temptation," he wrote Coates after Sexton's suicide. "I sometimes feel that I am approaching an abyss." He had to leave Ossining, he said, but hadn't arrived at a destination. Boston was terrible, he wrote Sara Spencer. His building had been robbed seven times. To the Friday Club, he was still more explicit. "This place is straight asshole," he wrote them.

Over the Christmas break he came home to Ossining, but spent much of the holiday in Phelps Memorial with a recurrence of his drastically irregular heartbeat and severe shortness of breath. The symptoms were bad enough to confine him to intensive care for a few days. He was then moved to a hospital room whose window curtains were painted with poppies and foxglove. There, or so he imagined, a young priest knocked on his door. "I've come to give you Holy Communion," the priest said. "Shall I kneel?" Cheever asked, the priest said, "Yes, please," and he knelt on the cold linoleum in his hospital pajamas and received Communion. The priest then left, and Cheever never knew who he was or where he had come from. On release from the hospital, he immediately resumed drinking. He seemed determined to drink himself to death. When he went back to Boston, Susie feared she would never see him alive again.

The second semester in Boston was a disaster. Dean Doner, a

writer and Boston University administrator, took Cheever to lunch one day. Midway through lunch Cheever mentioned that it was the date of *The New Yorker*'s fiftieth anniversary party. "You're not going?" Doner asked in astonishment. No, Cheever bitterly replied, he hadn't been invited, though he'd written "more god-damn words" for the magazine than anyone else. He'd never gotten along with Shawn, and perhaps that was why he hadn't been asked. Or maybe people at the magazine were afraid that he'd cause them some embarrassment because of his drinking. (In fact, only full-time staff were invited to the fiftieth anniversary: no contributors, and not even spouses. Either Cheever did not know that, or did not want to know it.)

As they parted, Doner realized how down and out Cheever was. When he'd parked the car before lunch, Doner had dropped a quarter in the gutter, full of dirty water from a hard rain, and decided to leave it there. After lunch they went back to the car together, and Cheever said he'd rather walk home than get a ride. Doner then drove off, and looked back to see Cheever hunkered down, scraping around in the dirty water for the quarter. When Eddie Newhouse brought John a care package of food from Mary, he found him "sodden drunk," reduced to crawling up the steps on all fours. Newhouse tried to get him to a doctor, but Cheever said not to bother, he was all right. One day, according to an autobiographical story, Cheever tried to put a hat atop the statue of the President of the Argentine on a walk down Commonwealth Avenue. The weather was frigid, but he wore no overcoat. "Gentlemen never wear overcoats," his father had told him. Then he spied a bum drinking out of a brown paper bag and sat down with him. They were sitting there, drinking "some kind of fortified wine" out of the brown paper bag, when a policeman came along and threatened to arrest them. "Don't be ridiculous," Cheever rather grandly said. "My name is John Cheever." The cop was unimpressed.

When he finally did go to see a doctor, Cheever affected a similar hauteur. He arrived poorly groomed and sloppily dressed, Dr. Robert A. Johnson recalls, and could not articulate his words clearly, but what words they were! Even drunk, he spoke quite beautifully. Most of all, though, he was concerned that everyone should know who he was. He was not a common drunk, he insisted, not a bum. Whoever he was, Dr. Johnson told him, he would have to stop drinking or his cardiomyopathy would kill him.

In the last months in Boston he was unable to cope with his social and financial obligations. Sally Swope drove up with Mary to help clean the apartment, and asked John to a dinner party at her father's house in Louisburg Square. Cheever arrived at that distinguished address, slipped and banged his head on the newel post, and appeared at the dinner table bloody and dirty. He also stopped paying his bills. When the telephone man came to take the phone away early in March, Cheever ripped it off the wall.

His classes turned into exercises in pathos. At one of the last sessions, a male graduate student contemptuously removed his shirt and strode around the room while Cheever—and the others—pretended not to notice. By the end of March it was clear that he could not go on, and Updike was recruited to meet his classes for the few weeks that remained of the semester. On April 2, Cheever left Boston. In his file at the university there were two unpaid bills from doctors, one from New England Telephone, and a humorous letter from Gurganus describing the gay scene in San Francisco.

Appropriately, it was his brother, Fred, who picked Cheever up and drove him to Phelps for detoxification. Now divorced and living alone on the South Shore, Fred had been supportive of his younger brother throughout his long siege in Boston. He called every day "to see," as John put it, "if I am still alive." At least once a week he took John to lunch, often with a third person accompanying them. Jane Cheever Carr, Cheever's favorite niece, and Rick Siggelkow, one of his undergraduate students, remember those lunches as pleasant occasions. John would order a roast beef sandwich and then ignore it in favor of his double martinis, but Fred did not chastise him. Instead he went out of his way to restore his brother's ego. Wasn't John a wonderful writer? he asked Jane. Wasn't he a marvelous teacher? he asked Rick.

Dr. Mutter admitted him to Phelps, where he suffered an episode of delirium tremens during the drying-out period. Then Mutter, Dr. Jewett, and Mary persuaded him to undergo treatment at the Smithers Alcoholism Center in New York City. The center, on East Ninety-third Street, is located in a palatial town house once owned by the flamboyant promoter Billy Rose. The house has an elevator, of course, and its huge octagonal bathroom designed for Eleanor Holm has been converted into a communal washroom for half a dozen men. Smithers was one of the first institutions to provide low-cost care for alcoholics, whether they could pay for it or not. When Cheever was there, his fellow patients included "freaks, cons, Irish policemen, whores, dismal gays . . . sand-hogs and seamen." He shared a room with five other men. One was a German delicatessen owner who kept calling out in his sleep, "Haff you been taken care of?" Another was a lame black who brandished his knitting needles and shouted, "I can make anything under the sun with these." To Cheever it seemed as if he were imprisoned, and he longed to escape.

The treatment cycle at Smithers runs twenty-eight days, and it took almost all of them for Cheever to acknowledge, first, that he was an alcoholic, and second, that he had to quit drinking if he wanted to survive. In the beginning he simply denied that he needed help, and linked the denial with expressions of grandiosity. He seemed more concerned with impressing others than with acknowledging his own vulnerability. His heart wasn't bothering him, he said. He had no trouble breathing. He wasn't depressed. Perhaps the others needed assistance, but he was perfectly able to deal with his own problems. After all, wasn't he a world-renowned novelist? He also seemed very class-conscious, and held himself aloof from the other patients. Criticized for this in group sessions, he became sarcastic but not overtly angry. It was difficult for him to recognize that no matter what he had done or where he came from, he was every bit as much at risk as the failed con man or the sandhog he beat at backgammon. Staff psychologist Carol Kitman urged him "to drop his John Cheeverdom and see himself as a vulnerable human who could easily be killed by his disease."

In conferences with his personal counselor, Ruth Epstein, Cheever struck an attitude of emotional detachment. He admitted to no feelings at all, and she began to wonder whether he actually had any. The clue was the curious little chuckle he produced at inappropriate moments. He spoke, for example, of trying to teach Fred to ride a bicycle, and of how he must have been cruel with the boy, and then chuckled. This was his way, she came to understand, of disguising what was most important to him. It was not that he didn't care but that he didn't want others to know how much he cared. He would not even declare that he wanted to live rather than die, but in the end he decided he cared about that most of all.

His correspondence from Smithers traces a gradual awakening to his responsibility to shake off his addiction and survive. During much of his stay he insisted that he was at Smithers only on the orders of his internist and his wife, and that he resented the way he was treated. On Sundays, Cheever was released to go to church and spend the afternoon away from the clinic with family and friends. He visited Leonard and Virginia Field on April 26, and delivered a tirade against the cruelty of the group leaders at Smithers, who brutalized him before the others and did so in the worst possible grammar. Gradually, though, the experience of his fellow patients began to sink in. The delicatessen man finished his twenty-eight days and left; he had lost "his wife, his children, his house . . . his everything." By the end of the third week, Cheever was beginning to accept his obligation to cure himself. "You can judge the worth" of this process soon, he wrote Laurens Schwartz on April 29. The following day he walked into Ruth Epstein's office and told her he'd never drink again. Only a few days before he had claimed that he could write as well as ever when drinking, and she had asked him, "But can you make sense of it the next day?" He'd been thinking about that, he said.

When Cheever was discharged on May 6, the prognosis at Smithers was "guarded." The consensus was that he was so wrapped up in himself that there was no room for anything else. He was prepared to attend Alcoholics Anonymous meetings, but unless he arrived at some internal change and a more realistic self-appraisal, the Smithers staff was not optimistic about Cheever's chances. Few of them thought he would stay sober. They did not reckon with his strength of will or his delight in being alive. He went home to Cedar Lane, where everything was in bloom: "apples, dogwood, wisteria, lilac, me."

REBIRTH

1975-1977

CHEEVER emerged from Smithers weighing twenty pounds less and feeling twenty years younger than he had four weeks earlier. It was as if he had been reborn, to begin a new life at sixty-three.

When John came home sober, Mary Cheever recalls, he was as happy as a prisoner released from bondage. "It was like having my old father back," Susan writes, except that now he was kinder and more alert and more helpful around the house than before. His pattern of social behavior had to change, for liquor forever threatened to pull him into the abyss. On his second day out of Smithers, he warned himself against "the euphoria of alcohol when I seem to walk among the stars." Yet drinking was very much part of the social world he and Mary continued to inhabit. The hardest part of the day came at twilight, especially the early-stealing dark of fall and winter afternoons that summoned up cocktail hours of the past. Once he had loved large parties; now he detested them. He and Mary sometimes arrived in separate cars, so that he could leave as the level of hilarity rose. At Jane and Barrett Clark's Christmas Eve party, he stayed only five minutes. When the Cheevers themselves entertained, he poured generous drinks for guests, but thought it would be "terribly nice" if they left early.

When Cheever quit drinking he quit taking pills: no Valium to get through the day, no Seconal to bring on sleep. Instead he drank large quantities of iced tea and chain-smoked cigarettes. (In the spring of 1979, he finally shook off his addiction to tobacco.) He chose not to sedate himself, and stuck to that choice with a remarkable fierceness of will. The choice, he knew, was really no choice at all, for by giving up alcohol he opted to live rather than die. But he reminded himself anyway that drink could do nothing to ease his daily passage, that it ruined his writing, that it robbed him of his dignity.

It was the drinking, he came to understand, that brought on his phobias about bridges and trains and crowds, if only to justify further drinking as a way of combating these anxieties. No encounter could be prepared for by liquor; the minutes beforehand simply had to be checked off. Nor did alcohol stimulate invention or liberate imagination; it only dulled the senses. Everywhere he detected the ill effects of drink on other writers' prose. "You can practically smell the bourbon" in Faulkner's worst work, he thought, and he sniffed it as well in the novels of contemporary writers he otherwise admired. And he repudiated the popular notion that great art derived from a torment that eventually led the artist to destroy himself. Certainly artists suffered, and perhaps more than most people. But that did not mean that they had to destroy themselves. Nor did they have to give up all their dignity, like the proverbial drunken poet at the campus reading. Hayden Carruth, himself a poet who long ago stopped drinking, asked Cheever why he quit so late in life. "At your age I think I'd have gone out loaded," Carruth said. "Puking all over someone else's furniture?" Cheever answered, in wonderful condensation.

Cheever set joyfully to work upon release from Smithers. In

Boston he had been unable to write much of anything. Updike recalls visiting his apartment on Bay State Road early in the fall and spying a page in the typewriter. It was the beginning of *Falconer*, describing the entrance to the prison. But "from month to month the page in the typewriter never advanced." His muse, as Cheever said, had been in Portugal while he was in Boston. In May 1975 they were reunited on Cedar Lane, and he threw himself into the composition of *Falconer*. He was overjoyed to be working again, and enchanted with what he was producing. He had been throwing "high dice" since May, he wrote Denny Coates in October 1975.

Rising early and working until one or two in the afternoon, he streaked along on the book, seven pages a day, and finished it in less than a year. He knew from the beginning what he wanted to create: a novel about confinement "as dark and radiant" as possible. Yet there were blissful discoveries along the way. He awoke one morning and it suddenly struck him that Farragut had to escape. "He's going to get out," he went shouting through the house. "Hey! Hey! He's going to get out." Never had his writing given him so much happiness.

Still, there was the rest of the day and some of the night to get through without drinking. He kept himself busy with a variety of activities, some old and some new. As always he swam in Sara Spencer's pool, or Maurie Helprin's, or Sally Swope's, during the summer months. He skated not only in the winter—the ice in the winter of 1975–76 was the best in a decade—but year-round at a nearby indoor rink with Donald Lang and two black girlfriends of Lang's. Occasionally he hiked to the Croton dam with the dogs. He also discovered new forms of exercise such as biking and cross-country skiing. John Dirks was with him the day they went into Barker's and Cheever hauled the assembled bike on display up to the counter and insisted on taking it home with him. Thereafter he worked out two routes—one long and one short—for the daily bike ride. The long route, eight miles, took him by Marion Ascoli's estate on Teatown Lake in Croton, where he would stop to buy some of the brown eggs laid by the free-ranging chickens and to chat with John Bukovsky, who was in charge of the chickens and the farmland and the orchards. The first time he pedaled up, the German shepherd Fritz charged out of the lilac bushes and nipped at his rear. Thereafter Bukovsky knew Cheever was on his way when he heard his voice calling "Fritzie, Fritzie" soothingly.

Cheever began to grow vegetables of his own—beets, leeks,

chard, spinach, tomatoes, beans—around the house on Cedar Lane. Roger Willson, who had grown up on a farm in Iowa, helped introduce him to the mysteries of gardening. "He loved to dig in the dirt," Willson remembers. Willson also took him fishing out in Long Island Sound. Their first time aboard the *Klondike VI*, the FM radio played Chopin, and between them Cheever and Willson hauled in a hundred pounds of mackerel in two hours. It was not always like that. The next time, they left New Rochelle at midnight on a beautiful night, but when they reached open water the seas were rough. Nobody caught any fish, and almost everyone on board got sick. On other evenings the Willsons took Cheever to the monthly fights at the Westchester County Center in White Plains. He loved it all: the fat sportswriters with their cigars, the floozie who paraded around the ring with the placard announcing the upcoming round, the toughs in the audience, the local hero with the cauliflower ear.

Occasionally Cheever drove down to Yankee Stadium for a baseball game. More often he watched on television, taking part as a spectator in the national pastime his father had failed to instruct him in. He heard the right-field fans turn ugly when Yankee outfielder Roy White dropped a fly ball. He watched in fascination as Jim Lonborg pitched a one-hitter. He agonized when pitcher Luis Tiant defected from the Red Sox to the Yankees, for like "all literary men" he was a Boston Red Sox fan. "To be a Yankee fan in literary society," he declared, "is to endanger your life." It was the game itself that drew him along, a game that seemed almost perfect in its unfolding. At World Series time he could not be pried loose from the television. And other television shows became virtually obligatory viewing also: the Sunday-night *Masterpiece Theatre* (*Poldark* was his favorite), and the glamorous soap opera *Dallas*.

Two or three nights a week Cheever attended meetings of Alcoholics Anonymous. He was a member of the Briarcliff chapter, but there was a meeting every night of the week in one or another of the communities nearby. He needed to go to these meetings, for he never got over the desire to drink. Simply saying the mantra "My name is John and I am an alcoholic" made him feel better. So did listening to the stories of others, as they traced their descent into degradation through drink. Cheever rarely spoke himself, instead smoking, drinking coffee, and sometimes striking up a conversation with someone who might prove to be a friend or confidant. In his new life he required new friends, and found some of them through AA.

Those who knew him before and after he quit drinking detected a substantial change in his attitude. As his writing in the late 1960s turned dark, he became even darker in person. There was an element of viciousness in what he said of others, including family and friends. This changed when he stopped drinking. Still intolerant of slowness and stupidity in others, he nonetheless acquired a new generosity of spirit. He learned from AA, with its membership drawn from all levels of income and education, how vastly different people could help one another. Characteristically, he would not wash dishes after AA meetings, but he would turn out at four in the morning to talk with someone afraid of backsliding. He also went out of his way to help young friends in trouble with alcohol, playing the role of a surrogate parent who had been through it all and who cared about them. "I have too much faith in you and your promise to let you do this to yourself," he told David Lange, Hope's brother. "You're an alcoholic like me," he told young Dudley Schoales. "I'm going to take you to Phelps and that's going to be it."

By such means, Cheever coaxed several of his acquaintances into Smithers. The therapy did not always work. Truman Capote, for example, appealed to Cheever for help in a series of drunken telephone calls. "Truman, the world will lose a great writer if you lose yourself," John said in some exaggeration. "Let me book you into Smithers." In due course this was arranged. Capote completed the program at Smithers. Soon thereafter he appeared on the Johnny Carson show, drunk, to sing the praises of his treatment.

Travel provided another way for Cheever to work off his restored supply of energy. He resumed frequent visits to Yaddo, working on *Falconer* there—for instance—both in the summer of 1975 and in the winter of 1976. He took trips whenever he had completed "a lump" of the novel: to Boston early in December 1975, to Stanford with son Fred late in January 1976. During the subsequent half-decade, he journeyed to Romania, Bulgaria (twice), Russia, the Netherlands, Venezuela. He became much sought after on the visiting writer circuit, reading his stories at Harvard and Bennington and Cornell, Syracuse and Oswego and Bradford, Ottawa and Montreal and Toronto, Stanford and Southern Methodist and Utah. As his fame grew, so did the local demands on his time from libraries, colleges, and civic and cultural associations. In addition, there was a substantial volume of correspondence that he answered himself, and promptly. So he passed many hours of his days.

Coming back to Yaddo, Cheever told Nora Sayre in a voice bursting with pleasure, was like "coming home again." It was still the one "positively ideal" place to work through the long mornings. In the afternoons he bicycled to Schuylersville and back, or cross-country skied the six-mile run through the golf course. At dinner he was in his element, engaging, convivial, full of anecdotes and good humor. Afterward he lost at Ping-Pong, shone at charades, or went into town to nurse his ginger ale and watch the young writers drink. Allan Gurganus was in residence in September of 1975, and so was the poet Philip Schultz. Cheever admired Schultz's poetry and soon was throwing the football back and forth with him in his fathers-playing-catch-with-sons ritual. It meant a great deal to Schultz to be befriended by so well established a writer as Cheever. At the time he was virtually broke, and was planning to move from Cambridge to New York with no job in prospect. Cheever assured him that better days lay ahead, and rejoiced with him when that turned out to be true. He enjoyed taking an interest in the careers of writers whose work he liked, whether he knew them or not. One of the pleasures of growing old, as he remarked, was that sometimes you could call attention to young people's work.

After Thanksgiving, Cheever went to Boston to read for the *Harvard Advocate.* To begin with he was apprehensive about revisiting what he thought of as "a sinister, provincial and decadent" part of the world, but he had something to prove. "I must repair my farewell scenes there," he wrote. In Cambridge he had dinner with Rob Cowley before the reading, and afterward there was a reunion with Jim Valhouli and Phil Schultz. The cabdriver, recognizing Cheever, refused to collect his fare. "Hot shit," the cabbie said. "*Apples, Bullet Park,* the Wapshots." Oddly, another cabdriver in New York later surfaced as one of Cheever's greatest fans. Sometimes it seemed as if he were "driving straight through a Cheever story" in his taxi, New York cabbie Patrick Coyne thought. The next day, Schultz got word of a four-thousand-dollar grant from the Council for the Arts, and to celebrate Cheever took him to lunch at Locke-Ober's. He liked watching Schultz—and others—drink, so long as there was no hint of alcoholism in the air.

The glow of redemption was still on him when Cheever accompanied his son Fred on a week's visit to Stanford in January. Fred looked over the university he hoped to attend—and ended up attending—while his father performed his "cultural soft-shoe" (a classroom visit and evening reading) for the English department. The two of them arrived in identical preppy dress—tweed sport coats, button-down shirts with crew-neck sweaters, gray slacks, brown penny loafers. In these clothes, with his face "reddened and polished, as if by a brisk wind," Cheever looked at least ten years younger than his sixty-three years. While Fred decamped at once to stay with friends from Andover, John was put up in the institutionally drab guest room of Florence Moore (Flo Mo) House. Instructor Dana Gioia, the poet-in-the-making who was asked to look after Cheever during his visit, was struck by the older man's unusual air of physical calm. His conversation was remarkable for its sensitivity and sudden surprising turns of phrase, but there was nothing of the performance about it. He listened intently to the Flo Mo undergraduates who were his companions at meals, and they were eager to sit at his table. "He gave off," Gioia wrote, "that almost visible aura of joy and serenity that people have just after they have experienced a genuine religious conversion or suddenly recovered from a long life-threatening illness." It was the joy of resurrection from alcohol, resurrection from the dead.

For most of the week, Cheever had little to do. He lingered over meals in the Flo Mo cafeteria, spent long hours smoking in the huge Naugahyde chairs of the lounge, and went on meandering walks and drives with Gioia. The undergraduates, Gioia discovered, knew nothing of his writing, so he rounded up some remaindered copies of *The World of Apples* and distributed them to freshmen. Cheever's reputation was at its nadir. The younger generation was reading his contemporaries, sometimes as class assignments, while his work was virtually forgotten.

The literary lion at Stanford that week, however, was not John Cheever but Saul Bellow. Bellow's wife, a mathematician, was being recruited for a position in the math department, and the administration and English department were courting her husband as well. Bellow's star was in the ascendant. *Mr. Sammler's Planet*, his last novel, had won the National Book Award. Before the year was out, *Humboldt's Gift*, his widely praised new novel, was to win the Pulitzer Prize, and he himself would receive the Nobel Prize. His visit to campus was as overscheduled as Cheever's was the opposite, but John betrayed no trace of resentment at the greater attention paid his co-artist and friend. There was warmth between them, and mutual admiration. Both understood, in Cheever's oft-repeated phrase, that "literature is not a competitive sport."

So Bellow read one night and Cheever the next, in as impressive a bit of campus programming as one could wish. Both were small, graceful men, but Cheever projected a relaxed amiability that contrasted with Bellow's dignified reserve. He was also capable of making fun of himself. Before leaving Stanford, Cheever was persuaded to tape an interview for the literary magazine. He always sounded funny on such tapes, he said. Even on telephone recording machines, his voice came out an octave lower, with a pronounced English accent. One day he'd phoned Sara Spencer and left a message on her machine: "I'm coming swimming in about twenty minutes." When he arrived, Sara played the recording back to him. "Who's that old fruit with the English accent?" Cheever asked, and dived into the pool.

However curious the accent—and when combined with his characteristic mumble it could render his speech extremely difficult to follow—Cheever's greatest charm lay in his command of language. He was hardly prepossessing physically. Trimly built with nut-brown hair, he looked at sixty-four, John Hersey reported, rather like a thirty-four-year-old who had been to "a hilarious but awfully late party the night before." At Iowa he was mistaken for a janitor in the basement of the English and Philosophy Building, at Knopf for a deliveryman, at the Ossining public library for an employee of Mr. Cheever come to Xerox portions of the *Falconer* typescript. Yet in good spirits and good company, there was a joyous quality about him that communicated itself in brilliant speech and infectious laughter. At such times, Mary said, people were crazy about him.

One of the problems confronting him after he solved the worst problem of all was who to be crazy about. As a side effect of his liberation from drink, he reacquired a powerful sex drive and continued to seek outlets for it outside his marriage. After the trip to Stanford, for instance, he put Fred on a plane to Andover and went down to Los Angeles to see Hope Lange. It was a very successful reunion. Hope looked marvelous. As soon as they sat down to dinner in a restaurant, Cheever reported, both of them took off their shoes. John had just read *Humboldt's Gift*, in which Charles

Citrine and the gorgeous Renata make surreptitious love to each other under cover of a tablecloth. "My," the hostess said, "you two surely enjoy your food." Much of Hope's appeal for him derived from her position as Hollywood and Broadway and television star, as the woman Norton Simon sent his jet to fetch across the continent to his birthday party. Proud of her and proud of their affair, he took her to meet John and Harriett Weaver in Hollywood, Bob Gottlieb in New York. He also tried to persuade her to travel with him to Romania and to Venezuela, but she turned him down. He was married, they could both be recognized, and she did not intend to slink around corners incognito. And over an extended period marked by long separations, the passion in the affair dwindled away.

Hope was not the answer, then, and it became increasingly clear that no woman could be. Soon after the drinking stopped, Cheever became more actively homosexual. What he yearned for was a loving manly relationship that did not demand too much of either party. In this way he could avoid accommodating, say, a particular woman's taste for "scalding bathwater and pink wallpaper." At the same time he was repelled by displays of the gay subculture. There *they* were mincing along in the Arcadian shopping center: the old one with his dyed hair, the youth in all his beauty. He was not like that at all, and could never be, Cheever thought. He had an occupation, he supported his family, he loved his wife and children, and nothing that he might do in the company of another man—he insisted—could diminish that.

Privately he worried that homosexuality might be only a ruinous form of self-love. When he was attracted to a young man, wasn't it a long-ago image of himself, naked on the beach at Quincy, that called out to him? And he was unable, like most men of his generation, to confess his inclinations. What would his sons think? What would his friends think? What effect would it have on his reputation? He worked out the answer in his journals. "Have you heard? Old Cheever, crowding seventy, has gone Gay. . . . Old Cheever has run off to Bessarabia with a hairy youth half his age." Unable to face such talk, he stayed in the closet and made his confessions in the fiction, where most readers chose to ignore them.

In February 1976, Cheever was back at Yaddo, jamming away on *Falconer.* He was called home early in March to mind the dogs while Mary and Fred went to Boston to reenact history's first telephone call. Susan Grosvenor, the great-great-granddaughter of Alexander

Graham Bell, telephoned Federico Cheever, great-great-grandson of Thomas Watson, from across the hall at MIT. "Mr. Watson, come here, I need you," Susan said, just as her great-great-grandfather had a century earlier. "I heard every word you said," Fred replied, just as his great-great-grandfather had one hundred years before. No interruption could slow *Falconer* for long. The novel came pouring out of him as if it had a volition of its own. On Good Friday, Cheever wrote the last word ("Rejoice") and went to church to offer a prayer of thanks.

Providence seemed to be in his corner, and with the novel at the typist Cheever turned happily to other matters. He began making plans for a midsummer trip to Romania under the sponsorship of *Travel & Leisure* magazine. He wrote Cowley proposing to nominate John Updike to the American Academy. At the academy ceremonial in May, Erica Jong kissed him and a man said that meeting Cheever made him feel like Cinderella—tomorrow the ball would be over and he'd have to go back to work.

His pleasure in these encounters—his joy in the regular round of daily life—was soon diminished by the shadow of death. Sara Spencer suffered a heart attack in April and spent months in the hospital. Cheever wrote her with fragments of neighborhood gossip and reports on her pool and garden. Finding her pool busy with relatives one day, he went to the Helprins for a swim and had a long talk with their son Mark, who was soon to become a novelist himself. The greatest of virtues, he told Sara, was to love one's neighbor, especially since she was that neighbor. She eventually recovered, but early in June the drumbeat of mortality sounded twice more.

The counterfeit phone call came at 3:30 A.M. on June 1. "This is the CBC," the voice said. "John Updike has been involved in a fatal automobile accident, and we were wondering if you had any comment." Cheever began to sob. "Oh," the voice said, "I didn't know it was personal." "He was a colleague," Cheever explained. The call was a hoax perpetrated by a rival novelist with a sinister sense of humor. But Cheever did not know that, and neither did Updike's former wife, Mary, who received a similar phone call a few minutes earlier. It was midmorning before Updike was located, in the best of health.

Cheever was already an emotional wreck when the hoax call reached him. The day before, his one and only brother, Fred, had died. The man he had lived with during his youth in Boston, the person he had loved and hated all his life, was gone, and in the wake of his passing John had only tender thoughts for the nurturing brother who had once meant more to him than anyone else in the world.

Despite periodic dry spells, Fred had never been able to stop drinking permanently. Alcoholism had cost him several jobs and dissolved his marriage. Toward the end he was selling space for a newspaper on the South Shore and living, alone and divorced, in a furnished room in North Scituate. Desperately ill, he came to see his younger brother in May. "I killed you off in *Falconer*, " John told him. "Oh good, Joey, good," Fred replied, "you've been trying all these years." It was, both brothers knew, a final meeting.

The funeral was held in Hingham on June 3, in a church whose windows opened on the surrounding fields and the salt smell of the sea beyond. The other mourners bothered Cheever. The men all had "sailboat tans, white hair, and mannered wives." As he strode down the aisle in his cuffless pants, he heard one of them mutter, "He must be a Spanish dancer." But the ceremony itself caused him no pain. A psychologist might say, he speculated afterward, that while he parted easily from his brother he might for the rest of his life seek in other men the love that Fred had bestowed on him.

Not even death could dampen his spirits. He had sloughed off the depression that had plagued him for so long. In a bicentennial comment for *Newsweek*, he took issue with those who played the role of Seeksorrow. The Yale literary magazine had written him asking if he thought things were going to get worse. "If people ask questions like that," he answered, "things are *bound* to get worse." Optimism and pessimism were interwoven through his life, but he no longer granted pessimism the last word. "The decline of the west is the easiest thing in the world to prove," he observed, but still one was alive, one could love, one could find usefulness in work, and one could walk in woods "full of light and cool clean air."

The future looked bright to him, not bleak, despite his reservations about the ill consequences of progress. In Romania he had discovered the roads of the past all but obliterated in an America crisscrossed with interstate highways. They took him back to the two-lane highways of his youth, to a serene human scale where you could see the geraniums in the farmhouse windows and the roadway followed the contours of the land. He visited Dracula's castle in Transylvania and the monastery at Voronet: everywhere the passing scenes seemed to signify another, earlier time. The four-teen-hour return trip brought him back to the twentieth century with a jolt. The 747 from Frankfurt was crowded and noisy. When he finally arrived at Kennedy, exhausted, there was some trouble in customs and it looked as if no one had come to meet him. Then he felt Federico's hand on his shoulder and the world righted itself.

On a bike ride a few weeks later, Cheever ran into some soft gravel and went "cock-a-hoop over the handlebars." The accident opened a nasty gash on his forehead. Phil Schultz, who had been riding along with him, was aghast, but Cheever declined all assist-ance. He would not be taken to the doctor, he would not go to the hospital, he would not even accept help with cleaning the wound. They walked their bikes back to Cedar Lane to wait for Mary and Susie. When the women returned from a walk, they looked at the two men in the living room—John with his bloody forehead, Phil with his ashen countenance—and both of them rushed over to comfort Schultz. He looked absolutely stricken. As it happened, Cheever's wound healed nicely, leaving only a small scar. It did nothing to interrupt his busy schedule of campus visits.

The Bennington trip in November began with a comedy of errors. Stephen Sandy, the poet in charge of Cheever's campus appearance, told him that he'd be met at the Amtrak station by an attractive young lady, Melissa Fish. At the last minute she could not run the errand, and Sandy sent another student, a tall young man named Peter Pochna, in her stead. Sandy instructed Pochna to look for a small, sprightly man with a twinkle in his eye, proba-bly natty in tweeds and chinos and "no longer young." Unfortu-nately, Pochna took in only those last three words and did not espy Cheever getting off the train. After the crowd dispersed, Cheever sat in the station looking for Melissa Fish and watching a tall young man approaching the seedy-looking habitués of the station one by one. Eventually Pochna asked an old codger sitting near Cheever if he was by any chance John Cheever, and the two identified each other at last. Matters improved only slightly after that inauspicious beginning. The dinner before the reading, with Bernard and Ann Malamud among the guests, lasted much too long, and Cheever took the platform half an hour late. Yet the next day Cheever generously returned his check to Pochna and Sandy. He didn't need the money *that much*, he said, and he wanted it used for support of the student literary magazine. This was a gesture he repeated often on college campuses, always to the surprise and delight of his hosts.

At Cornell early in December, Cheever not only gave his customary reading ("The Death of Justina" and "The Swimmer"), he also read a paper on Chekhov. The writer James McConkey invited him to speak on Chekhov as the first among a number of contemporary authors who, McConkey thought, would feel a particular affinity for the great Russian. He was right about Cheever, who in fact had already been compared with Chekhov for his portrayal of a provincial world sensitive to divisions of social class and inhabited in part by genial eccentrics, where people and things contrived to seem funny and sad at the same time. In preparing his eleven-page paper, Cheever could find little in Chekhov to quote. What he did instead was to fashion two stories—one as the Russian master might have written it, brilliant in its perfect ear for talk and illuminated by the significant detail, the other an example of modern imitators of Chekhov who ruined the effect by accumulating too many details.

In the imitation a woman dresses and leaves her home. "We are told the color of her dress, the shape of her door key, the condition of her front porch." She goes to a store and buys a deck of cards. The clerk tells her that his favorite cockatoo has died. She returns home and puts the deck of cards in the refrigerator. The telephone rings and she has a long conversation with a neighbor about making celery soup. Then she decides to play solitaire, but can't remember where she put the cards. "On this note of mystery . . . the story ends," except that the would-be contemporary Chekhov might throw in sexual intercourse or perversion to attract reader attention. Not even crypto-pornography could rescue such vulgar parodies, imitations that lacked Chekhov's "discipline, his wit and stamina."

People sometimes complained, he observed, that nothing happened in Chekhov. Alone in the empty house, Firs can hear the ax at the end of *The Cherry Orchard* and the world will never be the same again, but no one has been murdered and the plans to the nuclear submarine have not been stolen. The question to ask about the short story, Cheever insisted, was not "Does anything happen?" but "Is it interesting?" On these grounds one could not do better than Chekhov.

When it was time to leave Cornell Sunday morning, Frederica Kaven—a student in McConkey's graduate creative writing class who greatly admired Cheever's work—volunteered to drive him to the airport. But the plane was delayed an hour, "for mechanical reasons" the ticket agent said, and Cheever decided on the spot to find some other means of transportation. He arranged to take a bus that left Ithaca about 1:00 P.M., giving Kaven and himself a few hours to kill. In the course of that time he rather poignantly demonstrated his vulnerability.

Over coffee Kaven told him, for example, that she would laugh so hard reading some of his stories that she could scarcely go on. Just at that moment, she caught a glimpse of the hurt in his eyes. "It was clear that I had wounded him," she recalls, and the way he looked so disturbed her that she could not bring herself to say what she knew to be true: that his stories were not only funny but serious and moving, that her own laughter often hovered on the edge of tears.

They arrived at the bus station well in advance, and began looking for a nearby restaurant where they could buy a sandwich for Cheever's trip. About the only places open, on Ithaca's west side, were workingmen's bars. They tried several of these, but none would fix a sandwich for the road. At their last stop Cheever, dressed in impeccable tweeds, pleaded unsuccessfully with the bartender while the morning drinkers in plaid shirts and jeans regarded him askance. He looked small and defeated in the hazy blue light that filtered in through the windows, as the bartender slowly shook his head no. "Let's go," Cheever finally said. "I don't want anything." So back they went to the bus station, where he put some quarters into the vending machine, pushed the button for chicken soup, and out came . . . hot chocolate. It was that kind of a day.

Back in Ossining, he entered into a letter-to-the-editor debate with Elizabeth Hardwick, who had written an article for the *New York Review of Books* proposing that the widespread paranoia in contemporary society threatened to devalue the importance of anyone's personal downfall and to render guilt impotent. Could the novel well survive without the prospect of individual ruin and private guilt? In response, Cheever cited his own lively awareness of original sin, and moved on to a generalization. Each generation was liable to claim that its own parlous times were such as to invalidate the novel, yet the generations passed and the novel survived. In fact he thought the novel "the only art form we possess that has approached any mastery" of the complexities of contemporary life. About the novel as about the story one should ask if it was interesting, with "interest" connoting "suspense, emotional involvement and a sustained claim on one's attention." That was the standard that counted. That was what he had been aiming at in *Falconer*.

Waiting for the novel to come out, Cheever spent a week at the University of Utah late in January. On the surface, there was nothing to indicate that this trip would drastically change the rest of his life. As on other campuses he read students' stories, met them in conferences and classrooms, and gave the obligatory public reading. The poet Dave Smith, then head of the university's creative writing program, offered Cheever a choice of accommodations: he could stay at the rather grungy Lake City Motel on the edge of campus or at a hotel in Salt Lake City five miles away. Cheever chose the motel, to be within walking distance of campus. Every day he complained about how crummy his room was, and every day Smith offered to move him downtown. Cheever would not be moved, though; he seemed to enjoy the bitching. Otherwise Smith thought Cheever an ideal guest, insightful with the students, generous with his time, and a delight in conversation. For exercise during Cheever's stay, Smith arranged for a couple of sturdy skiers to take him cross-country skiing. His heart was in good condition, now that he'd stopped drinking.

It was after a morning of cross-country skiing and an afternoon seminar that Cheever met and fell in love with a young man named Max Zimmer, a teaching fellow at the university who was working toward his doctorate in creative writing. John had looked over the work of the more talented students in advance, was impressed with Zimmer's story "Utah Died for Your Sins," and asked to meet him. Zimmer was not particularly enthusiastic about the meeting. He knew the story was good, and had been told so by other visiting writers, including Grace Paley and E. L. Doctorow. Doctorow had even asked to see his projected novel. Nonetheless he turned up in the hallway after the seminar, and off they went in Max's car. "I've got to make two stops," Cheever said. "Liquor store and supermarket." At the liquor store he bought a quart of Jim Beam for Zimmer, and at the supermarket two six-packs of Diet 7-Up for himself. Then the two men went to Cheever's motel room and talked into the night about writing and reading, love and sex, and Max's future.

According to Smith, Zimmer was the sort of student no teacher ever forgets, "the kind of person about whom legends accrete." He was the product of a combative Mormon family, and his academic relationships were sometimes volatile (he and Smith had quarreled, briefly). Yet everyone liked him, and clearly the talent was there as well. Cheever was irresistibly drawn to him. "Lonely and with my loneliness exacerbated by travel, motel rooms, bad food, public readings and the superficiality of standing in reception lines," he wrote in his journal, "I fell in love with Max in a motel room of unusual squalor. His air of seriousness and responsibility, the bridged glasses he wore for his near sightedness and his composed manner all excited my deepest love." Max did not consider himself a homosexual, then or later, and felt an initial revulsion when John made sexual overtures. But they got along perfectly otherwise—their senses of humor meshed well—and for the remainder of Cheever's visit Max more or less took over as host, coming by for breakfast each morning and driving him around campus and into the surrounding mountains.

Before he left Utah, Cheever had persuaded Zimmer to come to New York. Much as E. E. Cummings had told him to get out of Boston, he advised Max to give up Salt Lake City in favor of New York City. A Ph.D. would do Zimmer no good as a writer, and might be actually harmful, Cheever argued. New York was still the best place for writers to get their work recognized. Max did not need much convincing. He had stayed in Utah long enough, and was ready to cut his ties to the university. Besides, Cheever offered help in getting him started in the East. He seemed to regard him as a kind of surrogate literary son, Max thought. In correspondence he reassured Max that he genuinely liked his work. "That I love you has nothing to do with the case," he declared. Still he did what he could for the younger man's career. He tried to place "Utah Died for Your Sins" with *The New Yorker:* it was rejected, primarily because of its use of one rather common but indisputably obscene word. More successfully, he lobbied for and got an invitation for Max to spend the summer at Yaddo. "If you don't take him," he told the Yaddo board, "I quit." So it was settled that Max would come to New York as soon as classes were over in June. The arrangement was confirmed when Max came East briefly in March and he and his sister visited the Cheevers in Ossining. After lunch John took him to see the Croton dam. They became lovers then, and remained so until the end.

SUCCESS

1977-1980

Falconer came out amid a barrage of publicity. Cheever had dodged *Time*'s reporters in 1964; now he cooperated fully with *Newsweek* on its cover story. He even participated in a question-and-answer piece with his daughter, Susan, a *Newsweek* staffer herself. To accommodate Susie, he cut short his Saturday-morning visit with Sara Spencer, but he was uneasy about the interview: "Would Coleridge have been interviewed by his daughter?"

He lacked a "public personality" and the rewards that came with it, Cheever used to say, but with the *Newsweek* story he acquired one. To the public at large, he became the writer who had kicked alcohol and

written a book about prison. In this new dispensation, he seemed
to shake off his native Yankee reserve. In magazine interviews and
television appearances he spoke openly about his terrible alcoholism, his troubled marriage, his conflicted relationship with his
brother. Mail poured in from *Newsweek* readers and viewers of *The
Dick Cavett Show*. At parties, even close to home, everyone wanted
to talk to him and to shake his hand. In New York, people recognized him on the street, and not because they mistook him for
David Wayne or Burgess Meredith. For the first time John Cheever
became a famous man, and found that he liked it. *Falconer* also
brought him a great deal of money. He had been almost broke when
he finished the novel. The book sold very well, however, and Paramount spent forty thousand dollars for a movie option and then
decided not to make the film. That was "the best of all possible
worlds," he said. "It was like finding money in the gutter."

"There are writers whose last novels are very like the first," Saul
Bellow remarked, but Cheever "was a writer of another sort, altogether . . . one of the self-transformers." After *Bullet Park*, he knew,
he had to find fresh subject matter and a new voice. He found them
in *Falconer*, a book radically different in setting, style, and theme
from anything he had yet written. Gone were the masterfully
evoked backgrounds of upper-middle-class life—the New York
apartment, the Yankee village, the exurban retreat. Instead the
action takes place in Cellblock F of Falconer prison, where the
protagonist, a drug addict and college professor named Ezekiel
Farragut, has been confined for killing his brother, Eben, with a
fire iron. For a cast of characters the Farquarsons and Merrills and
Bentleys and Weeds of his earlier writing were replaced by prison
inmates who were not allowed the dignity of last names: Chicken
Number Two, a tattooed folk-singing jewel thief; Tennis, an airplane hijacker who wrongly expects to "leap the net" to freedom
any week now; Cuckold, who finally "iced" his wife one night after
she had betrayed him a hundred times. Presiding over this crew is
the obese guard Tiny, who slaughters dozens of cats—prison population two thousand inmates, four thousand cats—after one makes
off with his London broil. The people in the prison talk as they
might be expected to: "fuck" is one of the basic verbs. And they are
full of self-justifications and improbable claims of innocence.

Yet in this unlikely environment Farragut somehow earns redemption. First, he kicks the heroin habit. Then he learns to love
his fellowman—not only sexually, as in his affair with the young

prisoner Jody, but compassionately, as when he cares for the bereft and dying Chicken Number Two. As Cheever often pointed out, the theme of the novel was confinement, and he used the word to signify social and psychological as well as physical restrictions. People could get stuck in elevators, trapped in airports, or locked into "sentimental or erotic contracts" that were extremely difficult to get out of. Even our homes, however much longed for, could make us captives. In that sense, he said, confinement had always been his subject. Falconer prison was his third "metaphor for confinement." The first had been St. Botolphs, a New England village that constrained its natives through the appeal of traditional values and nostalgia, and the second the comfortable suburban town, like Bullet Park and Shady Hill. But he was far from advocating total freedom in *Falconer*. Like an astronaut, he reveled in periods of weightlessness, but knew he would soon yearn for gravity. Only through love could one escape his bonds.

Falconer describes a new kind of love—a love without possessiveness that moves beyond eros to agape. To reach that ideal, Zeke Farragut must first rid himself of the cancer of self-hatred symbolized by his alter ego, Eben. The immediate cause of the fratricide is an argument in which Eben tells Zeke his father had tried to have him aborted. "Your own father wanted you to be killed," he screams, and Farragut strikes him with the iron. When he kills his detestable brother, he truncates that part of himself that prefers no to yes, cynicism to belief, sorrow to joy, hate to love. The crime represents a necessary first step in his eventual redemption. In prison he fears that in loving Jody he is only loving himself, but in fact the affair teaches him how to love without tying down the loved one. Jody is the beloved in the relationship, and Farragut waits for him "as he had waited for the sound of Jane's heels on the cobbles in Boston, waited for the sound of the elevator that would bring Virginia up to the eleventh floor, waited for Dodie to open the rusty gate in Thrace Street, waited for Roberta to get off the C bus in some Roman piazza. . . ." The difference is that when Jody is unfaithful—as he often is—Farragut feels no real pangs of jealousy. And when Jody miraculously escapes in a helicopter, Zeke misses him yet is genuinely glad for his freedom.

"There is nothing on earth as cruel as a rotten marriage," Farragut reflects, and his disastrous marriage to Marcia stands in sharp contrast to his love for Jody. "I don't have to listen to your shit anymore," his wife screams at him as he is about to be incarcerated.

He is astonished not because she is hysterical but because she took the words out of his mouth. When she visits him in prison, she pulls her hand away from his touch, says that it's been "nice to have a dry toilet seat" in his absence, observes that prison has turned his hair becomingly snow-white, and explains that she thinks it unwise to let him see his much-loved son Peter. "No one," as John Gardner commented, "has ever written down a more deadly wife than Farragut's." She is every bit as hateful and murderous as his brother had been. In his quest for love, Farragut must look beyond holy matrimony.

He achieves his redemption—and his own miraculous escape from Falconer—by caring for Chicken Number Two in his dying days. He takes the emaciated and pitiful Chicken into his cell, bathes him, and puts him to bed between clean sheets. He's not at all afraid to die, Chicken says. He hates to leave the party, for "even franks and rice taste good when you're hungry, even an iron bar feels good to touch." Yet he will die a happy man because, as he tells Zeke, he is "intensely interested in what's going to happen next." Zeke tenderly takes the old second-story man's hand, and seems to draw from it "a deep sense of freeness . . . something that Chicken Number Two was lovingly giving to him." Then he feels a slight discomfort in his buttocks and finds that he has been sitting on Chicken's false teeth. "Oh, Chicken," he says, "you bit me in the ass," and his laughter turns to sobs as Chicken dies.

The medics come, put Chicken in a shroud, and leave. Cunningly Farragut removes Chicken to his bed and takes his place in the shroud. By this means, reminiscent of *The Count of Monte Cristo*, he is delivered from prison. At the end, a stranger on a bus gives him a raincoat to protect him from the wet. As he alights from the bus, Farragut realizes that he has lost "his fear of falling and all other fears of that nature." He walks in the rain, head high and back straight, rejoicing in his release.

Cheever drew liberally on his own experience in the novel. His alcoholism supplied him with the authentic detail of withdrawal from addiction that Farragut suffers through, for example. Moreover, Farragut's family situation closely resembles that of his creator. The dark underside of the self represented by the evil brother, the father who invited the abortionist to dinner, the mother who neglected him, the wife who scorned him—all these characters from his family background, real and imagined, are presented in exaggerated form in *Falconer*. Yet the novel goes far beyond these

traces of autobiography, and it makes the most affirmative statement in all of Cheever's work. *Falconer* is his testament that only
love—selfless love, love for the least worthy and most flawed of our
fellowmen—can make us free.

Cheever was apprehensive about the reception of *Falconer*—he
well remembered the devastating Sunday *Times* review of *Bullet
Park*—but almost all of the reviews were favorable. Most welcomed
Falconer as a substantial advance on Cheever's previous work. One
of the things a great writer can do in a mad time, John Gardner
observed, is simply to write down things as they are. And in *Falconer* Cheever "simply copied down reality at its fiercest, making
no excuses." Bellow reached much the same conclusion. The novel,
he wrote Cheever, was "much the toughest book you ever wrote—
warlike, nothing softened." What he felt throughout was "an en-
raged determination to state the basic facts." Joan Didion, praising
the novel in the *New York Times Book Review*, emphasized that despite its dismal setting, *Falconer* nonetheless represented another
chapter in Cheever's ongoing concern with exile and estrangement.
Joyce Carol Oates sounded the sole negative note. The victories in
the novel came too easily, she maintained, and its transcendence of
pain and misery seemed "glib." Her critique echoed the old *"New
Yorker* writer" stereotype of Cheever: that he was too graceful and
brilliant, that he did not suffer convincingly enough on the page.
Yet in *Falconer* he found new and more basic ways of expressing
himself. "My prose is much closer to the substance," he remarked
in his interview with his daughter. "I've rid myself of persiflage.
It's like having a voice and finally finding the right music." Most
reviewers were disposed to agree with Margaret Manning of the
Boston Sunday Globe that the only thing wrong with *Falconer* was
that it had to end. "I wanted it to go on forever," Manning wrote.

To be sure, Cheever's depiction of marriage in *Falconer* stretches
the limits of believability. It may be that like Zeke's brother, Eben,
Marcia is supposed to symbolize some odious corner of himself that
he must obliterate or at least escape in order to become healthy and
whole. Yet the venom in the portrait unmistakably derives in part
from Cheever's own disturbed marriage. According to Fred, both
of his parents seemed driven by perversity, "always going in opposite directions" and capable of saying terrible things to and about
each other along the way. They were both highly articulate and
unusually contrary people, as John himself admitted. Even standing next to each other at a party, they could manage to look es-

tranged. At home they often kept their distance. When Dennis Coates or Allan Gurganus or Phil Schultz came to visit, Mary busied herself at the opposite end of the house. They were John's protégés, after all, and she had her own life to live. She constructed a separate life of her own, with different friends, while sticking to the marriage with determination. In the process, Susan believes, her mother became "really autonomous."

Publicly, Cheever called the marriage vows "the most inspired and the most preposterous of all propositions." In rural societies men and women might be bound for life because they had to work together to survive. But in modern life only "the imponderable of love" could bind a man and a woman, and in his view such love was "neither strong enough nor even enough in most cases to last a lifetime." In their case, he told more than one interviewer, there had scarcely been a week during forty years together that he and Mary did not contemplate divorce.

Despite what must have been the sting of reading and hearing her husband's words on the subject, and despite his sexual philandering and jealousy, Mary Cheever stuck it out. They had bad times, she acknowledges, but "bad times make it easier to hang on for people like me because in bad times you know you have to hang in and help." John's life, she understood, lay in his writing. Her job was to take care of him, especially when he was in the depths. According to Aline Benjamin, who knew both Cheevers well, "Mary was a strong, loving, indomitable, and funny wife." Almost always, they could laugh together. Once John brought her along to see the Ascoli farm and noticed a new chicken. "Where did it come from?" he asked John Bukovsky. "Oh, people drop them over the fence," Bukovsky explained. It was an easy way to get rid of Easter chicks who had grown too big or troublesome or uncute to keep. "I bet you'd like to drop me over the fence sometimes," John said to Mary.

With *Falconer* successfully launched, Cheever was ready to move on to something different. He thought of his career as a journey or voyage, and there was no going back. But he did not yet know where the road might lead. While he waited for the next part of his literary journey to declare itself, he resumed his own restless wayfaring and attended to his ceremonial obligations.

Elizabeth Ames died on March 28. The death certificate listed her age as ninety-two, but Malcolm Cowley suspected she was ninety-six and Cheever thought her ninety-nine. The last time John saw her at Yaddo, she sat in her chair fully dressed, with her handbag at her feet as if in a train station. Quite senile, she recognized Cheever but thought of him as the twenty-two-year-old she had first met in 1934. It was a pleasant visit, for he got her started telling stories about the old days. When they parted, she said she'd see him in Minneapolis—the city she had grown up in and left more than sixty years before. In recognition of the bond between them, Cheever was asked to speak at her memorial service in the music room at Yaddo. The audience included members of the Yaddo corporation, former artists who had been guests there, cooks and groundskeepers. With a gentle humor born of love, Cheever paid homage to her unusually useful and happy life. Even her senility was remarkable, he said at the end. "Well into her nineties she decided that the people she loved and admired—many of them long dead—were alive and working in the mansion. The fools and bores, she decided, were dead."

In June, Max Zimmer stopped at Cedar Lane on his way to Yaddo. He had driven forty-five hours straight through from Utah to New York, and was somewhat disoriented. Nor did he work well at Yaddo. He was put off by the rather genteel atmosphere of the place and by the pretensions of some of the guests. He was also annoyed to find that he was regarded as having been invited solely because of Cheever's influence. He could and should have made it on his own, he felt. At Yaddo, however, he met Lewis Turco, poet and professor at the State College of New York at Oswego, and Turco offered him a job teaching creative writing at the college. He taught at Oswego from the fall of 1977 to the spring of 1979. During this period Max was first married to a young woman studying medicine at Johns Hopkins and then divorced. He saw Cheever only three or four times a year, but was ever assured in conversation and correspondence of John's love for him.

Late in the spring, Cheever traveled to Bulgaria to attend an international conference titled "The Writer and Peace: The Spirit of Helsinki and the Duty of the Masters of Culture." The American participants—William Saroyan and Gore Vidal in addition to Cheever—had been recruited by Lyubomir Levchev, a charming Bulgarian poet and first deputy chairman of his government's committee on art and culture, during a whirlwind visit to the United States in late January and early February. Cheever was repeatedly advised not to make the trip. Robert Penn Warren and Eleanor Clark thought he was "almost criminally naive" to validate such a

repressive regime by his presence. Amnesty International sent him
lists of Eastern European writers recently thrown in jail. Tanya
Litvinov, living in London, strongly advised him not to go. But he
believed, as he told Raphael Rudnik, that any art that was any good
was by its nature heretical, and to expose any people to art was
therefore to act against a totalitarian state.

Mary Cheever accompanied her husband on the Bulgarian trip.
First they stopped in the Netherlands, to visit the Rudniks. On
June 4, Cheever gave a highly successful reading at the United
States Information Service Center in Amsterdam and delighted the
American ambassador and others by refusing an honorarium.
Then it was on to Bulgaria, where the conference turned into the
expected "love feast, stage-managed from opening speeches of self-
congratulation to final resolutions on peace." The American writers were unanimous in thinking that as political propaganda the
gathering was ineffective. The Russian delegates, including Yevtushenko and Vosnesensky, virtually surrounded the Americans, cutting off their access to writers from other countries. And press
reports were so carefully manipulated that the reporter from *Le
Monde* returned to Paris after the first day of the three-day meeting.

As envoys of goodwill, however, the hosts could hardly have
been more ingratiating. There were elaborate dinners "and always," Cheever observed, "a string trio in long gold dresses."
Saroyan's work was well known in Eastern Europe, his plays often
performed. "If this bus overturns," Vidal said during an outing,
"Saroyan is the only one the Bulgarian papers will feature." On the
return trip to the United States the Cheevers changed planes in
Frankfurt, and Denny Coates—stationed in Germany—tracked
them down at the airport. He found Cheever standing in line,
wearing the rattiest, dirtiest raincoat he had ever seen. As they
chatted together, Coates spied a familiar face half a dozen places
away in line. It was Mary, of course, and he went to greet her, then
came back to resume talking with John. They were traveling on the
same plane, but not really together.

Cheever spent two weeks of the summer signing copies of the
Franklin Library's special edition of *The Wapshot Chronicle*. The
Franklin people offered to dispatch him to any island in the world
to perform this chore, doubtless expecting him to opt for Bali. He
chose Nantucket instead, where he and Mary stayed at the Wauwinet House, which they knew well from other visits. He spent part
of each day at his desk, writing his name in the books and trying

to hold the pen at the angle recommended to avoid hand fatigue. Such were the penalties of fame. The benefits worked out to two dollars a signature.

He also went to Yaddo, more to see Max than to write. It was obvious, Grace Schulman remembers, that he was in love with Max, but the reunion went badly. When Max moved to Oswego in the fall, Cheever began a relationship with Steve Phillips (not his real name), one of his former students at Boston University. This liaison was not as intense as that between Cheever and Zimmer. Steve occasionally came to Ossining, and the two of them would bicycle along the aqueduct to the Croton dam or drive off to lunch together. On these occasions Cheever commented wittily on books and authors for the benefit of the aspiring young author. In return Phillips gave him the intimacy he required. "Brightness falls from the air" was the Joycean refrain that ran through John's head after their meetings. It was "a summons to life." Both of them were content to keep the affair easygoing. Cheever, perhaps thinking of Max, worried about its becoming a relationship whose every parting would seem intolerable.

As with Max, he saw to it that Steve had more than enough to drink and smoke. Sometimes Phillips ended up back in Grand Central Station barely able to drag himself off the train. Cheever seemed to take a vicarious pleasure in watching these young men drink. And liquor functioned to relax inhibitions, even for the entirely sober Cheever. He remained agonizingly ambivalent about his homosexual desires, and unwilling to declare them overtly. He liked cultivating an air of illicit intrigue, Phillips thought, but sometimes this led to awkwardness. Once the two of them were biking together when John spied some friends in the distance. "You go on ahead," he told Steve, and stopped to talk with the friends as if he and Steve had not been companions at all. At times his needs overcame him. When he went into New York to see Ned Rorem, for example, he became embarrassingly insistent almost at once. Ned escaped him, but then Rorem's companion James Holmes came in and Cheever transferred his attentions. After that, he saw Holmes occasionally for backgammon or lunch at the Edwardian Room of the Plaza, where John seemed to be in his element. It was not a fulfilling friendship, however. Holmes thought him childishly self-centered in his attitude toward sex.

During the fall of 1977, Cheever was persuaded by David Clarke, a visiting scholar at Yale, to write a piece about architectural preservation. Clarke asked Cheever to undertake the job because he admired the way he characterized places in his fiction. Shady Hill and St. Botolphs were so vividly presented, he thought, that like Thomas Hardy's Wessex they came to function as characters in his fiction. Pleased by that observation, Cheever dashed off a brief essay titled "The Second Most Exalted of the Arts" for the *Journal of Architectural Education.* The burden of his message was that most contemporary buildings would hardly deserve preservation. Architecture revealed the character of the architect, he observed, and current housing developments and motel projects proclaimed nothing so loudly as the avariciousness and stupidity of those who designed and built them. He was also distressed by the incursion of Route 9A on his own property, where it cut within thirty-five feet of his apple orchard. He reposed his hope in the independence and pride of individual craftsmen. On his way to church one Sunday morning, he spied a lone workman on the roof. "Something has to be done *right,*" the Sabbath laborer told him, and he was doing it on his own time.

In November he broke off his long professional alliance with Candida Donadio, a separation that caused both author and agent some pain. In a parting letter of regret, Cheever thanked her for her faith in *Falconer* and for seeing him through some difficult times. Nonetheless he severed the tie, and before hiring another agent tried to handle his literary business by himself, with dubious success. In July 1978, for instance, he turned down a request from X. J. Kennedy to include "The Swimmer" in his popular Little, Brown textbook *An Introduction to Fiction,* and so made that magnificent story unavailable to hundreds of thousands of college students. He was overwhelmed by such requests, he told Kennedy by way of explanation, with "no agent, no secretary."

The last months of 1977 were punctuated by a series of public appearances and hometown awards. The Reformed synagogue in Chappaqua named Cheever Man of the Year. He and Mary were honored by the Ossining public library. He paid a return visit to Iowa for a reading and a workshop session. Once again he went to Harvard to read on behalf of the *Advocate,* except that this time the magazine charged a two-dollar fee for the right to witness the author of *Falconer.* The following day he wowed the students at Bradford, brightening everyone's day with his "warmth, wit, and boundless laughter." He appeared at a mass benefit reading in Alice Tully Hall, performing after John Ashbery and Donald Barthelme and before Richard Eberhart, Allen Ginsberg, and Eugene McCarthy, among others. Phil Schultz prevailed on him to read at the YM-YWHA in New York to an overflow audience. Grace Schulman threw a party afterward at her University Place apartment in Greenwich Village. John and Mary's friends attended, the men in business suits and the women in high collars and hats. It seemed to Schulman as if a nineteenth-century soirée had been transplanted to the avant-garde precincts of the Village.

After the new year the Cheevers were off on another overseas journey, her first and his third trip to the Soviet Union. In a kind of perverse preparation they dined with the Romanovs in mid-December. "My grandmother sent a battleship for me," Vassily said in explaining how he survived the revolution. In Moscow two weeks later, they were met by Frieda Lurie, a colonel in the KGB and a Russian of another color. Cheever's third Russian sojourn was not as auspicious as the others. He came back exhausted; Mary acquired a stomach parasite it took months to purge. The trip was not without its moments, however. The Novgorod high school band greeted them with a version of "Hold That Tiger." As always Cheever was impressed by the serious attention paid to writers. They treated him, he told Dick Cavett in a television interview, with as much respect as an investment banker commanded in the United States.

Cheever readjusted to Western time and customs at Yaddo. He was sometimes rude at dinner to those who betrayed the least trace of pretentiousness, Hayden Carruth noted. But he also renewed his old friendship with cook Nellie Shannon and watched *Little House on the Prairie* with caretakers George and Helen Vincent. Afternoons he and Carruth skied the seven-mile cross-country course twice over. At first Cheever had trouble keeping up with Carruth, ten years his junior, but by the end of a week he was staying with him and even pushing the pace. Neither of them was getting much writing done.

Much of Cheever's time was spent answering the correspondence that came in from those lonely and intelligent readers, unassociated with journalism or publishing or academia, that he welcomed as his ideal audience. He did not save their letters. He saved no one's letters, for "saving a letter is like trying to preserve a kiss." But he faithfully and promptly answered them, usually on the same day they arrived. He was also busy with the organizational and ceremonial duties that devolved upon him in his growing eminence. In 1977 he was elected to the board of the American Academy; by 1978 he was serving as secretary of that august body. The academy called on him, in May 1977, to present Saul Bellow with its gold medal. Then in February 1978 he and Bernard Malamud were asked to make laudatory remarks when the National Arts Club awarded Bellow *its* gold medal. That made two gold medals in nine months, and later he was to bestow still other honors on his friend Saul. At the academy ceremony, Cheever commented on the "genuine brilliance and civility" with which Bellow had faced the hullaballoo surrounding the Nobel Prize. At the National Arts Club dinner, he called Bellow "the master of his time" and singled out *The Adventures of Augie March,* particularly, as a book that "has stayed with me all of my days."

Much has been written about the competitiveness of writers, yet as Eileen Simpson wondered in connection with John Berryman and Delmore Schwartz and Randall Jarrell and Robert Lowell, were poets really "more competitive than astronauts, art collectors, assistant professors, jockeys, hostesses, ballet dancers, professional beauties?" In Cheever's case he was subject to twinges of resentment when authors he regarded as inferior were honored out of proportion to their accomplishment. He felt nothing of the sort, however, with respect to the writers—Saul Bellow and John Updike among them—whose work he most valued. Among the three of them and such others as Malamud and Robert Penn Warren there grew up a kind of fellowship that made rivalry seem ridiculous.

Cheever and Bellow first met in Eleanor Clark's railroad apartment in New York, shortly after World War II. From the beginning there was mutual admiration between them, and it lasted. Bellow repeatedly placed Cheever atop lists of writers he admired, citing his extraordinary "sleight-of-hand." As for Cheever, he had thought Bellow the most interesting writer he knew since first reading his description of a woman washing window glass in the 1944 *Dangling Man.* In reading Bellow, Cheever sensed a spirit of brotherhood. "We share not only our love of women but a fondness for rain." The affinity extended beyond the fiction to the authors themselves. A real friendship sprang up between them, though they saw each other infrequently. "On both sides there was instant candor," Bellow said. Nothing was held back behind costumes or masks. The very difference in their backgrounds—the Yankee prep schooler versus the son of Jewish immigrants—seemed to tie them together, because both proceeded beyond their origins to become, more simply and importantly, American writers. Toward Bellow, Cheever displayed none of the snobbery of certain Yankee WASPs. Instead, Bellow observed, he put "human essences in the first place: first the persons—himself, myself—and after that the other stuff, class origins, social history." Once Cheever told him that if he had the choice, he would wish to be born the child of Jewish immigrants in the United States. That might bring them closer together.

As writers, though, what counted was not where they came from but where they let their writing take them. And Cheever, Bellow felt, had transformed himself through his fiction, growing and developing in the process. It was what he aimed to do himself and gave them a commonality of purpose shared by few others. "I felt *connected* with John," he said emphatically.

The tie between Cheever and Updike was complicated by the public tendency to confuse the two writers and their work. Cheever was sometimes put off when an acquaintance would say how much he or she admired his latest book—*"Rabbit Redux,* wasn't it?" Once he was actually invited to do a reading at Notre Dame by a professor who complimented him on the masterful "Maple stories." Updike was the victim of similar mistakes, and he cannot have been pleased by the bad pun that characterized him as an under- or an over-a-Cheever. Yet there was mutual respect between them from the time Updike wrote Cheever a fan letter about the hang of Cousin Honora's dress and Cheever recognized the unmistakable indications of genius in Updike's first work. "He's a winner," Cheever invariably said of the writer who was nearly twenty years his junior. He admired Updike's willingness to take chances in his fiction and his capacity to move easily from story and novel to essay and poem. They were in fact "colleagues," just as Cheever had said in response to the false report of Updike's death, and that collegiality gave their friendship an importance out of all proportion to the rare occasions on which they met. In 1977, John and Mary Cheever drove to Boston for Liz Updike's wedding. He would have gone to Korea to see Liz married, Cheever wrote Updike afterward. Such ceremonies enabled him to recognize the bond between them.

At another significant ceremony in June 1978, Cheever was awarded an honorary degree by Harvard. "A master chronicler of his times," the citation read, "he perceives in the American suburb a microcosm of the divisions, tensions, and incongruous ecstasies

of twentieth-century life." The recognition meant more to him
than to most. He was undoubtedly the only recipient that year
whose academic career had ended with his expulsion from prep
school. The other honorees included the Russian writer Alexander
Solzhenitsyn and Ephraim Katzir, the former president of Israel.
"Did you graduate from Harvard?" Madame Katzir innocently
asked Cheever. No, Cheever replied, nor from high school either.
He'd spent most of what might have been his college years, he said,
in furnished rooms on the Lower West Side of Manhattan, cold and
hungry and lonely.

"Ah," Madame Katzir said, "but that's all behind you."

"No," said Cheever. "I'm not sure that it is."

At sixty-six, he might soon be on his own again, he hinted. The
overseas trips with Mary were over. Now he traveled alone, or with
others. In the summer of 1978, he visited Bulgaria again and took
Ben and Linda along. According to Ben, he apparently had an affair
with his interpreter on this journey, a young woman named Andrea. He insisted on Andrea's accompanying them on a trip to
Varna, on the Black Sea. There he arranged a champagne-and-
caviar celebration in honor of her birthday. The next day, Ben and
Linda saw the two of them sunning on the beach in casual intimacy, Andrea topless. It seemed clear that they had spent the night
together.

In the fall he was on the reading circuit again, this time on a tour
of Canadian cities for the State Department. Word came in October
that Susan, who had been spending a year in France for that purpose, had finished her first novel, later published as *Looking for
Work*. He was proud of her, John wrote: completing a novel was
a great accomplishment. He was happy that Susie was not ashamed
of being the daughter of a novelist, and that she had not resorted
to crypto-autobiography. In her book, he pointed out, the father
rode to hounds and parted his hair in the middle. "I wouldn't be
caught dead with a center part," he said. He was even gladder that
she hadn't taken a couple of years off waiting tables in Aspen to find
herself. She "knows damn well" who she is and what she wants to
do, he observed with approval.

At the end of October, Knopf brought out *The Stories of John
Cheever*, a comprehensive collection of sixty-one of Cheever's stories. The book was a triumph, but it might not have existed at all
but for the foresight of Bob Gottlieb. When Gottlieb first proposed
the collection, Cheever resisted the idea. Almost all the stories had

already appeared in both magazine and book form. "Who's going to buy a book just to read them again?" he argued. But Gottlieb saw the potential of a large volume of stories after the success of *Falconer*. Moreover, he did most of the work in putting the book together. All Cheever did was "pull the stories out from under the bed." Gottlieb read through them, made his choices in consultation with Cheever, and worked out a tentative table of contents. The result was a brilliant assemblage of the best of Cheever, with some significant omissions among his early work and such other stories as the autobiographical "The National Pastime" and the explicitly homosexual "The Leaves, the Lion-Fish, and the Bear." The stories were presented mostly in chronological order of composition. Cheever decided to lead off, however, with the masterly "Goodbye, My Brother" (1951), though several other stories in the book were written earlier.

The Stories of John Cheever, nearly seven hundred pages in its bold red jacket, had about it the atmosphere of a magnum opus, a valedictory statement from a writer approaching the end of his threescore and ten. To the general reader and even to reviewers who should have known better, the book came as a surprise. Few realized how many excellent stories Cheever had written, or how many in different keys: some dark, some light, some "written from the outside" in an ironic tone, some "written from the inside" and illuminated by the sunny vision of the narrator, some realistic, some magical. Most of the reviews were ecstatic. "John Cheever is a magnificent storyteller," Anne Tyler advised, "and this is a dazzling and powerful book." The appearance of Cheever's *Stories,* John Leonard asserted, was "not merely the publishing event of the 'season' but a grand occasion in English literature." Cheever was "one of the two or three most imaginative and acrobatic literary artists now alive," Stephen Becker proclaimed. Commercially, the book did extremely well. The local Books 'n Things store in Briarcliff sold almost nine hundred hardcover copies at a book-signing party, and sales were high throughout the nation. His new agent, Lynn Nesbit at ICM, negotiated a five-hundred-thousand-dollar advance from Knopf toward his next two books. He had no need ever to feel poor again.

Cheever welcomed the recognition as much as the money, and for good reason. Early in 1978 his name had been left off a list of three nominees for the American Academy–National Institute Gold Medal in the Short Story. The names submitted to the members were Mary McCarthy, Peter Taylor, and John Updike, distinguished artists all (Taylor won), with Cheever conspicuously absent. His name had come up in the deliberations, and was then dropped on the grounds that he had already received the Howells Medal for the novel from the organization and it was time to recognize someone else. Bill Maxwell propounded this view to the other members of the nominating committee, and it carried the day. To some extent, Maxwell was simply stating what he believed—that it was a good idea to spread the honors around—but he was also motivated by Cheever's ill-spirited remarks about him.

He was particularly incensed by the "Telephone Story"—the tale circulated by Cheever in newspaper and television interviews. In one version of the story, Maxwell recalls, Cheever said he had come to see his editor back in the mid-1950s when he was dead broke and asked if the editor would give him some money in exchange for a share in the royalties of the as yet unpublished *Wapshot Chronicle*. The editor supposedly offered him three thousand dollars, and when Cheever asked if he couldn't make it a little more, picked up the telephone and held it toward him, as if to say, "See if you can do better anywhere else." No one who knew the gentlemanly Maxwell was likely to take that story seriously, but nonetheless it angered him. "Why should I further John's career when he tells those whoppers about me?" he thought. His part in this decision, Maxwell acknowledges, has subsequently "remained somewhat on my conscience. Maybe more than somewhat." For the fact was that he thought Cheever the best short-story writer in America.

Malcolm Cowley, another who felt the same way, was outraged at not finding Cheever's name on the ballot circulated to members, and conducted a behind-the-scenes correspondence among officers of the American Academy–National Institute chastising them for letting such an oversight come to pass. Cheever would have been a shoo-in had his name been proposed, Cowley thought, and there was plenty of precedent for awarding the gold medal to those who had already won the Howells. Faulkner had been so honored, as had Cather and Welty. Naturally disappointed, Cheever insisted that he wasn't. He would much rather have written "The Swimmer," he said, medal or no medal. Still, it must have seemed something like a vindication when *The Stories of John Cheever* received both the National Book Critics' Circle Award and the Pulitzer Prize for 1978, while narrowly missing the National Book Award.

The Pulitzer was the biggest prize so far, and it meant a great deal to Cheever. The news came through on Patriots' Day, when the Cheever family had assembled in Boston for Ben's first Boston Marathon. When the telephone call reached the desk of the Ritz, Ben was midway between Hopkinton and the Prudential Center, while his father and his son, Joshua—Cheever's first grandchild— were riding the swan boats in the public garden. Ben got back first, finishing the marathon in just over three hours and running on to the Ritz, where he brought the message for his father up to the room. When John returned, he opened it and discovered that he'd won the Pulitzer. For the Cheever family, as Mary pointed out, "it was a day to remember."

Many in the literary community inclined to think that Cheever's Pulitzer was overdue. Also in the running for that year's prizes was John Irving's immensely popular *The World According to Garp*. Irving was asked in an interview how it felt to be edged out by Cheever. "When I was learning how to write," Irving said, "John Cheever was one of the few people who made me realize that the kind of writing I loved could still be done. I can't imagine resenting any honor paid him." Rumors about a potential Nobel Prize for Cheever began to circulate, rumors that were repeatedly brought to his attention. "When the house fills up with Swedish reporters," he said, "I'll damned well know I'm up for a Nobel." In the meantime, he didn't want to speculate on his chances.

Though the Nobel did not come through, John Cheever was by 1979 a wealthy and famous man. "The mail was thick" with invitations, Susan reported. It seemed that everyone who mattered wanted him to come to lunch, to dinner. All that attention rather turned her father's head, Susan felt. He began to talk about himself more than before, to take on airs, and to expect special treatment, she believed. Certainly there were times when he enjoyed his celebrity.

Knopf threw a gala dinner for *The Stories of John Cheever* at Lutèce, where Cheever's immediate companions were actresses Maria Tucci (Gottlieb's wife) and Lauren Bacall. Bacall was then engaged in writing her memoirs, and was delighted when Cheever encouraged her in that effort. Later, he attended a book-launching party for Bacall. "God, you're so terrific to me," she told him. "You've really given me a boost." Just don't write a novel, he responded; if she did, he might not be so nice. Much of this was flirtation, but the flirting was innocent enough. "He did give off an aura of being a terrific gent," Bacall said. Perhaps if she'd known him in his younger days, well . . . In any event, Cheever was delighted with the Knopf party. It was good to have a publisher, he said, who didn't think writers should sleep on straw. And he was also appreciative when Gottlieb introduced his work to such British authors as David Cornwell (John le Carré), Harold Pinter, and Antonia Fraser. Cornwell wrote him fan letters. Pinter and Fraser took to fighting over who would get to read *Stories* at bedtime.

Contrary to democratic dogma, Cheever believed in the existence and importance of social class, and sneakingly admired the upper class. When Allan Gurganus used the phrase "very rich" in a story, he lined out the adverb. You were or you weren't, he said. "Rich" was one of the few words in the language that did not require qualifying. So he reveled in lunching with the Rockefellers in Pocantico Hills and dining at Mrs. Vincent Astor's. Her diamonds, he wrote in comic exaggeration, were so heavy she couldn't get up by herself. She asked him what he used his little shit-brown Volkswagen Rabbit *for*. "It's so *unbecoming*," she pointed out. Cheever thought she was "glorious."

Similarly he was in his element at the races in Saratoga, where he was invited along with Eugene and Clayre Thaw to sit in James Gaines's box. He mingled with the Gaineses and the Whitneys, the Palamountains and Ned Rorem came by to greet him, and he was even winning at the windows. Cheever was "like a little kid" bubbling over with high spirits, Thaw recalled, and was virtually shaking with pleasure as they walked down to the paddock between races.

He also delighted in the eight-thousand-dollar Rolex Oyster Perpetual Day-Date Superlative Chronometer he was given for appearing in an advertisement. It seemed incongruous for a reticent understated Yankee like Cheever to wear this heavy ostentatious gold watch. So Cheever kidded himself about it, joyfully. He shot his cuffs in Dallas to display the massive timepiece, he said, but no one was impressed, because "everybody in Dallas has one." Sara Spencer teased him about his Rolex-bearing arm growing longer than his other one, and he liked that too. Here was success such as his father only dreamed of.

Enjoying fame is one thing, and becoming conceited because of it quite another. Not everyone agreed with Susan that her father misplaced his dignity in going through "a kind of adolescence of celebrity." As his son Ben remarks, he has "known stationery store proprietors who are more self-important than his father was." Hayden Carruth at Yaddo detected no pretensions or stuffiness about Cheever at all. "He never made the kind of egotistical remarks that most writers—almost all writers of whatever merit—do," Carruth recalls. He was far more likely to make himself the butt of jokes. And longtime maid Iole Masullo thought him a humble and simple man, "not like a peacock at all, you know." What seems indisputable is that he grew more aware of his public image, and more willing to use the media to shape the contours of that image. In "The Cheever Chronicle," a long article in the *New York Times Magazine,* he cooperated with author Jesse Kornbluth in rearranging a number of details about his family, his post-Thayer years, his army career, and his relationship with *The New Yorker.* He posed on horseback for *People* magazine, encouraging the widespread misconception that he was a kind of country gentleman who kept horses. Margaret Mills at the academy-institute assumed as much when he came by the office in a hacking jacket. Normally, now that he could afford it, he dressed elegantly in well-tailored suits and sport coats accented by large floppy bow ties. He was generous with others, too. In the summer of 1979, Fred was jilted by a girl who told him to grow up and get a car. He was saving up for a Volkswagen when his father bought him a BMW to take back to Stanford.

Much as he was gratified by his acceptance among the elite, Cheever never lost the common touch. He practiced a kind of social schizophrenia, the Thaws concluded. In one aspect he was a snob with a strong sense of propriety and a nostalgia for the days when Boston ladies had their hats and men wore fedoras. On the other hand, he really liked and identified with working people. What he hated was the Sleepy Hollow country club crowd, a cast of moneyed nonaristocratic suburbanites who told off-color jokes in loud voices. The Thaws took him to the country club once, and for weeks he entertained everyone with wickedly sarcastic vignettes of his "dinner at Sleepy." Aside from these people, he had a gift for talking to anyone and a genuine interest in what they had to say.

At Yaddo, he had for so long been a member of the family that cook Nellie Shannon finally decided to ask him to dinner at her house. He was the first and only guest so honored, for Elizabeth Ames was very much opposed to fraternization between employees and artists. On the appointed evening Cheever arrived with flowers and an autographed copy of his *Stories* for Nellie, and the dinner was a great success. At Yaddo itself, she played a maternal role toward him. When he stuck his head in the kitchen—the first guest down—and said "Good morning, Nellie," she knew the reply he was hoping for. "Yes, John," she'd answer, "the coffee's ready." Through the long years she regularly chided him for his drinking. "Don't you know you're killing yourself?" she said while others remained silent. Even after he quit, the routine continued. On one of his last visits, she fixed him an early-morning breakfast and packed some cookies and a Thermos of orange juice for his drive back to Ossining. "I hope you haven't got any gin in that car," she warned him. "Now, Nellie," he said, "my own mother wouldn't lecture me the way you do." And off he drove, grinning.

It was in Ossining, however, that Cheever showed himself most plain. He came to love the town toward the end, for both its physical beauty and its lack of pretentiousness. In the fall of 1979 he wrote a short piece for the original Ossining Marathon. From his bicycling, he noted, he shared with the marathon runners "an intimate knowledge of the road bumps, and the weeds and wild flowers along the shoulders," along with an appreciation for the views offered by High Tor and the Tappan Zee Bridge. As he hiked or biked or drove around town, he saw a great many people he knew, but Ossining was not the kind of town where people interrupted his dinner to ask for an autograph. No amount of publicity could induce his fellow citizens to treat him like a celebrity. He was simply "old Mr. Cheever on his bike or old Mr. Cheever with his dogs, which is precisely what one would want." If he was seen as different from his neighbors, it was largely because he didn't have a job that kept him riding the trains.

In this community he made some of his friends among others— tradespeople, mostly—who also did not have to commute. For nearly fifteen years he bought his gas from and took his car for servicing to Dominick Anfitreatro at Dom's Friendly Service in Croton, and each winter Dom plowed the Cheever driveway clear of snow. Sometimes Cheever drove in just to talk—to tell stories about what happened on his trips, for instance. Dom could hardly wait for Cheever to come by. "When he left," he said, "he left me on a high for a good part of the day." Cheever was a regular, too, at the Highland Diner in Ossining, where he'd arrive with a book or newspaper to read and then look around for someone to talk to.

At the Ascoli Farm, he and John Bukovsky would perch on the stone wall for fifteen minutes of conversation about the crops and the fox in the henhouse and somewhat deeper spiritual matters. He knew and was liked by so many people in the town that his family used to call him the Mayor of Ossining. He never ran for office, of course, but there was an abortive movement in the wake of the Pulitzer to name a street after him. Cheever was pleased and self-deprecatory about this at the same time. He and Mary and the children sat around the dinner table thinking of what else might be named after him. "Let's see," he proposed, "how about the John Cheever Memorial Dump?"

He felt a strong obligation to accept invitations to read or speak from Ossining and nearby communities, even when they cut into his time at the typewriter. The Newburgh Kiwanis Club or the Friends of the Peekskill Library or the White Plains Rotary Club would ask him to appear, for example, and he would ask bookman Bev Chaney whether he had to go. He showed a kind of little-boy quality in asking for such elementary advice, Chaney felt, rather as if it were a big world out there and he felt lost in coping with it. What Chaney told him, in any event, was that he didn't even have to *answer* that kind of mail, but usually Cheever did and usually he agreed to go. He wanted to please, and was willing to forgive others their mild trespasses against him. Herbert Hadad recalls one Cheever reading at a public library where the man introducing him went on and on for ten minutes enumerating his own accomplishments, finally ending with an "exquisitely remembered moment" of glory in his career. "And at that second," the introducer concluded at last, "if there was anyone in the world who could have done it better, it was John Cheever. I give you John Cheever." With extraordinary charity Cheever simply said, "Thank you for the elaborate introduction," and the evening's pleasures could then commence. He demonstrated a generosity of spirit in befriending Maureen Willson's son Michael and daughter Hannah. When Michael won a high school literary prize, Cheever wrote him a letter of congratulation, said he'd just won a prize himself (the Pulitzer), and enclosed a check for fifty dollars.

In his post-Pulitzer euphoria, Cheever quit smoking. It was not easy to end a fifty-year, up-to-two-pack-a-day habit, and for a time he was terribly irritable. But the advantages were obvious. He felt much better when he woke up, as his morning smoker's cough disappeared. His sense of smell sharpened, and food tasted wonderful. In a surge of physical vigor, he discovered that he could bicycle up hills in third gear that he'd previously been able to negotiate only in seventh or eighth. Like many reformed smokers, he tried hard to convert others—notably Max Zimmer, who came back into his life as a frequent and much-loved companion in the summer of 1979.

During the September 1977–June 1979 period, their friendship had been conducted at long distance. Zimmer was teaching and living in Oswego, but now he moved with his girl to Dobbs Ferry in Westchester, only a few train stops south of Ossining on the Hudson line. He and Cheever began to see each other three or four times a week, and oftener during Mary's annual visit to Treetops. Zimmer drank a lot during these meetings. Cheever would ask him up for lunch, and hand him a glass of vodka when he arrived. The drinking continued during the activities that followed: the lunch, the bike ride, the backgammon game, the discussion of a story Max had written, the lovemaking. He sometimes consumed a quart of vodka by the end of the afternoon, when he went back to the Dobbs Ferry station to meet his girl, coming in on the train from her job in New York City.

As the drinking suggested, Zimmer felt somewhat uncomfortable about the relationship. He tremendously admired Cheever and came to feel love for him, yet he also wanted to break away, to assert his independence, to say goodbye. Cheever sent out conflicting signals in that regard. His love for Max was "totally unprecedented," he said. He didn't fully understand his own feelings. It was essential, Cheever sometimes said, that their relationship end, and end happily. Max had to live his own life, after all. Yet it would devastate him, he said at other times, if Max should leave. Eventually Zimmer thought of himself as trapped by his ties to Cheever. And he was scared to death around Mary, though he and John were never caught in the act or chastised. He sometimes hoped that they would be caught, and that she would blow up. That didn't happen, at least not overtly. Once when he and John returned from making love in the woods, Mary was berating the gardener for cutting flowers along with weeds. Her anger was really directed at him and her husband, Max thought. He would have felt better about being John Cheever's lover if their essentially furtive and unacknowledged liaison had not been integrated into the fabric of his family, his house, his woods. At the end of the summer, Max and his girl and another former student from Oswego rented a house in Southampton, well out on Long Island, and thus eliminated the possibility of casual visits to Cedar Lane.

By mid-August, when Cheever flew up to New Hampshire to receive the MacDowell Colony medal, he knew that Max was about to leave and felt very much bereft. John Leonard, in charge of the award committee, spent much of a pretty awful weekend with Cheever. The administrative staff at MacDowell seemed to vanish, leaving their guest of honor to fend for himself. Cheever had to borrow a car to drive himself to the award ceremony from Hillcrest, the handsome old house of Mrs. MacDowell, where he was staying. That night there was a big dance where Cheever kept looking for "someone short enough to dance with." Perhaps bored and certainly sober among the merrymakers, he slipped away and walked the long way back to Hillcrest in the dark. Leonard found him sitting alone at ten o'clock, drinking the instant coffee he had brought along with him. They talked away much of the night. At first it was Cheever the charmer and Leonard the admirer, but then—and for the rest of the night—all that Cheever could talk about was his loneliness and his need for love. "Sex is very important to me," he said, "and there is no sex in my marriage." He was, that night, the most unhappy person Leonard had ever seen.

Among other things he told Leonard that he was thinking of moving to New York City. What he was seeking was a place where being homosexual (or bisexual, more accurately) would not make him conspicuous, but he did not spell this out. Could Leonard help him find an apartment? The proposed move to New York was something he often spoke of in the fall and winter of 1979–80 to Hope Lange, to his children, to Eugene and Clayre Thaw. In due course the Thaws located a furnished apartment on a quiet side street in Murray Hill, ideal as a place to write and close to the Century Club and Grand Central. No, Cheever said, he couldn't stand the idea of living with someone else's furniture. Always there were obstacles preventing him from leaving home. If he left, wouldn't he end up "a lonely old man with a dog on a leash?" If he left, what would he do with his bicycle, and wouldn't he miss his friends and should he come back on weekends? How could he leave Cedar Lane when he'd "turned every square inch" of its soil? In public and private, he proclaimed his and Mary's incompatibility. They did not sleep together, they did not get along well, they did not even like each other. Yet he also suggested that this basic tension made for a "much more workable relationship" than most conventional marriages. Presented with a concrete alternative, he decided to stay where he was.

CANCER

1980–1982

FOR the most part, the prospect shone bright as Cheever turned a corner into the 1980s. He had achieved wealth and fame, those desiderata he promised his parents never to seek, and frankly enjoyed the recognition that came with them. In March, Ambassador William Luers invited him to come to Venezuela for a week of interviews and appearances and dinners. He stayed at the ambassador's residence, and was feted everywhere. In that cordial atmosphere he was his charming best, fatherly with the children, flirtatious with Luers's wife, Wendy, and virtually aglow aboard the yacht that took them to Margarita island, escorted by a destroyer. In May he flew to Chicago to present yet another prize to Saul Bellow at St. James Episcopal Cathedral. There he was delighted over breakfast at the McDonald's on Michigan Avenue when other patrons recognized him, thanked him for his writing, and asked him to autograph their paper napkins. He showed up at Sara Spencer's one Saturday clutching the day's bundle of mail. "I'm rich and famous," he announced gaily, waving his letters in the air. Yet the Yankee in him understood that celebrity was as dross to the gold of literary accomplishment, and in that area he had unmistakably slowed down.

As always, Cheever continued to think in narrative. "To spend an afternoon with Cheever," Steve Phillips observed, "is to hear about forty stories begin to take shape." But the three-day frenzies that produced many of his stories visited him no longer: he could not concentrate with that kind of intensity. Sometimes, too, he was afflicted with what he called spells of *otherness*. Fixing breakfast, sitting at his desk, or dawdling over dinner, his mind would trip a wire and transport him across time and space to a realm where he knew not who he was. After a few terrifying moments the short circuit would mend itself and he would be back in the house at Cedar Lane, shaken and fearful of madness. How could he write if his mind was not right? His diminished capacities combined with the distractions of fame to retard his writing. It grew harder and harder to get the words down on paper. But as never before—now that he was sober, now that he understood how important it was to his audience as well as to himself—he wanted to write. It was what gave his life meaning.

Along about 1977, it occurred to Cheever that he was as dependent on his readers as they were on him. "Writing is very much like a kiss," he said. "It's something you can't do alone." Armed with that realization, he was willing to do readings and attend book signings almost anywhere. Only once did he rebel, when a rather elegantly dressed woman brought him an old copy of *The Wapshot Scandal* that the dog had obviously gotten to. She presented the chewed and be-saliva'd copy for signature. He flatly refused to sign. "Buy one of the new books," he suggested, "and I'll inscribe it any way you want, but preferably to the dog, obviously the only Cheever lover in your household." The woman stormed away. Otherwise, he felt a real sense of communion with "the fourteen or eighteen or twenty people who live in the woods and read my books," as he said on *The Dick Cavett Show*. Actually there were perhaps two hundred thousand people in the United States and England who would read and understand and like his work, and that wasn't counting the international audience he commanded in translation. He liked to think that they were "intelligent, well informed, serious, and mature," but he did not know who they were in the sense that Virginia Woolf, for instance, knew exactly whom she was addressing in her best books. From RFD return addresses he discovered that some of his readers lived in remote areas and that among them was the president of the True Value hardware store in Eau Claire, Wisconsin, and a woman from New York who thanked him for brightening the very day that her canary, "a glorious Yorkshire cock," had died. Earlier he had thought they were all *New Yorker* readers, but that proved to be less true with *Falconer* and the collected *Stories* than the earlier books. His audience was expanding, and he wanted to reach still more. In an effort to do so, he turned to television.

To begin with, Cheever had his reservations about the medium. Late in 1979 the Public Broadcasting Service's *Great Performances* series presented one-hour adaptations of three Cheever stories: "The Sorrows of Gin," adapted by Wendy Wasserstein; "O Youth and Beauty!" adapted by A. R. Gurney; and "The Five Forty-Eight," adapted by Terrence McNally. Cheever declined the chance to do the adaptations himself. "A short story completed is rather like a baseball game," he said. "You can't do anything else with it." He was also convinced that no really fine novel or story could be translated to film. A fourth-rate story like *Poldark* made an excellent television series, while *The Mayor of Casterbridge* fizzled. You could not film *The Great Gatsby*, though people kept trying. "Literature goes to where the camera is not." He admired J. D. Salinger for sticking to his guns on this issue. When *The Catcher in the Rye* came out, Salinger was approached to sell the motion-picture rights. He wouldn't do that, Salinger replied. *Catcher* wasn't a film, it was a novel. According to Cheever, Hollywood doubled the ante "and even sent a piano to soften Salinger up. He sent it back. The issue was not negotiable."

The only way Cheever saw of writing for television was to write an original script. The problem here was that in commercial television as in the films, the writer was often regarded as a functionary whose work might be twisted entirely out of shape in the process of production. Such writers were at the mercy of the producer and the director, the network and the sponsor, and he was unwilling to give up his independence in that way. Jac Venza, executive producer of New York's WNET, solved the problem. When Cheever told him he wasn't interested in adapting his own stories but might like to do an original screenplay, if only he could be guaranteed the independence he wanted, Venza said to go ahead. He'd do his best to prevent any interference. This was in mid-1973, and for six months Cheever sweated over the first draft of *The Shady Hill Kidnapping*. In February 1979 there was a reading of the tele-play at Joseph Papp's Public Theatre. "It was an exciting experience," Cheever remarked, but Venza and Ann Blumenthal, who was eventually to produce *Kidnapping*, knew that the script still needed work. For the time being all parties let it simmer while Cheever returned to fiction. By the start of 1980, he was working with painful slowness on *Oh What a Paradise It Seems*. It was intended, he told interviewers, to be a "big book."

Cheever's personal relationships stabilized early in 1980. Fred was happy and doing well at Stanford. Ben, separated from his wife, came home to Cedar Lane in December 1979. Thereafter he and his father were closer than ever before. Susan's first novel was in press, and her second in the typewriter. She and Ben alike were soon forging other alliances, Ben with Janet Maslin, film critic for the *New York Times*, Susan with Calvin Tomkins, art critic for *The New Yorker*. "You know, my kids find very interesting people to shack up with," Cheever said irreverently, but he was pleased for them nonetheless.

In the spring of 1980, Max Zimmer moved back to Westchester from Long Island and resumed his thrice-weekly calls at the Cheever house. This time Max was on the payroll as general factotum: chauffeur and secretary, bike rider and backgammon opponent, friend and lover. When Mary left for Treetops in August, Max moved in and even did the cooking sometimes. He also continued to bring his fiction to Cheever for comments. "I learned an enormous amount from him about craft," he says, "about scenes, paragraphs, story construction." As time went on, the roles even reversed somewhat. When Cheever struck a rough patch on *Paradise* or *Kidnapping*, he and Max would bounce alternative passages back and forth.

With Max nearby, John could better abide the waning of his affair with Hope Lange. Hope loved seeing him, but had progressively less interest in the physical side of their association. She turned him down when he tried to persuade her to accompany him to Venezuela. And when they had lunch in New York, she would arrange to do some shopping or go to an exercise class immediately afterward. John took Ben along for one such lunch date in the summer of 1980. "It did not look as if things were going to work out for Daddy that day," he recalls. Finally there was no sex at all. The last time he saw her, Cheever told Max Zimmer, they rendezvoused at Bloomingdale's and then walked to her hotel. Cheever got undressed hopefully, while she busied herself making phone calls. Deciding that flowers were called for, he got dressed, went downstairs, bought flowers, came back up, put the flowers in a vase, and removed his clothes again. But Hope stayed on the phone, and finally—defeated—he got up, dressed, and left. Hope does not remember this scene. Certainly, she says, she would not have wanted John to feel dismissed. But that was the way he characterized it for Max, and pretty much the way he later presented it in a fictionalized version in *Paradise*.

In the fall, Cheever drove up to Saratoga Springs for his last, and worst, stay at Yaddo. Looking backward, it was easy enough to detect omens of the trouble ahead. In October "the small season" had begun at Yaddo, with the number of artists reduced to a fraction of the summer crowd. At dinner, Cheever was very much king of the hill and excessively short-tempered. He was also unconscionably rude to the writer and doctor Richard Selzer. Still no one was prepared for what happened.

Cheever was headquartered in Hillside Cottage, a studio nestled in a grove of locust trees. He went to some trouble to get a television set installed there so that he could watch the World Series between the Philadelphia Phillies and the Kansas City Royals, and invited Mary Ann Unger, Joan Silver, and Lee Hyla to watch the third game—a night game—with him. The game followed an exhausting day for Cheever. After his morning's work, he bicycled twenty-two miles around Saratoga Lake, passing cottages—he was able to remember—called Gud Enuff and Dun Roamin. After dinner he attended an Alcoholics Anonymous meeting, and returned in time to watch the ball game with his guests. In the seventh inning, he stood watching the game and holding a plastic glass of ginger ale. As Joan Silver watched, he crushed the glass with his hand. At first she thought it was a joke, but the grimace on Cheever's face arrested her laugh. With his mouth twisted, he slipped, fell on the couch, and continued to convulse. Hyla ran to West House to summon help, while the two women stayed with the unconscious Cheever.

The ambulance arrived in about ten minutes. Dr. Selzer, alerted to the emergency, rode along to the hospital with Cheever, where he saw to it that he was not subjected to any "invasive tests." He was unconscious for several hours and troubled by loss of memory for many more. The hospital diagnosed his malady as a "ministroke." Silver and Unger thought it might have been a heart attack. It was a grand mal seizure.

In conversation and correspondence, Cheever treated the incident lightly. The game itself had been very dull, he told Silver, and was not to be blamed for his seizure. Even after a second episode six weeks later, he continued to make light of his affliction. During the "aura" that preceded his collapse, the image that sprang into his mind was of a bishop on the beach in Nantucket, bestowing his blessing in a forgotten language. Then he began to "chew on grandmother's Oriental rug and woke up in the emergency room." He was willing to accept his seizures as somehow ordained by God, and not by a vindictive God, for they helped bring about a knitting together of the threads of his marriage. In his distress the still-beautiful Mary cared for him with love and tenderness, and he responded to her nurturing with gratitude. Stein & Day had just published her *The Need for Chocolate & Other Poems*. And she was also branching out artistically, developing her drawing skills under the tutelage of Millie Adler. She needed an etching press and a studio with good light, John decided. He commissioned architect Don Reiman to plan such an addition and bought her an Edward Hopper print for Christmas.

When writer and psychologist Eugene Kennedy came to see Cheever on December 21, he unburdened himself about his seizures. He was grateful that they had brought his wife back to him, but terribly afraid that they had cost him his imaginative powers. He had signed a contract with Knopf and was not at all sure that he could fulfill it. His memory seemed to be going. He could not organize his thoughts. Even reading required more concentration than he could manage. Kennedy tried to reassure him as the two men spent the shortest day of the year together. Cheever had been cautioned against driving, but on their way to lunch he took the wheel and sped with abandon across the icy hills of Westchester. He seemed to Kennedy a combination of Peck's Bad Boy and dignified Brahmin, at one moment a genteel landowner and at the next a schoolboy on truancy. When they reached the restaurant, the bravado was gone and Cheever spoke again of the terror of surrendering consciousness, of losing his creative gifts. From the windows they could see the hills across the Hudson, and Kennedy reminded him of what Tony Nailles said in *Bullet Park*, "Give me back the mountains."

"Yes," Cheever said, his eyes glistening as he gazed out the window, "that's what I want. I want somebody to give me back my mountains."

Cheever was childlike in his uncommon need for affection, Kennedy thought. Now that he was successful, he said, only two kinds of people wanted to see him: those with scandalous stories to tell about other people, and those who asked for favors. Occupied by their private agendas, they hardly noticed that the famous man they spoke to was reaching out for friendship. Kennedy listened, understood, and cared.

As if to dispel doubts about his creative ability, Cheever worked hard the first six months of 1981 on *The Shady Hill Kidnapping* and *O What a Paradise It Seems*. Jac Venza called in director Paul Bogart, well known for his success with *All in the Family*, to work with Cheever on revising the script for *Kidnapping*. As an admirer of Cheever's fiction, Bogart was pleased to get the assignment, and still more pleased when the author proved to be not at all defensive about making changes. "They'll do the script the way it is, just because it's yours," Bogart said at the outset, "and they damned well should." But, he added, "I think your audience needs more than you've given them." The plot revolves around the disappearance of a small boy, and his family's frantic attempts to find him and bring him home. Cheever was clearly more interested in the way this crisis drew the family together than in the fate of the boy, however, and that threatened to confuse the television audience. In first draft, for example, the family assumes at once that the boy has been kidnapped, but for no good reason. Bogart encouraged Cheever to work on scenes of comic contrast: the boy happily riding his little red wagon, the family discovering his absence, the boy eating popcorn and watching television with the lonely housewife who invites him in, the family trying to get the police to take an interest. Initially Cheever did not bother to return the missing boy to his family. "You've got to bring the kid back," Bogart told him. "The audience is going to say, where's the kid? Where's

Binxie?" Cheever nodded, seeing a lot of rewriting ahead, and did nothing. In the end Bogart reunited Binxie (a name Cheever used for a young male child three times in his fiction) and his mother. "Yes, do it," Cheever told the director. "Go ahead and do it." Nor did he object to minor changes in dialogue. "The bigger the artist, the less they fuss about it," Bogart observed.

This is not to say that Cheever was passive or uninterested in his play. According to *Kidnapping* producer Ann Blumenthal, he participated in three areas where writers are rarely involved: in casting, where he asked for and got the same casting director who had worked on the adaptations of his stories; in locations, where he chose the most rural of the three possible sites Blumenthal located for a Department of Motor Vehicles office; and in voice-over, where he himself recorded the coda at the end of the film. Bogart had to do some coaching on the voice-over. "You need a pause there," he'd suggest, "and a little more volume here." Cheever balked briefly. "I'm not an actor, you know," he said. As an emergency measure Bogart had George Grizzard, the leading actor in the play, make a dummy recording of the voice-over. The final decision, though, was to go with Cheever's own, idiosyncratic voice.

During his work on *Kidnapping*, Cheever became fascinated with the technical side of television. At parties he began buttonholing *CBS News* producer Bud Benjamin with questions about the most detailed mechanics of the craft. And had he lived, Ann Blumenthal felt sure, he would have written more for television. "He was very good at it, and learning very fast." Both she and Bogart remain enthusiastic about *Kidnapping.* "It's a very odd, very angular, very literary film," Bogart says. "I love it." Cheever was proud of it too.

With *Kidnapping* in production, Cheever wrote one last very short story for *The New Yorker.* Called "The Island," it told of a small imaginary island in the Caribbean—well off the routes of the cruise ships—where were assembled "the greatest trombonist, the movie queen, the ballplayers, trapeze artists, and sexual virtuosos of yesterday leading happy and simple lives." They were engaged in catching shellfish, weaving baskets, and reading good books. "We were only on the island for a few hours," the narrator concludes, "but I keep thinking about this little-known place where everybody was having such an easy time of it, reading the classics and eating shellfish." Perhaps that was where Cheever was headed, too.

His energy was on the wane, and *Paradise* turned out to be a much shorter book than he had anticipated: only one hundred pages. In May he interrupted his writing briefly to accept an honorary degree from Skidmore. As an old man, he wrote Joe and Anne Palamountain afterward, he enjoyed "accomplished men and women." More and more, his remarks took on a valedictory tone. "I am an old man nearing the end of his journey," he had been telling his children for twenty-five years. Now that comment lost some of its humor as a succession of physical ailments—possibly related by metastasis to his seizures—conspired to weaken him.

On April 20, Cheever went to Phelps Memorial Hospital for a prostate operation. At that time, Dr. Marvin Schulman detected blood in the right renal pelvis, but thought that the bleeding had probably been caused by the passing of a kidney stone. Back home from the operation, he managed to finish *Kidnapping*. He was determined to get that job done, he told John Updike with casual indelicacy, "even if his prick fell off." In fact he passed blood with his urine long after the effects of a kidney stone should have ceased. Still, Cheever was casually upbeat when he wrote Schulman on July 3 about collecting urine samples. Two specimens of his "vin ordinaire" were in the refrigerator, he said. And his "plumbing" seemed to be in good working order. A week later he was back in Phelps, first for exploratory surgery and then to have his cancerous right kidney removed. A carcinoma the size of a walnut came out with the kidney. His doctors hoped they had caught the cancer in time. They had not.

There is no human difference so great, someone has observed, as that between the sick and the well. After his July operation, it was clear to everyone who saw him that Cheever was unwell. Soon after his return from the hospital, the Updikes swung through Westchester on a research trip for *Bech Is Wed* and stopped for lunch at Cedar Lane. Ravaged by pain, Cheever had no appetite but sat through the meal with his guests, courtly and witty as ever, and afterward took them on an excursion to the Croton dam. In August, Professor Robert G. Collins of Ottawa and his wife, May, came to make a tape recording. Collins, who had seen a vibrantly healthy Cheever in Canada in 1978, was startled at the transformation that age and disease had wrought. Thinner now and shaky of limb, Cheever was nonetheless genial and cheerful throughout the visit. He spoke with satisfaction of having just sent off the galleys for *Paradise,* as if completing that chore had somehow qualified him for last things. There was a "sunset quality" about him, Collins thought. At the same time he looked like a little boy alongside the patently fit Max Zimmer, there to care for him during Mary's vacation at Treetops.

Mary had offered to stay in Ossining to nurse her husband, but John said, "No, I can get Max to stay with me." He had followed the same pattern when it was time to come home from Phelps. Mary could have come to get him, but she had an etching session that morning and he did not want her to miss it. Ben could have taken a half day off from work to run the errand, but John did not want to disrupt his routine. Instead he called on Max to fetch him home. The younger man, "the beloved" in the relationship, felt increasingly circumscribed by his services to Cheever, the more so now that he was compensated for them. It began to seem as if he were being held captive. John was, naturally, sensitive to those feelings. He was torn between wanting to bind Max to him as strongly as possible and wanting him to achieve his own independent future. On some days he told Max that if he left, it would certainly not kill him but would make his life terribly hard. On others he joked with him about appropriate farewell speeches Max might use. "Goodbye, old man," he might say, "you can't even change a flat tire."

As summer wore on into fall, Cheever's cancer spread to bone and robbed him of his vigor. The bicycle trips and hikes that he depended upon for their restorative effects became exercises in agony, and had to be curtailed. Almost daily he grew weaker. On a crisp autumn day late in September, Eudora Welty came to read at the Katonah library and the literary establishment turned out to do her homage. Robert Penn Warren and Eleanor Clark were there, along with William Maxwell, Robert Fitzgerald, and John and Mary Cheever. Dana Gioia spoke to Cheever in the line outside the library, but Cheever sounded so tired and looked so painfully frail that Gioia soon excused himself. "He seemed half a century older than the quick, boyish man" Gioia had met at Stanford in 1976.

Cheever knew when he left the hospital that the tumor was malignant, and his body told him every day that his cancer was still accomplishing its deadly work. As the disease pervaded his system, he became terribly depessed. Dr. Schulman sent him to see Dr. D. J. Van Gordon in Croton for counseling. Twice a week for four months, Cheever talked to Van Gordon, a psychiatrist. He made less resistance to impending death and less protest against it than any other terminally ill patient Van Gordon had treated. Of the classic stages of dying—shock and denial, anger, bargaining, depression, preparatory grief—he seemed to bypass anger entirely. He did not, like most patients, "fight back." He did not fly into rages or talk volubly about it or drive too fast. If Cheever had one constantly recurring thought, Van Gordon remembers, it was how nice it would be to take a drink. But he did not do that either, and even resisted taking drugs for depression. He kept his dignity and was "kind of relieved" at the prospect of dying, Van Gordon thought. "There wasn't any emergency in it for him."

Family weddings and two television shows in the fall helped keep his mind off his illness. Susan was married to Calvin Tomkins on October 1, and plans were under way for Ben's marriage to Janet Maslin at Christmastime and Fred's to Mary McNeil in February. On Halloween, WNET arranged for a screening of *The Shady Hill Kidnapping,* and Cheever invited a substantial company of friends to attend. When the lights went down he was as nervous as George S. Kaufman on opening night. "It's really rather good, isn't it?" he whispered to Bud Benjamin only a few minutes into the one-hour screening. Then he could not sit still, and paced up and down outside the screening room with Ann Blumenthal. Afterward the author said a few words. He liked to think of his one-shot, low-budget show, he said, as Westchester's answer to *Dallas.*

Soon thereafter he appeared on *The Dick Cavett Show* again, this time in company with John Updike. The two authors outdid themselves in admiring each other's work. Cheever had just finished reading *Rabbit Is Rich* in bound galleys, and thought it was one of the best American novels in years. Updike was driven almost to stuttering in his eagerness to praise Cheever's excellence. Both of them were conscious of the older man's failing health. Updike was at the peak of his powers, while Cheever—as he said of himself for the thousandth time—was indeed "nearing the end of his journey." He looked the part on the screen. Besides the continuing discomfort of pain, he discovered at showtime that his zipper was stuck and so he kept his legs virginally crossed during the entire show. On November 17 the Cavett show aired, and Cheever watched it alone in the kitchen at Cedar Lane. He looked like a viper trying to break wind, he wrote Updike.

On December 4, Cheever was back in Phelps for another operation. Dr. Schulman found at least thirty small superficial tumors all over the bladder, and burned them off with electric current. Now

there was no question that the cancer was spreading. It fell to
family doctor Ray Mutter to tell the Cheevers what they had
known and tried not to admit since midsummer: John had perhaps
six months to live and could not expect any improvement. Cheever
had but one question. "My son Fred is getting married in California on Valentine's Day," he said. "Will I at least be able to go to
his wedding?" It was a promise Mutter could not make.

Max Zimmer was at the house when John and Mary returned
from the doctor's office. Both looked completely gray and drained.
Cheever managed to smile. "The news is all bad," he said. "The
news is very bad." He took off his coat, settled in the wing chair
in the living room, and asked for a glass of tea. Max knew then that
he was in for the duration, and because he wanted to be.

A long winter lay ahead. First there was Christmas to get
through. On December 24, Ben and Janet were married at Cedar
Lane. Edgar, John's favorite dog, perched on the newlyweds' feet
throughout the wedding. Mary had to prop John up during the
standing parts of the ceremony. The next day he wrote her a brief
note arranged as verse:

CHRISTMAS MORNING 1981

> You gave your son his wedding
> In an old House, impeded
> by a Hamstrung husband you
> gave him a ceremony that was
> positively shimmery.

> You gave your son his wedding
> to a twice-chosen bride. Sitting in
> a mulberry tree in New Haven
> you may never have wished to
> bear a handsome man and give
> him a wedding but this is what
> you have done.

When Bud and Aline Benjamin came to call on Christmas afternoon, they went up to see Cheever in his bedroom. Aline grasped
his big toe, briefly. Parchment-thin, John made a valiant attempt to
be his usual charming self.

With the new year he began to receive state-of-the-art treatment
for his cancer: chemotherapy, cobalt radiation, platinum. Max

drove him down to Sloan-Kettering Cancer Center on East Sixty-eighth Street for his initial stay. Susie met them at the hospital, and waited with her father while his room was being made up. Dressed elegantly in a tweed suit and cashmere overcoat, he spoke quietly of suicide. He'd saved up his pills until he had enough, he told her, and hid them in the drawer of his bedside table. Then he told Don Ettlinger about them, that seemed to make him feel better, and he put the pills back in the medicine cabinet.

He and Ettlinger, close friends since the mid-1940s, met occasionally for lunch on days when Cheever could manage the outing. One day when he could barely stand up—the cancer had metastasized to his left hip and right rib cage—they met at a diner near the Tappan Zee Bridge, and Cheever unburdened himself.

"I'm frightened," he told Don. "I wake up at night and I'm calling out Daddy, Daddy, help me. The thing is, I've never called anybody Daddy in my whole life."

After that first stay at Sloan-Kettering, treatments continued on a three-times-a-week basis. Max, living in Manhattan, took an early-afternoon train to Ossining, spent an hour or two there, and drove Cheever to the hospital in his Volkswagen Rabbit. He dropped Cheever off at the entrance while he parked the car, and then took him up to the treatment room. There he helped John out of his clothes—he invariably dressed in suit and tie for these trips—and into his hospital gown. Waiting for his turn, they watched the other cancer victims in gowns, Magic Markers indicating where they would be irradiated that day. One beautiful Puerto Rican woman, with only a single breast, walked around trying to cheer people up. As always, Cheever spoke about what the others must be thinking and feeling, imagining their stories, hypothesizing the details of their lives. He was writing in his mind right up to the end.

At 7:00 or 8:00 P.M. it would be time for Cheever to go into the cobalt room. He came out looking as if he'd walked out of the desert. Sometimes he did not know who or where he was. Limping badly from his hip and leg pain, he walked with Max down a long corridor, took the elevator to the ground floor, and returned to Ossining. Sometimes they stopped en route to make love. Even when he was in acute distress, Cheever's sex drive remained active. At Cedar Lane, Mary kept dinner waiting for the two of them, and then Max would catch the late train back into the city.

This numbing routine gave way by mid-February to daily treatments at Northern Westchester Hospital Center in nearby Mount

Kisco. These were successful in arresting some of the pain, but he was far too ill to travel to California for Fred's wedding. On many days it was difficult for him to get as far as his typewriter in Ben's old bedroom. The only way he could motivate himself to work, he told Bill Luers, was to create characters—young girls, old men— who somehow managed to overcome cancer.

On rock-bottom days he could write nothing at all, and Max was assigned to answer correspondence. Cheever's work was finally getting considerable critical attention. A fifteen-thousand-word discussion of his fiction appeared in the Scribner's *American Writers* series. Samuel Coale and Lynne Waldeland both wrote monographs about him for other established series. Father Hunt was working on a long book, eventually to appear as *John Cheever: The Hobgoblin Company of Love* (1983). Robert G. Collins was collecting material for *Critical Essays on John Cheever* (1984).

While this academic recognition was gratifying, Cheever was not at all receptive to the idea of a critical gala in celebration of his seventieth birthday on May 27—a proposal advanced by professors Collins, Frederick Karl, and, spearheading the effort, Richard Rupp. Rupp's letter to Cheever about the proposal could hardly have been more ill-timed. It arrived less than a week after Cheever got the bad news from Ray Mutter. Rather brashly, Rupp suggested that following a day-long symposium at the New York Public Library on his birthday, Cheever might receive his diploma from Thayer Academy, say a few words about his life as a writer, and adjourn with the celebrants for dancing until midnight in Bryant Park to old Benny Goodman and Glenn Miller recordings. As a point of honor, Rupp observed, the organizers would "not accept a nickel of Cheever's own money toward this enterprise." Unimpressed, Cheever scotched the plans in two curt letters to Collins, the second signed by Max.

Cheever's mood darkened with the sudden decline and death of his favorite dog, Edgar. Edgar, a.k.a. Shithead, was in reality a spayed female whose original name was Tara. "I changed his name," Cheever explained, "because I was an old man and thought I ought to have a male dog." Edgar was "very accommodating," he added, "urinates on trees and all that." They were close companions, dog and master. For breakfast Cheever fixed English muffins and bacon for both of them. They took walks together in the afternoon, Edgar's jaws clamped around a tennis ball. On trips to Carvel's after dinner Cheever bought Flying Saucers and Lollapaloozas for Edgar and the other family dogs, Bathsheba and Maisie. So he was naturally distressed after his return from Sloan-Kettering when Edgar abandoned his accustomed sleeping place at the foot of his master's bed. After that the dog rapidly weakened, losing mobility and appetite and coughing frighteningly. Within a month, Edgar was dead of lung cancer. Cheever took it hard.

Not knowing the news, Ben called his father. "How's Edgar?" he asked.

"Edgar died," Cheever answered. Silence.

Later that evening, Ben called again. "I'm sorry about Edgar," he said.

"That's all right," Cheever said. And hung up.

Preparing for the end, Cheever rarely permitted himself such incivilities. Instead he was eager to cement old friendships. He sent a conciliatory note to William Maxwell. He played backgammon regularly with Arthur Spear and Roger Willson and Bud Benjamin. Alerted to his condition, Updike called with words of encouragement and support. Bellow offered to fly to New York whenever it was convenient. His illness, Cheever pointed out in interviews, linked him with thousands of others "seeking some cure for this deadly thing." It was neither depressing nor exhilarating, he said. It was simply "a critical part of living, or the aspiration to live."

He also joked about his baldness, brought on by chemotherapy. "I had a full head of hair a few weeks ago," he said. "Then I woke up one morning and there it was on the pillow." When he showed up at the barbershop in Briarcliff, he reported, the barbers nearly died laughing. Exposed to landscapes of pain he had never imagined, he was determined to be upbeat in public. Moreover, he would no longer resign himself to the inevitable. In letter after letter he insisted that he fully intended to recover. Late in March he wrote Jim McConkey that he planned to celebrate his eightieth birthday "by walking to Croton dam." When Susie produced his granddaughter Sarah in April, he declared that his cancer was finished. "I've licked it," he told his daughter. He had two months left to live.

ENDINGS

C HEEVER'S last two major works conveyed the powerfully affirmative statement of a dying man. It was as if the prospect of leaving this life confirmed his appreciation of its great gifts. Both *The Shady Hill Kidnapping* and *Oh What a Paradise It Seems* hymn the glory of the natural world and the wonder of family love. The teleplay (first shown on January 12, 1982, as the opening performance in the *American Playhouse* series) begins with a series of spats among members of the Wooster family. Father quarrels with son, mother with daughter, and finally father with mother. "We must stay together for the sake of the children," the senior Woosters say, but this is an old family joke and it is love that keeps them together through all arguments and trials. George Grizzard, as the father, most clearly speaks for his creator in two early passages. "What a paradise," he says, stepping outside his home on a beautiful summer morning. And later, from the heart, "How wonderful it is to have so many people I love sleeping under one roof."

After a number of comic complications, all the Woosters are together at the end, bound by the force of love. At dusk they go to the station where the daughter is to greet the man she loves coming in on the train. In the closing voice-over, Cheever warns that "we cannot overlook the universal loneliness of our times." Some of the people getting off the train will be met by dark houses, recriminations, and cruel mates, others by beautiful women who will serve them drinks on a tray. Yet there can be nothing more moving than a homecoming, he concludes, even if "not many of those getting off the train have achieved what one could call home." Home was what Cheever had been seeking all his life, though other objectives distracted him along the way.

His most striking innovation in *Kidnapping* was to intersperse five fake "commercials" into his script. At well-calculated breaks in the plot, the actress Celeste Holm—Cheever had wanted Hope Lange, but she was unavailable—appears on screen to hymn the virtues of Elixircol. Elixircol, the same expensive nostrum Moses wrote advertising copy for in "The Death of Justina," claims to restore youth, assure fame and social success, and protect against atomic waste. But the panacea will not work to ward off loneliness, and may have disastrous side effects. As Holm cattily purrs in the final commercial, the surgeon general has discovered that Elixircol causes cancer in animals, "but who knows the surgeon general or his wife?" Then she shifts from plugging the product to a message from the heart. Supposedly reading the ingredients from the bottle, she articulates sentiments very much like those in the ritual grace Cheever fashioned for himself: "We should consider that the soul of man is immortal, able to endure every sort of good and every sort of evil. Thus may we live happily with ourselves and each other and the gods, whoever they may be. Thank you, and good night."

Cheever was proud of *Kidnapping,* and particularly pleased with Holm's insinuating style in reading the commercials. He was much less sure of *Oh What a Paradise It Seems,* which Knopf published early in March. It was not up to his best, he feared, and he was right. *Paradise* reads rather like a reprise of earlier Cheever fiction and lacks the power of a full-length novel. Yet there are many wonderful passages, even in this novella written under siege. "The tone" of it, as Allan Gurganus observed, is quintessential Cheever. Like *Kidnapping,* this book sings the joy of creation. And it goes beyond *Kidnapping* and even *Falconer* in its portrayal of the capacity of love to work miracles.

The old man Lemuel Sears, living alone in the city after the death of his wife, comes back to his former suburban home to go ice skating on Beasley's Pond. It is an invigorating experience. "Swinging down a long stretch of black ice" gives him a sense of homecoming. "At long last, at the end of a long, cold journey, he was returning to a place where his name was known and loved and lamps burned in the rooms and fires in the hearth." So he is appalled to discover that commercial interests are conspiring to turn this pond into a dump. He sets out to battle against those interests, and in the end, after a complicated struggle in which he is aided by a young mother named Betsy Logan, he is victorious and the pond is restored to its pristine beauty.

At this stage the narrator delivers a generalization. "The liveliness of the landscape had been restored. It was in no way distinguished, but it could, a century earlier, have served as a background for Eden or even the fields of Eleusis if you added some naked goddesses and satyrs." In effect, *Paradise* drifts back to mythical times, bypassing nostalgia en route. More than anything Cheever ever wrote, it rejects celebration of a historical past in favor of the present. He was as aware in 1982 as in 1962 of the depredations that nomadism and money-grubbing were causing. "That things had been better was the music, the reprise of Sears's days," Cheever writes, but he recognizes the futility of looking to an idealized past for relief. If miracles are to be worked, they must come through love, and through a love for the creation and all those who inhabit it.

The experience of Sears exemplifies the point. He is not entirely successful in erotic love. The lovely Renee seems to care for him, but rejects him with a repeated catch phrase: "you don't understand the first thing about women." Eduardo, the elevator man in Renee's building, then becomes his lover, but when their idyllic fishing trip is over, Eduardo goes back to his wife and that, presumably, is the end of that. The satisfactions of sex give life savor, but change nothing. Where Sears triumphs is in a wider devotion to his fellow human beings and the world they jointly inhabit. "Sears means to succeed in loving usefulness," Cheever said of his principal character, "and actually he is quite useful. He purifies a large body of water. There really is little one can do that's comparably useful today." In his writing, though, he was striving toward a similar usefulness, with considerable success.

On April 27, Cheever received the National Medal for Literature (and fifteen thousand dollars) in a ceremony at Carnegie Hall. William Styron was chosen to make the presentation, and the two writers foregathered backstage in advance of the ceremony. There Cheever caught a glimpse of the two pages of copy Styron had prepared. "Are you going to say all that?" he asked. "Ah, Bill, just tell them I'm short." Then he held his hands over his ears in embarrassment while Styron, onstage, praised him as one of those "undislodgeably established in the wonderful firmament of American literature." When he first began reading Cheever's "marvelous early" fiction—"beguiling tales of apartment dwellers and suburbanites"—Styron did not realize that he was being "lured into another, more difficult territory: the landscape of the human condition." Now he knew better.

In prose "as sweet and limpid as Mozart," he went on, Cheever

has told us many things about America in this century: about the untidy lives lived in tidy households, about betrayal and deception and lust and the wounds of the heart, but also about faith and the blessings of simple companionship and the abiding reality of love. Only the greatest of writers have this gift: which is to write of these familiar and homely matters with such understated but powerful insight as to cause us to pause and realize, in wonder, that we have been told secrets about ourselves that we have never known.

Hawthorne had this gift, Styron said, and Chekhov, and John Cheever, and therein lay his usefulness. The National Medal for Literature was being awarded to him, he said in conclusion, "because of our great love for all you have written, which will always be useful to us beyond all measure—and because you are a lord of the language."

There was an audible gasp when Cheever came out onstage to receive the medal. The sprightly Cheever many in the audience had once known was now a sick old man, bald, and carrying a cane to support his limp. Yet when he spoke his voice was strong. And in his response, he made the case for the ultimate, the cosmic, useful-

ness of his art. "A page of good prose is where one hears the rain,"
he said. "A page of good prose is when one hears the noise of battle.
A page of good prose has the power to give grief a universality that
lends it a youthful beauty. A page of good prose has the power to
make us laugh." Then, finally: "A page of good prose seems to me
the most serious dialogue that well-informed and intelligent men
and women carry on today in their endeavor to make sure that the
fires of this planet burn peaceably." Literature had rescued the
damned, inspired lovers, and routed despair. Now, perhaps, it
could save the world from nuclear holocaust.

Time and again in his last half dozen years, Cheever tried to
express what he had been aiming for in his life's work. "Literature," he proclaimed, "is the only continuous and coherent account
of our struggle to be illustrious, a monument of aspiration, a vast
pilgrimage." "Fiction," he insisted, "is our most intimate and acute
means of communication, at a profound level, about our deepest
apprehensions and intuitions on the meaning of life and death. And
that is what binds us together, . . . the bond of agreement that
. . . keeps us from flying to pieces." His favorite definition of fiction,
he told John Hersey, came from Cocteau: "Literature is a force of
memory that we have not yet understood." The writer presents the
reader "with a memory he has already possessed, but has not com-
prehended." (Hersey was asked by his Yale colleague Peter Brooks,
chairman of the French department, to find out where in Cocteau
he'd found that quotation. "Come, John," Cheever said when Hersey inquired, "you know I made that up.") "Nothing in our civilization is more important than the welfare of literature," he declared
in 1979, for literature helped us make sense of an otherwise bewil-
dering world, and without it "we would have no knowledge of the
meaning of love." Certainly writing helped him make sense of his
own life. "Upon being bewildered by any turn of events . . . ," he
said, "I've tried to put it into the language of a story—to see if I
could comprehend it." In the process, he might very well aid others
in puzzling out their own confusing lives. And at last he came
around to the assertion that literature might save the world.

This barrage of near pontifications suggests how strongly
Cheever felt the need to justify his art. It is probably significant that
he uttered almost all of these statements in interviews that took
place after achieving wealth and fame. He may have felt a pang of
guilt that his writing gave him so much pleasure and brought him
so much success. It was not enough to do what he was born to do.

As a Yankee he felt it imperative to be useful, to serve the common good.

Critics have often tried to classify Cheever by comparing him with other writers, and it was a measure of his accomplishment that most such comparisons rapidly break down. For example, he was sometimes likened, early in his career, to such social realists as Marquand and O'Hara. But his suburbia is an archetypal version of the real. Open the front door and the god Pan slips past. Open the back and the Angel of Death sneaks in. And so, though he is often criticized for the narrowness of his fictional world—"Where is politics? Where is history? The ghetto and the camps?"—the mythical and the miraculous give his fiction the universal resonance of fables.

In assessing his work, critics have variously called him "a satirist, a Transcendalist, an existentialist, a social critic, a religious writer, a trenchant moralist, an enlightened Puritan, an Episcopalian anarch, a suburban surrealist, Ovid in Ossining, the American Chekhov, the American Trollope for an age of angst, and a toothless Thurber." He has been compared with Thoreau and Emerson for his sensitivity to nature and distaste for the unlived life, and with Hawthorne and Melville for "the shadowy and troubled undergrowth" of his stories and for a powerful sense of morality that has little to do with conventional standards.

The fact is that each of the critical characterizations and each of the comparisons has at least some validity. In his work the transcendental consorts with the real and Chekhov lies down with Kafka. What distinguishes Cheever from the minor writers is that throughout the assimilative process he kept his own distinct and idiosyncratic voice. You can pick up a Cheever story or novel anywhere and know within a paragraph or two who is speaking. The proof of the style is that it can be parodied but not re-created. "Anyone can write a Barthelme story," Tom Boyle says. "No one can write a Cheever story."

In acknowledging his literary debts, Cheever bowed in all directions. There were so many influences, he said, that it was difficult to single out only a few. The thread ran from the Egyptian Book of the Dead through the Greeks to Flaubert and the Russians. "Then the generation before mine—Hemingway, Fitzgerald, Faulkner—was also terribly important," he said. Of the three, his closest affinity is with Fitzgerald.

In both writers there is a strain of romance that seems oddly out

of place in the midst of busy quotidian life, and much the same
tenderness and lyricism of style. Some writers feel thinly and others pretend to feel, as Bernard Malamud remarked, but "Cheever's
fiction is always informed by feeling." So, too, is Fitzgerald's.
Cheever "wrote prose fiction in a manner more common with poets
and their poetry," Updike observed, "as a kind of dictation that
flowed, when it did, effortless and compact." He might have said
exactly the same thing of Fitzgerald, for both were granted the
rhetorical capacity to evoke epiphanies. As early as the mid-1960s,
both Elizabeth Hardwick and Stanley Kauffmann drew attention
to the Cheever-Fitzgerald connection. It's almost like tracing a
family tree, Kauffmann wrote, "for it is difficult to imagine the later
writer exactly as he is without the existence of the earlier one."
Something of that family bond must have been in John le Carré's
mind fifteen years later when he told Cheever, over the telephone,
that he thought him "the best American writer since Scott Fitzgerald." The strongest evidence of the link between them, however, emerges in the short biography of Fitzgerald that Cheever
wrote for *Atlantic Brief Lives* (1971). It is significant, to begin with,
that Cheever chose to write about Fitzgerald and no one else. And
there is no disputing the fact that in composing his brief life of
Fitzgerald, Cheever was writing about himself.

Both writers had unsuccessful fathers and strong mothers: that
much is true of almost all major American male writers. But
Cheever shapes his version of Fitzgerald's parents to suit his own.
"His mother was the ruthless and eccentric daughter of a prosperous Irish grocer. His gentle father belonged to the fringe aristoc-
racy of the commercial traveler. . . . " No one else has ever
characterized Mollie McQuillan Fitzgerald as "ruthless": eccentric,
to be sure, but hardly ruthless. Against her, Fitzgerald's father, like
Cheever's own, is outmatched, too gentle yet somehow still a prince
of the road. As for Fitzgerald's career, Cheever comments on certain "appalling lapses in discipline" but in the same breath characterizes him as "a serious writer working to support a beautiful and
capricious wife" and as one who never quite lost "his singular
grace." Above all in Fitzgerald, Cheever pointed out, "there is a
thrilling sense of knowing exactly where one is—the city, the resort, the hotel, the decade and the time of the day." His stories were
not mere vignettes or overheard conversations "but real stories
with characters, invention, scenery and moral conviction." This
was true despite his notoriety as a drinker given to "pranks, prat-

falls and ghastly jokes." Fitzgerald's last fiction uncannily predicted Cheever's own. Though he wrote often of the poignancy of
loss and sorrow, Fitzgerald "remained astonishingly hopeful," so
that there is no more trace of darkness in *The Last Tycoon* than in
Oh What a Paradise It Seems.

The similarity of the two writers, both in their lives and in their
work, extends well beyond what Cheever wrote about Fitzgerald
in his brief biography. Both of them, for instance, grew up with an
acute social sensitivity that derived from living in the best section
of town while debarred from acceptance among the community's
elite by the failure of their fathers. Both were poor students,
though Fitzgerald at least finished prep school and by virtue of
makeup examinations was eventually admitted to Princeton. Both
found their vocation early and stuck to it. They were writers first,
last, and always, with no other apparent gifts. Neither was in the
least intellectual. Both were small men of great charm, when sober.
Both were alcoholics who managed late in life to stop drinking.
Both had difficult marriages that they remained true to, in their
fashion. Both fell in love with motion-picture actresses. Both were
exceedingly fond of their children. Both achieved a final dignity.

Professionally the parallels are also striking. Cheever and Fitzgerald produced almost exactly the same body of work: four and
one half novels and one hundred and eighty stories. Each was
denigrated in his own time for the company his fiction kept—
Fitzgerald for his ties to the well-paying middlebrow *Saturday Evening Post,* Cheever for his long affiliation with *The New Yorker.* Both
were criticized for not writing enough about the sociopolitical
crises of their times. Both were superlative story writers who found
the longer form of the novel difficult to master. Yet both succeeded
in doing so at least twice—Fitzgerald with *Gatsby* and *Tender Is the
Night,* Cheever with *The Wapshot Chronicle* and *Falconer.* It remains
to be seen whether Cheever's posthumous reputation will follow
the ascending course of Fitzgerald's.

No forerunner was responsible for the work that Cheever left.
He would have written more but for drink, and a lot less if he had
not put in his hours at the desk, on good days and bad. Even in his
last weeks, as his lethal disease extended its dominion, he tried to
write and tried to take exercise. The will to live was there very
powerfully at the end. He and Mary watched a television show
about the Irish patriots Parnell and Kitty O'Shea. "That made me
want to live so," he told her afterward, "to walk across that field

the way they did." If will alone had been sufficient to save him, he might have outlived his cancer. He was "a man of iron will," Mary thought. When he decided to quit drinking, he quit, and that was that. He quit smoking the same way. But he could not stop dying.

Mary cared for him in his extremity as never before. Max came to Cedar Lane only occasionally in Cheever's final illness. Now it was Mary who nursed him and fed him and cared for him at home. The two of them even played a kind of courtship game. Even toward the end, Ben recalls, John was always trying to get into Mary's bed. One morning John, feeling better, fixed her breakfast and took it up to her along with a flower in a long vase. That evening, father winked at son when Mary started making straw-berry jam from a recipe in a cookbook he'd bought her. "A good sign," he told Ben. He retired with high hopes for the morrow, when once more he brought her breakfast in bed. The technique did not work. "You know what she said," he told Ben, " 'That cookbook you bought me, it's a pack of lies.' " The strawberry jam had not set. But there was good humor about all this, a kind of shared male camaraderie about the unfathomable ways of woman-kind.

Humor welded the marriage together. In a 1981 interview of both Cheevers, John was asked to describe his life with Mary.

"She has displayed an extraordinary amount of patience," he began.

After a pause he continued. "Women are an inspiration. It's because of them we put on clean shirts and wash our socks. Because of women we want to excel. Because of a woman, Christopher Columbus discovered America."

"Queen Isabella," Mary murmured.

"I was thinking," John said, "of Mrs. Columbus."

Cheever had less than two months to live after the award of the National Medal for Literature on April 27. During those last weeks, a number of friends and admirers made the pilgrimage to Ossining. Raphael Rudnik came on a brilliant day early in May, to be greeted by a Cheever he hardly knew. He was wearing old clothes, and for the first time Rudnik noticed an intricate map of lines on his face. He said something about Cheever's being "disheveled," and knew immediately that was wrong. "Yes, I'm intrinsically disheveled," Cheever answered. At Cedar Lane he took out the scythe, though he didn't have much strength, and maneuvered it down the slope by letting inertia work for him. Miraculously, the scythe left a jack-in-the-pulpit uncut. It was his favorite flower, Cheever said.

Later they drove up to see the Croton dam in full flow. Anyone who was excited by the dam overflowing was all right, John said. Raphael saw a lot of smoke or white hair in the coursing water, a Dionysian image. But for Cheever the fire seemed to be going out. Here was someone who had won a series of battles, a singer of the tribe, Rudnik thought. It seemed wrong that he should be physically beaten, defeated.

Cheever also took Allan Gurganus to see the dam on his last visit in May. Allan went "Ah" at the sight of the falls, and John said you could always tell what kind of orgasms people had by the way they Ahed. "I guess I won't see you again . . . ," Gurganus said at the station upon parting, and then hurried on after watching Cheever's face collapse, "until I come back from Yaddo." He was at Yaddo on the morning he heard of John's death, and found a letter from him on the mail table. "There is something that I must tell you," it said. Perhaps it was the same thing he told Steve Phillips on their final trip to the dam. He revealed how sick he was and extracted a vow. "No matter what," Cheever said, "promise me you'll have a family." Whatever his homosexual feelings, they were only tolerable within the context of a conventional family life. After Phillips left, Cheever took Ben aside to confess that he'd made love to a number of men in his life. Ben allowed that he'd suspected as much.

Max Zimmer came when called. Once John awoke in the middle of the night and said, "Charlie's at the station. I have to go down and get him." Mary quieted him down. "Charlie"—a nickname for Max—couldn't possibly be there, she told him. No trains ran at that hour. The next morning she telephoned to suggest that Max come for a visit. He also chauffeured Cheever on his now infrequent trips to the hospital in Mount Kisco. Cheever still had some good days, as good as they had been before his kidney operation ten months earlier, and then there were terrible days. Max found there were two things he could say to cheer him up. First was to tell him he'd be back on his bicycle soon. Second was to paraphrase favorite scenes from his fiction, as when in *Bullet Park* Nellie Nailles finds the Swami to cure her son, Tony, and the Swami and the boy chant "Love" and "Hope" together.

During the third week in May, Max drove Cheever to Mount Kisco for a blood transfusion. At the clinic he held John's ice-cold hand, and felt it warm as the blood began to travel through him. Cheever was so inactive now that his Rolex kept stopping. On June

2, Mary picked Max up at the station and drove him to Cedar Lane. "Go up and see him," she said, and Max went through all the bedrooms looking for him except Mary's and there he was, restored to her bed after many years of separate bedrooms. He was always cold now, and the electric blanket warmed his bones. Mary brought lunch up to the room—the first time Max had seen John unable to make it downstairs for a meal. After lunch he slept, after that Max took him outside for the sun, and after five minutes in the sunshine he asked to go inside again.

The two men met only once more. "The last time I saw your face," Max wrote in his journal months later, "it resembled a young bird's in the way your blue skin clung to the prominent bones and the fine nose and the way it was pulled away from your usually narrow eyes. You were on your back in what you once said was your marriage bed, your head propped up on a pair of pillows" and the carpenters working on Mary's studio outside. Desperately ill as he was, Cheever got out of bed and into the bathroom, where, protected from the possible view of the carpenters, he was brought to climax. "Adiós," John said when Max left. "Adiós."

Death came swiftly, and Cheever met it with dignity. On June 9, he signed his last will and testament, leaving everything to Mary and appointing her executrix of his estate, with her brother Dr. William Winternitz and Roger Willson as alternates. Early the following week, on the last good day of his life, he called to ask Willson to bring him a double order of "ants in the trees" from the Chinese restaurant in Pleasantville. When Willson arrived, Cheever spoke optimistically of plans for his garden and about getting another dog to replace Edgar. He was reluctant to accept the inevitable, or if he did, it was with intimations of the beyond. On his ideal next-world island he would see Edgar again, along with the men and women he loved best. "I expect we will renew our connection later," he wrote Bellow.

On June 15, now enfeebled and fragile, he broke his leg while trying to get out of bed and walk. He went on morphine after that, while the family gathered round. Late in the afternoon of June 18, one of the longest days of the year, Cheever died in an overheated bedroom in his own home. Mary was at his side, as were Susan and Ben. Fred, in California, could not be there. The Reverend George Arndt of Trinity Episcopal Church came to administer last rites. The dying man was in physical turmoil, and struggling to breathe. But when Arndt made the sign of the cross on his forehead, he became absolutely peaceful, took one last breath, and died. For a moment longer Ben gasped for his father, trying to get him to breathe again.

It was decided to hold two memorial services, the first in Massachusetts, where Cheever was to be buried in what he used to call "the family hole," the second in Ossining. The burial service was set for 1:00 P.M. Tuesday, June 22, at Norwell First Parish Unitarian Church, directly across the street from the cemetery. John's niece Jane Carr made the arrangements, vying with a canny Yankee undertaker to keep things simple. Susan insisted on three don'ts: no gladioli, no fake grass, and no little wheels on the casket. As it happened, the aisles of the church were so narrow that the casket had to be rolled up and down, with the wheels concealed beneath the United States flag.

The afternoon provided much the same mixture of the comic and the serious, the irreverent and the deeply felt, that characterizes Cheever's fiction. It was a fine summer day, hot in the sunshine, pleasant in the shade. A spring runs through the middle of Norwell, and the sound of water was audible everywhere. The church itself is New England austere, a white wooden building with a square steeple containing a clock that works. Inside are no statues, no paintings, no stained glass. Mary and the children arrived fifteen minutes late after their four-hour drive from Westchester. About fifty mourners came, and half as many photographers were admitted to the balcony by the undertaker. Each of the children spoke. After wrestling to unlatch the door to the pew, Ben repeated Leander Wapshot's wonderful passage of advice to his sons. Susan read from Romans. Fred said a few words about what it meant to be John Cheever's son: "Part of him lives in me and in the other people who knew him well. So, though in one sense his journey has finally ended, in another it continues." In mid-ceremony Max Zimmer was admitted to the Cheever pew. Then Updike, boyishly lean in a soft gray suit, rose to present the tribute, and the photographers filled the church with the exploding of flashbulbs. Updike spoke of "the magic certainty" of Cheever's prose and of the "willed act of rebirth" that made his last seven years triumphant. After the service the pallbearers accompanied the casket on the slight downhill trip to the cemetery across the street. They were practically running by the time they reached the family burial site. There Cheever was laid to rest between a noble maple tree and a parking lot. Susan touched the coffin as it was lowered into the ground. Ben and Fred and Calvin Tomkins each shoveled in some dirt. "You can tell it's New England," someone said, as the topsoil they dug up was full of stones. While the prayers were being read, John Hersey saw a group of people emerge over the crest of the hill in the graveyard. Suddenly a teenage boy, overcome with exuberance, tossed off a couple of cartwheels. That, he knew, Cheever would have loved.

Back in Ossining, Cheever's adopted hometown mourned his passing. By administrative fiat, flags flew at half-mast for ten days. (Ben and Janet Cheever lowered the flag at the Highland Diner themselves.) It was "as if the heart of Ossining were gone," Aline Benjamin observed. "Cheever was as closely associated with Ossining as Emerson with Concord or Tolstoy with Yasnaya Polyana," the local newspaper proudly pointed out.

On Wednesday, June 23, the day after the service in Norwell, two hundred friends and colleagues gathered at Trinity Episcopal in Ossining to pay their respects. Ben shyly introduced each of the three speakers. Saul Bellow spoke of his admiration for Cheever's growth as a writer and of the marvelous friendship between them that fed on air, "like a hydroponic plant." Burton Benjamin remembered Cheever as "marvelous, funny, unpredictable, full-of-life John," a graceful ice skater and formidable backgammon opponent who "could captivate a child with a smile and a story." Life without Cheever would be difficult to imagine, Eugene Thaw said, for there was an abiding sense of "radiance" about him. It was the very word Updike had chosen on the Cavett show the previous fall, when challenged to say how he felt about Cheever's fiction. Then he had second thoughts. "I kept saying radiant on Cavett," he wrote Cheever, "but it's more like the little star inside a snowball on a sunny day." There were greater writers than Cheever, the *Boston Globe* acknowledged, "but painfully few of whose work it can be so emphatically said: It delighted us."

Only a childlike man, perhaps, would have been capable of feeling such joy all his life, intermingled though it often was with a strain of sadness. He never lost his capacity for wonder, or his appreciation for "the great benefice of living here and renewing ourselves with love." Cheever was "a blessed man," Raphael Rudnik felt as he sat through the stolidly overlong service in Ossining. Life would be lonelier for a vast number of people now that he was gone, not just for those who knew him. Among the messages of condolence that came to Mary Cheever were letters from former students of his and hers, from friends going back to the mid-1930s in New York, from fellow soldiers during the army days, from admirers in Bulgaria and Italy and England and Russia, from their close friends through the Westchester years, and from a great many people who had never met Cheever at all but who wanted to say a word about how much his writing had meant to them.

His threescore years and ten were not easy ones. Alcohol dimmed his days, depression dogged his path, and sometimes he could be cruel. Yet he was on balance "a *good* man," as Malcolm Cowley wrote Mary, and one who grew as a human being just as he did as a writer. In the great judgment hall of Anubis where accusations were made, defenses offered, and souls finally measured on the scales, John's good deeds would surely outweigh his transgressions, Cowley thought. And that was to say nothing of Leander in full glory, Zeke rejoicing, and kings and elephants crossing the mountains.

ACKNOWLEDGMENTS

THIS book is based on interviews and correspondence with those who knew John Cheever well; on his published writings, a few of his journals, and several fragmentary typescripts; on more than a thousand letters he wrote, along with a smaller number of letters written to him; and on discussions of the man and his work in memoirs, recorded interviews, and articles and books.

About 170 interviews yielded both information and insights, and I am grateful to those who were kind enough to talk with me, often at considerable length and sometimes on several occasions, about their memories and impressions of John Cheever: Vassily Aksyonov, Shana Alexander, Marion Ascoli, Lauren Bacall, Stephen Becker, Saul Bellow, Aline Benjamin, Burton Benjamin, Anne Bernays, Connie Bessie, Simon Michael Bessie, Dr. LeClair Bissell, Ebie Blume, Peter Blume, Ann Blumenthal, Paul Bogart, Susan Boyd, Mimi Boyer, Philip Boyer, T. Coraghessan Boyle, John Bukovsky, Hortense Calisher, Henry Carlisle, Jane Cheever Carr, Hayden Carruth, Burnham Carter, Susan Carter, Raymond Carver, Bev Chaney, Jr., Ben Cheever, Federico Cheever, Mary Cheever, Susan Cheever, Robert Chibka, Barrett Clark, Eleanor Clark, Jane Clark, Dennis Coates, May Collins, Robert G. Collins, Molly Malone Cook, Malcolm Cowley, Muriel Cowley, Robert Cowley, John Crutcher, John Dirks, Mary Douglas Dirks, Candida Donadio, Nina Engel, Don Ettlinger, Katrina Ettlinger, Frederick Exley, Dorothy Farrell, Leonard S. Field, Daniel Fuchs, Sue Fuchs, John C. Gerber, Tom Glazer, Robert Gottlieb, Allan Gurganus, Pauline Hanson, Curtis Harnack, Dr.

David S. Hays, Shirley Hazzard, John Hersey, Sandra Hochman, James Holmes, Eugenia Hotchkiss, Joseph W. Hotchkiss, Father George W. Hunt, Lee Hyla, Elizabeth Janeway, Dr. Frank Jewett, Dr. Robert A. Johnson, E. J. Kahn, Jr., Virginia Rice Kahn, Justin Kaplan, Eugene Kennedy, Carol Kitman, Donald C. Lang, David Lange, Hope Lange, John Leggett, Christopher Lehmann-Haupt, John Leonard, Frances Lindley, Tanya Litvinov, Elizabeth Logan, Robert F. Lucid, William H. Luers, Morris Lurie, Norman Mailer, Ann Malamud, Bernard Malamud, Janet Maslin, Iole Masullo, Ruth Maxwell, William Maxwell, James McConkey, Mary McNeil, Margaret M. Mills, Ted Mills, Lucy Miner, Peggy Murray, Dr. Raymond Mutter, Edward Newhouse, Charles Newman, Anne Palamountain, Frank Perry, Lila Refrigier, Don Reiman, Ginger Reiman, Natalie Robins, Ned Rorem, Philip Roth, David Rothbart, Raphael Rudnik, Dudley Schoales, Dudley Schoales, Jr., Grace Schulman, Dr. Marvin L. Schulman, Philip Schultz, Laurens R. Schwartz, Nellie Shannon, Charles Shapiro, Judith Sherwin, Rick Siggelkow, Joan Silver, Dr. J. William Silverberg, Dave Smith, Gray Smith, Arthur P. Spear, Stella Spear, Anthony Spencer, Sara Spencer, Susan Spencer, Gayatry Spivak, George Starbuck, Francis Steegmuller, Richard G. Stern, Ezra Stone, Sally Swope, Clayre Thaw, Eugene V. Thaw, James Valhouli, Dr. D. J. Van Gordon, Aileen Ward, Robert Penn Warren, Lillian H. Wentworth, Hazel Hawthorne Werner, Margot Wilkie, Alan D. Williams, Maureen Willson, Roger Willson, Will Wyatt, and Max Zimmer.

Among those whose letters have been invaluable in helping to fill in the gaps are Rollin Bailey, Helen Barolini, Stephen Becker, Livingston Biddle, Peter Blume, William S. Boice, Mimi Boyer, Philip Boyer, Frederick Bracher, Josiah Bunting III, Hortense Calisher, Hayden Carruth, Bev Chaney, Jr., Federico Cheever, Mary Cheever, Eleanor Clark, David Clarke, Samuel Coale, Hennig Cohen, Robert G. Collins, Blanche W. Cook, Malcolm Cowley, Robert C. Daugherty, Robert L. deVeer, James Dickey, Mary Douglas Dirks, Dean B. Doner, Frederick Exley, Sherry Farquharson, Daniel Fuchs, Dr. Bernard C. Glueck, Gordon Godfrey, Dana Gioia, Allan Gurganus, Ron Hansen, Hugh Hennedy, John Hersey, L. Rust Hills, Sarah Irwin, Dr. Robert A. Johnson, Eugene Kennedy, X. J. Kennedy, John Leggett, Christopher Lehmann-Haupt, Frances Lindley, Tanya Litvinov, Bernard Malamud, Jerre Mangione, William Maxwell, James McGraw, Paul Moor, E. W. Nash, Edward Newhouse, James O'Hara, Grace L. Osgood, Anne Palamountain, David C. Robertson, Jr., Raphael Rudnik, Stephen Sandy, Nora Sayre, Laurens R. Schwartz, Arthur P. Spear, Elizabeth Spencer, Leonard Spigelgass, George Starbuck, Wallace Stegner, Richard G. Stern, Caskie Stinnett, Lewis Turco, John Updike, James Valhouli, Gore Vidal, Aileen Ward, Larry Watson, Mary Weatherall, John D. Weaver, Lillian H. Wentworth, and Beatrice Wood.

Some of those named above have been kind enough to let me see copies of their letters from Cheever. In addition, I am indebted to a number of major research libraries for the opportunity to read portions of his correspondence. Particular acknowledgment goes to Margaret M. Mills and Nancy Johnson of the American Academy and Institute of Arts and Letters; Victor A. Berch of the Brandeis University library; Bonnie Hardwick of the Bancroft Library, University of California, Berkeley; Maggie Fusco of the Regenstein Library, University of Chicago; Nora J. Quinlan of the University of Colorado at Boulder library; Bernard R. Crystal of the Butler Library, Columbia University; Dolores Altemus of the University of Delaware library; Elizabeth Ann Falsey of the Houghton Library, Harvard University; Carolyn A. Sheehy of the Newberry Library; Lola L. Szladits of the Berg Collection, New York Public Library; Carolyn A. Davis and Kathleen Mainwaring of the George Arents Research Library, Syracuse University; and Steve Jones of the Beinecke Rare Book and Manuscript Library, Yale University.

In his later years Cheever was frequently interviewed. Sessions in recorded or printed form with Joseph Barbato, Bruce Benidt, Jo Brans, John Callaway, Dick Cavett, Susan Cheever Cowley, Robert Cromie, Dana Gioia, Millicent Dillon, Michael Stillman, Annette Grant, John Hersey, Christopher Lehmann-Haupt, Lewis Nichols, Christina Robb, Jaqueline Tavernier-Courbin and Robert G. Collins, James Valhouli, and Will Wyatt have been extremely useful.

The most important book dealing with Cheever's life is Susan Cheever's *Home Before Dark*, a sensitive memoir that provides fascinating quotations from his journals and letters. Scholarly books on his work have been written by Samuel Coale, Father George W. Hunt, and Lynne Waldeland. Robert G. Collins has edited a collection of critical essays, and written some of the ablest criticism himself. Others who have done first-rate articles on Cheever's fiction include Frederick Bracher, John W. Crowley, Robert Morace, Stephen C. Moore, and James O'Hara. Doctoral dissertations by Dennis Coates and James Valhouli proved of particular value, partly because of the authors' friendship with Cheever. Reminiscences by Samuel Coale, Malcolm Cowley, and Dana Gioia provided intimate glimpses into Cheever's personality. David Rothbart's World War II journal, Laurens Schwartz's journal covering the mid-1970s, and Max Zimmer's journal of 1981–82 furnished essential background data and contributed significant perceptions.

Assistance was also rendered by a number of people in ways not easily categorized. Among these benefactors are Harold S. Crowley, Jr., Robin Dougherty, Carl Dolmetsch, Judith Ewell, James L. Greenfield of the *New York Times*, Thomas Heacox, H. Hobart Holly and Doris Oberg of the Quincy Historical Society, Charles M. Holloway, David F. Morrill, Emil P. Moschella of the Federal Bureau of Investigation, DeLois L. Ruffin of the U.S. Department of State, Lee S. Strickland of the Central Intelligence

Agency, Gene vonKoschembahr of the Smithers Alcoholism Rehabilitation Center, and Aileen Ward and the members of the Biography Seminar of the New York Institute for the Humanities. A grant from the National Endowment for the Humanities financed a year of the four years' work that went into the making of the book. In the summer of 1984, Arthur and Stella Spear were kind enough to rent us their home in Briarcliff Manor while they made their annual pilgrimage to Maine. During those warm-weather months, living just four miles from Cheever's home, I talked to a number of his closest friends and began to get acquainted with the territory. A research grant from the College of William and Mary subsidized that summer's work, and the college has been generous since in allowing me time to write. David Raney stayed with the project through the last year, bringing his literary intelligence to the mundane task of getting the book down on paper. Vivian Donaldson's encouragement kept me going at times when it would have been easy to stop.

Finally, *John Cheever: A Biography* would not have been possible without the cooperation of the author's widow and executor, Mary Cheever. She submitted to long hours of questions, suggested additional sources, and opened a number of doors—as, for example, to her husband's literary friends and his doctors and psychiatrists—that might otherwise have remained closed.

None of the people listed above is in any way culpable for errors of fact or interpretation in this biography.

NOTES ON SOURCES

CHEEVER rarely dated his letters, but their contents usually make it possible to estimate when they were written. Citations for stories and articles not collected in book form are to their first periodical appearance; otherwise, citations are to the first book appearance. Where the text makes the source of information clear, the source is not repeated in these notes.

Abbreviations: JC = John Cheever, MC = Mary Cheever, SD = Scott Donaldson.

PREHISTORY

FICTIONALIZING TENDENCY AND RETICENCE ABOUT BACKGROUND: Interview William Maxwell, 9 April 1985; interview Arthur Spear, 17 July 1983; interview Edward Newhouse, 5 June 1984; interview Tom Glazer, 3 June 1984; interview Hortense Calisher, 17 September 1984; interview Katrina Ettlinger, 4 June 1984; JC, BULLET PARK notes, Brandeis library.

EZEKIEL CHEEVER LEGEND: Elizabeth Porter Gould, EZEKIEL CHEEVER, SCHOOLMASTER (Boston, 1904); Joshua Coffin, A SKETCH OF THE HISTORY OF NEWBURY, NEWBURYPORT AND WEST NEWBURY (Boston, 1845), p. 221: it was thought that the sufferings endured by the people of Massachusetts during King Philip's War were inflicted upon them for the affectation of wearing wigs; Ralph Ellison quoted in Alwyn Lee, "Ovid in Ossining,"TIME, 27 March 1964, p. 67; JC quoted in Christina Robb, "Cheever's Story," BOSTON GLOBE SUNDAY MAGAZINE, 6 July 1980, p. 27; Lewis Turco to SD, 19 September 1985.

REAL ANCESTRY: Patricia Gross to Susan Cheever, 19 August 1983, Quincy Public Library; "The (Genealogical) Research Notes of Mary Adams Rolfe," The Historical Society of Old Newbury; Robert K. Cheney, MARITIME HISTORY OF THE MERRIMAC (Newburyport, 1964), pp. 51, 241; John J. Currier, HISTORY OF NEWBURYPORT, MASS., 1764–1909 (Newburyport, 1909), Vol. I, pp. 539–41, Vol. II, pp. 330–31; JC quoted in Susan Cheever, HOME BEFORE DARK (New York, 1984), p. 27; JC to John and Mary Dirks, September 1974; JC to Elizabeth Ames, 1 February 1937.

AARON WATERS CHEEVER: John Callaway, "Interview with John Cheever," 15 October 1981; Alan Dawley, CLASS AND COMMUNITY: THE INDUSTRIAL REVOLUTION IN LYNN (Cambridge, 1976), pp. 78–83; JC, typescript 21; JC, "Homage to Shakespeare," STORY, November 1937, pp. 73–81; RECORD OF DEATH, Commonwealth of Massachusets Archives, 1882, Vol. 339, p. 195, item 5221; Robin Dougherty to SD, 4 October 1985 and 15 November 1985.

FREDERICK LINCOLN CHEEVER: JC to John Updike, 15 June 1976; JC, THE WAPSHOT CHRONICLE (New York, 1957), p. 99 and throughout: Leander Wapshot in the Wapshot novels is supposed to represent "a loving picture" of his father; Melissa Baumann, "John Cheever Is at Home," BOSTON MONTHLY, September 1979, p. 14; JC, typescript 21; JC, journal, Brandeis library; Christopher Lehmann-Haupt, interview with JC, February 1969; Callaway, interview with JC, 15 October 1981.

MOTHER, GRANDMOTHER, AND AUNT: JC to William Maxwell, 1968; Frederick L. Cheever, Jr., to Dennis Coates, 20 October 1973; Coates, interview with Frederick L. Cheever, Jr., 22 September 1973; "John Hersey Talks with John Cheever," YALE ALUMNI MAGAZINE, December 1977, p. 21; JC, typescript 21; JC, journal, Brandeis library; Shirley Silverberg, "A Talk with John Cheever," WESTCHESTER, May 1976, p. 67; JC to Laurens Schwartz, 3 January 1976; J. W. Savage, "John Cheever: The Long and the Short and the Tall," CHICAGO TRIBUNE MAGAZINE, 22 April 1979, p. 31.

QUINCY, MORTON, AND ADAMS: H. Hobart Holly, ed., QUINCY 350 YEARS (Quincy, 1974); Louise Randall Pierson, ROUGHLY SPEAKING, New York, 1943; the misbehavior of Thomas Morton is depicted in Hawthorne's story "The Maypole of Merry Mount"; Henry Adams, "Quincy," the first chapter of THE EDUCATION OF HENRY ADAMS; JC to Max Zimmer, 1977.

CHILDHOOD

FIRST YEARS, WORLD WAR I, MAIDS: JC, typescript 21; John Hersey, "John Cheever, Boy and Man," NEW YORK TIMES BOOK REVIEW, 26 March 1978, p. 31.

MOVE TO WOLLASTON, ATMOSPHERE: City directories, Quincy; Rollin Bailey to SD, 2 September 1985 and 23 September 1985, provided details about the way of life in Wollaston during the early 1920s.

CHEEVER AND PLAY, THEATRICS: Rollin Bailey to SD, 25 August 1985, 30 August 1985, 2 September 1985, and 23 September 1985; Baumann, "At Home," pp. 13–15; Mrs. Richard S. Dennison to SD, 9 August 1985; interview Dr. Raymond Mutter, 22 June 1984; interview Tanya Litvinov, 2 November 1986; Helen Perry to Patricia Hoxie, 1983.

EARLY STORYTELLING, COMMITMENT: Jo Brans, "Stories to Comprehend Life: An Interview with John Cheever," SOUTHWEST REVIEW, Autumn 1980, p. 338; Marcia Seligson, "Portrait of a Man Reading," BOOK WORLD, 9 March 1969, p. 2; JC to Frederick Bracher, 15 July 1962; Helen Perry to Patricia Hoxie, 1983; Robert C. Daugherty to SD, 29 November 1984; Lloyd Moss, interview with JC, WQXR, 12 January 1980; according to his brother, Fred, at the age of fourteen Cheever won a short-story contest sponsored by the BOSTON HERALD-TRAVELER: Dennis Coates, "The Novels of John Cheever," Duke University doctoral dissertation, 1977, p. 25.

BOYHOOD RELATIONSHIP WITH FATHER: Savage, "The Long and the Short," p. 31; Coates, dissertation, pp. 17–21; interview MC, 6 June 1983; JC, "The National Pastime," NEW YORKER, 26 September 1953, pp. 29–35; interview Dr. David S. Hays, 14 January 1985; Federico Cheever's remarks at father's memorial service, 22 June 1982.

SUMMERS IN NEW HAMPSHIRE, CAMP MASSASOIT: JC to Josephine Herbst, 1954; Baumann, "At Home," p. 14; Rollin Bailey to SD, 27 August 1985; interview MC, 10 April 1985; interview H. Hobart Holly, 4 July 1985; interviews Harold Crowley, Jr., 15 July 1985 and 22 July 1985.

THAYER AND ANNA BOYNTON THOMPSON: THE THAYER ACADEMY: ONE HUN-DRED YEARS, 1887–1987; [Lillian H. Wentworth], "Anna Boynton Thompson," THAYER ACADEMY MAGAZINE, Spring 1984, pp. 3–5; Lillian H. Wentworth to SD, 30 May 1985 and 1 August 1985; JC, "The Temptations of Emma Boynton," NEW YORKER, 26 November 1949, pp. 29–31; JC, "Thanks, Too, for Memories," NEW YORK TIMES, 22 November 1976, p. C6.

JC AT THAYERLANDS: Grace L. Osgood to SD, 23 August 1985; JC quoted in Coates, dissertation, p. 23; JC on the Charlie Rose show, Dallas–Fort Worth television, late 1979; THE [THAYERLANDS] EVERGREEN, April 1925, pp. 20, 22, and April 1926, p. 24; Lillian H. Wentworth, " . . . And Recalled: John Cheever at Prep School," PARENTS LEAGUE BULLETIN 1984, New York, 1984, pp. 42–43, quotes "The Brook" and "The Stage Ride" in full; THE [THAYER-LANDS] EVERGREEN, commencement issue 1926, p. 13; JC, talk at the Peekskill (N.Y.) library, 21 April 1974.

ADOLESCENCE

FATHER'S ECONOMIC COLLAPSE: Frederick Lewis Allen, ONLY YESTERDAY, New York, 1931, pp. 159–61; Winfield Townley Scott, "Shoetown," COLLECTED POEMS, New York, 1962, p. 31; Susan Cheever, HOME BEFORE DARK, p. 9; Robb, "Cheever's Story," p. 13; Beatrice Wood to SD, 26 May 1985; Mrs. Gordon S. Mustin to Lillian H. Wentworth, 21 March 1983; Robert C. Daugherty to SD, 29 November 1984; Rollin Bailey to SD, 4 September 1985.

FATHER'S DRINKING: Robb, "Cheever's Story," p. 12; JC, "The President of the Argentine," ATLANTIC MONTHLY, April 1976, p. 44; JC, journal, Brandeis library; JC, typescript 21; JC to Frederick Exley, 21 July 1972; JC, "The Folding Chair Set," NEW YORKER, 13 October 1975, p. 38; JC, FALCONER (New York, 1977), pp. 60–62.

MOTHER'S REPUTATION: Robert C. Daugherty to SD, 29 November 1984; Beatrice Wood to SD, 26 May 1985; Mrs. Gordon S. Mustin to Lillian H. Wentworth, 21 March 1983; Rollin Bailey to SD, 23 September 1985.

MOTHER'S BUSINESS CAREER: Thayer Academy transcripts; interview Doris Oberg, 5 June 1985; Rollin Bailey to SD, 4 September 1985; "Open Little Shop Around the Corner," QUINCY PATRIOT-LEDGER, 30 September 1929, p. 2; JC, typescript 21; interview Eugene and Clayre Thaw, 15 July 1984; interview Robert Penn Warren and Eleanor Clark, 10 July 1984; Allen, ONLY YESTERDAY, p. 97.

MOTHER'S DOMINATION OF FATHER: Interview Dr. J. William Silverberg, 18 June 1984; interview Virginia Rice Kahn, 5 June 1985: Jinny Kahn suggested that the Christian Science doctrine "There is no father or mother except God" stood in the way of showing affection—she and Cheever used to spiel off the Scientific Statement of Being at parties; JC, typescript 21; JC, CHRONICLE, p. 126; Callaway, interview with JC, 15 October 1981; interview Dr. David S. Hays, 14 January 1985; JC, "Publick House," THE WAY SOME PEOPLE LIVE (New York, 1943), pp. 182–83; JC, "The Jewels of the Cabots," THE WORLD OF APPLES (New York, 1973), p. 26; JC, "The Edge of the World," THE WAY SOME PEOPLE LIVE (New York, 1943), pp. 75–77: the boy in this story is flunking out of school in his emotional distress; JC quoted in HOME BEFORE DARK, pp. 3–4.

EFFECT ON JC OF FATHER'S WEAKNESS: JC to Max Zimmer, 25 May 1977; interview Dr. D. J. Van Gordon, 30 June 1984; interview MC, 26 July 1984.

KEEPING UP APPEARANCES, DANCING SCHOOL: JC, "Thanks, Too . . . ," pp. C1, C6; interview Don Ettlinger, 4 June 1984; Baumann, "At Home," p. 14; Rollin Bailey to SD, 23 September 1985; Eleanor Munro, " 'Not Only I the Narrator, but I John Cheever . . . ,' " Ms., April 1977, p. 75; interview MC,

28 November 1984; JC, "In the Beginning," NEW YORKER, 6 November 1937, pp. 77–80: this piece of straight reminiscence, not presented as fiction, provided an illuminating view of the social mores of the time and place.

JC AT THAYER ACADEMY: Baumann, "At Home," p. 13; Gordon Godfrey to SD, August 1985; Thayer Academy transcript: during that time the Thayer school required five years of high school study for graduation; Robert C. Daugherty to SD, 29 November 1984; Callaway, interview with JC, 15 October 1981; Grace L. Osgood to SD, 23 August 1985.

"EXPELLED" AND REACTION: John Cheever, "Expelled," NEW REPUBLIC, 1 October 1930, pp. 171–74; Lillian H. Wentworth, " . . . And Recalled," pp. 44–46; interview Lillian H. Wentworth, 15 October 1984; Lillian H. Wentworth to SD, 1 August 1985; Rollin Bailey to SD, 4 September 1985; Hugh Hennedy to SD, 9 October 1985.

CAUSE OF EXPULSION: Lillian H. Wentworth to Susan Cheever, 4 March 1983; Hersey, "Boy and Man," p. 3; JC, "Jewels," p. 15; interview Tom Glazer, 27 July 1984; interview Edward Newhouse, 5 June 1984; Beatrice Wood to SD, 26 May 1985. Some at Thayer feel that Cheever was not officially expelled, but fell so far behind in his grades that he could not recover. A note in his vertical file in the school library reads: "John Cheever, ex '31, was not expelled, but in the interests of drama considered himself to be."

BROTHER

PHYSICAL RETICENCE, SEXUALITY: Interview MC, 10 April 1985; JC, CHRONI-CLE, pp. 79, 126–27; Baumann, "At Home," p. 14; interview Federico Cheever, 11 February 1985; Mrs. Gordon S. Mustin to Lillian H. Wentworth, 21 March 1983; JC quoted in Susan Cheever, HOME BEFORE DARK, pp. 174–75; Susan Cheever Cowley and JC, "A Duet of Cheevers," NEWS-WEEK, 14 March 1977, p. 69.

READING: H. Hobart Holly, ed., QUINCY, pp. 53–54; Callaway, interview with JC, 15 October 1981; Seligson, "Portrait," p. 2.

FRED HOME, FATHER'S DECLINE: Interview Dennis Coates, 8 October 1984; Coates, dissertation, pp. 21, 25–26, 29; Frederick L. Cheever, Jr., to Dennis Coates, 20 October 1973; JC to Elizabeth Ames, 4 May 1935; JC to Malcolm Cowley, 1931; "Chronicler of Suburbia," MD., March 1978, p. 109; JC, "Jewels," p. 23; JC, "National Pastime," pp. 14, 22–24; interview MC, 12 July 1984; JC, typescript 21.

BOSTON BOHEMIA, RADICALISM: Coates, dissertation, pp. 27–28: this dissertation is particularly valuable because it is based in large part on conversations and correspondence with John Cheever and his brother, Fred;

Frederick Bracher, notes from a meeting with JC, 9 February 1965; Rollin Bailey to SD, 30 August 1985 and 23 September 1985; JC, "President," pp. 43–44; JC to Malcolm Cowley, 1933; Lee, "Ovid," p. 69; Daniel Aaron, WRITERS ON THE LEFT, New York, 1961, pp. 70–71, 367; Robin Dougherty to SD, 4 October 1985; Jon Cheever, "Fall River," THE LEFT, Autumn 1931, pp. 70–72; JC to Allan Gurganus, 21 March 1974; Samuel Coale, JOHN CHEEVER (New York, 1977), p. 5; Susan Cheever, HOME BEFORE DARK, p. 24.

BOSTON LITERARY CAREER: JC to Richard Johns, 1930, 1931, and 17 October 1967; JC, "Late Gathering," PAGANY, October–December 1931, pp. 15–19; JC, "Bock Beer and Bermuda Onions," HOUND AND HORN, April–June 1932, pp. 411–20; interview Hazel Hawthorne Werner, 1 July 1984; Father George W. Hunt, interview with JC, fall 1979; Michael Janeway, "Glimpses of Cheever," BOSTON SUNDAY GLOBE, 27 June 1982, p. A22; JC to Laurens Schwartz, 16 October 1975. In the light of Cheever's later image as a sort of country gentleman of letters, it is interesting that the editors of HOUND AND HORN cited his name, among others, as evidence that all their contributors did NOT belong to the leisure class: Mitzi Berger Hamovitch, THE HOUND AND HORN LETTERS (Athens, Ga., 1982), pp. 20–21.

INTIMACY OF FRITZ AND JOEY: Interview James Valhouli, 15 October 1984; interview Candida Donadio, 15 June 1984; Quincy city directories, 1930–35; Boston city directories, 1932–35; Savage, "The Long and the Short," p. 31; JC, "In Passing," ATLANTIC MONTHLY, March 1936, pp. 339–42; Charles Flato to MC, 19 June 1982.

YADDO, ELIOT: JC to Elizabeth Ames, 24 April 1933; JC to Malcolm Cowley, late spring 1933; Peter Ackroyd, T. S. ELIOT: A LIFE (New York, 1984), pp. 192–98; JC to Elizabeth Ames, spring 1934; YADDO, pamphlet distributed at the artists' retreat; Stephen Altman, "Paradise Regained," CULTURAL POST (National Endowment for the Humanities), March/April 1977; Marjorie Peabody Waite, YADDO YESTERDAY AND TODAY (Albany, 1933), pp. 27–37; interview Dorothy Farrell, 9 April 1985.

LEAVING FRED, BOSTON: Susan Cheever Cowley and JC, "A Duet," p. 69; Hersey, "Boy and Man," p. 31; Robb, "Cheever's Story," pp. 27–28, 35; interview Rick Siggelkow, 23 October 1984; interview Hazel Hawthorne Werner, 1 July 1984; JC, "The Brothers," THE WAY, pp. 155–75; interviews Jane Cheever Carr, 27 September 1983 and 5 June 1984; interview Ben Cheever, 19 October 1984.

STARTING

COWLEY AND WERNERS: Interview Frances Lindley, 17 September 1984; JC, CHRONICLE, pp. 106–9; Malcolm Cowley to JC, 29 November 1979; Malcolm Cowley, "John Cheever: The Novelist's Life as a Drama," SEWANEE RE-

VIEW, Winter 1983, pp. 1–2; Robb, "Cheever's Story," p. 28; interview Hazel Hawthorne Werner, 1 July 1984; Frederick Bracher, notes from a meeting with JC, 9 February 1965; JC to Dennis Coates, 1974.

MGM, HUDSON STREET: Annette Grant, "John Cheever: The Art of Fiction XXII," PARIS REVIEW, Fall 1976, p. 52; Callaway, interview with JC, 15 October 1981; JC to Whit Burnett, 2 November 1961; JC to Rick Siggelkow, 1977; JC to Elizabeth Ames, late summer 1934.

REVIEWING, BOOK PROPOSAL: Malcolm Cowley, "Novelist's Life," p. 2; Malcolm Cowley, THE DREAM OF THE GOLDEN MOUNTAINS: REMEMBERING THE 1930S (New York, 1980), pp. 260–62; JC, "While the Fields Burn," NEW REPUBLIC, 26 September 1934, pp. 191–92; interview Malcolm Cowley, 12 June 1984; JC to Malcolm Cowley, 1934.

YADDO, LONG WINTER: Interview Arthur Spear, 19 July 1983; JC to Max Zimmer, 25 May 1977; JC, typescript 8; JC to Elizabeth Ames, fall 1934; Archie Hobson, ed., REMEMBERING AMERICA: A SAMPLER OF THE WPA AMERICAN GUIDE SERIES (New York, 1985), pp. 74, 76; Joseph Barbato, interview with JC, 27 October 1978; JC to Malcolm Cowley, 8 January 196—.

STORIES, *NEW YORKER*: JC to Elizabeth Ames, late 1934–early 1935; JC, "Of Love: A Testimony," THE WAY, p. 66; Malcolm Cowley, "Novelist's Life," pp. 3, 11; interview Malcolm Cowley, 12 June 1984; Dana Gioia et al., interview with JC, 23 January 1976.

HARD TIMES IN FICTION: Malcolm Cowley, DREAM, ix–xii; JC, "Brooklyn Rooming House," NEW YORKER, 25 May 1935, pp. 76–77; JC, "In Passing," pp. 159, 331–43. Almost all of Cheever's fiction during the mid-1930s dealt with working-class characters or with middle-class characters fallen on hard times.

SUMMER AT YADDO: JC to Elizabeth Ames, late 1934–early 1935, 22 April 1935, and 4 May 1935.

WORKING FOR WALKER EVANS: JC to Elizabeth Ames, fall 1935; interview Hazel Hawthorne Werner, 1 July 1984; WALKER EVANS AT WORK (New York, 1982), p. 117; interview Frances Lindley, 17 September 1984.

FWP TURNDOWN, YADDO, NOVEL: Monty Noam Penkower, THE FEDERAL WRITERS' PROJECT (Urbana, 1978), p. 159 and throughout; JC to Malcolm Cowley, 23 October 1935; interview Frances Lindley, 17 September 1984; Daniel Fuchs to SD, 8 May 1984; interview Daniel and Sue Fuchs, 11 February 1985; interview William Maxwell, 9 April 1985; interview Robert Penn Warren and Eleanor Clark, 10 July 1984; JC to Elizabeth Ames, 25 May 1936; JC to Dennis Coates, 9 July 1974.

LILA REFRIGIER, LADIES' MAN: Interview Dorothy Farrell, 9 April 1985; interview Lila Refrigier, 14 January 1985; JC to Eleanor Clark, 21 September 1977; interview Frances Lindley, 17 September 1984; interview Elizabeth Logan, 2 July 1984; JC to Allan Gurganus, 28 March 1974.

LITERARY FRIENDS, *HOLLY TREE*: Interview Laurens Schwartz, 29 July 1985; Dana Gioia et al., interview with JC, 23 January 1976; Coates, dissertation, p. 36; JC to Josephine Herbst, 1936; JC to Malcolm Cowley, 16 December 1936; Samuel Coale, "John Cheever: A Portrait"(unpublished paper, 1982), p. 7; JC to Elizabeth Ames, 1 February 1937; interview Jane Cheever Carr, 19 October 1984; JC "Way Down East," NEW REPUBLIC, 11 December 1935, p. 146.

SPANISH CIVIL WAR AND WRITING: Interview Lila Refrigier, 14 January 1985; interview Dorothy Farrell, 9 April 1985; JC to Malcolm Cowley, 25 May 1937 and 8 January 196__; interview Malcolm Cowley, 12 June 1984; JC, "Behold a Cloud in the West," NEW LETTERS IN AMERICA, ed. Horace Gregory and Eleanor Clark (New York, 1937), pp. 125–44; Dana Gioia et al., interview with JC, 23 January 1976.

MARY

COMMERCIAL FICTION, JOINING FWP: JC, "His Young Wife," COLLIER'S, 1 January 1938, pp. 21–22, 46; Daniel Fuchs to SD, 8 March 1985; Hobson, REMEMBERING AMERICA, pp. 1–11; JC to Josephine Herbst, 1938; Penkower, FEDERAL WRITERS' PROJECT, pp. 20–21, 51; Jerre Mangione, THE DREAM AND THE DEAL (Boston, 1972), pp. 102–03.

WASHINGTON FWP: JC, "Washington Boarding House," THE WAY, pp. 116–21; JC to Josephine Herbst, 1938 (two letters), 1942 (two letters), 1950; JC, CHRONICLE, pp. 130–36; JC to Elizabeth Ames, 1938; Jerre Mangione, AN ETHNIC AT LARGE (New York, 1978), p. 237; Jerre Mangione to SD, 23 September 1985.

NEW YORK FWP: Penkower, FEDERAL WRITERS' PROJECT, pp. 43, 70–71, 160, 170–71, 194–95; Mangione, DREAM AND DEAL, pp. 119, 188; NEW YORK CITY GUIDE (New York, 1979 reprint), front matter; transcription of federal service record, John W. Cheever, National Personnel Records Center, 21 February 1986; interview Ted Mills, 17 October 1985; Jim McGraw to SD, 6 June 1984.

TRIUNA: JC to Josephine Herbst, fall 1939 (two letters); "Not for Publication," QUINCY PATRIOT-LEDGER, 17 March 1938, p. 9.

IMMINENCE OF WAR, MARRIAGE PROSPECTS: JC to Malcolm Cowley, 8 January 196__; JC, "I'm Going to Asia," HARPER'S BAZAAR, 1 September 1940, pp. 61, 114; interview Elizabeth Logan, 2 July 1984; interview Frances Lindley,

17 September 1984; Rick Siggelkow to SD, 8 August 1984; interview MC, 7 June 1984.

MC's FAMILY, YOUTH: Tanya Litvinov to SD, 31 January 1984; Callaway, interview with JC, 15 October 1981; interviews MC, 6 June 1983, 2 June 1984, 7 June 1984, 20 October 1984, 10 April 1985, and 30 May 1985; Marge Leahy, "Mary—the Other Cheever," SUBURBIA TODAY (Westchester), 19 April 1981, pp. 6–10; MC, "Silverface," THE NEED FOR CHOCOLATE AND OTHER POEMS (New York, 1980), p. 78; JC to Josephine Herbst, 1953; interview Dr. J. William Silverberg, 18 June 1984; JC to John Updike, 2 April 1977; Lee, "Ovid," p. 70; MC, "Prospect Street," THE NEED FOR CHOCOLATE, p. 91.

DECIDING ON MARRIAGE: JC to Elizabeth Ames, 26 December 1939; interviews MC, 7 June 1984 and 16 June 1984; Lloyd Moss, interview with JC, WQXR, 12 January 1980; interview Edward Newhouse, 5 June 1984.

SUMMER SEPARATION, NOVEL OUTLINE: JC to MC, summer 1940 (thirteen letters); Mabelle Fullerton, "Quincy Youth Is Achieving New York Literary Career," QUINCY PATRIOT-LEDGER, 6 August 1940. pp. 1, 7.

JC's RESERVATIONS: Interview Dorothy Farrell, 9 April 1985; interview Elizabeth Logan, 2 July 1984; JC, "A Present for Louisa," MADEMOISELLE, December 1940, pp. 126–27, 154–57. For a record of Cheever's publications, see Dennis Coates, "John Cheever: A Checklist, 1930–1978," BULLETIN OF BIBLIOGRAPHY, January–March 1979, pp. 1–13, 49.

YADDO IN AUTUMN: JC to MC, fall 1940 (four letters).

WEDDING, SOCIAL LIFE: Interview MC, 16 June 1984; "John Cheever, Quincy Author, to Wed Mary Winternitz Today in New Haven," QUINCY PATRIOT-LEDGER, 22 March 1941, p. 5; interviews MC, 7 June 1984, 16 June 1984, 28 June 1984, 12 July 1984, 26 July 1984, and 20 October 1984; interview William Maxwell, 9 November 1983; interview Elizabeth Logan, 2 July 1984.

ERWINNA, ENLISTMENT: JC to Josephine Herbst, summer 1941 and winter–spring 1942 (two letters); JC, "Run, Sheep, Run," THE WAY, pp. 93–100; interview Elizabeth Logan, 2 July 1984; JC to Malcolm Cowley, 3 January 1942.

ARMY

INDUCTION, CAMP CROFT, SOUTH: JC to MC, May–August 1942 (nine letters); David Rothbart, WORLD WAR II ARMY JOURNAL (Pittsburgh, 1977, privately published), p. 2; JC, "Introduction," THE WAPSHOT CHRONICLE (New York, 1965, TIME Reading Program special edition), p. xviii; JC to Josephine Herbst, 1954; JC, FALCONER (New York, 1977), pp. 36–37; JC to E. E. Cummings, summer 1942.

SERGEANT DURHAM: JC to MC, May–August 1942 (six letters); JC to Gus Lobrano, 8 September 1942; JC, "Sergeant Limeburner," NEW YORKER, 13 March 1943, pp. 19–25.

CAMP GORDON, ARMY JOBS: JC to MC, August 1942–March 1943 (twenty letters); JC to William Maxwell, 16 August 1942 and 24 December 1942; JC, THE WAPSHOT SCANDAL (New York, 1964), p. 70; JC to Elizabeth Ames, September 1942; Rothbart, ARMY JOURNAL, pp. 35–103; David Rothbart to SD, 10 October 1985; interview David Rothbart, 15 October 1985; JC to Josephine Herbst, 24 October 1942; JC to E. E. Cummings, 8 October 1942; JC to Marion Morehouse, 5 September 1962; JC to Bennett Cerf, 15 October 1942; JC, "Dear Lord, We Thank Thee for Thy Bounty," NEW YORKER, 27 November 1943, pp. 30–31; JC, "The Invisible Ship," NEW YORKER, 7 August 1943, pp. 17–21.

THE WAY SOME PEOPLE LIVE: On dust-jacket copy, Bennett Cerf to JC, 19 October 1942; JC to Bennett Cerf, February 1943 and 14 March 1943; William DuBois, "Tortured Souls," NEW YORK TIMES BOOK REVIEW, 28 March 1943, p. 10; JC to MC, April 1943 (two letters); Struthers Burt, "John Cheever's Sense of Drama," SATURDAY REVIEW OF LITERATURE, 24 April 1943, p. 9; Weldon Kees, "John Cheever's Stories," NEW REPUBLIC, 19 April 1943, pp. 516–17; Random House profit and loss report, THE WAY, 31 October 1944.

UPTOWN

22ND INFANTRY AND JC: Dr. William S. Boice, HISTORY OF THE TWENTY-SECOND UNITED STATES INFANTRY REGIMENT IN WORLD WAR II (U.S. Army Military History Institute, 1959), pp. 1–3, 16–24, 28, 102–4, 110–11, 176–78; Jesse Kornbluth, "The Cheever Chronicle," NEW YORK TIMES MAGAZINE, 21 October 1979, p. 103; Robb, "Cheever's Story," p. 28; interview John and Mary Dirks, 16 July 1984.

CHELSEA, BIRTH OF SUSAN: Interview Elizabeth Logan, 2 July 1984; JC to Josephine Herbst, 9 August 1943; JC to Natalie Robins, 3 December 1968; Hersey, "John Hersey Talks," p. 23.

ASTORIA, PROPAGANDA: John D. Weaver to MC, 19 June 1982; John D. Weaver (ghostwriter for Colonel Emanuel Cohen), "Film Is a Weapon," BUSINESS SCREEN, 1946; Ted Mills to SD, 19 March 1985; interview Ted Mills, 17 October 1985; Leonard Spigelgass to SD, 11 September 1984; interview Edward Newhouse, 5 June 1984; interview Don Ettlinger, 4 June 1984; interview Peggy Murray, 11 June 1984; Caskie Stinnett to SD, 26 November 1985 and 12 December 1985.

COMMUNIST LEANINGS: Interview Ted Mills, 17 October 1985; interviews Don Ettlinger, 4 June 1984 and 9 November 1984; JC to Josephine Herbst, 1946 (two letters).

92ND STREET TOWN HOUSE: JC to Josephine Herbst, November 1944 and summer 1945 (two letters); MC to Josephine Herbst, 22 July 1945; interview Peggy Murray, 11 June 1984; interview MC, 16 June 1984; interview William Maxwell, 9 April 1985; interview Leonard Field, 18 September 1984; JC, "Town House" stories, NEW YORKER, 21 April 1945, 11 August 1945, 10 November 1945, 5 January 1946, 16 March 1946, and 4 May 1946.

GUAM, PHILLIPINES: Interview Dorothy Farrell, 9 April 1985; JC to MC, April–June 1945 (ten letters); Robert Cromie, interview with JC, BOOK BEAT, May 1973; JC, "Manila," NEW YORKER, 28 July 1945, pp. 20–23; JC, "Love in the Islands," NEW YORKER, 7 December 1946, pp. 42–44.

59TH STREET, DISCHARGE: MC to Josephine Herbst, late 1945; JC to Josephine Herbst, November 1945; interview Virginia Rice Kahn, 5 June 1985; interview Katrina Ettlinger, 4 June 1984; service records, National Personnel Records Center.

PARENTS, FATHER'S DEATH: Interview Dudley Schoales, Jr., 17 July 1984; interview Elizabeth Logan, 2 July 1984; interview Jane Cheever Carr, 5 June 1984; Hersey, "Boy and Man," p. 32, maintains that JC did read Prospero's speech at his father's funeral, whereas Susan Cheever, HOME BEFORE DARK, p. 9, asserts that he refused to do so—in any event, "We are such stuff as dreams are made on" is engraved on his father's tombstone; JC, typescript 21.

CANDLEWOOD, TREETOPS: Interview Don Ettlinger, 4 June 1984; JC to Josephine Herbst, 19 March 1946 and summer 1946; MC, "Happy Birthday, Susie," THE NEED FOR CHOCOLATE, pp. 30–31; JC to Don and Katrina Ettlinger, 17 August 1946; interview Joseph H. and Eugenia Hotchkiss, 15 January 1985; JC, "The Summer Farmer," THE ENORMOUS RADIO AND OTHER STORIES (New York, 1953), pp. 138–51; JC, "Vega," HARPER'S, December 1949, pp. 86–95; JC, "How Dr. Wareham Kept His Servants," REPORTER, 5 April 1956, pp. 40–45.

SUSIE AT SCHOOL, SOCIAL LIFE: JC to Don and Katrina Ettlinger, 2 October 1946; JC to Josephine Herbst, late 1946; interview Leonard Field, 18 September 1984.

FIELD VERSION: JC to Robert N. Linscott, September 1946; JC quoted in John D. Weaver, "John Cheever: Recollections of a Childlike Imagination," LOS ANGELES TIMES BOOK REVIEW, 13 March 1977, p. 3; JC to Robert N. Linscott, together with outline of novel, 16 December 1947; Robert N.

Linscott to JC, 22 December 1947; JC to Robert N. Linscott, January 1950 and 13 October 1950.

MARY TEACHING, BIRTH OF BEN: JC to Josephine Herbst, 24 February 1947, 6 June 1947, and May 1948; interview MC, 28 June 1984.

TOWN HOUSE ON BROADWAY: JC to Josephine Herbst, summer–fall 1948 (three letters); Mabelle Fullerton, "Former Quincy Boy Courting Miracle," QUINCY PATRIOT-LEDGER, 2 September 1948; JC, "The Origin of 'Town House,'" BOSTON POST, 5 September 1948; interview Don Ettlinger, 4 June 1984; the three "theater" stories are "O City of Broken Dreams," NEW YORKER, 24 January 1948, pp. 22–31, "The Opportunity," COSMOPOLITAN, December 1949, pp. 44, 174–76, and "The People You Meet," NEW YORKER, 2 December 1950, pp. 44–49.

LOWELL VS. AMES: Interview Elizabeth Logan, 2 July 1984; Elinor Langer, JOSEPHINE HERBST (Boston, 1984), pp. 270–71; Ian Hamilton, ROBERT LOWELL (New York, 1982), pp. 142–52; Eleanor Clark et al., "Statement to the Board of Directors of Yaddo" and letter to former Yaddo guests asking their support of Ames, both 21 March 1949; interview Robert Penn Warren and Eleanor Clark, 10 July 1984.

GUGGENHEIM: JC to Guggenheim foundation, 13 November 1950; Malcolm Cowley to Henry Allen Moe, 13 December 1950.

SCARBOROUGH

LEAVING NEW YORK: Interview Margot Wilkie, 25 June 1984; interview Allan Gurganus, 16 September 1984; JC, FALCONER, pp. 50–51; interview William Maxwell, 9 April 1985; William Maxwell to SD, 10 April 1985; JC, "Moving Out," ESQUIRE, July 1960, pp. 67–68; JC to Josephine Herbst, May 1951; JC, "The Journal of a Writer with a Hole in One Sock," REPORTER, 29 December 1955, p. 26; JC, "Where New York Children Play," HOLIDAY, August 1951, pp. 46–47, 86–89.

CITY VS. COUNTRY: JC to Don and Katrina Ettlinger, 1946; JC to Josephine Herbst, 30 July 1950, MC to SD, 15 June 1985; JC, "Moving Out," pp. 67–68.

BEECHWOOD AMBIENCE: E. J. Kahn, Jr., ABOUT THE "NEW YORKER" AND ME (New York, 1979), pp. 244–45; interview Dudley Schoales, 25 June 1984; Susan Cheever, HOME BEFORE DARK, pp. 81–85; interview MC, 7 November 1983; interview Edward Newhouse, 5 June 1984; JC to Malcolm Cowley, 28 January 1951; John D. Weaver, "Reminiscences," p. 3; JC to Josephine Herbst, 8 June 1951; interview Virginia Rice Kahn, 5 June 1985; interview Federico Cheever, 10 February 1985.

SUBURBIA, SUSAN, BEN: A. C. Spectorsky, THE EXURBANITES (Philadelphia, 1955), pp. 91–107; JC to Josephine Herbst, November 1951; JC, "Hole in One

Sock," p. 25; interview Margot Wilkie, 25 June 1984; JC to William Maxwell, 1953.

DRINKING, PARTIES: Interview Virginia Rice Kahn, 5 June 1985; interview Philip and Mimi Boyer, 8–9 July 1984; interview MC, 26 June 1984; JC to Eleanor Clark, 195—; interview Jane Cheever Carr, 27 September 1983; JC to Josephine Herbst, 29 December 1953; JC to Allan Gurganus, 24 February 1974; interview E. J. Kahn, Jr., 10 June 1984.

MUSIC, FIRE DEPARTMENT, SCHOOL: Mimi Boyer to SD, May 1984; JC to Josephine Herbst, 26 January 1955 and early 1956; interview Don and Ginger Reiman, 3 July 1984; E. J. Kahn, Jr., "NEW YORKER" AND ME, pp. 160–61; Arthur Spear to SD, 16 December 1983; JC, BULLET PARK (New York, 1969), pp. 225–28; interview Aline Benjamin, 5 July 1984; JC to Malcolm Cowley, early 1953.

MRS. VANDERLIP: JC to William Maxwell, 1958; interview Dudley Schoales, 25 June 1984; interview E. J. Kahn, Jr., 10 June 1984; JC, typescript 21; JC to Eleanor Clark, 4 November 1953.

ZINNY SCHOALES: Interview Dudley Schoales, 25 June 1984; interview Dudley Schoales, Jr., 17 July 1984; interview Robert Cowley, 20 June 1984; Susan Cheever, HOME BEFORE DARK, pp. 86–87.

AMBIVALENCE ABOUT SUBURBIA: JC to Josephine Herbst, 17 July 1951; JC to Eleanor Clark, 3 July 1952; JC to Malcolm Cowley, 12 January 1953, 8 February 1953, and 1 November 1953; Malcolm Cowley to JC, 22 January 1953 and 11 February 1953; JC to Josephine Herbst, late summer 1953; JC to Eleanor Clark, late 1953; JC to Josephine Herbst, 195—; interview Barrett and Jane Clark, 28 June 1984; interview MC, 26 July 1984; JC, "Moving Out," pp. 67–68.

CAREER

STORY VS. NOVEL: Callaway, interview with JC, 15 October 1981; JC, typescript 21; Harvey Breit, "In and Out of Books," NEW YORK TIMES BOOK REVIEW, 10 May 1953, p. 8; JC quoted in Elizabeth Janeway et al., "Is the Short Story Necessary?" SHORT STORY THEORIES (Athens, Ohio, 1976), pp. 96–97.

RANDOM HOUSE TURNDOWNS: Robert N. Linscott to JC, 7 June 1951; JC to Josephine Herbst, fall 1951 and spring 1952; interview William Maxwell, 9 November 1983; JC to Candida Donadio, January 1965.

LIFE WITH FATHER, TELEVISION: "Life with Father and Mother," CBS press release, 13 November 1952; interview Ezra Stone, 11 October 1985; JC, "Don't

Leave the Room During the Commercials," TV Guide, 9 January 1982, p. 20.

Enormous Radio, New Yorker tarbrush: JC to Malcolm Cowley, 29 December 1952; George Garrett, "John Cheever and the Charms of Innocence: The Craft of The Wapshot Scandal," Hollins Critic, April 1964, pp. 3–4; interview Richard Stern, 23 April 1985; interview Norman Mailer, 29 March 1985; interview William Maxwell, 9 April 1985; Kees, "Cheever's Stories," pp. 516–17; Taliaferro Boatwright, "Snapshots in the East Fifties," New York Herald Tribune, 24 May 1953, p. 16; Arthur Mizener, "In Genteel Traditions," New Republic, 25 May 1953, pp. 19–20; William DuBois, "Books of the Times," New York Times, 1 May 1953; James Kelly, "The Have-Not-Enoughs," New York Times Book Review, 10 May 1953, p. 21; Morris Freedman, "New England and Hollywood," Commentary, October 1953, pp. 390, 392; dust-jacket copy, British edition of The Enormous Radio; JC to Josephine Herbst, spring 1953; Malcolm Cowley to JC, 29 March 1952 and 27 April 1953; JC to Malcolm Cowley, April 1953.

"Goodbye, My Brother," Fred: JC, "Goodbye, My Brother," Enormous Radio, pp. 3–27; Malcolm Cowley to JC, 22 January 1953; JC to Malcolm Cowley, 8 February 1953; interview JC, August 1977; interview MC, 20 October 1984; interview Virginia Rice Kahn, 5 June 1985; interview E. J. Kahn, Jr., 10 June 1984; interview Ben Cheever, 19 October 1984; interview Edward Newhouse, 5 June 1984; Susan Cheever Cowley and John Cheever, "A Duet," p. 69.

"The Country Husband," Nabokov: JC, "The Country Husband," Enormous Radio, pp. 49–83; Vladimir Nabokov, "Inspiration," Saturday Review of the Arts, 1 January 1973, p. 32.

McCarthy, Herbst: Langer, Herbst, pp. 294–95, 360–61; JC to Josephine Herbst, 1954 (two letters).

Barnard, teaching: JC to William Maxwell, 1955; David Robertson to SD, 23 March 1985; interview MC, 12 July 1984; interview Judith Sherwin, 18 January 1985.

Health problems: Interview Dr. Raymond Mutter, 22 June 1984; interview Aline Benjamin, 5 July 1984; JC ("Cassie") to Philip and Mimi Boyer, 1954; Dr. Bernard C. Glueck to SD, 11 March 1985; JC to William Maxwell, 1955; JC to Josephine Herbst, 1955; JC to Eleanor Clark, 24 June 1955; Susan Cheever, Home Before Dark, p. 167.

Chronicle sold: Interview Simon Michael Bessie, 6 June 1984; Random House memo, Tony Wimpfheimer to Bennett Cerf, 21 January 1965.

ITALY

AWARDS, MOTHER'S DEATH: Benjamin Franklin award, NEW YORK TIMES, 29 May 1955; O. Henry award, NEW YORK TIMES, 4 January 1956; JC to Josephine Herbst, 18 May 1955 and 22 February 1956; Robb, "Cheever's Story," p. 12; interview Jane Cheever Carr, 27 September 1983; JC, typescript 21; Susan Cheever, HOME BEFORE DARK, p. 6; Smithers Center notes, 10 April 1975.

WAPSHOT NOVEL, INSTITUTE: JC to Josephine Herbst, summer 1954; Malcolm Cowley, citation, 23 May 1956; JC to Elizabeth Ames, 1956; JC to Eleanor Clark, 26 June 1956; MC to Malcolm Cowley, 4 October 1982.

FRIENDSHIP, SUMMER PLACES: JC to William Maxwell, 1955, summer 1956 (three letters), 1961; JC to Josephine Herbst, 26 June 1956; JC to Jean Stafford, 26 June 1956.

MEETING BESSIE: Reminiscences of Simon Michael Bessie, Oral History Research office, Columbia, pp. 82–84.

PREPARING FOR ITALY, TRIP ACROSS: Stephen Becker to SD, 30 April 1985; JC to Eleanor Clark, 3 October 1956; JC to William Maxwell, October 1956; JC, "Atlantic Crossing," Ex Ophidia, 1986.

PALAZZO DORIA, IOLE: Interview Peter and Ebie Blume, 12 June 1984; JC to William Maxwell, 5 November 1956, 10 November 1956, 12 November 1956, 24 November 1956, and 7 December 1956; JC to Philip and Mimi Boyer, 17 November 1956; JC to Josephine Herbst, 4 January 1957; JC to Malcolm Cowley, 7 January 1957; Elizabeth Spencer to SD, 11 December 1985 and 17 January 1986.

ROMAN SOCIETY, LANGUAGE, SCHOOLS: JC to Josephine Herbst, 24 November 1956 and 2 December 1956; JC to Malcolm Cowley, 25 November 1956; Weaver, "Reminiscences," p. 3; Susan Cheever, HOME BEFORE DARK, pp. 109–10; interview MC, 2 June 1984; JC to Francis Steegmuller, 13 June 1957; Elizabeth Spencer to SD, 11 December 1985; tape recording, Ben and Susan Cheever, n.d.; JC to Philip and Mimi Boyer, 17 November 1956; JC to Mary Dirks, 17 December 1956; Stephen Becker to SD, 30 April 1985; interview Peter and Ebie Blume, 12 June 1984.

STORIES WITH STAFFORD ET AL.: JC to Jean Stafford, July 1955 and 24 July 1956; interview William Maxwell, 9 April 1985; JC, Author's Note, STORIES (New York, 1956), unpaginated; Richard Sullivan, "A Talented Quartet," NEW YORK TIMES BOOK REVIEW, 23 December 1956, p. 10; William Peden, "Four Cameos," SATURDAY REVIEW OF LITERATURE, 8 December 1956, pp. 15–16.

ELECTION TO INSTITUTE: Jacques Barzun, nomination to institute, 1956; Louise Bogan to JC, 21 January 1957; Malcolm Cowley to JC, 23 February

1957; Susan Cheever, "Remembering John Cheever," NEW YORK TIMES BOOK REVIEW, 9 September 1984, p. 51; JC to Felicia Geffen, 9 October 1957; JC, file at American Academy and Institute of Arts and Letters.

PROTECTING REPUTATION: Interview Simon Michael Bessie, 6 June 1984; JC, correspondence with Curtis Brown, 1956–57.

BIRTH OF FEDERICO: JC to William and Emmy Maxwell, 22 March 1957, 4 April 1957, 5 April 1957, and late April 1957; JC to Robert Penn Warren and Eleanor Clark, 29 February 1957, 9 March 1957, and 28 March 1957; JC to Josephine Herbst, 17 March 1958; interview Peter and Ebie Blume, 12 June 1984; interviews MC, 28 June 1984 and 20 October 1984; interview Ben Cheever, 19 October 1984.

WAPSHOT CHRONICLE: JC to Malcolm Cowley, 26 February 1957; JC to William Maxwell, 22 March 1957; William Esty, "Out of an Abundant Love of Created Things," COMMONWEAL, 17 May 1957, p. 187; Joan Didion, "A Celebration of Life," NATIONAL REVIEW, 22 April 1961, p. 255; Richard Rupp, "John Cheever: The Upshot of Wapshot," CELEBRATION IN MODERN AMERICAN FICTION (Coral Gables, Fla., 1970), p. 31; Maxwell Geismar, "End of the Line," NEW YORK TIMES BOOK REVIEW, 24 March 1957, p. 5; Donald Malcolm, "John Cheever's Photograph Album," NEW REPUBLIC, 3 June 1957, pp. 17–18; JC, Introduction, CHRONICLE (TIME Reading Program special edition, 1965), p. xviii; JC to Granville Hicks, 10 April 1957; JC to Frederick Bracher, 15 July 1962; Carlos Baker, "Yankee Gallimaufry," SATURDAY REVIEW OF LITERATURE, 23 March 1957, p. 14; Coates, dissertation, pp. 54–56; Malcolm Cowley, "Novelist's Life," pp. 4–5; JC, "Independence Day at St. Botolph's," NEW YORKER, 3 July 1954, pp. 18–23; interview Jane Cheever Carr, 27 September 1983; Jo Brans, "Stories to Comprehend," p. 340; interview Stephen Becker, 26 March 1986; "Quincy Son's First Novel Wins National Book Prize," QUINCY PATRIOT-LEDGER, 12 March 1958; interview William Maxwell, 9 April 1985; interview Francis Steegmuller, 17 January 1985.

TRAVELING, LA ROCCA: JC to William Maxwell, summer 1957 (seven letters); JC to Malcolm Cowley, 14 June 1957; JC to Arthur Spear, 15 June 1957; JC to Peter and Ebie Blume, 24 June 1957 and July 1957; interview Robert Penn Warren and Eleanor Clark, 10 July 1984; JC, typescript 21; interview Iole Masullo, 23 June 1984.

LURE OF ITALY, TASSO: Baumann, "At Home," p. 15; interview MC, 6 June 1983; Augustus J. C. Hare, WALKS IN ROME (London, 1909), pp. 644–48; C. F. Brand, TORQUATO TASSO: A STUDY OF THE POET (Cambridge, 1965); interview Peter and Ebie Blume, 12 June 1984; Peter Blume to SD, 18 April 1986.

HOUSE

FIGURE OF IMPORTANCE, NBA: JC to Morton Dauwen Zabel, 25 January 1958; JC to Cabell Greet, 6 October 1958; JC to William Maxwell, fall 1958; JC, acceptance remarks, National Book Award ceremony, 11 March 1958; interview Bernard Malamud, 18 January 1985; Brans, "Stories to Comprehend," p. 338.

HOUSEBREAKER, SUBURBIA: JC, THE HOUSEBREAKER OF SHADY HILL AND OTHER STORIES (New York, 1958); JC, "Don't Leave the Room," p. 20; Richard Gilman, "Dante of Suburbia," COMMONWEAL, 15 December 1958, p. 320; Irving Howe, "Realities and Fictions," PARTISAN REVIEW, 1959, pp. 130–31.

ITALIAN STORIES, IOLE: JC, "The Bella Lingua" and "Clementina," THE BRIGADIER AND THE GOLF WIDOW (New York, 1964), pp. 106–32, 133–55; SD, "Americans in Italy: The Clash of Cultures in John Cheever's Stories," LETTURE ANGLO-AMERICANE IN MEMORIA DI ROLANDO ANZILOTTI (Pisa, 1986), pp. 113–26; interview Iole Masullo, 23 June 1984; interview Dudley Schoales, 25 June 1984; JC to William Maxwell, 16 July 1958; JC to Morton Dauwen Zabel, 9 February 1959.

YADDO, SARATOGA: Interview MC, 7 November 1983; interview Allan Gurganus, 16 September 1984; interview Pauline Hanson, 17 October 1984; JC to Morton Dauwen Zabel, 9 February 1959; JC to William Maxwell, 1960; JC, typescript 21; JC to Josephine Herbst, fall 1957 and winter 1958; JC to Malcolm Cowley, 1960; Susan Cheever, HOME BEFORE DARK, pp. 33–35.

WINTER'S DEATH, EUROPE: JC quoted in Susan Cheever, HOME BEFORE DARK, pp. 132–33; JC to Josephine Herbst, September 1959; JC to William Maxwell, summer 1959 (two letters); JC to Peter and Ebie Blume, summer 1959; interview Simon Michael Bessie, 6 June 1984.

MIDDLE-CLASS LIFE: Interview Lila Refrigier, 14 January 1985; interview Elizabeth Logan, 2 July 1984; Dana Gioia, "Meeting Mr. Cheever," HUDSON REVIEW, Autumn 1986, pp. 419–34.

NEW YORKER FLAREUP, ROSS, MAXWELL: Dana Gioia et al., interview with JC, 23 January 1976; JC to Robert Gottlieb, 8 July 1976; Grant, "John Cheever: The Art," pp. 52–53; interviews William Maxwell, 9 November 1983 and 9 April 1985; Susan Cheever Cowley and JC, "A Duet," p. 69; JC to William Maxwell, December 1960; interview MC, 10 April 1985; Susan Cheever, "Remembering," p. 51.

GUGGENHEIM, SAN FRANCISCO: JC to Mrs. Leighton (Guggenheim application), 21 January 1960 and 30 January 1960; Wallace Stegner to SD, 16 September 1984; "Publisher's Page," ESQUIRE, October 1960, p. 6; interview Philip Roth, 18 July 1984; Robert Gutwillig, "Dim Views through Fog,"

New York Times Book Review, 13 November 1960, pp. 68–69; JC, "The Death of Justina," Some People, Places, and Things That Will Not Appear in My Next Novel (New York, 1961), pp. 1–19.

Cedar Lane mortgage: JC to Josephine Herbst, 17 March 1958; JC to William Maxwell, 1960 (two letters); JC to Malcolm Cowley, 16 September 1960; Susan Cheever, Home Before Dark, p. 123.

Hollywood, Jerry Wald: JC to Josephine Herbst, 10 October 1958; John D. Weaver to SD, 26 February 1985 and 12 April 1986; John D. Weaver, "Recollections," p. 3; Daniel Fuchs to SD, 8 May 1984; interview Daniel and Sue Fuchs, 11 February 1985; interview Barrett and Jane Clark, 13 July 1984; interview Ben Cheever, 19 October 1984; JC to William Maxwell, 17 November 1960, Thanksgiving 1960, December 1960, and 1961; JC to Malcolm Cowley, 22 December 1960.

Ossining, house: Dr. George Jackson Fisher, "Ossining," History of Westchester County (Philadelphia, 1886), Vol. II, pp. 321–65; Martha Smilgis, "The Dark Moments of His Life Rival—and Perhaps Inspire—John Cheever's Stories," People, 23 April 1979, p. 78; interviews MC, 7 November 1983 and 10 April 1985; interview Charles Shapiro, 11 April 1985; interview Barrett and Jane Clark, 28 June 1984; Carl Oechsner, Ossining, New York (Croton-on-Hudson, N.Y., 1976), p. 7; interview Marion Ascoli, 5 July 1984; JC quoted in Susan Cheever, Home Before Dark, pp. 123–24; JC, "A Vision of the World," Brigadier, pp. 241–42; JC to Max Zimmer, February 1977; MC to Malcolm Cowley, 4 October 1982; interview Saul Bellow, 10 July 1984.

OSSINING

Social life, Boyer, Spear: Interview Alan Williams, 18 September 1984; JC to William Maxwell, June 1964; JC to John Hersey, 196__; JC to Frederick Bracher, 16 March 1963; interview Philip and Mimi Boyer, 8–9 July 1984; JC to Frederick Exley, 1 June 1965; interviews Arthur and Stella Spear, 19 July 1983 and 10 November 1983; Arthur Spear to SD, 31 March 1986.

Sara Spencer, Rudnik, Robins: Interview Sara Spencer, 10 November 1983; interview Anthony and Susan Spencer, 15 September 1984; interview Arthur and Stella Spear, 19 July 1983; JC to Sara Spencer, 196__ (two letters); interview Raphael Rudnik, 18 January 1985; interview Christopher Lehmann-Haupt, 26 July 1984; interview Natalie Robins, 22 October 1984.

Physical life, pool, dogs, cats: JC quoted in Robb, "Cheever's Story," p. 12; interview Federico and Mary Cheever, 10 February 1985; tape recording, Christopher Lehmann-Haupt interview with JC, February 1969; JC to Allan Gurganus, 24 January 1974; JC to Laurens Schwartz, 26 June 1977;

Nora Sayre to SD, 8 April 1985; JC to Malcolm Cowley, late 1961 and 1962; Malcolm Cowley to JC, 13 January 1962; JC to Josephine Herbst, 6 December 1963; Susan Cheever, HOME BEFORE DARK, pp. 144–45; Susan Cheever Cowley and JC, "A Duet," p. 70; Ron Hansen to SD, 25 June 1984; JC, "The Geometry of Love," THE WORLD OF APPLES (New York, 1973), p. 150; JC, FALCONER, pp. 38–41.

SOME PEOPLE REVIEWS: Malcolm Cowley to JC, 10 February 1961; David Boroff, "A World Filled with Trapdoors into Chaos," NEW YORK TIMES BOOK REVIEW, 16 April 1961, p. 34; Frank J. Warnke, "Cheever's Inferno," NEW REPUBLIC, 15 May 1961, p. 18; JC, "Some People, Places, and Things That Will Not Appear in My Next Novel," NEW YORKER, p. 55; JC to Frederick Bracher, summer 1962.

MAXWELL, BRACHER, CUMMINGS, O'HARA: Interview William Maxwell, 9 November 1983; Grant, "John Cheever: The Art," pp. 53–58; JC to Frederick Bracher, 20 September 1962 and October 1962; interview Curtis Harnack and Hortense Calisher, 17 September 1984; JC to Marion Morehouse, 5 September 1962; Susan Cheever, HOME BEFORE DARK, pp. 61–62; JC to ——— ———, 2 May 1963.

DRINKING, FRED: Max Zimmer journal; JC, typescript 21; Paul Moor to SD, 29 October 1984; interview Nina Engel, 21 June 1984; interview Virginia Rice Kahn, 5 June 1985; interview Simon Michael Bessie, 6 June 1984; JC to Frederick Bracher, August 1964; interview MC, 26 July 1984; interview Robert Penn Warren and Eleanor Clark, 10 July 1984.

RELATIONSHIP WITH MARY: Kenneth Shelton to MC, 27 July 1982; interview Raphael Rudnik, 18 January 1985; MC to Malcolm Cowley, 2 October 1982; Samuel Coale, "John Cheever: A Portrait" (unpublished paper, 1982), p. 8; interview John and Mary Dirks, 16 July 1984; interview Edward Newhouse, 5 June 1984; interview MC, 22 October 1984; MC, "To Emily Dickinson in Heaven," THE NEED FOR CHOCOLATE, p. 75; JC, "The Chimera," WORLD OF APPLES, pp. 96–97; MC quoted in Alwyn Lee, "Ovid," p. 72.

SUSAN, BEN, FEDERICO: Interview Susan Cheever, 21 September 1983; Seligson, "Portrait," p. 2; JC to William Maxwell, 1962 and 1963 (three letters); interview Charles Shapiro, 11 April 1985; interview Ben Cheever and Janet Maslin, 19 October 1984; interviews MC, 6 June 1983 and 20 October 1984; JC, typescript 21; interview Federico and Mary Cheever, 10 February 1985.

PHOBIAS, DEPRESSION: JC, "The Angel of the Bridge," BRIGADIER, pp. 23–35; JC, "A Vision of the World," BRIGADIER, pp. 238–47; JC to Frederick Bracher, September 1962, 25 June 1963, and 12 January 1964; tape recording, Christopher Lehmann-Haupt interview with JC, February 1969; Grant, "John Cheever: The Art," p. 42; JC to Robert Gottlieb, 21 August 1968; JC to Malcolm Cowley, 1964; interview Susan Cheever, 21 September 1983.

WAPSHOT SCANDAL, REVIEWS: Garrett, "The Charms of Innocence," pp. 4, 8; Stanley Edgar Hyman, "John Cheever's Golden Egg," NEW LEADER, 3 February 1964, pp. 23–24; Glenway Wescott, "A Surpassing Sequel," NEW YORK HERALD TRIBUNE BOOK REVIEW, 5 January 1964, pp. 1, 9; interview Dennis Coates, 8 October 1984; JC, notes for SCANDAL in Coates, dissertation, pp. 55, 140, 141–42; Malcolm Cowley to JC, 22 October 1963.

CONFRONTATION WITH *NEW YORKER:* Kornbluth, "Cheever Chronicle," pp. 29, 102; Susan Cheever, HOME BEFORE DARK, pp. 138–40; interview William Maxwell, 9 April 1985.

RUSSIA

TIME COVER STORY: "A Letter from the Publisher," TIME, 27 March 1964, p. 11; Paul Moor to SD, 29 October 1984; Bruce McCabe, "The Inner Realm of John Cheever," BOSTON GLOBE, 23 October 1974; JC to Malcolm Cowley, winter 1963–64; JC to Frederick Bracher, spring 1964; JC to Eleanor Clark, 1964; interview Robert Penn Warren and Eleanor Clark, 10 July 1984; JC to William Maxwell, 1964; John W. Aldridge, "John Cheever and the Soft Sell of Disaster," TIME TO MURDER AND CREATE (New York, 1966), p. 172; JC quoted in Susan Cheever, HOME BEFORE DARK, p. 154; JC, typescript 21.

WAPSHOT FILM, HOPE LANGE: Interview Hope Lange, 24 October 1984; interview David Lange, 6 June 1985; JC, typescript 21.

OLD FRIEND, MARY, ITALY: JC, typescript 21; JC, "Boy in Rome," SOME PEOPLE, pp. 138–39, 161; JC to Frederick Bracher, July 1964.

"THE SWIMMER": JC, "The Swimmer," *BRIGADIER,* pp. 61–76; JC to Alan Pakula, 1964; interview Frank Perry, 6 June 1985; Lewis Nichols, "A Visit with John Cheever," NEW YORK TIMES BOOK REVIEW, 5 January 1964, p. 28; Grant, "John Cheever: The Art," pp. 62–63; Munro, "Not Only I," p. 77; Dana Gioia et al., interview with JC, 23 January 1976, pp. 2–3, 10; tape recording, Joseph Barbato interview with JC, 27 October 1978.

TRIP TO RUSSIA, *BRIGADIER* REVIEWS: Orville Prescott, "John Cheever's Comedy and Dismay," NEW YORK TIMES, 14 October 1964, p. 43; interview MC, 6 June 1983; interview Vassily Aksyonov, 23 January 1986; interview William H. Luers, 22 August 1985; JC to Josephine Herbst, 14 December 1964; Tanya Litvinov to SD, 31 January 1984 and 15 February 1984; JC to Frederick Bracher, 12 February 1965.

YEVTUSHENKO, UPDIKES: John Updike to SD, 25 June 1984 and 18 July 1984; interview MC, 20 October 1984; Robert Cromie, interview with JC, BOOK BEAT, May 1973; Grant, "John Cheever: The Art," p. 46; JC to Paul Moor, 30 December 1984; JC to John Updike, 1963; JC to Malcolm Cowley, 1963; John Updike, PICKED-UP PIECES (New York, 1976), pp. 5–6; John Updike, memorial tribute to JC, 23 June 1982; Mary Weatherall to SD, 17 December 1984.

LAST DAYS IN RUSSIA: JC, typescript 5 and typescript 21; interview Eugene and Clayre Thaw, 15 July 1984; interview Raymond Carver, 23 October 1984.

INWARD

MOOR, RUSSIAN CORRESPONDENCE: Paul Moor to SD, 20 November 1984 and 30 November 1984; JC to Paul Moor, 3 February 1965; JC to Laurens Schwartz, 2 December 1975; JC to William Maxwell, 1965; Lee S. Strickland (CIA) to SD, 10 June 1986.

WASHINGTON, BROWN, CHICAGO, TRAINS: JC to Frederick Bracher, 23 February 1965; James Dickey to SD, 1 January 1985; interview Richard Stern, 23 April 1975; JC to Richard Stern, 1964 and 1965; Mrs. Donald H. Farquharson to SD, 19 January 1985 and 5 April 1985; interview Ben Cheever, 19 October 1984.

HOWELLS, WHITE HOUSE, DENTISTRY: Glenway Wescott, report on THE WAPSHOT SCANDAL, American Academy and Institute files; JC to William Maxwell, 1965; JC to Richard Stern, 1965; Ralph Ellison, presentation of the Howells Medal, and JC, acceptance of the Howells Medal, 19 May 1965, American Academy and Institute files; "Cheever, John," CURRENT BIOGRAPHY, 1975, p. 76; interview Ben Cheever and Janet Maslin, 8 November 1983; JC to Frederick Exley, 1965 (two letters).

"GEOMETRY," MLA: JC to Frederick Exley, 4 October 1965 and late fall 1965; JC to Frederick Bracher, 5 October 1965, late fall 1965, and 4 January 1966; interview William Maxwell, 9 April 1985; JC, typescript 21; Hennig Cohen to SD, 15 December 1984; interview Raphael Rudnik, 18 January 1985; JC to Richard Stern, late 1965; Richard Stern, "Report from the MLA," NEW YORK REVIEW OF BOOKS, 17 February 1966, pp. 26–28; Richard Stern to SD, 13 September 1984; interview Richard Stern, 23 April 1985; interview Norman Mailer, 29 March 1985; Hilary Mills, MAILER: A BIOGRAPHY (New York, 1982), p. 314; Norman Mailer, CANNIBALS AND CHRISTIANS (New York, 1966), pp. 95–103; interview Robert F. Lucid, 2 April 1985.

POLITICAL RADICALISM OF CHILDREN: JC quoted in Susan Cheever, HOME BEFORE DARK, p. 142; JC to William Maxwell, 1965; JC to Josephine Herbst, May 1965; JC to Tanya Litvinov, 23 May 1966.

FRIDAY CLUB: Interview Tom Glazer, 27 October 1983; interview Arthur Spear, 19 July 1983; interview MC, 6 June 1983; Betsy Brown, "The Friday Club, A Cheever Salon," NEW YORK TIMES (Westchester section), 27 June 1982, pp. 1, 8; JC to Barrett Clark, 19 January 196__.

"SWIMMER" FILM, ROREM: Interview Frank Perry, 6 June 1985; Vincent Canby, "Lancaster Takes Suburban Swim," NEW YORK TIMES, 16 July 1966; JC to Richard Stern, 17 August 1966; JC to Frederick Bracher, 15 September 1966; interview Ned Rorem, 20 September 1984.

TROUBLES WITH MARRIAGE, LIQUOR, DR. HAYS: JC, typescript 21; JC, journal, Brandeis library; JC to Frederick Bracher, September 1965; JC to Richard Stern, 18 February 1966; JC to Robert Gottlieb, 21 August 1968; interview Dr. David S. Hays, 14 January 1985; interview MC, 2 June 1984; JC to MC, summer 1966; Anatole Broyard, "Fiction That Lies About Its Dreams," NEW YORK TIMES BOOK REVIEW, 12 January 1986.

SUSIE AND ROB'S WEDDING: Interview Alan Williams, 18 September 1984; interview Robert Cowley, 21 June 1984; JC to William Maxwell, 1967; JC, typescript 21; interview Sally Swope, 8 November 1983; "Susan Cheever Wed to Robert Cowley," NEW YORK TIMES, 7 May 1967, p. 93; Malcolm Cowley, "Novelist's Life," p. 7.

LOREN, WARD, PALAMOUNTAIN, AMES: JC, journal, Brandeis library; interview Carl Dolmetsch, 25 May 1984; JC to Frederick Bracher, 14 September 1967; JC, "Sophia, Sophia, Sophia," SATURDAY EVENING POST, 21 October 1967, pp. 32–35; interview Aileen Ward, 23 October 1984; interview Anne Palamountain, 17 July 1985; interview Nellie Shannon, 17 July 1985; JC, "Elizabeth Ames," minutes of the meeting of the corporation of Yaddo, 7 September 1968; JC, "The Hostess of Yaddo," NEW YORK TIMES BOOK REVIEW, 8 May 1977, pp. 3, 34–35.

PROSTATITIS, THANKSGIVING: Interview Dr. Raymond Mutter, 22 June 1984; JC to Dr. Raymond Mutter, 10 November 1967; JC, journal, Brandeis library; JC, "Thanks, Too, for Memories," pp. C1, C6; JC to Natalie Robins, 3 December 196—; interview Christopher Lehmann-Haupt and Natalie Robins, 22 October 1984; Christopher Lehmann-Haupt, "Authors' Creative Ways to Get Out of Writing," NEW YORK TIMES, 6 June 1985, p. C22.

BEN'S ARREST, KING'S DEATH: Interview Ben Cheever, 19 October 1984; JC to Josephine Herbst, early 1968; Dana Gioia et al., interview with JC, 23 January 1976, pp. 17–18; JC, journal, Brandeis library.

DOUBLING

BOURGEOIS ARTIST DIVISION: Interview Christopher Lehmann-Haupt, 26 July 1984; interview Molly Malone Cook, 2 May 1985; interview Aline Benjamin, 5 July 1984; JC, typescript 21; interview Tom Glazer, 3 June 1984;

interview Mrs. Wallace Boyd, 29 April 1985; Father George W. Hunt, JOHN CHEEVER: THE HOBGOBLIN COMPANY OF LOVE (Grand Rapids, Mich., 1983), pp. 176–77; JC to Dennis Coates, 29 June 1974.

HOPE LANGE AFFAIR: Interview Virginia Rice Kahn, 5 June 1985; interview Edward Newhouse, 5 June 1984; interview Dr. J. William Silverberg, 18 June 1984; JC, journal, Brandeis library; interview Hope Lange, 24 October 1984.

JOURNAL CONTENTS, SELF-LOATHING: James Valhouli, interview with JC, 2 December 1977; Elizabeth Hardwick, "Cheever, or the Ambiguities," NEW YORK REVIEW OF BOOKS, 20 December 1984, p. 3; Richard Stern to SD, 11 May 1985; JC, BULLET PARK notes, Brandeis library; JC, journal, Brandeis library; Susan Cheever, HOME BEFORE DARK, p. 67; interview John Leonard, 23 October 1984; interview Federico Cheever, 6 April 1985; interview Max Zimmer, 19 July 1984; interview Dr. Raymond Mutter, 22 June 1984; interview Frances Lindley, 17 September 1984; JC, typescript 21; JC to Arthur Spear, October 1968; JC to Frederick Exley, 1968.

STERN, STYRON, EXLEY, NOBEL, BOM: Interview Richard Stern, 23 April 1985; JC to Josephine Herbst, May 1968; JC to Frederick Exley, 1968 and 14 May 1969; Cheever file, American Academy and Institute; Weaver, "Recollections," p. 8; JC, journal, Brandeis library.

IRELAND: JC to William Maxwell, 9 August 1968 and late August 1968; JC to Josephine Herbst, 21 August 1968; interview John and Mary Dirks, 16 July 1984; Mary Dirks to SD, 6 August 1984.

SWITCH TO KNOPF, SPENDING: Interview Candida Donadio, 15 June 1984; JC to Frances Lindley, 17 September 1968; JC to Robert Gottlieb, September 1968; interview Connie Bessie, 19 July 1984; interview Robert Cowley, 21 June 1984; interviews MC, 7 November 1983 and 20 October 1984; JC to Frederick Exley, December 1968.

DUALITY OF VISION: Samuel Coale, "Cheever and Hawthorne: The Romancer's Art," CRITICAL ESSAYS ON JOHN CHEEVER, ed. Robert G. Collins (Boston, 1982), pp. 193–209; John W. Crowley, "John Cheever and the Ancient Light of New England," NEW ENGLAND QUARTERLY, June 1983, pp. 270–71; (John Updike), "Notes and Comment," NEW YORKER, 12 July 1982, pp. 27–28; John Gardner, "Witchcraft in Bullet Park," NEW YORK TIMES BOOK REVIEW, 24 October 1971, p. 2.

BULLET PARK: TECHNIQUE, ENDING: JC, journal, Brandeis library; JC, BULLET PARK notes, Brandeis library; Robert Gottlieb to JC, 5 September 1968; JC to Robert Gottlieb, Labor Day 1968 and 8 November 1968; Gardner, "Witchcraft," p. 2; Lee, "Ovid," p. 72.

Bullet Park, religion: Lee, "Ovid," p. 68; Mircea Eliade, The Sacred and the Profane (New York, 1969), pp. 11–12; JC, journal, Brandeis library; Dana Gioia, "Meeting Mr. Cheever," pp. 425–26.

Divided selves: Hammer, Nailles, Tony: JC, journal, Brandeis library; JC, Bullet Park notes, Brandeis library; tape recording, Christopher Lehmann-Haupt interview with JC, February 1969; Leslie Aldridge, "Having a Drink with Cheever," New York, 28 April 1969, p. 49; Lynne Waldeland, "John Cheever's Bullet Park; A Key to His Thought and Art," Critical Essays, pp. 266–68; Coates, dissertation, pp. 171, 187.

Reaction to *Bullet Park:* JC to Marion Morehouse, 9 April 1969; Aldridge, "Having a Drink," pp. 48–50; Benjamin DeMott, "A grand gatherum of some late 20th-century American weirdos," New York Times Book Review, 27 April 1969, pp. 1, 40–41; Anatole Broyard, "You Wouldn't Believe It," New Republic, 26 April 1969, pp. 36–37; Stephen C. Moore, "A Text Already 'Deconstructed': Bullet Park"(paper given at Modern Language Association meeting, 1985); interview Philip Roth, 18 July 1985.

Depression, Dr. Silverberg: Stephen Becker to SD, 30 April 1985; JC to William Maxwell, 6 March 1969; JC to John Updike, 13 May 1969; JC and Federico Cheever quoted in Susan Cheever, Home Before Dark, p. 155; interview Dr. J. William Silverberg, 18 June 1984; interview John and Mary Dirks, 16 July 1984; JC to Allan Gurganus, 11 February 1977.

BOTTOMING

Drunkenness, parties: Interview Robert Cowley, 21 June 1984; interview John and Mary Dirks, 16 July 1984; interview Leonard Field, 18 September 1984; Robert Cromie, interview with JC, Book Beat, May 1973; JC to Malcolm Cowley, spring 1971; Malcolm Cowley to JC, 14 May 1971; Susan Cheever, Home Before Dark, pp. 182–83; interview MC, 26 July 1984; interview Curtis Harnack and Hortense Calisher, 17 September 1984; interview Robert Penn Warren and Eleanor Clark, 10 July 1984; interview Gray Smith, 11 September 1984; interview John Hersey, 18 October 1984; interview Francis Steegmuller and Shirley Hazzard, 17 January 1985; Shirley Hazzard to SD, 13 January 1987; James O'Hara, "John Cheever," Dictionary of Literary Biography Yearbook 1982, ed. Richard Ziegeld (Detroit: Gale Research, 1983), p. 132; Mary Dirks to ————, 10 September 1972; interview Tom Glazer, 27 October 1983.

Marriage tensions, infidelity: JC quoted in Susan Cheever, Home Before Dark, pp. 182–83; interview Sandra Hochman, 17 January 1985; JC, typescript 21; interview Dr. J. William Silverberg, 18 June 1984; interview Frederick Exley, 9 July 1984; interview MC, 12 July 1984.

BRIARCLIFF, POETRY: Interview Roger and Maureen Willson, 29 July 1984; interview Charles Shapiro, 11 April 1985; MC, "Wisteria Morning," THE NEED FOR CHOCOLATE, pp. 61–64; Marge Leahy, "Mary—the Other Cheever," SUBURBIA TODAY, 19 April 1981, pp. 6–10; Robin Thrush Jovanovich, "Mary Cheever on Her Own," MOUNT KISCO PATENT TRADER, 4 January 1985, p. A3; MC to Malcolm Cowley, 3 June 1971 and mid-June 1971; Malcolm Cowley to MC, 10 June 1971; interview Bernard Malamud, 18 January 1985; JC to Bernard Malamud, 10 June 197__ ; Aldridge, "Having a Drink," p. 50; interview MC, 12 July 1984.

OTHER WOMEN: Mary Dirks to SD, 9 October 1984; JC to Candida Donadio, 26 January 1970; interview Candida Donadio, 15 June 1984; interview Shana Alexander, 21 September 1985; interview Eugene and Clayre Thaw, 15 July 1984; interview Curtis Harnack and Hortense Calisher, 17 September 1984; JC, typescript 21; Susan Cheever, HOME BEFORE DARK, pp. 125–26; interview Robert Penn Warren and Eleanor Clark, 10 July 1984; interview MC, 12 July 1984.

FATHER-SON, FRED: Interview Robert Cowley, 21 June 1984; interview Ben Cheever, 19 October 1984; interview MC, 2 June 1984 and 26 July 1984; JC, typescript 21; interviews Federico Cheever, 10 February 1985, 11 February 1985, and 6 April 1985; interview Sara Spencer, 10 November 1983.

KOREA, RUSSIA: JC to William Maxwell, 1970; JC, typescript 21; John Updike to SD, 25 June 1984; MC to John Updike, 1970; John Updike to MC, 30 September 1970; JC, "The Melancholy of Distance," *Chekhov and Our Age*, ed. James McCarkey (Ithaca, 1984), pp.125–35; interview Curtis Harnack and Hortense Calisher, 17 September 1984; Virginia M. Grinager, "Cheever Finds Russians Full of Warmth, Hospitality," OSSINING CITIZEN REGISTER, 20 December 1973; interview Federico Cheever, 10 February 1985; Tanya Litvinov to SD, 7 March 1984 and 6 December 1984; JC, typescript 21; tape recording, Father George W. Hunt et al., interview with JC, April 1980; Federico Cheever quoted in Susan Cheever, HOME BEFORE DARK, p. 158.

PLAYBOY, CHICAGO: Richard Todd, "Gathering at Bunnymede," ATLANTIC MONTHLY, January 1972, pp. 86–88; Richard Stern to SD, 13 September 1984; interview Richard Stern, 23 April 1985; JC to Frederick Exley, 1 June 1971; interview Saul Bellow, 10 July 1984.

SING SING, LANG: Diane Hofkins, "Cheever: Literature a Key," OSSINING CITIZEN REGISTER, 2 November 1977, p. A3; interview Donald Lang, 20 September 1984; "The Attica Tragedy," NEWSWEEK, 27 September 1971, pp. 22–38; interview John and Mary Dirks, 16 July 1984; Mary Dirks to SD, 6 August 1984; Mary Dirks to ————, 21 February 1972 and 7 December 1972; interview Robert Cowley, 21 June 1984; JC to Allan Gurganus, 15 March 1974 and 27 April 1974; interview Gray Smith, 11 September 1984;

interview Barrett and Jane Clark, 28 June 1984; interview Federico Cheever, 11 February 1985; JC to Candida Donadio, 18 July 1972; Callaway, interview with JC, 15 October 1981; interview Philip and Mimi Boyer, 8–9 July 1984; JC to Robert Gottlieb, 28 August 1982; "Chronicler of Suburbia," MD., March 1978, p. 114.

COMPETITION, TELEVISION: Interview Philip Roth, 18 July 1984; JC to Malcolm Cowley, 26 April 1972; interview Curtis Harnack and Hortense Calisher, 17 September 1984; interview Morris Lurie, 16 December 1985; Jacqueline Tavernier-Courbin and R. G. Collins, "An Interview with John Cheever," THALIA, 1978, p. 7; Susan Colgan, " 'Literature in Peril': Cheever," OSSINING CITIZEN REGISTER, 24 May 1972, p. 3; JC to John Updike, 197—.

IOWA, JOHN VS. MARY: Interview Frederick Exley, 9 July 1984; Frederick Exley, "On Cheever, Styron, and That Place," unpublished typescript; JC to Frederick Exley, late 1972 and 22 March 1973; interview Federico Cheever, 10 February 1985; interview MC, 26 July 1984; MC, "Gorgon," THE NEED FOR CHOCOLATE, pp. 18–21; interview Rick Siggelkow, 24 July 1984.

CARDIOMYOPATHY, HOSPITALIZATION: Interview Dr. Raymond Mutter, 22 June 1984; interview Dr. Robert A. Johnson, 18 December 1984; interview Robert Cowley, 21 June 1984; Susan Cheever, HOME BEFORE DARK, pp. 181, 184–85; MC to Malcolm Cowley, 4 October 1982; JC to Candida Donadio, May 1973; JC to Robert Gottlieb, 26 May 1973; JC to Dr. Raymond Mutter, 4 June 1973; JC to Mrs. Burnham Carter, Jr., 5 June 1973; interview Dr. Frank Jewett, 29 June 1984.

ACADEMY, *APPLES*: Robert Penn Warren et al., nominating petition for JC's membership in the American Academy, 16 May 1973; L. Woiwode, "Cheever at His Best, As If He Were Growing Younger," NEW YORK TIMES BOOK REVIEW, 20 May 1973, pp. 1, 10, is a representative review.

IOWA-BOSTON-SMITHERS

IOWA WELCOME, IRVING, CARVER: JC, "An Afternoon Walk in Iowa City, Iowa," TRAVEL & LEISURE, September 1974, pp. 32, 50; JC to John and Mary Dirks, 20 September 1973; interview Allan Gurganus, 16 September 1984; Frederick Exley, PAGES FROM A COLD ISLAND (New York, 1975), pp. 246–47; Ron Hansen to SD, 25 June 1984; JC to Sara Spencer, 4 October 1973; JC to Arthur Spear, 29 October 1973; John Irving, "But what you always remember . . . ," SEEMS LIKE OLD TIMES (Iowa City, 1986), pp. 114–16; Mona Simpson, "Raymond Carver: The Art of Fiction," PARIS REVIEW, Summer 1983, pp. 204–5; interview Raymond Carver, 23 October 1984.

DRINKING, TEACHING: Interview John Leonard, 23 October 1984; interview T. Coraghessan Boyle, 11 February 1985; Ron Hansen to SD, 25 June 1984; Sarah Irwin to SD, 18 July 1984; JC to Laurens Schwartz, 9 October 1975; interview Bob Chibka, 5 June 1985; interview Allan Gurganus, 16 September 1984; JC on Dick Cavett show, 21 March 1978; interview John C. Gerber, 29 April 1985.

MINER, IRWIN, SPIVAK, GURGANUS: Interview Lucy Miner, 18 October 1984; Lucy Miner to SD, 28 January 1987; interview John Leggett, 28 April 1985; interview Mrs. Wallace Boyd, 29 April 1985; interview Federico Cheever, 10 February 1985; Sarah Irwin to SD, 18 July 1984; interview Gayatry Spivak, 28 December 1984; interviews Allan Gurganus, 31 May 1984 and 16 September 1984; Allan Gurganus to SD, 18 February 1986; interview Bob Chibka, 5 June 1985.

ATTACK, ACADEMY, RETURN: JC to Dr. Raymond Mutter, 8 September 1973; Sarah Irwin to SD, 18 July 1984; Aaron Copland to JC, 23 November 1973; Margaret Mills to JC, 20 November 1975; JC, typescript 21; Caskie Stinnett to SD, 26 November 1985; JC to Candida Donadio, 16 April 1974.

SEPARATION, GURGANUS STORY: JC to Frederick Exley, 31 January 1974; JC to Allan Gurganus, 21 February 1974, 5 March 1974, and 8 March 1974.

BOOZE, COATES: Interview John and Mary Dirks, 16 July 1984; interview Aline Benjamin, 5 July 1984; JC to Dennis Coates, 11 March 1974 and 11 April 1974; interview Dennis Coates, 28 May 1984 and 8 October 1984; JC, "The Leaves, the Lion-Fish and the Bear," ESQUIRE, November 1974, pp. 110–11, 192–93, 195–96.

TALK OF DIVORCE: Interview John and Mary Dirks, 16 July 1984; Mary Dirks to SD, 6 August 1984.

DEGRADATION, PROVINCETOWN, FRED AS PROTECTOR: Interview Gayatry Spivak, 28 December 1984; Mary Dirks to SD, 9 August 1984; interview Christopher Lehmann-Haupt and Natalie Robins, 22 October 1984; interview Molly Malone Cook, 2 May 1985; interview Virginia Rice Kahn, 5 June 1985; interviews Federico Cheever, 10 February 1985 and 11 February 1985; Lucy Miner to SD, 17 March 1987; interview Dr. Raymond Mutter, 22 June 1984.

BOSTON—"A NEW LIFE": Interview Dr. Frank Jewett, 29 June 1984; interview MC, 20 October 1984; JC to John and Mary Dirks, 11 September 1974; JC, typescript 15; David Robertson to SD, 23 March 1985; George Starbuck to SD, 28 October 1983; interview George Starbuck, 16 October 1984; John Malcolm Brinnin to SD, 9 May 1984; JC to William Maxwell, 3 September 1974; McCabe, "The Inner Realm."

VALHOULI, SCHWARTZ, UPDIKE: Interview James Valhouli, 15 October 1984; interview Laurens Schwartz, 29 July 1985; Laurens Schwartz to SD, 1 August 1985; MC to SD, 15 June 1985; John Updike to SD, 25 June 1984 and 13 November 1984.

CALLS FOR HELP, DOWN AND OUT: Interview Allan Gurganus, 31 May 1984; JC to Dennis Coates, 14 October 1984, 2 November 1984, and 2 December 1984; JC to Sara Spencer, early 1975; JC to Friday Club, 12 February 1975; interview Dr. Raymond Mutter, 22 June 1984; Dana Gioia et al., interview with JC, 23 January 1976; Dean Doner to SD, 22 October 1984; interview William Maxwell, 9 April 1985; interview Edward Newhouse, 5 June 1984; JC, "The President of the Argentine," ATLANTIC MONTHLY, April 1976, pp. 43–45; Hersey, "John Hersey Talks," p. 24; Susan Cheever Cowley and JC, "A Duet," p. 70; interview Dr. Robert A. Johnson, 18 December 1984; interview Sally Swope, 8 November 1983; JC to Mary Gormley, spring 1975; JC file, Boston University; interview Rick Siggelkow, 24 July 1984; JC to John Updike, 2 June 1975.

DETOXIFICATION, WITHDRAWAL: Interview Rick Siggelkow, 24 July 1984; interviews Jane Cheever Carr, 27 September 1983 and 5 June 1984; patient history and patient progress notes, Smithers Alcoholism Center, 9 April 1975 to 6 May 1975; interview Carol Kitman, 5 September 1984; interview Ruth Maxwell, 17 September 1984; JC to Allan Gurganus, 10 May 1975; JC to Arthur Spear, April 1975; JC to Candida Donadio, 21 April 1975; JC to William Maxwell, 25 April 1975; interview Leonard Field, 18 September 1984; JC to Laurens Schwartz, 29 April 1975; Robert L. deVeer to SD, 26 September 1984; JC to Candida Donadio, 20 May 1975.

REBIRTH

STRAIN OF SOBRIETY: Interview MC, 10 April 1985; Susan Cheever, HOME BEFORE DARK, pp. 198–99; interview Sara Spencer, 10 November 1983; interview Hope Lange, 24 October 1984; interview Nina Engel, 22 June 1984; interview Barrett and Jane Clark, 28 June 1984; JC to Allan Gurganus, summer 1976; Max Zimmer journal; June Beisch, "John Cheever Comes Home," BOSTON HERALD, 28 August 1977; Kornbluth, "Cheever Chronicle," pp. 28–29; Brans, "Stories to Comprehend," p. 345; Hayden Carruth, "The Incorrigible Dirigible."

WRITING A STREAK: John Updike, remarks at memorial service, 22 June 1982; JC to Laurens Schwartz, 7 October 1975; Jan Herman, "John Cheever Never Plays Celebrity Role," CHICAGO SUN-TIMES "Show" section, 17 April 1977, p. 9; JC to Dennis Coates, 6 October 1975 and 11 February 1976; Hersey, "John Hersey Talks," p. 24.

SKATING, BIKING, GARDENING, SPECTATING: JC to Dennis Coates, 31 October 1975 and 5 May 1976; JC to Laurens Schwartz, 19 January 1976; interview John and Mary Dirks, 16 July 1984; interview John Bukovsky, 5 July 1985; interview Roger and Maureen Willson, 29 July 1984; JC to Laurens Schwartz, April 1978; JC to Allan Gurganus, 26 May 1976; JC, journal, Brandeis library; JC to Max Zimmer, 197—; "A Fan Fans Tiant," NEW YORK TIMES, 29 November 1978; Grant, "John Cheever: The Art," pp. 40–41.

AA MEETINGS, ACTIVITIES: Interview Bev Chaney, Jr., 6 June 1984; interview Eugene and Clayre Thaw, 15 July 1984; interview John Crutcher, 22 June 1985; interview David Lange, 6 June 1985; interview Dudley Schoales, Jr., 17 July 1984; Laurens Schwartz to SD, 26 March 1986; interview Grace Schulman, 16 September 1984.

TRIPS, YADDO, BOSTON: JC to Dennis Coates, 11 February 1976; Nora Sayre to SD, 8 April 1975; JC to Laurens Schwartz, 11 November 1975, 1 December 1975, and 9 March 1976; JC to Candida Donadio, winter 1976; interview MC, 6 June 1983; Dana Gioia et al., interview with JC, 30 January 1985; interview Robert Cowley, 21 June 1984; JC to James Valhouli, 6 December 1977; interview Philip Schultz, 27 June 1984; Patrick Coyne to MC, 1983; Burton Benjamin, "Cheever Quotes Pay Cab Fare," WHITE PLAINS REPORTER DISPATCH, 7 June 1983.

STANFORD, BELLOW: Dana Gioia, "Meeting Mr. Cheever," pp. 419–34; Dana Gioia et al., interview with JC, 23 January 1976.

APPEARANCE, CHARM, HOPE: John Hersey, "Talk with John Cheever," NEW YORK TIMES BOOK REVIEW, 6 March 1977, p. 1; interview Allan Gurganus, 16 September 1984; JC to Laurens Schwartz, 10 February 1976; interview MC, 6 June 1983; interview Margot Wilkie, 25 June 1984; JC to Allan Gurganus, 11 February 1976; JC to James Valhouli, 3 February 1976; JC to Max Zimmer, early 1977; interview Robert Gottlieb, 27 June 1984; interview William H. Luers, 22 August 1985; interview Hope Lange, 24 October 1984.

HOMOSEXUAL LEANINGS: Interview Saul Bellow, 10 July 1984; JC, typescript 15; JC to Max Zimmer, 12 May 1977; interviews Max Zimmer, 27 June 1984 and 19 July 1984; JC quoted in Susan Cheever, HOME BEFORE DARK, p. 208; interview Allan Gurganus, 15 September 1984.

PLEASURES OF SPRING 1976: JC to Dennis Coates, 9 March 1976; "Teens Re-Dial Forebears' 1876 Call," OSSINING CITIZEN REGISTER, 11 March 1976; JC to Allan Gurganus, 23 April 1976; JC to Malcolm Cowley, 24 April 1976; JC to Laurens Schwartz, 19 April 1976 and 23 May 1976.

SHADOWS OF DEATH: JC to Sara Spencer, 23 April 1976, 16 June 1976, 3 July 1976, and 4 July 1976; Susan Cheever, HOME BEFORE DARK, p. 189, 205–6; JC to Allan Gurganus, June 1976; interview Barrett and Jane Clark, 28 June 1984; Howard Kissel, "John Cheever Maintains Family Prestige," Ossining Citizen Register, 20 April 1980, p. D3; JC to Candida Donadio, 5 June 1976.

Optimism, Romania, bike accident: "The Novelist," Newsweek, 4 July 1976, p. 36; Bruce Benidt, "Conversations with John Cheever," Minneapolis Star, 30 December 1978, p. 10; JC, "Romania," Travel & Leisure, March 1978, pp. 86–87; JC to Laurens Schwartz, 7 August 1976; interview Philip Schultz, 27 June 1984; JC to Allan Gurganus, 1976.

Bennington, Cornell, Hardwick: Stephen Sandy to SD, 22 September 1984; JC to Allan Gurganus, 30 November 1976; interview James and Gladys McConkey, 10 July 1984; JC, "The Melancholy of Distance"; interview Frederica Kaven, 31 January 1987; JC, "An Exchange on Fiction," New York Review of Books, 3 February 1977, p. 44.

Utah, Max: Interview Dave Smith, 30 January 1985; interview Max Zimmer, 27 June 1984; JC quoted in Susan Cheever, Home Before Dark, p. 207; JC to Max Zimmer, 24 February 1977; Max Zimmer journal.

SUCCESS

Falconer, Newsweek: JC to Max Zimmer, winter 1977; "John Cheever: Did Newsweek Make Him a Bestseller?" Coda: Poets & Writers Newsletter, 5, i (1977), p. 26; interview Burton Benjamin, 19 June 1984; John Firth, "Talking with John Cheever," Saturday Review, 2 April 1977, p. 23.

Falconer: change, confinement, love: Saul Bellow, "On John Cheever," New York Review of Books, 17 February 1983, p. 38; interview Curtis Harnack and Hortense Calisher, 17 September 1984; SD, "John Cheever: Redemption in Cellblock F," Minneapolis Tribune, 3 April 1977, p. 140; John Hersey, "Talk," p. 24; JC, typescript 19; Hunt, Hobgoblin, pp. 272–73; interview James and Gladys McConkey, 10 July 1984; Robert G. Collins, "From Subject to Object and Back Again: Individual Identity in John Cheever's Fiction," Twentieth Century Literature, Spring 1982, pp. 9–10; Peter Costa, "A Wasp Author Discusses Wasps," Boston Herald American, 4 May 1977.

Reviews of Falconer: Interview John Leonard, 23 October 1984; interview Morris Lurie, 16 December 1985; John Gardner, "On Miracle Row," Saturday Review, 2 April 1977, p. 20; Saul Bellow to JC, 23 November 1976; Joan Didion, "Falconer," New York Times Book Review, 6 March 1977, pp. 1, 22; Joyce Carol Oates, "An Airy Insubstantial World," Ontario Review, fall–winter 1977–78, pp. 99–101; Susan Cheever Cowley and JC, "A Duet," p. 68; Margaret Manning, "I Wanted It to Go On Forever," Boston Sunday Globe, 20 March 1977.

MARRIAGE OF PERVERSITY, STAYING POWER: Interview Federico and Mary Cheever, 10 February 1985; Callaway, interview with JC, 15 October 1981; JC, typescript 19; interview Francis Steegmuller and Shirley Hazzard, 17 January 1985; interview Dennis Coates, 8 October 1984; interview Grace Schulman, 16 September 1984; interview Allan Gurganus, 16 September 1984; interview Rick Siggelkow, 24 July 1984; Susan Cheever, "Mothers by Daughters," Channel 4 television show, New York, January 1985; Shirley Silverberg, "A Talk with John Cheever," pp. 67–68; Susan Cheever Cowley and JC, "A Duet," p. 69; interviews MC, 28 June 1984 and 20 October 1984; interview Aline Benjamin, 5 July 1984; interview John Bukovsky, 5 July 1984; Jovanovich, "Mary Cheever on Her Own," p. A3.

LANG, AMES, ZIMMER: Tape recording, Joseph Barbato interview with JC, 27 October 1978; Mary Dirks to ———, 25 April 1977; Malcolm Cowley to JC, 30 March 1977; JC to Malcolm Cowley, 4 April 1977; JC, "The Hostess of Yaddo," NEW YORK TIMES BOOK REVIEW, 8 May 1977, pp. 3, 34; Stephen Sandy to SD, 22 September 1984; interview Max Zimmer, 27 June 1984.

BULGARIA: Interview Robert Penn Warren and Eleanor Clark, 10 July 1984; JC to Max Zimmer, spring 1977; interview Raphael Rudnik, 18 January 1985; twelve U.S. Department of State telegrams, January–June 1977; JC to Laurens Schwartz, 26 June 1977; Gore Vidal to SD, 16 October 1984; interview Dennis Coates, 28 May 1984.

WAUWINET, YADDO, ZIMMER, PHILLIPS, ROREM, HOLMES: Interview Raphael Rudnik, 18 January 1985; interview Grace Schulman, 16 September 1984; JC to Steve Phillips, fall 1977 and 1 November 1977; interview Steve Phillips, 24 July 1984; interview Ned Rorem, 20 September 1984; interview James Holmes, 20 October 1984.

ARCHITECTURE, AGENTLESS: JC, "The Second Most Exalted of the Arts," JOURNAL OF ARCHITECTURAL EDUCATION, November 1977; David Clarke to SD, 1 February 1984; JC to Candida Donadio, 17 February 1977 and 27 November 1977; X. J. Kennedy to JC, 16 July 1978; JC to X. J. Kennedy, 23 July 1978; X. J. Kennedy to SD, 16 October 1985.

AWARDS, APPEARANCES, RUSSIA AGAIN: JC to Max Zimmer, fall 1977; JC to John Leggett, 17 September 1977 (two letters); James Valhouli to SD, 27 February 1985; interview Grace Schulman, 16 September 1984; JC to Laurens Schwartz, 13 December 1977; JC to T. Coraghessan Boyle, 14 February 1978; JC on Dick Cavett show, 21 March 1978.

YADDO, ACADEMY, COMPETITIVENESS: Interview Hayden Carruth, 10 October 1985; JC to MC, winter 1978; Albin Krebs, "Notes on People," NEW YORK TIMES, 1 January 1977, p. 12; JC to Margaret Mills, 11 May 1977; Eileen Simpson, POETS IN THEIR YOUTH (New York, 1982), p. 149; interview Robert Gottlieb, 27 June 1984.

BELLOW, UPDIKE: Interview MC, 12 July 1984; JC, typescript 21; "Writers' Writers," NEW YORK TIMES BOOK REVIEW, 4 December 1977; Saul Bellow, "On John Cheever," p. 38; interview Saul Bellow, 10 July 1984; interview Bev Chaney, Jr., 26 June 1984; JC to John Updike, 1977 and 11 July 1979; tape recording, Christopher Lehmann-Haupt interview with JC, February 1969; interview Tom Glazer, 27 October 1983.

HARVARD, BULGARIA, SUSAN'S NOVEL: Robin Dougherty to SD, 23 April 1986; Joseph Barbato, "Cheever: Stories of Dreams Gone Awry," DETROIT NEWS, 28 November 1978; interview Ben Cheever, 19 October 1984; JC to T. Coraghessan Boyle, 21 October 1978; Callaway, interview with JC, 15 October 1981; Susan Cheever, "My Father's Life," ESQUIRE, June 1984, p. 179; JC, "My Daughter, The Novelist," NEW YORK, 7 April 1980, p. 53.

STORIES, REVIEWS: Interview Robert Gottlieb, 27 June 1984; MC to Malcolm Cowley, 2 October 1982; Anne Tyler, "Books Considered," NEW REPUBLIC, 4 November 1978, pp. 45–47; John Leonard, "Books of the Times," NEW YORK TIMES, 7 November 1978, p. 43; Stephen Becker, "John Cheever's Short Glories," CHICAGO SUN-TIMES, November 1978; interview Charles Newman, 23 July 1984.

GOLD MEDAL controversy: Interview William Maxwell, 9 April 1985; William Maxwell to SD, 10 April 1985: another version of the "Telephone Story" appeared in Kornbluth, "Cheever Chronicle," 21 October 1979, p. 29; Malcolm Cowley to "Members of the Nominating Committee for the Gold Medal in the Short Story," 5 February 1978; Richard Wilbur to Malcolm Cowley, 20 February 1978; Malcolm Cowley to Richard Wilbur, 25 February 1978; JC to Malcolm Cowley, 1 March 1978.

PULITZER, NOBEL RUMORS: Interview Philip Schultz, 27 June 1984; interview Jane Cheever Carr, 27 October 1983; Linda Gilbert, "Marathon Day for Cheever Yields Prize," OSSINING CITIZEN REGISTER, 17 April 1979; Jim Morse, "A Happy Twist to Cheever Chronicle," BOSTON HERALD AMERICAN, 18 April 1979; John Irving quoted in Stephen Becker to SD, 26 June 1985; Savage, "The Long and the Short," p. 30.

CELEBRITY AND ITS EFFECTS: Susan Cheever, HOME BEFORE DARK, pp. 210–11; JC to Max Zimmer, 6 December 1978; interview Lauren Bacall, 17 January 1985; JC to Robert Gottlieb, 26 January 1979; interview Robert Gottlieb, 27 June 1984; interview MC, 26 June 1984; interview Allan Gurganus, 16 September 1984; JC to Rick Siggelkow, fall 1977; interview Rick Siggelkow, 23 October 1984; interview Eugene and Clayre Thaw, 15 July 1984; Coale, "Portrait," p. 3; interview Sara Spencer, 10 November 1983; interview Curtis Harnack and Hortense Calisher, 17 September 1984; interview Ben Cheever, 8 November 1983; interview Hayden Carruth, 10 October 1984;

interview Iole Masullo, 23 June 1984; Smilgis, "Dark Moments," pp. 78–79, presents Cheever on horseback in PEOPLE magazine: he was capable of kidding himself about this supposed equestrian background—strangers kept asking him "where his horse was," he wrote Max Zimmer, May 1979; interview Margaret Mills, 19 September 1984; interview Federico Cheever, 10 February 1985.

COMMON FOLK, OSSINING: Interview Eugene and Clayre Thaw, 15 July 1984; interview Nellie Shannon, 17 July 1985; JC, "The Ossining Marathon," 1979–80; interview Burton Benjamin, 19 June 1984; "Author Cheever Loves Ossining Life," OSSINING CITIZEN REGISTER, early 1979; Benidt, "Conversations," p. 9; Susan Merrill, "The Everyday Ossining Haunts of John Cheever," MOUNT KISCO PATENT TRADER, 14 March 1986, pp. 12–13, 34; interview John Bukovsky, 5 July 1984; interview Susan Cheever, 21 September 1983; interview Rick Siggelkow, 23 October 1984; interview Bev Chaney, Jr., 6 June 1984; Herbert Hadad, "Goodbye to a Man of Patience," OSSINING CITIZEN REGISTER, 4 July 1982; interview Roger and Maureen Willson, 29 July 1984.

SMOKING, MAX: Max Zimmer journal; interviews Max Zimmer 27 June 1984, 25 July 1984, and 19 September 1984.

MACDOWELL, STAYING AT HOME: Interview John Leonard, 23 October 1984; interview Hope Lange, 24 October 1984; interview Susan Cheever, 21 September 1983; interview Eugene and Clayre Thaw, 15 July 1984; interviews Max Zimmer, 27 June 1984 and 19 July 1984; interview Bev Chaney, Jr., 6 June 1984; interview Rick Siggelkow, 23 October 1984; interview Robert Penn Warren and Eleanor Clark, 10 July 1984; JC on the Charlie Rose show, Dallas–Fort Worth television, late 1979.

CANCER

PLEASURES OF FAME: Interview William H. Luers, 22 August 1985; interview Eugene Kennedy, 23 April 1985; Eugene Kennedy, "America Has Lost a Mountain in John Cheever," CHICAGO TRIBUNE, 30 June 1982, Section 3, p. 1; interview Sara Spencer, 10 November 1983.

SLOWING DOWN, AUDIENCE: Interview Steve Phillips, 24 July 1984; Susan Cheever, HOME BEFORE DARK, pp. 226–27; Valhouli, interview with JC, 2 December 1977; Stephen Sandy to SD, 8 October 1984; JC on Dick Cavett show, 21 March 1978; Hunt et al., interview with JC, fall 1979; Gioia et al., interview with JC, 23 January 1976; interview John Crutcher, 22 June 1985; Saul Bellow to JC, 23 November 1976; Callaway, interview with JC, 15 October 1981; JC to Sara Spencer, 2 April 1977; JC to Robert Gottlieb, 20 July 1973 and 16 March 1977.

TELEVISION VENTURE: Ralph Tyler, "How a Trio of Cheever Stories Made It to TV," NEW YORK TIMES, 14 October 1979, p. B33; Barbato, interview with JC, 27 October 1978; Callaway, interview with JC, 15 October 1981; tape recording, Lloyd Moss interview with JC, "This Is My Music," WQXR, 12 January 1980; Jack Thomas, "Cheever Leads Showcase Series," BOSTON GLOBE, 10 January 1982, TV Week, p. 2; JC, "Breaking Into Television at the Age of Seventy," THE DIAL, January 1982, pp. 13–16.

CHILDREN, MAX, HOPE: Interview Dr. J. William Silverberg, 18 June 1984; interview Leonard Field, 18 September 1984; interview Max Zimmer, 27 June 1984 and 19 July 1984; interview Ben Cheever, 19 October 1984; interview Hope Lange, 24 October 1984.

UNION LEAGUE MEDAL: JC, acceptance speech, Union League gold medal, 1980, typescript 11.

SEIZURE, AFTEREFFECTS: Interview Allan Gurganus, 16 September 1984; interview Lee Hyla and Joan Silver, 16 January 1985; JC quoted in Susan Cheever, HOME BEFORE DARK, pp. 228–30; JC quoted in Hunt, HOBGOBLIN, pp. xiii–xiv; interview Sally Swope, 8 November 1983; interview Eugene Kennedy, 23 April 1985; Jovanovich, "Mary Cheever on Her Own," p. A3; Kennedy, "Mountain," p. 6.

KIDNAPPING REVISION, "ISLAND," SKIDMORE: Interview Paul Bogart, 11 February 1985; interview Burton Benjamin, 19 June 1984; interview Ann Blumenthal, 15 January 1985; Jonathan Black, "Directing Cheever," THE DIAL, January 1982, p. 17; JC, "The Island," NEW YORKER, 27 April 1981, p. 41; JC to Joseph and Anne Palamountain, 25 May 1981.

OPERATION, CANCER, DEPRESSION: Dr. Marvin Schulman, record of operation, Phelps Memorial Hospital, 20 April 1981; John Updike to SD, 25 June 1984; JC to Dr. Marvin Schulman, 3 July 1981; Dr. Marvin Schulman, operative reports, Phelps Memorial Hospital, 10 July 1981 and 14 July 1981; interview Robert G. and May Collins, 26–27 September 1985; Updike, tribute at memorial service, 22 June 1982; Max Zimmer journal; Gioia, "Meeting Mr. Cheever," p. 434; interview Dr. Marvin Schulman, 26 June 1984; interview Dr. D. J. Van Gordon, 30 June 1984.

SCREENING, CAVETT: Interview Rick Siggelkow, 24 July 1984; Burton Benjamin, tribute at memorial service, 23 June 1982; Steven Hager, "Cheever on Writing for TV," HORIZON, December 1981, p. 56; Joshua Gilder, "John Cheever's Affirmation of Faith," SATURDAY REVIEW, March 1982, p. 17; interview Father George W. Hunt, 29 June 1984; interview Rick Siggelkow, 24 July 1984; JC to John Updike, 18 November 1981.

DECEMBER DEATH NOTICE: Dr. Marvin Schulman, record of operation, Phelps Memorial Hospital, 4 December 1981; Dr. Marvin Schulman to JC,

25 March 1982; interview Father George W. Hunt, 29 June 1984; interview Max Zimmer, 27 June 1984; JC, "Christmas Morning 1981"; interview Aline Benjamin, 5 July 1984; Susan Cheever, HOME BEFORE DARK, pp. 97–98; interview Don Ettlinger, 4 June 1984.

TREATMENT: Interview Max Zimmer, 27 June 1984; interview William H. Luers, 22 August 1985; interview MC, 10 April 1985.

CRITICAL ATTENTION, PROPOSED GALA: Samuel Coale, JOHN CHEEVER (New York, 1977); Lynne Waldeland, JOHN CHEEVER (Boston, 1979); SD, "John Cheever," AMERICAN WRITERS: A COLLECTION OF LITERARY BIOGRAPHIES, ed. Leonard Unger, Supplement I, Part 1 (New York, 1979), pp. 174–99; Hunt, HOBGOBLIN; CRITICAL ESSAYS ON JOHN CHEEVER, ed. Robert G. Collins (Boston 1982); Richard Rupp to JC, 2 December 1981; JC to Robert G. Collins, 24 January 1982 and 3 March 1982.

EDGAR, FRIENDSHIPS, OPTIMISM: Benidt, "Conversations," p. 10; interview Ben Cheever and Janet Maslin, 8 November 1983; Susan Cheever, HOME BEFORE DARK, pp. 148–49; JC to William Maxwell, 31 January 1982; interview Arthur Spear, 19 July 1983; Saul Bellow to JC, 9 December 1981; Malcolm Cowley, "Novelist's Life," pp. 15–16; Geoff Walden, "Illness Aside, Cheever Full of Surprises," OSSINING CITIZEN REGISTER, April 1981, p. A12; JC to Allan Gurganus, 10 February 1982; JC to James McConkey, 31 March 1982; JC quoted in Susan Cheever, "My Father's Life," p. 172.

ENDINGS

SHADY HILL KIDNAPPING, HOME: THE SHADY HILL KIDNAPPING, produced by Ann Blumenthal, directed by Paul Bogart, written by JC, shown 12 January 1982 as the opening production of AMERICAN PLAYHOUSE; interview Paul Bogart, 11 February 1985; interview Father George W. Hunt, 29 June 1984.

PARADISE: Interview Allan Gurganus, 16 September 1984; interview Robert G. Collins, 26–27 September 1985; Gilder, "Affirmation," p. 18.

NATIONAL MEDAL CEREMONY: Interview Max Zimmer, 19 July 1984; William Styron, presentation speech, April 1982; interview Father George W. Hunt, 29 June 1984; JC, "A Page of Good Prose," quoted in Edwin McDowell, "ABOUT BOOKS AND AUTHORS," NEW YORK TIMES BOOK REVIEW, summer 1982; JC quoted in Susan Cheever, HOME BEFORE DARK, p. 234.

LITERATURE AND ITS USES: JC quoted in Hunt, HOBGOBLIN, p. xi; Gioia et al., interview with JC, 23 January 1976; Hersey, "John Hersey Talks," p. 22; John Hersey to SD, 22 July 1984; JC, "Mailer's 'Song,' " CHICAGO TRIBUNE BOOK WORLD, 7 October 1979, p. 1; JC, "My Friend, Malcolm Cowley," NEW YORK TIMES BOOK REVIEW, 28 August 1983, p. 18; JC quoted in Michiko

Kakutani, "In a Cheever-like Setting, John Cheever Gets MacDowell Award," NEW YORK TIMES, 11 September 1979, p. C7; Brans, "Stories to Comprehend," p. 338.

COMPARISONS: Robert A. Morace, "Long-Distance Thoughts on 'Cheever Studies,'" paper read at Northeast Modern Language Association meeting, March 1986; Eugene Chesnick, "The Domesticated Stroke of John Cheever," NEW ENGLAND QUARTERLY, December 1971, pp. 531–32; John W. Crowley, "John Cheever and the Ancient Light of New England," NEW ENGLAND QUARTERLY, pp. 551–52; Updike compares the penultimate paragraph of PARADISE with the end of WALDEN in his letter to JC, 15 November 1981; Elizabeth Hardwick, "Cheever, or the Ambiguities," NEW YORK REVIEW OF BOOKS, 20 December 1984, p. 3; Samuel Coale, "Cheever and Hawthorne: The Romancer's Art," CRITICAL ESSAYS, pp. 193–209; Saul Bellow, "On John Cheever," p. 38; interview T. Coraghessan Boyle, 11 February 1985.

FITZGERALD CONNECTION: Barbato, interview with JC, 27 October 1978; interview Bernard Malamud, 18 January 1985; John Updike, tribute at memorial service, 22 June 1982; Elizabeth Hardwick, "The Family Way," NEW YORK REVIEW OF BOOKS, 6 February 1964, pp. 4–5; Stanley Kauffmann, "Cheever, Fitzgerald, Hemingway," WILSON LIBRARY BULLETIN, May 1965, 766–67; John le Carré to MC, 27 June 1982; JC, "F. Scott Fitzgerald," ATLANTIC BRIEF LIVES, ed. Louis Kronenberger (Boston, 1971), pp. 275–76.

WILL TO LIVE, MARY, HUMOR: Interview MC, 6 June 1983; interview Ben Cheever, 19 October 1984; Leahy, "Mary," p. 10.

LAST VISITS: Interview Raphael Rudnik, 18 January 1985; interview Allan Gurganus, 16 September 1984; interview Steve Phillips, 23 October 1984; interview Ben Cheever, 19 October 1984; interviews Max Zimmer, 27 June 1984, 19 July 1984, and 25 July 1984; Max Zimmer journal.

FINAL DAYS, DEATH: Interview MC, 26 July 1984; interview Roger and Maureen Willson, 29 July 1984; interview Saul Bellow, 10 July 1984; Susan Cheever, HOME BEFORE DARK, pp. 234–35; Merrill, "Everyday Haunts," p. 34; interview Ben Cheever, 19 October 1984.

NORWELL SERVICE, BURIAL: Interview Jane Cheever Carr, 27 September 1983; Allan Gurganus to Pauline Hanson, July 1982; Coale, "Portrait," pp. 1–2; mimeographed schedule of memorial service, First Parish of Norwell, 22 June 1982; Federico Cheever, remarks at memorial service, 22 June 1982; interview Allan Gurganus, 16 September 1984; John Updike, tribute at memorial service, 22 June 1982; interview Max Zimmer, 27 June 1984; interview Susan Cheever, 16 January 1985; John Hersey to MC, 23 June 1982.

OSSINING SERVICE, CONDOLENCES: Geoff Walden, "Area Remembers Man Who Loved Ossining," OSSINING CITIZEN REGISTER, 20 June 1982; "Ossining Loses Literary Treasure," OSSINING CITIZEN REGISTER, 22 June 1982; interview Robert Cowley, 21 June 1984; Saul Bellow, "On John Cheever," p. 38; Burton Benjamin, remarks at memorial service, 23 June 1982; Eugene Thaw, remarks at memorial service, 23 June 1982; John Updike to JC, 11 December 1981; "John Cheever," BOSTON GLOBE, 22 June 1982, p. 18; Raphael Rudnik journal, late June 1982; Malcolm Cowley to MC, 28 September 1982.

INDEX

ABOUT THE AUTHOR

After graduating from Yale, SCOTT DONALDSON received his master's degree and Ph.D. at the University of Minnesota. He served in the Far East during and after the Korean War and then began a ten-year career in the newspaper business as reporter, editor and publisher.

Since 1966, he has been affiliated with the College of William and Mary and became the Louise G. T. Cooley Professor there in 1984. He is the author of *Poet in America* about Winfield Townley Scott; *By Force of Will*, about Hemingway; and *Fool for Love*, about F. Scott Fitzgerald. He lives in Williamsburg, Virginia.